B&T
50
'78
W9-AEP-861

# Enculturation in Latin America

# An Anthology

UCLA Latin American Studies

Volume 37

*Series Editor*

JOHANNES WILBERT

*Editorial Committee*

ROBERT N. BURR
HELEN F. CALDWELL
JOHN E. ENGLEKIRK
EDWARD GONZALEZ
THOMAS J. LA BELLE
MILDRED E. MATHIAS
STANLEY L. ROBE
JONATHAN D. SAUER
ROBERT M. STEVENSON

# ENCULTURATION IN LATIN AMERICA

## An Anthology

JOHANNES WILBERT, EDITOR

UCLA LATIN AMERICAN CENTER PUBLICATIONS

University of California, Los Angeles • 1976

Wingate College Library

UCLA Latin American Center Publications

University of California, Los Angeles

Copyright © 1976 by The Regents of the University of California
All rights reserved
Library of Congress Catalog Card Number: 76-620078
ISBN: 0-87903-037-2
Printed in the United States of America

The research for chapters 2, 3, 5, 8, 9, 10, 12, and 13 was
made possible, in part, through the financial support of
the Agency for International Development, Grant 211(d).
The information and conclusions contained therein do
not necessarily reflect the position of AID or the U.S.
government.

# Contents

073547

# Preface

In 1970 the Latin American Center of the University of California, Los Angeles, received a five-year "Institutional Centers to Aid Foreign Development" grant authorized by the Foreign Assistance Act of 1966 and administered by the Agency for International Development. The grant was designed to develop and strengthen a multidisciplinary competence at UCLA for the analysis of effective alternatives to processes of education in Latin America. This innovative grant-in-aid program enabled UCLA to decide what substantive questions and topics would be pursued through research, training, and service within the objectives of the grant. During this period, UCLA faculty and students, in collaboration with individuals and institutions in Latin America, conducted research on the teaching-learning process as a continuum from the individual to the group, from face-to-face interaction to the use of media, from tribal to industrial, from rural to urban, and from informal to the formal. The research orientation stressed empirical investigations based on conceptual and theoretical knowledge rather than descriptions or inventories of disparate educational phenomena. Some of the results are scheduled for publication as contributions to four anthologies by the Latin American Center.

The first volume, edited by Thomas J. La Belle, *Educational Alternatives in Latin America* (1975), is primarily concerned with nonformal education in Latin America. The present volume, *Enculturation in Latin America,* deals with indigenous education; the third volume, edited by Gerardo Luzuriaga and entitled *Popular, Educational, and Political Theater in Latin America*, has been completed and will appear in 1977; and David O'Shea is editing the fourth volume, *Education and Social Change in Latin America,* also to be published in 1977.

All of the articles comprising *Enculturation in Latin America* represent contributions based on fieldwork or, in two cases, on library research, when, because of the extinction of the peoples under study, there is no other way of getting at the basic data. The portion of the total grant allotted to the study of indigenous education was rather limited, so that the papers presented in this volume make no pretext at covering the topic or the area of Latin American enculturation comprehensively. Yet a research model designed for the specific purpose of studying tribal education was discussed with many of the researchers and kept in mind by several of them during the data collecting and write-up phases.

Summaries in the Introduction of the individual papers are based on abstracts supplied by the authors.

The grant has had a major impact on research and training activities in the field of enculturation at UCLA. Nine of the fourteen authors are present or former UCLA personnel. We are grateful to AID for having given us the opportunity to become active in this area of inquiry. As editor of this volume, I am particularly grateful to Thomas J. La Belle, the principal coordinator of the grant, for his guidance and personal encouragement, to James Wilkie who served on the Advisory Board, to Hubert Smith who introduced me to the field of ethnographic research film as a promising methodology in the study of enculturation, and to the students in the Latin American Studies Seminar, who enthusiastically helped me review the extensive literature on traditional education and conceptualize a model for the study of enculturation. A special vote of gratitude is due the Center secretaries, Nelly Williams and Sofía Speth, for their work on the volume, and to Colleen Trujillo and Teresa Joseph for editing and designing it. To all my heartfelt thanks.

J.W.

*University of California, Los Angeles*
*June, 1976*

# Introduction

## JOHANNES WILBERT

### Historical Antecedents

Enculturation among Indians of Latin America is a gravely neglected field of studies. In contrast with other world areas like North America, Africa, and Oceania systematic treatises on such educational processes in Latin America are sparse. Lindquist (1971:307–384) excludes Latin America altogether from his "World Bibliography of Anthropology and Education," while Middleton (1970:xvii–xx) laments the fact that in his survey of studies in the anthropology of education there were fewer sources to be quoted on South and Central America than on most other areas of the world. For South America he lists only the studies by Hilger (1957) on the Araucanians and by the Reichel-Dolmatoffs (1961) on the "Indians" of Colombia. For Middle America he mentions Redfield (1943) on rural communities in the highlands of Guatemala and Hunt and Hunt (1967) for rural Mexico. If one draws on Burnett's (1974) bibliography, *Anthropology and Education,* it is possible to include in this list also the works by Romney and Romney (1963) on a Mixtecan barrio of Juxtlahuaca, Mexico; Driver and Driver (1963) on the Chichemeca-Jonaz of northeastern Mexico; Hotchkiss (1967) on a Ladino community in Chiapas, Mexico; and Modiano (1969) on Indians of the Chiapas Highlands. But, with the exception of Hilger's monograph, these studies are concerned primarily with Ladino and Mestizo communities rather than with tribal societies. And although this is true also for some of the essays in the present collection, the novel dimension that this anthology adds to the study of educational processes in Latin America is that it concentrates primarily on tribal Indians.

The general unpopularity of the topic of enculturation becomes starkly manifest in Frederick and Alice Dockstader's (1957–1974) bibliography, *The American Indian in Graduate Studies.* Of the total inventory of 7,446 titles, covering approximately eighty years of research by degree candidates of 274 colleges and universities in the United States, Canada, and

1

Mexico, only 32 theses and dissertations concern themselves with tribal education. Of those less than a dozen deal with Latin American Indians and they mainly with the Aztec, Maya, and the Inca. Neither is there much encouragement in store for those who consult compendia less specific for our topic, like Paulston (1972), Poston (1976), and the *Handbook of Latin American Studies* (1936——) or the *Handbook of Middle American Studies* (Wauchope, 1964-1976).

It is true that the ethnographic literature on Latin America contains much general information on enculturative learning among various Indian tribes. Consulting the *Handbook of South American Indians* (Steward, 1946-1958), for example, one can profitably examine general chapters on life cycle with sketches on childhood, puberty rites, and initiations. Chapters on religion, lore, and learning contain tantalizing snatches of interesting information on education. Yet the compilers of the seven-volume *Handbook* did not provide within its framework a special section on education. Under the education entry in the index the reader will find merely a dozen or so pertinent references. Thus one gets the distinct impression that, except for some more or less accentuated training during transitional rites and initiations, the process of culture transmission was assumed to take care of itself and that because it lacked certain formal aspects considered prerequisite, this automatic process of enculturation could not rightfully be called education. It was actually not before the mid-twentieth century that textbooks in anthropology began to treat enculturation as a special area of application. But, as Spindler (1963:53) observed, by the time Kroeber (1953) edited the comprehensive volume *Anthropology Today* it had as yet not come into its own right.

The same is true for the field of education. Wooton (1946) demonstrated in his review that texts in educational history like Davidson, 1901:19, Monroe, 1905:1-11, Graves, 1909, Knight, 1940, Wilds, 1936, and Mulhern, 1946 all maintained a more or less evolutionist nonempirical and prejudiced stance vis-à-vis a supposedly nonexistant or incipient indigenous education. Down to the middle of the present century these authors have ignored anthropological literature on enculturation which had since become available and which should have suggested otherwise (cf. Hedenus, 1933; Raum, 1940: 23-53; Middleton, 1970; Burnett, 1974).

It is not difficult to isolate several reasons why enculturative education has remained a nontopic for so long. To be sure, it was not for lack of early advocates who pleaded for the inclusion within the fields of "history of humanity" and emerging ethnology of child education (Meiners, 1785: 17, 30), and the transmission of culture and cultural learning (Klemm, 1854-1855:37, 217). But these voices were either muted or their original intent diverted, once modern evolutionism came to fruition in the latter half of the nineteenth century. Early protestations by Waitz (1858-1871), for instance, who rejected the notion that primitives were born copyists (hence close to apes), made little impression on the scholarly world. Nor did Boas's (1896) first challenge of the basic assumptions of evolutionary theory upset it in any way. What was accomplished by these dissenting scholars was that below the surface of the evolutionist wave they nurtured an undercurrent that as of the 1930s gained the upper hand through the empirical studies of their students and followers.

One factor that interfered with promoting indigenous education as a field of studies in its own right was philosophic in nature, which, in the context of idealistic evolutionism, focused on education as a means of spiritual emancipation from the conditions of existence. Controlled by their lower instincts, primitive or "nonhistoric" peoples lacked education because they lacked spiritual goals.

Schmid (1873:59-68), a proponent of this principle of Hegelian derivation, did admit that the struggle for spiritual liberation was discernible among nonhistoric societies in their conscious efforts at transmission of tribal lore, fortification tests, and the preparation of their youth for self-sacrifice on behalf of the society. Yet a study of the ethnographic literature, such as it was, convinced him that indigenous education was essentially countereducation. It developed the child physically and morally in a distorted way. Evidence of insubordination sanctioned in the name of courage and love for freedom and the practice of physical mutilation of children betrayed all too clearly the true nature of such education (Raum, 1940:4). As a result, scholars like Schurtz (1902:627) uncritically adopted the dictum that among "primitives" education was lacking because the older generation had nothing of value to transmit to their children: nothing in terms of knowledge, nothing in terms of discipline. And it was quite customary among social scientists to work under the assumption that in the absence of an emancipating or value oriented curriculum there was no need to be concerned with ethnopedagogy (Smith, 1934:319).

Furthermore, while it became increasingly fashionable under the influence of Spencer and social Darwinism to describe the history of education in terms of biological evolution, a second reason why primitive peoples were believed to lack education was because they were deficient in intelligence, hence only conditionally educable. To give just one example, Sutherland (1898:I, 126-127) explained that animals like birds, cats, dogs, and monkeys took to training their young even earlier than man.

> But with the dawning intelligence of man the practice of
> education tends to become a leading feature of social life. It is
> not so to any very marked extent in the lower savages [like
> Bushmen, Negritos, Semang, and other peoples of small
> stature], though even . . . there is of necessity something in
> the way of a rude education given to the young. But with the
> middle savage [like the Indians of Tierra del Fuego, many
> other South American Indians, and most North American
> Indians], the process assumes a more conscious nature even
> though yet only embryonic.

The primitive child is "left to pick up merely what he can on his own
account." And the parent, strictly according to whim, amuses himself
"in a passing way by showing what he happens to know."

According to the author, barbarian farmers and herders, because of
their more sedentary life, experienced "an increase in home-life and all
its warm associations, with multiplied parental affection." Education on
this level becomes more systematic [as among the Aztec, Maya, and
Inca.]

With the nonliterate peoples around the world considered either savages or barbarians, what was there to study but some unintelligent
manifestations of embryonic education? In the words of Müller-Lyer
(1924:19) these were too reminiscent of the instructional training "higher
animals (birds, mammals) give their young." The lowest form of human education articulating with that of higher animals, as it were,
"we simply deal here with the exercising of nature-given instincts and
drives."

Instead of being gauged against his own ambience, the intelligence,
that is, educability, of the indigenous child was measured by its ability
to acquire Western knowledge (Hedenus, 1933:159). Even scholars of
the stature of Tylor (1881:74-75) failed to realize this mistake, as is
apparent in one of his occasional lapses into evolutionary *Zeitgeist*.

> There seems to be in mankind inbred temperament and inbred
> capacity of mind. . . . In measuring the minds of the lower
> races, a good test is how far their children are able to take a
> civilized education. The account generally given by European
> teachers who have had the children of lower races in their
> schools is that, though these often learn as well as the white
> children up to about twelve years old, they then fall off, and
> are left behind by children of the ruling race. This fits with
> what anatomy teaches of the less development of brain in the
> Australian and African than in the European.

Efforts to educate the natives were doomed to failure simply because they were genetically less gifted than the civilized. Consequently, whatever education one designed for them could only improve their inferior potential but not elevate them to higher levels of intelligent humankind. Steinmetz (1935:50–51) suggested that "a better result we can only effect by the employment of means that operate deeper and influence heredity. What these means are, we do not know as yet, we are just beginning to study them." But the author throws us a hint by pointing out that selection of racial stock "fortunately does not always necessitate the annihilation of the living but only the impairment of their fertility."

A third, more apparent, reason for believing that primitive peoples had no education was that they had no schools. The African bush schools, the schooling of shamans throughout aboriginal America, or the prolonged nonformal courses of puberty training given to boys among the Indians of Tierra del Fuego and to girls among the Guajiro, for instance, did not qualify for the name education. The closest the New World populations ever got to schooling worthy of the appelation was that practiced by indigenous civilizations where some method of formal training was recognized to occur, hence the theses and dissertations mentioned above.

In sum, within the global schemes of evolutionary educational history of "man in his upward career," indigenous education came to serve the base line function of illustrating a state of nonextant education at the dawn of civilization. Primitive man was "on the average less than man as we know him" (Spencer, 1882:I, 53), his culture as retarded as his intelligence arrested. He was present-oriented and conformist, living a simple life in stagnated cultures and, motivated by the basic drives of fear and hunger, learned by blind imitation in an atmosphere of general disaffection.

South American Indians, in particular, got off to a limping start in the study of enculturation. In part this was attributable to the negative influence of the dean of evolutionary theory himself. Darwin was shocked to the very roots of his Victorian existence by the Indians of Tierra del Fuego. He was amazed, in 1832, at the "miserable, degraded savages" he met there. This was "man in his lowest and most savage state . . . men, whose very signs of expression are less intelligible to us than those of domesticated animals; men, who do not possess the instincts of these animals, nor yet appear to boast of human reason . . ." (Darwin, 1962: 501). These savages were cannibals (!) with hideous faces, discordant voices, whose languages scarcely deserved to be called articulate. Typical of savages around the world, he went on, they seemed to possess the power of mimicry to an uncommon degree.

Based entirely on hearsay, Darwin (p. 217) projected a most devastating image of the Indians of Tierra del Fuego. "Was a more horrid deed ever perpetrated, than that witnessed on the west coast by Byron, who saw a wretched mother pick up her bleeding dying infant-boy, whom her husband had mercilessly dashed on the stones for dropping a basket of sea-eggs!" He concluded that the Fuegians, among whom this horrible deed was observed, "cannot know the feeling of having a home, and still less that of domestic affection, for the husband is to the wife a brutal master to a laborious slave." Said Raum (1940:1) in this regard: "The man who in his own study took the step to a positive rule only after a painstaking examination of its negative instances took little trouble to analyze into various antecedents of a fact of educational import."

That Darwin later revised his thinking did little to repair the damage, and it is no coincidence that his countryman Sutherland (1898:I, 103–108), recounting the incident of cruel parental behavior among the Fuegians, proceeds to describe them as ranking below all other Indians of the Americas. In fact, in doing so, he only adopted Darwin's (1962:231) belief that: ". . . in this extreme part of South America, man exists in a lower state of improvement than in any other part of the world." It was soon to happen that Indian hunters began with the extermination of the Fuegian Indians and were commended, as for instance in the necrologue for one of the exterminators, as precursors "in the victories of civilization over barbarism" (Lopez, 1893:219–220).

Much to the contrary of Darwin, Wallace, the coinventor of the theory of evolution through natural selection, was not horrified by the natives he visited, in 1851, on the Amazon. He showed not only sympathy and admiration for their culture but also understanding for the intrinsic values of language and customs in culture-specific terms. This scientific attitude allowed him to see, possibly for the first time in scholarly literature, that despite apparent differences between Indians and Europeans, the cultural distance between primitives and civilized was not as abysmal as was commonly believed. The Indians were definitely educable because they possessed a brain that rather than being only a few degrees superior to that of an ape was "very little inferior to that of a philosopher" (Wallace, after Bronowski, 1973:302). Proponents of evolutionary theory and eugenics found no support here. The Indian was not the dawn-of-civilization creature Western intellectuals wanted him to be. He was not beyond educability and not doomed, at least not on account of his feeblemindedness and bad habits, "to disappear and leave room for others" (Sutherland, 1898:I, 108).

Lost in an atmosphere of self-fulfilling prophecy, one of Darwin's suggestions that might have served to stimulate research into indigenous education unfortunately went unheeded by the scholarly world. Darwin had suggested that "group cohesion was of paramount importance in the struggle for existence, that it was the product of sympathy expressing itself in mutual fidelity and unselfish courage. These factors were conceived by him to have developed from sensitiveness to praise and blame (Giddings, 1926:45), in other words, their emergence presupposed some sort of educative effort" (Raum, 1940:6). But ideas such as this were not adopted as guidelines for the study of indigenous educative processes for more than a generation to come. Instead, attention concentrated on corporal punishment and on life-crises situations in child life (Ploss, 1884). The psychological factors involved in the crises rituals that covertly affect the child's education were largely ignored.

The first to reverse this trend for South American Indians was Martin Gusinde who, from 1918 to 1924, shortly before the extinction of the Fuegian Indians, succeeded in contacting and studying them. To Gusinde we owe the first comprehensive account of child-rearing and child-enculturation processes of South American Indians (1927, 1931, 1937, 1974). Not only did he rectify the misrepresentation of family life and affection among Fuegians, he also documented the existence among them of nonformal education for shamans and of what amounts to one of the best-developed initiation training programs for adolescent youth anywhere in South America. As early as 1926, Gusinde issued a special call for in-depth field studies on the children in primitive societies. Unfortunately, this call failed to attract the attention of ethnologists, educationists, or any others engaged in the study of Latin American Indians. We hope that this anthology will at least renew that plea. Admittedly, our contribution can represent but a first step toward recognizing the informal and nonformal modes of Latin American indigenous enculturation as effective methods of cultural transmission. Eventually, however, we trust that this recognition will establish more firmly the study of enculturation as a legitimate field of inquiry well deserving of concentrated scholarly effort. For as Klemm (1854-1855:37, 217) already pointed out, it is in "the transmission of past experience to the new generation" that culture manifests itself. And, we may add, since cultural transmission is the societal vehicle of personal learning and since both, transmission and learning, are the principal elements of enculturation, it follows that an examination of these processes through the study of enculturation opens important avenues to a deeper understanding of man and his culture.

Furthermore, since these processes operate in culturally patterned ways, they are arbitrary and vary from one society to another. Therefore, enculturation studies conducted on a comparative basis promise significant insights into the plasticity of the phenomenon of culture—of humankind. Available studies indicate that indigenous cultures, far from being uniform and static, reveal through their child-rearing practices considerable individual, subcultural, and temporal variability. Enculturation studies scan the spectrum of variant practices and put the finger on the fine pulse of continuous culture change through internally dynamic forces.

Yet another reason why the study of enculturation deserves increased scholarly attention is because it helps design practical guidelines for the assimilation of indigenous societies into the national ambit. Much naïveté on the part of scholars, bureaucrats, and technicians is displayed in this area, and much heartache could be avoided by making detailed knowledge of enculturative processes and their ranges of tolerance available to the change agents concerned.

## *Enculturation Defined*

Enculturation was first defined by Herskovits (1960:39). According to him, "The aspects of the learning experience which mark off man from other creatures, and by means of which, initially, and in later life, he achieves competence in his culture, may be called *enculturation.*" More specifically, enculturation is the process by which the individual through informal and nonformal modes of cultural transmission learns the language, the technological, socioeconomic, ideational, as well as the cognitive and emotional patterns of culture. It is a lifelong learning process that lasts from an individual's infancy to adulthood and "which can be said to end only with his death" (ibid., p. 40).

Characteristically, enculturation with its two modes, informal (observational) and nonformal (noninstitutional systematic), is a highly culture-specific affair, much more so than formal (institutional) education or schooling (Scribner and Cole, 1973). The former two processes of learning are more peculiar than schooling to tribal societies which, generally speaking, lack formal educational institutions. Coombs and Ahmed (1974:8) define *informal education* as "the lifelong learning process by which every person acquires and accumulates knowledge, skills, attitudes and insights from daily experiences and exposure to the environment." *Nonformal education* is defined by the same authors as "any organized, systematic, educational activity carried on outside the framework of the formal system to provide selected types of learning to particular subgroups in the population, adults as well as children." Finally, *formal education* is defined by them as referring to the "institutionalized, chronologically graded and hierarchically structured educational system, spanning lower primary school and the upper reaches of the university."

Informal and nonformal learning occurs throughout a person's life, although one or the other mode may receive the greater emphasis at a given time. Studies show that in traditional societies both modes occur simultaneously according to a pattern of alternating articulation.

Enculturation is a universal process of behavior. It is bound to occur in all societies simply because it is the process by which culture is transmitted from one generation to another. Shimahara (1970:143-154) includes in the enculturative process not only the transmission of culture but also its transmutation throughout human growth. The former is defined as the "process of acquiring the traditionally inherited culture," the latter as the process "of psychosocial transmutation through deliberate, reflective functional, yet occasionally incidental processes of learning (ibid., p. 148). According to Shimahara, the learner is not only a passive receiver of the culture tradition but also actively engaged in creating change through transmutation. The author sees enculturation as "a bipolar process of cultural transmission and transmutation." Yet it may not be necessary to understand enculturation as a bipolar process of this kind. I view it as the development of one process (transmutation) out of the other (transmission). And since the concept of enculturation denotes a cultural process of learning, it may be preferable, as Brown (1970:150) suggests, to exclude from it the changes in culture content brought about by enculturation and to limit the term "enculturation" to the "process by which culture is transmitted (by society) and received (by the individual)." Changes in cultural content, whether creatively brought about through invention, accidentally through tentation, imitatively through cultural borrowing, or simply as a result of gradual variation, become part of the cultural matrix only after they have been socially accepted and integrated. They will then become subject to enculturative learning and part of the personality makeup of the new generation.

Finally, it may be helpful in this connection to reiterate that enculturation is not identical with "growing up," although both processes of change, the cultural and the biological, are interrelated to such a degree that one cannot exist without the other (Cohen, 1964). Instead, "both these kinds of change, change through organic mechanisms and change through learning, combine to generate the process of personality development" (Fend, 1969:46). Enculturation produces the culture-related changes which occur in the individual throughout his lifetime and which are only one part of the total changes that occur in the process of personality formation.

It is because of the interrelationship of changes produced during the stages of maturation and enculturation of a person that the essays of this anthology have been arranged from infancy and childhood through puberty and from adolescence to adulthood.

## The Essays

The anthology opens with a paper by SANDRA McCOSKER on infant and child enculturation among the Cuna Indians. This largely pre-puberty informal education for boys and girls takes place whenever a mother perceives the need to comfort her baby.

The setting of the idyllic scenario is the family corner where the mother, cradling the baby in her lap, shakes a rattle and sings a lullaby as she swings in the hammock to the rhythm of her song. Nothing could be more informal, nothing more casual and unpretentious. Yet through McCosker's research, as also through the facts exposed in Hatley's paper, it becomes evident that lullabies are powerful agents of Cuna enculturation.

Several factors can account for their extraordinary effectiveness. First is the total nurturance provided the child in the lullaby context. Daily, for periods of considerable length, the child enjoys the intimate presence and affection of its mother. She not only holds the baby against her body but also comforts and nurses it whenever desirable.

Second is the rocking motion synchronous with the rhythm of the mother's breathing, singing, and rattling that implants the early extension patterns of Cuna personal and social life for him (Hunt, 1976:61–73).

Third is the texts of the lullabies. Unlike parents in other societies, Cuna mothers sing impromptu songs, not formal ones, freely invented while singing along. Instead of the more common pastoral scenes or the specters of bogeyland, Cuna lullabies portray tribal social organization and values. From the very dawn of consciousness, they imprint on the child's mind the outlines of male and female life, as the case may be. True, the meaning of the texts may be lost on the infant. But who can doubt the intensity of the enculturative imprinting when listening to the singing of girls six to thirteen years old, or watching them playing house or, better still, substituting for mother or aunt. They sing lullabies to their younger siblings or cousins which contain a full complement of social and moral messages.

One must not overlook the fact that the audience of Cuna lullabies is not solely the baby, nor only the child under four who joins mother and infant for an occasional ride in the hammock. Rather the audience for this course in informal enculturation comprises all the children of the family plus their friends playing around the house. Even teen-agers and adults cannot fully escape the instructional impact the songs have as a confirmation of their achieved statuses and roles.

Ultimate proof of the effectiveness of lullabies as a means of enculturation is derived from a comparison of transmitted lullaby messages with
actual behavior of Cuna children and adults. Almost complete congruence
between the two sets of evidence has been observed by different investigators, especially in the areas of differential sex statuses and roles, personal
relationships, division of labor, and inter- and extra-familial cooperation.

Cooperative behavior and enculturation among the Cuna is the main
topic of NANCY HATLEY's paper. The study was triggered by the observation that the Cuna Indians display the kind of cooperative behavior many
others do not. Ventures to establish cooperatives among Indians have
frequently failed because they were premised on the mistaken assumption
that Indians are naturally cooperative. Consequently research and applied
work related to cooperatives in Latin America have markedly declined.

In order to discover why the Cuna make an exception and what prepares
them to manage cooperatives successfully, Hatley examines behavior
systems that are of particular relevance like nurturance, sociability,
self-reliance, achievement, and responsibility. Special attention is given
to the inculcation of these variables through child-rearing practices.

The author confirms the importance of the lullaby for identity definition
and behavior imprinting. Beyond this, however, she finds Cuna enculturation strongly oriented toward dependent relationships among kinfolk
and the community at large rather than toward independent ones. The
dependency is based on the strong emphasis placed on nurturance,
sociability, and responsibility rather than on self-reliance and achievement.

The behavior systems enforced by Cuna culture provide a solid foundation for cooperatives which in turn lend relevance to behavioral training. The secret of successful cooperatives among these Indians is found in
the existence of functional enculturation and the behavior-enforcing effect
co-ops have as concordant need-fulfilling institutions.

PETER FURST and MARINA ANGUIANO also concentrate on prepuberty
enculturation for boys and girls. Among the Huichol Indians, the
youngest children—up to the age of five—are introduced to the core
tradition of the primordial peyote quest on which much of the tribal
ideology rests. Although reported on by previous ethnographers, Furst
and Anguiano are first to reveal the actual content and meaning of this
ceremony. Its significance is said by the elders to be nothing less than
to teach their children the meaning of being Huichol.

To conduct this intensive, nonformal training with pupils at a tender
age the Huichol, like the Cuna, choose as a medium percussion music
and chant. For the "Dance of our Mother" ritual, the children are
gathered in the temple where they are taught to adopt prescribed positions

and to act in tradition-honored ways. In a lengthy and repetitive chant of hundreds of verses their teacher, the officiating shaman, magically transforms the participating children into little birds and leads them on a "flight" that resembles the peyote pilgrimage of adults. Incessantly beating the drum, the teacher and his assistants describe the sacred landmarks along the journey which they will take as adults in order to "find their life." The Huichol Indians consider these pilgrimages prerequisite to cultural survival guaranteed through the teachings of their ancestors and legitimized through peyote visions of the cultural matrix.

Again the learners in this enculturative effort are not solely the actively participating boys and girls below five. The other prepubescent children also join the circle of spectators. Only postpuberty children are excused from active or passive participation but by then the geography and itinerary of the mystical journey through peyote land—through life itself—has been indelibly etched into their minds.

The paper by E. RICHARD SORENSON, KAL MULLER, and NICOLAS VACZEK on the context of Huichol enculturation supplements Furst's and Anguiano's data, but more than that and particularly interesting in connection with the topic of the anthology, it describes the innovative methodology provided by the ethnographic research film; more on this later.

The authors' objective is to arrive at an understanding of the dynamics of culture transmission through the analysis of extensive film records. In their report they concentrate primarily on the context in which patterns of Huichol traditional life evolve.

Huichol child life develops in a context of socially benevolent community life. From childhood on the individual is encouraged to establish personal contacts with his fellowmen and the Supernaturals. Children have access to ceremonial life and participate actively in ritual and ceremonies. Infants and children are enculturated in daily life informally and mainly through observational learning. Competitiveness is uncommon and aggressiveness left to subside without parental intervention. Enculturation in general develops those faculties propitious for harmonious life.

The essay by MARIA-BARBARA WATSON-FRANKE examines puberty enculturation and the nonformal vocational training a Guajiro girl undergoes for several years following her first menstruation. Information on female education among Latin American and other Indians is exceedingly sparse. Specific data on Guajiro enculturation for girls are sporadic and not of the depth demanded in view of their uniqueness for lowland South America. Moreover, besides being superficial in nature, a good number of previous authors on Guajiro female enculturation undercut its importance by displaying a peculiar chauvinism. We are told, for instance, that besides acquiring certain technical skills, the girl has to learn "all the knick-knacks Indians love so well" (Simons, 1885:791–792); "how to satisfy her husband erotically and always to be ready, when he is excited" (Bolinder, 1957:107); and "to cook meat which always has to be her husband's favorite" (Tello, 1930:20–21). Other authors, notably Polanco (1958) and Gutiérrez de Pineda (1950), a female anthropologist with field experience, are considerably more enlightening. But to have worked out the special value the Indians place on the education of their female youths is Watson-Franke's specific contribution.

The paper focuses on the enculturation process and its social consequences for the girl on the threshold of womanhood, a transition that begins at the end of childhood with the onset of menstruation. While adulthood is achieved physiologically, the girl is now taught how to cope and how to achieve it socially.

Enculturation of the Guajiro girl at and following puberty takes place in two phases. First she learns about the physiological changes that take place in her body. She is also introduced to the use of native methods of birth control.

The second phase, beginning soon after the activities related to the first menses have been concluded, may last for several years. Throughout this time the young woman is separated from the community and her family. She is confined to a special hut or to a partitioned corner of the house and may not interact with anybody except with her mother and a selected number of individuals.

The family contracts for the services of an experienced kinswoman or, if unavailable, of a qualified unrelated woman. She functions as a special teacher to the girl. Under her tutelage the pupil undergoes rigorous vocational training toward becoming an expert weaver. She is prepared to fulfill the expectations of an adult woman, how to gain economic independence and self-sufficiency as a provider for herself and her future family. The latter goal, particularly, provides an interesting alternative to female education and role expectations in many other societies, traditional or modern. Guajiro culture programs for the adolescent girl a specific set of behavior adjustments to occur concomitantly with biological changes in the person, to guarantee that growing up and acquiring new knowledge combine to produce a competent woman.

An example of puberty enculturation of boys is treated in the paper by DOUGLAS SHARON on Inca initiation for nobility. To arrive at the basic information and to evaluate its enculturative significance as objectively and as free from historical bias as possible, Sharon synthesizes the major ethnohistorical sources and examines a hitherto unpublished document

Wingate College Library

by the chronicler Molina. He delineates the major events of the ceremony
and the way it was used to teach the young the roles and values of Inca
society and ideology.

The lengthy ritual, lasting for several months, began with the preparation of costumes, in October, and a pilgrimage to the sacred hill of
Huanacauri, in November. The boys underwent initiation in December.

The rituals consisted of pilgrimages to the sacred shrines of four
"hills," Huanacauri, Anahuarque, Sabaraura, and Yavira, where llama
sacrifices were performed. Before and after each pilgrimage the initiates
paid homage to the Inca, the ancestors, and to the deities of the Inca
pantheon in the main square of Cuzco. They received their halberds
before the second pilgrimage to Anahuarque, where a downhill race was
staged. On the last pilgrimage to Yavira the candidates were given their
breechclouts and, following a ritual bath, they received the remainder
of their arms. Then they had their ears pierced. The last days of the month
saw the performance of a feline dance and the burning of ritual firewood.
The month closed with llama sacrifices on Puquin hill.

At the beginning of January the new knights staged a mock battle as
a test of strength. Sharon concludes with a discussion of Inca creation
myths indicating that the initiates were imitating the paradigmatic actions
of their creator-god and their deified royal ancestors in order to promote
the total regeneration of nature and culture.

FRANCES BERDAN's reexamination of Aztec education reveals that in
this society, as in other nonindustrial imperial societies, enculturation
became institutionalized in the larger political system. By the time the
Spanish arrived, the Aztec state had developed methods of informal and
nonformal education for children of both sexes as well as a system of
formal schooling for the education of males.

Nobles and commoners were segregated in separate schools, each with
different goals, duties, and manner of instruction. The state took
particular interest in preparing the male nobles for high-ranking political
and religious positions and in fostering their allegiance to the state as a
whole rather than any component unit of it. Male commoners were trained
primarily for military activities, as conquest and expansion were important goals of the Aztec state.

Every child, male and female, noble and commoner, was instructed
in the skills appropriate to his or her position, as well as in the ideological
training that provided the moral underpinnings for the performance of
those specific tasks.

Little doubt remains that the Aztec had developed one of the most
formal systems of education anywhere in Latin America, with its specific
school buildings, specialized faculty, age-graded student body, and

differentiated curricula. Besides preparing the children and adolescents for their various positions in daily and professional life, the educational system, institutional and noninstitutional, provided effective means by which the state defined and maintained social positions, and also channeled loyalties to the state itself.

The next four essays focus on the occurrence of career training in traditional societies and in rural Peru. The existence of career training in tribal context may come as a surprise to those who consider indigenous cultures too simple to require specialists. Yet the Kogi Indians of Colombia, as GERARDO REICHEL-DOLMATOFF demonstrates, submit their male candidates for the priesthood to an exacting course of specialized training. In fact, Kogi priestly training gets close to formal schooling.

Reichel-Dolmatoff explains that ideally the predestined child is surrendered to the priest-teacher's household soon after birth. Living in the temple compound, separated from his family and community, he and one or two other boys undergo up to eighteen years of continuous career training under the tutelage of a master priest. The novice is subjected to the strictest rules of temperance in food, drink, sex, sleep, and any form of overindulgence. To enforce strict obedience the priest is assisted by a resident warden in charge of discipline.

Religious education among the Kogi is imparted in two phases, prepuberty and postpuberty training, and the curricular objectives are calibrated according to the physical and mental maturation of the novice. During the initial phase, instruction concerns itself with dancing, chanting, and the recital of myths. In the second phase, it turns to cosmology, the definition of moral values, and the use of ritual mechanisms by means of which a balance between opposed but complementary forces can be established.

Reichel-Dolmatoff lists nine major areas of religious training which together make up the curriculum that assists the aspirant to the priesthood achieve the supreme goal of a Kogi man and priest: a balance between good and evil and old age in a state of tolerance and wisdom. This comprehensive religious career training and the all-pervading educational influence of the native priest are certainly fundamental factors in preservation of traditional Kogi life.

To produce a leader of great wisdom is also the prime purpose of the very lengthy and exacting course of political training for Guajiro youths aspiring to the chieftainship. LAWRENCE WATSON found that a Guajiro chief usually selects a candidate for his successor from among his maternal nephews. He may be only a child or an adolescent, but he must display from early on desirable personality traits such as responsibility, compliance, unaggressiveness, and respectfulness.

Preliminary tests of potential candidates begin early in a boy's teens and may last from five to ten years. The boy is given the opportunity to demonstrate his skill at managing livestock and is judged according to how he relates to peers and elders. When a decision is finally made, the apprentice is often separated from his family to live henceforth avunculocally.

Training of the young man concentrates at this stage on the performance of economic duties, leadership, and the theoretical understanding of the complicated legal system of Guajiro society. The mode of instruction shifts from informal to nonformal when verbal teaching during special sessions of instruction becomes more prevalent.

Following this first period of apprenticeship in the theory of chieftainship, enculturation continues as in-service training. Witnessing actual court cases, the apprentice learns how theory becomes reality. One day the uncle officially presents his chosen successor to the leaders and to the community at large, thereby instilling in the candidate a sense of commitment and moral motivation. Throughout the phase of in-service training, as also during the subsequent one of role experimentation, the apprentice may still lose his uncle's favor. Only after he has successfully handled several minor disputes by himself will he eventually become a master and leader. Political education among the Guajiro is thus an effective means of teaching the personality traits required in a chief for exercising political power and of guaranteeing the continuity of authority through public recognition.

The JOHANNES WILBERT paper on career training among the Warao is an attempt to illustrate the lifelong process of enculturation certain male members of the tribe are subjected to who choose to become master carpenters of canoes. The comprehensive question underlying the study is: how are skill-training, socialization, and moral education of boat makers effected by the Warao during infancy, childhood, and adulthood within their particular environment, society, and culture? The paper is part of a larger study being prepared for publication on Warao enculturation which also includes an examination of career training for girls who become expert weavers of baskets and hammocks.

Skill-training of boys begins with an informal conditioning during childhood, develops into postpuberty and early adulthood in-service training for practical skills, and is complemented during a man's prime and old age by esoteric skill-training. Skill-conditioning takes place in the house, the neighborhood, in the forest, and on the river. At no time does instruction occur within a specially assigned area or building. The form of instruction is visual learning, demonstration, and participation in real-life situations. Verbalization during conditioning and technical skill-training is nonexistent or highly uncommon. Esoteric skills, on the other hand, are transmitted and learned in the context of initiation schooling. A special room may be set aside for this purpose and a curriculum of esoteric lore underlies the training process. Instruction is predominantly verbal.

Socialization is effected by seeking and finding acceptance in a number of different social groups ranging from the small nuclear family, through large children's cohorts and adolescent gangs, adult work teams, and finally the tribal elite. In all these the artisan has to achieve the social status prescribed by the culture and play the role society expects.

Moral education is the result of lifelong conditioning imparted mainly by the parents, the father-in-law, and the tribal mythology. Nonformal (noninstitutional formal) education in ethical standards and moral conduct is provided by a hired expert during a ritual initiation for canoe makers. Fear of supernatural punishment serves as primary reinforcement for proper moral conduct. There are also indications that strict alignment with ethical standards may bring mystic experience as a reward. Such an experience will make the artisan pine for repeated encounters with the Mother Goddess, a yearning that turns him into a harsh proponent of the canoe maker's code lest he jeopardize his transcendental personal (and collective) purpose of life.

Douglas Sharon's paper on career training of modern *curanderos* in Peru illustrates the survival power of traditional knowledge systems in the face of drastic cultural change. Shamanism or folk healing is still very much alive in northern Peru, and Sharon studies the way in which it is transmitted without benefit of the mutually reinforcing systems of a tribal culture.

Characteristic for a shamanistic career, the biographical report of Eduardo Calderón, the Peruvian folk healer under study, begins with the call to the curing profession in the form of ritual sickness. In his case disturbing dreams during childhood were temporarily overcome in adolescence through the development of artistic and scholarly abilities. The tragedy and culture shock experienced in adjusting to big-city life while in art school in the nation's capital brought on a severe case of "witchcraft."

Returning to the north, Eduardo was healed by a female folk healer. Once cured, he learned curandero therapy through in-service training as a wandering apprentice and assistant for several shamans. The informal learning and nonformal instruction were reinforced by a body of noninstitutionalized lore that typically serves as a highly adaptive charter for contemporary shamanism. Apprenticeship and exposure to curing lore eventually led Eduardo to a rediscovery of his cultural heritage and to the acceptance of his call as a curandero at the service of the members of his community.

The applied implications of shamanic training and folk healing are obvious. The cultural complex shows such power of survival mainly because its practitioners know how to adapt to modernization, including Western medicine, just as their ancestors knew how to adapt their careers and art to acculturation processes during the Conquest and subsequent eras. Considering the persistence and popular acclaim of *curanderismo,* Sharon suggests that modern Peru could benefit from the experience of Mexico and China in adopting paramedical programs that build upon available human resources and cultural traditions.

LINDA O'BRIEN's paper on music education among a contemporary Maya society is yet another example of cultural plasticity and adaptability in the face of modernization. Among the Tzutuhil-Maya of Santiago Atitlán, a community of 95 percent Indians and 5 percent Ladinos, traditional education is geared to the transmission and conservation of values through certain customs believed to be primordial in origin and power. Should these customs one day be discontinued, the Indians believe they will become divested of the power to influence nature in their favor. The world of the Tzutuhil would come to an end.

With the purpose of the customs and rituals thus clearly defined, the Atitecos entrust their performance to the stewardship of ritual specialists within the *cofradía* community: cofradía officers, midwives, shamans, and musicians. During a yearly cycle of observances, the cofradías require and sponsor the performance of traditional Tzutuhil music and dance, which survive exclusively in this ritual context.

Music is one of the most important vehicles of informal and nonformal enculturation in Atitlán. It forms an integral part of the cult of the ancestral heroes and deified saints and serves to transmit traditional concepts of the cosmic order and the economy of exchange between the gods and mankind. Through active participation from infancy to old age, every Atiteco learns and reinforces these fundamental Tzutuhil values as they are acted out in performances of dance dramas, shamanic prayer chants, processional instrumental music, and songs.

The extraordinary plasticity of indigenous culture becomes apparent in the fact that despite the conservatism of their tradition, the contemporary music of the Tzutuhil is an amalgam of alien and indigenous elements, welded into an integral whole. Harmonic, tonal, and rhythmic characteristics of the originals have been modified by the Tzutuhil musician, operating under his own aesthetic, into a unique style. What is especially remarkable is that the accommodation is accomplished with the existing symbol system of the culture. Through incremental syn-cretism, the adaptation of alien forms resulted in the identification and assimilation of the counterpart alien form with ancestral tradition. Once part of the tradition, music is tenaciously preserved in its accepted form.

Most of the learning process involved in skill-training, socialization, and moral education occurs throughout much of a person's life but appears to be largely informal. Nonformal instruction and learning of some of the instrumental and ritual skills most likely occur, but are considered negligible and unimportant.

With the continuing encroachment of Western civilization on tradi-tional indigenous societies it appears to be only a matter of time before the frontier will finally overrun the tribal territories and force the Indians to adjust their methods of enculturation to new educational practices. A relatively large number of Guajiro Indians are presently experiencing this transition because they have opted to leave their hunting grounds for a life in urban Maracaibo. The anthology, therefore, closes with a paper that examines the fate Indians face, once their autochthonous cultures cease to provide them with a traditional framework of en-culturation.

For many years LAWRENCE WATSON has been interested in observing the recent migrants and studying the difficulties of adjustment they experience. In his paper he identifies the cognitive, enculturational, and sociocultural variables that predispose successful educational adjustment especially among Guajiro urban schoolchildren. The study was designed to test the hypothesis that the Indian child develops appropriate attitudes toward his education only when the parents understand the requirements of the new urban environment and are able to convey an accurate pic-ture of the relevance of education for achieving valued urban goals. The accuracy of the parent's urban cognition, Watson hypothesized further, is positively associated with the level of acculturation the parents have achieved. Watson's findings are therefore of considerable applied value for indigenous populations undergoing acculturation under similar circumstances.

## The Study of Enculturation

The evidence presented in these papers makes absurd the denial of the existence of indigenous education on the basis that Indians are governed by "lower instincts." Recall the ideals to be realized by the Huichol pilgrim to find his life, the Kogi ascetic to balance good and evil, the Warao mystic to reach the land of the winter sun. If anything crystal-lizes in this anthology it is the transcendental ideal of enculturation: to preserve the people's way of life by providing the individual with purpose and meaning.

This goal has certainly little in common with the instinctual behavior of higher animals, as evolutionists had it. The indigenous learner is first to admit that his elders have much to teach him. In fact, learning the lessons may take the better part of a lifetime. But enculturative learning is culture bound and students who perform well in a native context fail with a curriculum managed from outside. Faltering here is not symptomatic of any lack of intelligence but of the cultural disjointedness or irrelevance of the pensum. I am sure that native teachers would be quick to reverse Tylor's judgment about the educability of primitives by pointing out that ethnographers fall behind Indian fellow-students because they lack the "head" to comprehend advanced esoteric knowledge. Reichel-Dolmatoff has admitted to being humiliated more than once by impatient Kogi sages. To fathom the wisdom of a Warao canoe maker has taken me several years, and I have repeatedly suffered the scornful smile of my frustrated teachers.

To look at the reverse side of the coin, knowledge through enculturative learning, informal and nonformal, is not easily transferable. It is naïve to suppose that an expert carpenter of canoes can be retrained to become a carpenter of Western furniture. The technological skills are alike but in each case bound to the product of the artisan; the sociocultural constraints are altogether incompatible. It would be wrong to believe that the Guajiro lineage institution of training chiefs could be reprogrammed to produce community leaders in the city. And Tzutuhil musicians of the Song of the Face of the Earth perform badly at a Catholic mass. Conservatism and particularism are trademarks of informal and nonformal education, and these are positive traits for indigenous education, not detrimental ones. The efficacy of enculturation is in its cultural specificity.

Previous literature on enculturation has stressed that the bases of this form of learning were copying and imitation. The authors of this volume disprove that theory by providing considerable evidence for preplanned and systematic enculturative instruction. The rigorous study plans in Aztec and Kogi religious education and in Guajiro and Warao professional training are impressive. The longitudinal extent of this training, spanning years and even decades, is remarkable.

Enculturation, it is agreed, is a lifelong process; but not the haphazard kind that tumbles in as life goes on. The essays describe enculturation as a process in which informal and nonformal modes of teaching alternate in frequency and in intensity throughout the learner's life. And the shifting of gears from one mode to another far from being random is

Gusinde, Martin
  1927    "Wertung und Entwicklung des Kindes bei den Feuerländern." *Mitteilungen der Anthropologischen Gessellschaft* (Wien) 57:163-170.
  1931    *Die Feuerland-Indianer*. Vol. 1. *Die Selknam*. Mödling.
  1937    *Die Feuerland-Indianer*. Vol. 2. *Die Yamana*. Mödling.
  1974    *Die Feuerland-Indianer*. Vol. 3, part 1. *Die Halakwulup*. Mödling.

Gutiérrez de Pineda, Virginia
  1950    "Organización social en la Guajira." *Revista del Instituto Etnológico Nacional* (Bogota), vol. 3, part 2.

Hambley, W. D.
  1926    *Origin of Education among Primitive Peoples*. London: Macmillan.

*Handbook of Latin American Studies*
  1936—

Hedenus, H.
  1933    "Wesen und Aufbau der Erziehung primitiver Völker." *Baessler-Archiv* (Berlin) 16(3-4):105-163.

Herskovits, Melville J.
  1960    *Man and His Works*. New York: Alfred A. Knopf.

Hilger, Ines
  1957    *Araucanian Child Life and Its Cultural Background*. Smithsonian Miscellaneous Collections 133. Washington.

Hotchkiss, John C.
  1967    "Children and Conduct in a Ladino Community of Chiapas, Mexico." *American Anthropologist* 69:711-718.

Hunt, Edward T.
  1976    *Beyond Culture*. New York: Anchor Press.

Hunt, Robert, and Eva Hunt
  1970    "Education as an Interface in Rural Mexico and the American Inner City." In *From Child to Adult: Studies in the Anthropology of Education*. John Middleton, ed. New York: Natural History Press. Pp. 314-325.

Klemm, Gustav
  1854-   *Allgemeine Kulturwissenschaft*. Leipzig.
  1855

Knight, Edgar W.
  1940    *Twenty Centuries of Education*. Boston: Ginn.

Kroeber, Alfred L.
  1953    *Anthropology Today*. Chicago: University of Chicago Press.

La Belle, Thomas J.
  1976    *Nonformal Education and Social Change in Latin America*. Latin American Studies, vol. 35. Los Angeles: UCLA Latin American Center Publications.

Lindquist, Harry M.
  1971    "A World Bibliography of Anthropology and Education, with Annotations." In *Anthropological Perspectives on Education*. M. L. Wax, S. Diamond, and F. O. Gearing, eds. New York: Basic Books. Pp. 310-384.

Lopez, Lucio V.
  1893    "Julio Popper." *Boletín del Instituto Geográfico Argentino* (Buenos Aires) 14:217-220.

Meiners, C.
1785    *Grundriss der Geschichte der Menschheit.* Lemgo.

Middleton, John
1970    *From Child to Adult: Studies in the Anthropology of Education.* New York: Natural History Press.

Miller, Nathan
1928    *The Child in Primitive Society.* London: K. Paul, Trench, Trubner.

Modiano, Nancy
1969    *Indian Education in the Chiapas Highlands.* New York: Holt, Rinehart and Winston.

Monroe, Paul
1905    *A Text-Book in the History of Education.* New York: Macmillan.

Mulhern, James
1946    *A History of Education.* New York: Ronald Press.

Müller-Lyer, F.
1924    *Die Zähmung der Nornen.* Second part: Soziologie der Erziehung. Nach dem Manuskript überarbeitet und herausgegeben von B. Müller-Lyer. Munich: Albert Langen.

Paulston, Rolland B.
1972    *Nonformal Education: An Annotated International Bibliography.* New York: Praeger.

Ploss, H.
1884    *Das Kind in Brauch und Sitte der Völker. Anthropologische Studien.* 2 vols. Leipzig: Th. Grieben's Verlag. (L. Fernau.)

Polanco, José Antonio
1958    "Noticias guajiras por un Guajiro, 3: El blanqueo o majáyüráa." *Boletín Indigenista Venezolano* (Caracas) 6(1-4):131-136.

Poston, Susan L.
1976    *Nonformal Education in Latin America: An Annotated Bibliography.* Reference Series, vol. 8. Los Angeles: UCLA Latin American Center Publications.

Raum, Otto F.
1940    *Chaga Childhood: A Description of Indigenous Education in an East African Tribe.* London: Oxford University Press.

1957    "An Evaluation of Indigenous Education." In *Trends and Challenges in the Education of the South African Bantu.* Pretoria. Pp. 89-105.

Redfield, Robert
1943    "Culture and Education in the Midwestern Highlands of Guatemala." *American Journal of Sociology* 48:640-648.

Reichel-Dolmatoff, G., and A. Reichel-Dolmatoff
1961    *The People of Aritama.* Chicago: University of Chicago Press.

Romney, Kimbal, and Romaine Romney
1963    "The Mixtecano of Juxtlahuaca, Mexico." In *Six Cultures: Studies in Child Rearing.* Beatrice B. Whiting, ed. New York: John Wiley.

Schmid, Karl
1873    *Geschichte der Pädagogik.* 3rd ed.

Schurtz, Karl
1902    *Altersklassen und Männerbünde.* Berlin.

Scribner, Sylvia, and Michael Cole
1973    "Cognitive Consequences of Formal and Informal Education." *Science* 182:
        553-559.

Shimahara, Nobuo
1970    "Enculturation—A Reconsideration." *Current Anthropology* 2(2):143-154.

Simons, F. A. A.
1885    "An Exploration of the Goajira Peninsula, U. S. of Colombia." *Proceedings of
        the Royal Geographic Society* 7:781-796.

Smith, Edwin W.
1934    "Indigenous Education in Africa." In *Essays Presented to C. G. Seligman.*
        E. E. Evans-Pritchard, R. Firth, B. Malinowski, I. Schapera, eds. London:
        K. Paul, Trench, Trubner. Pp. 319-334.

Spencer, Frank Clarence
1899    *Education of the Pueblo Child: A Study of Arrested Development.* New York.

Spencer, Herbert
1882    *Principles of Sociology.* 3 vols. New York.

Spindler, George D.
1963    *Education and Culture: Anthropological Approaches.* New York: Holt, Rinehart
        and Winston.

Steinmetz, S. R.
1935    *Gesammelte kleinere Schriften zur Ethnologie und Soziologie.* 3 vols. Gron-
        ningen-Batavia: P. Nordhoff.

Steward, Julian H., ed.
1946-   *Handbook of South American Indians.* 7 vols. Smithsonian Institution. Bureau
1958    of American Ethnology Bulletin 143. Washington.

Sutherland, Alexander
1898    *The Origin and Growth of the Moral Instinct.* 2 vols. London: Longmans, Green.

Tello, Mejía Salvador
1930    *Selvas colombianas.* Medellin: Imprenta Editorial.

Tylor, Edward B.
1881    *Anthropology: An Introduction of the Study of Man and Civilization.* New York:
        D. Appleton.

Waitz, Theodor
1858-   *Anthropologie der Naturvölker.* Leipzig.
1871

Wallace, Alfred Russel
1889    *A Narrative of Travels on the Amazon and Rio Negro, with an Account of the
        Native Tribes, and Observations on the Climate, Geology, and Natural History
        of the Amazon Valley.* London: Ward, Lock.

Wauchope, Robert, ed.
1964-   *Handbook of Middle American Indians.* Austin: University of Texas Press.
1976

Wilds, Elmer Harrison
1936    *The Foundation of Modern Education.* New York: Farrar and Rinehart.

Wooten, Flaud C.
1946    "Primitive Education in the History of Education." *Harvard Educational Review*
        16(4):235-254.

# 1.

# San Blas Cuna Indian Lullabies: A Means of Informal Learning

SANDRA McCOSKER

## Introduction

The lullabies sung by the Cuna Indians of Panama are a vehicle for informal education. Whereas the lullabies of most cultures are learned in a formalized manner and serve primarily to tranquilize the child, Cuna lullabies are spontaneously invented at each sitting and do more than induce sleep. In fact, Cuna mothers use these lullabies as an effective tool of enculturation. They prepare the children for the different stages of their lives by describing how their daily activities and responsibilities will relate to their family and tribe. Rather than scaring the children to sleep by threatening descriptions of bogeys, a feature found in other Indian lullabies, Cuna lullabies are generally positive in nature as are the people who sing and listen to them.

The Cuna Indians have many cultural traditions. Their language is close to the Chibcha family of languages found in regions of northern South America (Mason, 1946; Loukotka, 1968), but considered by some scholars to have belonged to a group that is now extinct (Kramer, 1970). The Cuna are among the few surviving tribes indigenous to northern South America. They can be divided into three geographical populations: the Colombian Cuna who live in the lower Atrato River Valley and on the eastern shore of the Uraba Gulf; the Panamanian Cuna who gradually

AUTHOR'S NOTE: Travel funds and assistance were kindly provided by the following: Vic E. Breeden, California Academy of Sciences, Steinhart Divers, The Smithsonian Tropical Research Institute, and Thomas Tilton. I also thank Maurice Giles, Vernon Salvador, and Mari Lyn Salvador for photographic assistance, Víctor Pérez for aid with translations, and Mari Lyn Salvador and John E. McCosker for suggestions regarding this manuscript.

migrated from Colombia to the Pacific-slope rivers in eastern Panama and were first encountered there in the sixteenth century; and the San Blas Cuna who, in the midnineteenth century, came from mainland Panama to the offshore islands of the San Blas Archipelago on Panama's Caribbean coast. Data for this study were gathered by the author among the San Blas Cuna on several occasions during 1970–1971 and on two subsequent visits in May and October of 1974. Thirty-one lullabies, sung by ten individuals, were recorded. The translations were made by Víctor Pérez, a bilingual (Cuna/Spanish) Cuna from Ailigandi. The recordings are housed in the University of California Los Angeles Ethnomusicology Archives (McCosker collection 72.1) and at the California Academy of Sciences (McCosker collection 74.1). This material is supplemented by examples taken from seven lullabies collected by Nils Holmer in 1951.

Within the Cuna tradition, education is highly regarded and associated with social prestige. Since ancient times, the highest ranking officials have been shamans and chiefs who must undergo years of arduous training to learn the numerous and lengthy chants essential to their respective fields of knowledge. Because of the social recognition given to individuals who prove themselves in these native forms of education, the Cuna have been quick to accept recent Western forms of education as another means by which an individual may gain social prestige. Since 1930 the Panamanian government has established primary schools in most island villages, with secondary- and university-level schooling available in Panamanian cities (Stout, 1947). Whereas one might expect that the influence of Western education would eventually extinguish the native methods of learning and fields of knowledge, the two seem to coexist in Cuna society. A significant factor contributing strength to Cuna traditionalism in the face of rapid Westernization is the enculturation process inherent in their lullaby singing. The style, context, and function of lullaby singing are described herein with discussions of the attitudes their texts impart upon the children.

## The Lullabies

Cuna lullabies exhibit a balance between the freedom of improvisation and the restriction of style. The melodies and texts are invented spontaneously and sung in a style common to all Cuna lullabies (Reverte, 1968). The norms of style include shaking a rattle to establish either a duple or triple rhythm, singing in a normal speaking range (or less frequently, in a high, soft voice), using a narrow tonal range (no larger than the interval of a sixth), singing complete textual and musical phrases with each breath, and ending those phrases on the lowest melodic pitch (for specific melodic characteristics see McCosker, 1974). A musical example of the first few lines of a lullaby is shown in figure 1.

Fig. 1. Lullaby 35, phrases 1–4, ♩ = ca. 90 per minute.

The context of lullaby singing refers to the placement of lullabies within the social scheme. Lullabies are sung frequently during the day whenever a child needs to be comforted. This may amount to three or four times each day for the children of a single household. They are sung inside the house while the singer and child swing briskly in a hammock (fig. 2). Owing to their improvised nature, lullabies vary considerably in length; a singer will continue until her child is asleep or until she is interrupted. Thirty-two lullabies collected by the author in 1970 and 1974 ranged in length from fifty-one seconds to fifteen minutes (lullaby durations are provided in Appendix I).

An important consideration is the singer/listener relationship. This relationship usually falls within a family but can include women singing for neighboring children outside of their family. The first seven lines of this lullaby illustrate this:

> when mama leaves for the mountains
> you will cry for her
> you will cry for your mama
> mama will leave without knowing about her children
> little girl
> little boys
> always crying for your mama
>
> (McCosker, 39:1–7, lullaby number 39, lines 1–7. Full texts are provided in Appendix II)

Within a family, the singer can be an older sister or female cousin aged about six to thirteen years, the mother, an aunt, or grandmother. A restriction forbids a sister to sing who has passed her puberty rites but is without children. The principal listeners are boys and girls from infancy until the age of three or four. Older children are in no way restricted from listening although they are usually not found in the hammock with the singer.

The function of lullaby singing relates to the social needs that are fulfilled by the lullabies. The Cuna sing lullabies to quiet their children. The singer, in an impromptu manner, relates the reasons for her child's crying and then proceeds to describe the responsible behaviors and activities expected as the child grows older.

> little ones come here to the hammock
> you are crying come here
> mama is always here in the hammock
> mama sees you crying and will take you in her arms
>
> (McCosker, 35:1–4)

FIG. 2.   Ofelia Morres singing to her children Eloisa and Mario. Arretupo Island.

> In the hammock I sit swinging for you;
> Baby, don't cry, why do you want to cry?
> I sit swinging for you
>> (Holmer, c:1-3, lullaby number (c), lines 1-3. The punctuation com-
>> plies with Holmer's texts; full texts are provided in Appendix II.)

Lullabies are a positive way of directing a child's behavior. Crying seems
to be an acceptable behavior for an infant. The Cuna mother, however,
has good reason to find the behavior of a language-speaking child quite
unacceptable if it does not comply with the guidelines repeatedly sung in
her lullabies.

> if she were not a little girl
> she would not be crying in the house
>> (McCosker, 39:47-48)

> All you do is crying for the breast only, you see.
> If your mother goes to leave you for the woods, you will cry again
>     and again, all the time for the breast.
>> (Holmer, a:4-5)

Cuna lullabies thus introduce language, the norms of vocal singing styles, and, most importantly, the cultural attitudes that play a significant role in maintaining the Cuna's traditional integrity.

Furthermore, the textual subject of lullabies differs when addressed to girls or boys. In this way, the distinction between the work activities of the two sexes is clearly established for the children at an early age. Lullabies sung to girls describe their mother's work duties, which include house-cleaning, cooking, washing clothes, going to the nearby mainland for fresh water (as the small islands have none), and helping to beach the men's boats when they return from their daily work of fishing or farming.

> mama is doing the housework and she cannot attend to you
> mama is always washing the clothes of the people
> mama is thinking that you are my companion in housework and all
>     that you do
> mama is always in the house waiting for when the uncles will return
>     to the house, she is always in the kitchen working
> the uncle arrives with the boat and with the things that he brings
>     from the mountains, and he calls you to help him bring his boat
>     up on the beach
>            (McCosker, 13:5, 11, 13, 15, 26)

> your sisters and mama
> they are here to greet you
> mama will greet you and help to bring in the cayuco (boat)
>            (McCosker, 41:55-57)

> mama will clean the little fish
>            (McCosker, 39:16)

> Mother goes about taking care of the house for you, goes about
>     taking care.
> Your mother, your mother prepares food for you in the morning.
> You will just get to crying, you see.
> I spend the day for you, you see,
> Preparing food for you, you see,
>            (Holmer, $f$:6-7, 9-11)

Lullabies for boys describe their father's work activities of fishing (fig. 3) and farming. This work accounts for about seven hours each day, four or five times a week. The boys begin accompanying their fathers when they are about twelve years old (Arauz, 1970).

> papa goes to fish, he goes very far to fish
>            (McCosker, 39:24)

FIG. 3.   Three young boys learning to fish. Tupile Island. Photo by M. L. Salvador.

when the boys grow up
they will fish far out to sea
        (McCosker, 35:52–53)

Mario, soon you will grow and bring fishes to eat in the house
        (McCosker, 11:21)

Baby, when you come to grow up, when you have become a grown-
   up man,
You will go sailing on the sea, you will sail on the sea in your canoe.
For the sake of fish you will want to go sailing.
Now you are my baby, you see, you will go fishing porgy,
        (Holmer, *b*:1–4)

You will go about on the sea, you will grow up, won't you?
Mother is looking after you, you see,
You are fishing (where) there is fish, if you grow up,
Since you are a boy,
You receive (the heat of) the sun, you will grow up, won't you?
                    (Holmer, *f*:17-21)

you are all little boys
you will go with your father to the mountains to work
you are the boys who will grow up
at the side of your father you will go to the mountains
papa will teach you to work in the mountains
at the side of your father you are cutting small trees
                    (McCosker, 41:1-6)

soon the neighbors think that they too will have sons and they will
    work in the mountains; they will give them *madun* to drink, a
    drink for boys
                    (McCosker, 13:19)

Again you will go to the woods, because you are a man.
You are a man, you see, you will go working (at planting) the corn
    until the sun goes down.
Soon you will clear plantations below, you see.
                    (Holmer, *b*:5-7)

A typical extended family of the Cuna is headed by a married couple,
their unwed offspring, and their married daughters with their husbands
and children. Although Cuna residence rules are matrilocal, the society
is patripotestal because family decisions and village politics are controlled
by the men (Nordenskiöld, 1938; Wassén, 1949). The responsibilities of
girls and boys change after marriage. The young wife transfers her care
and attention from her siblings to her husband and subsequently to her
children (fig. 4). The young husband transfers his work responsibilities
from his family of orientation to that of procreation.

    my little girls
    you will grow up and marry a grown-up boy
    you will grow up
    when you are married, your mama will eat fish with you
                    (McCosker, 35:13-16)

Matrilocal residence is described in the lullabies by frequent reference
to the esteemed position women enjoy in Cuna society, and by the work
obligation men have to the women of their household.

FIG. 4.   Three young girls playing with their dolls in a hammock. Tigre Island.
Photo by M. L. Salvador.

mama has only daughters
little girls
I wanted that you would be girls
girls that you are
only the girls will walk about the house
like girls they should be
you will always be happy
happy since you are women
                    (McCosker, 48:6-11, 37-38)

mama will eat their fish
when the boys return
                    (McCosker, 35:54-55)

you fish only for me
mama will always be observing you
the fish you bring will be to eat
immediately you will be happy
                    (McCosker, 41:17-20)

> when you grow, it will be for me and you will work for me, for the
> house
>> (McCosker, 12:3)

> I am going to tell you, soon we will call our brothers,
> when they go to work, they are fishing for us
>> (McCosker, 11:10-11)

To reinforce this work obligation, the singer frequently remarks that the women at home are thinking of the men as they work.

> you are a boy who is going to grow up and fish; your grandmothers
>   are thinking that you will bring fish to the house
> mama is always attentive to what you do and what your needs are
>> (McCosker, 13:2, 4)

> your sisters in the house will be thinking of you
>> (McCosker, 41:7)

> (While) on the sea, I will stand watching for you, I will stand waiting
>   for you.
>> (Holmer, *f*:23)

Each lullaby tends to emphasize a single theme taken from individual or family work duties. From an early age, sibling responsibilities are established in the description of individual work duties. The girls are told how they will care for their brothers (fig. 5) by sewing and washing their clothes and by helping with their fishing.

> they will always greet you upon returning to the house
> your sisters will wash your clothes that you use for working
> for the boys who come at the side of papa
> your sisters will wash your clothes
>> (McCosker, 41:8-9, 50-51)

> Raquelita is a girl, and soon she will be helping her brother
>> (McCosker, 11:9)

> small child, you are growing up to receive your brother who comes
>   from fishing and to clean the fish that he brings
>> (McCosker, 13:1)

> quickly and for you the little river girl will go to look for fish and
>   thus she will always help you
> upon returning, mama will greet you and clean the fish
>> (McCosker, 41:15-16)

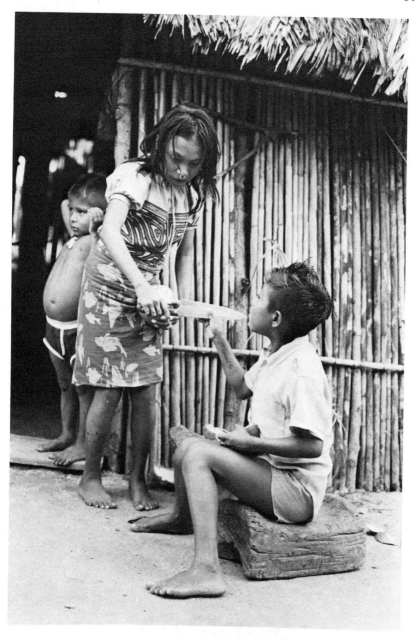

Fig. 5.  Sarah Serrano helping her cousin Cebaltito open a coconut. Tigre Island.

Later on you are going to take care of your brothers.
    (Holmer, *d*:3)

As the girls become older, they are expected to care for their younger siblings (fig. 6) and, in turn, to sing lullabies to them.

    the baby is crying and you will pick it up into the hammock and
        sing to it
        (McCosker, 13:17)

The boys are instructed to call upon their sisters for help at the appropriate times.

    brother, when are you going to call for help?
    when you are older, you will call me to wash the clothes
    the brothers are growing up and soon they will call us
        (McCosker, 11:3, 5, 20)

FIG. 6.    Sarah Serrano taking care of her younger cousin. Tigre Island.

The family responsibility most commonly described for girls is that of fetching fresh water from the river for daily household needs.

> mama is watching you, the uncles are going to call you to go fetch
> water in the river
>> (McCosker, 13:3)

> just your sisters will go to the river
> to fetch water
>> (McCosker, 41:53-54)

> you are the little girls
> many will go to the river, your mama will make you grow and then
> you will look for water at the river
>> (McCosker, 35:32-33)

> Soon when you will grow up, you will fetch water for me, you see,
> When I come to bring you up to be my little girl.
>> (Holmer, d:1-2)

The responsibility of caring for family visitors and guests, however, is one of the most important themes and is described at length in the lullabies. Young girls are expected to fulfill this role until they are married. They first learn how to make the elder family men comfortable when they return from a day's work in the mountains by giving them food and drink.

> the grandfather is going to the mountains; you don't know the work
> that he does in the mountains but you will receive him to see if
> he has brought something for you
> when the grandfather arrives, when he is in the house, because you
> are a girl, mama thinks that you will be well dressed, your mama
> always thinks this
> mama is thinking of the other person: you will not bring him
> sadness, you will serve him well; the grandfather is always
> working in the mountains for the girls
> the people are coming; you will always receive them because they
> come with hunger
> you are a girl who is growing to receive the family
> to receive the uncles when they arrive and to give them a drink
> small little girl who is growing up
> the uncle is always working in the mountains and you are here to
> receive him

come here, mama sees that the uncle is coming so that you can
   receive him
mama sees you growing up to receive the visitors
   (McCosker, 13:7-9, 12, 21-25, 30)

You will wash the clothes for your father, you will roast plantains
   for your grandfather, you see.
   (Holmer, *d*:4)

The girls are also told how to treat house guests hospitably by greeting
them, talking with them, sewing and washing their clothes, and serving
them food.

   you will serve to receive the visitors
   the visitors will be men
   they are born to receive the visitors in the house
   and to call on them
   the visitors will be men
   when you are older and unmarried
   you will sew clothes for them and greet them
   when the visitors come, upon arriving
   let them drink, do not make them suffer
   you are the women little girls
   when you greet them do it happily, do not let them suffer
   they are older visitors
   do not leave them without full cups
   you will always be at their side
   pay attention to what they say
   you will always be at their side
   you are old enough to cook and wash the clothes of the visitors
   you will greet the men
   you will greet the married men
      (McCosker, 48:4-5, 12-16, 18-26, 33-35)

One of the most important duties a young man has to his family is to
work in Panama. This subject seems to be one of the few themes presented in a negative way. Panama is referred to as the "house of the
devil" (*nia nega,* or *ila tola kana nega*), and is described in a foreboding
manner. The young boys first hear of other family men who are working
in Panama and subsequently of their own future work.

   when you grow up the uncles will call you to go to the foreigner's
      house to work
   the uncles are staying a long time in the foreigner's house
      (McCosker, 11:13, 16)

soon you will not be with us when you grow up
        (McCosker, 12:5)

the uncles will come to the house of the devil to learn to work and
    to learn to speak Spanish
you will grow up and will go to Panama to work
your brother will be working in Panama like his cousin Roberto
        (McCosker, 13:16, 18, 29)

Later on when you have become a young man, you will go to the
    negroes' houses,
You will buy shirts, you will go about taking care of your sister.
You (will be) far away, you see, you will be a man, you see.
        (Holmer, c:6-8)

To emphasize the work obligation in the family bond, the singer will
frequently ask for presents and money in her lullabies.

the sons will go
they will go to Panama
to work in order to earn money mama thinks
they will send mama things
they will send mama things
when the sons are in Panama
mama always thinks this, mama always thinks this
my little sons
you will go to Panama and send mama presents
        (McCosker, 41:35-43)

The financial importance of the work is stressed along with descriptions
of the loneliness and hardships involved.

when you go to the house of the devil you will leave me
when you go alone
you will leave me alone
your mama hopes that you will bring back presents, and mama
    who made you grow up
mama thinks of always sending you letters
        (McCosker, 41:21-25)

Through the descriptions of individual and family work responsibilities
the lullabies establish the social work patterns. The women stay close to
home while the men work in family groups outside of the home.

little girls
you are my daughters
you are growing up in the house
          (McCosker, 48:1-3)

when you are young girls, I say
you will stay with mama
you will go everywhere with mama
          (McCosker, 41:30-32)

you will be about the house
while mama is working
          (McCosker, 39:35-36)

Little girl, when I have brought you up, you (will be) always with
    me, helping me, cooking food, sweeping the house.
You are a girl, you see, watching the brothers, serving the uncles.
In the morning your father got up, he has gone to fetch you things,
    you see, you are girls, you see.
Washing clothes in the river, you see, fetching water.
You are girls, you see; when I have brought you up,
When you become big, you will sit sewing clothes in the house.
          (Holmer, $g$:2-7)

when you grow, you will visit various places, we are girls who cannot
    do what boys do, we stay in the house to work
we the girls stay in the house
we the girls are going to work in the house
          (McCosker, 11:8, 13-14)

You (little boy) (will belong) to the uncles, you see,
When I come to bring you up, you will come to work with the uncles,
    you see,
When you will come to pass the day (working outside), you are
    going to forget your home, you see.
(When) I get to bring you up, you see, you (will) fish for the uncles,
You will fetch food for the uncles.
          (Holmer, $e$:1-5)

Girls, the brothers are saying to you: "We will go for a while sailing
    on the sea,
Going to fish, stopping out at sea, turning the canoe,

There are fish, (we will) stop to fish."
Girls, you are watching the house, you see.
Out at sea, they are thinking of home; when the sun declines,
They are turning the boat homeward, hoisting the sails,
Getting wet from the waves, they return home.

(Holmer, *g*:10–16)

The lullaby descriptions of group work patterns are a reflection of the Cuna's traditional use of cooperative work societies. Cooperative work is organized within families to plant and harvest crops and to hunt. Within a village, cooperative work is used, among other things, to gather the necessary provisions for important village ceremonies, to build houses, and to maintain village property. It is interesting that the Cuna have successfully applied their traditional principles of the cooperative work society to deal with recently introduced activities such as store and hotel management.

The division of labor taught informally by the lullabies in San Blas agrees in all but one regard with the observations made by Arauz (1970, 1972) and Costales (1970) of the San Blas, Panamanian mainland (the Bayano), and Colombian (Arquia) Cuna (table 1). The discrepancy is found in the activity of sewing. Lullabies direct all sewing towards women while Arauz and Costales observed it to be an activity common to both sexes. The remaining work categories are in agreement. In San Blas and Arquia, farming is done by the men with the women assisting them during harvest. In the Bayano, men and women farm daily together. Ocean fishing is exclusive to men, while river fishing is common to both sexes. Food preparation, clothes washing, water gathering, and housework are exclusive to women.

Two work activities described in the lullabies which do not appear in the observations of Arauz and Costales are caring for houseguests (exclusive to young girls) and working in Panama (exclusive to men). Activities that I have not heard in lullabies are hunting (exclusive to men), house building (shared by both sexes), and the household crafts of woodworking, basket weaving (both exclusive to men), and ceramics (exclusive to women). This can be partly explained by the rarity of hunting among the San Blas Cuna.

## Summary and Conclusions

The lullabies of the Cuna Indians are a means of informal education and an effective tool of enculturation because of the social and cultural attitudes they impart upon the children. These attitudes reinforce the

TABLE 1.

DIVISION OF LABOR BY SEX AMONG THE CUNA

| | Men | | | | Women | | | |
|---|---|---|---|---|---|---|---|---|
| Activity | Lullabies | San Blas[a] | Bayano[a] | Arquia[b] | Lullabies | San Blas | Bayano | Arquia |
| Farming | X | X | X | X | | harvest | X | harvest |
| Fishing | ocean | ocean | rivers | rivers | rivers | rivers | rivers | ? |
| Hunting | | sometimes | X | X | | | | |
| Work in Panama | X | | | | | | | |
| Caring for guests | | | | | X | | | |
| House building | | X | X | X | | X | X | X |
| Sewing | | X | X | X | X | X | X | X |
| Food preparation | | | | | X | X | X | X |
| Clothes washing | | | | | X | X | X | X |
| Water gathering | | | | | X | X | X | X |
| Housework | | | | | X | X | X | X |
| Basket weaving | | X | X | X | | | | |
| Woodworking | | X | X | X | | | | |
| Ceramics | | | | | | X | X | X |

[a]Data from Arauz (1970).
[b]Data from Costales (1970).

traditional patterns of Cuna culture and serve to balance the acculturative changes introduced by Westernization. Cuna lullabies provide a history of Cuna human relations between men and women and between children and adults.

Cuna lullabies are freely improvised yet exhibit a standard singing style. Their texts are spontaneously invented but their melodies conform to a homogeneity of musical style found in all forms of Cuna vocal music. The lullabies, which average four minutes in length, are sung frequently each day during a child's first three or four years. The singer, who is usually the child's older sister or mother, describes the matrilocal organization of Cuna society and the responsibilities a child has to family and tribe as established in their division of labor. Via the lullabies, a Cuna child's first introduction to language and song provides a clear picture of his or her future roles in life.

The social attitudes conveyed by the lullabies include personal relationships and work duties. Intrafamilial relationships are stressed more than extrafamilial relationships, yet commonly the lullabies will teach girls how to serve houseguests respectfully, guests who may be foreigners or persons outside of the family. Intrafamilial relationships are established by the distinction between the work duties of men and women. The matrilocal bond is reinforced by frequent statements relating to the esteemed position of women in the family and the work obligation men have to their women. Girls are expected to care for younger siblings, to wash and sew their brothers' clothes, and help with their mother's housework. Boys are taught to call on their sisters for help when needed, and are prepared for work duties away from home. Thus, the girls are placed in a serving role and encouraged to stay close to home, while the boys are prepared for group work situations such as mainland farming with the family men, and participation in cooperative work societies.

The cultural attitudes that are transferred via the lullabies influence the Cuna attitudes toward their own tribe and other cultures. In preparing boys for necessary work periods in Panamanian cities, the lullabies describe the loneliness and hardships that accompany this task. Panamanian cities are referred to as "the house of the devil." The emphasis is placed on tribal allegiance nurtured by a strong ethnic pride. The lullabies emphasize the temporary nature of these sojourns and the importance of earning money for the family women. In so doing, they encourage the boys to leave for a short time only and reinforce their desire to return to the tribe.

Cuna lullabies perpetuate the social and cultural patterns essential to the survival of Cuna Indians in today's world. In fact, they can be likened to a perpetual motion device, which, once set in motion, would operate indefinitely. The lullabies teach girls songs to be sung in turn to younger family members; the songs teach boys to respect the needs and desires of the women. Thus, while the lullabies encourage boys to reach out for new experiences and knowledge in faraway places, they equip girls with the means by which to influence their men to remain loyal to their family and tribe by bringing these innovations back home.

## APPENDIX I

## DURATION OF LULLABIES IN
## McCOSKER COLLECTIONS

| Lullaby | Singer | Length (minutes) | (seconds) | Lullaby | Singer | Length (minutes) | (seconds) |
|---------|--------|---------|-----------|---------|--------|---------|-----------|
| | | | | 43 | Ya Pipi | 4 | 20 |
| COLLECTION 72.1 | | | | 44 | Siabibi | 3 | 10 |
| 24 | Ofelia | 3 | 34 | 45 | Siabibi | 5 | 50 |
| 26 | Sia | 0 | 51 | 46 | Siabibi | 5 | 6 |
| 27 | Sia | 2 | 44 | 47 | Siabibi | 3 | 44 |
| 28 | Olokwa | 4 | 6 | 48 | Siabibi | 4 | 27 |
| 29 | Olokwa | 4 | 17 | 49 | Siabibi | 4 | 37 |
| 30 | Ofelia | 5 | 58 | 50 | Siabibi | 7 | 43 |
| 31 | Eterpina | 3 | 25 | 51 | Ofelia | 7 | 13 |
| 32 | Ofelia | 3 | 28 | 52 | Ofelia | 6 | 48 |
| 35 | Leticia | 5 | 44 | 53 | Ofelia | 2 | 12 |
| 36 | Ikuatintile | 2 | 44 | 54 | Ofelia | 6 | 5 |
| 37 | Ikuatintile | 4 | 0 | 56 | Ofelia | 2 | 3 |
| 38 | Ikuatintile | 5 | 25 | | | | |
| 39 | Leticia | 4 | 13 | COLLECTION 74.1 | | | |
| 40 | Leticia | 1 | 49 | 11 | Eloisa | 9 | 15 |
| 41 | Leticia | 5 | 45 | 12 | Eloisa | 5 | 5 |
| 42 | Ya Pipi | 6 | 10 | 13 | Puna | 15 | 10 |

## APPENDIX II

## LULLABY TEXTS AND TRANSLATIONS

### McCOSKER COLLECTION 72.1, MADE IN 1970-71

The lines of the dialect follow the syllabic divisions established by the music using morphemic rather than word boundaries in most cases. Translations were made by Víctor Pérez, a Cuna Indian from Ailigandi. In a few of the lines, V. Pérez was unable to understand some of the words. The ideas that he noted about these lines appear in parentheses in the translations.

#### Lullaby 35, Leticia Fernández of Nalunega Island

pani kala pani poa nai tai ye
little ones come here to the hammock

poe pii poe pii pani tai maloye
you are crying come here

nana peka u kachi pa kine
mama is always here in the hammock

nana peka nai kucha pani nukku pa kine pani poa tii pa ye um
mama sees you crying and will take you in her arms


poe piipii na piipii pak
crying crying is the baby

naa pe a tummuwali malo
mama raises you in her arms

pani nukku pa ki pani
[refers to something that mama is doing while sitting]

nokku we ye
[refers to something that mama is doing while sitting]

nana peka
mama is sitting

u kachi pa kina
she is sitting in the hammock

nana peka nai kucha ye
mama is sitting while the little ones come

pani pii nana pani poa tii kpaa um
you [little girl] were crying


puna tola piipii maloye
my little girls

machi tola o kanapi
you will grow up and marry a grown-up boy

na pe o tumnotali maloye
you will grow up

naa peeka ua kune kolo ye
when you are married your mama will eat fish with you

pani puna tola kanka pani mola pukatii ye
for my daughters I will look for *molas* [blouses]

punolo piipii maloye um
molas for the little girls


pani machi tola kanapii pani walako pa na pe o tummutani malo
here are the little boys you [boys] are without brothers mama will raise you

um kolo ye
[no translation]

puna tola punti pani peka tii wale maloyee
your sisters will look for you at the river

nana tii pe a pinne
mama will greet you

ua pipi sasike maloye
when you bring and clean a baby fish

pani machi tola kanapii malo
you are the little boys

pe pa naa malayo tii kpe
she is thinking of greeting them

nana pinsa e ye um
mama thinks this

poa pii poa pii pani tai maloye
you are crying I always see you crying

ani ko pani poi nai maloye
you are crying

punaloa piipii maloye um
you are a little baby girl

pani nukku poi pina pani poe pii kpa ye
you were crying for the arms of your mother

pani nukku pake pani nukpe maloye ye
your mama will come to get you

puna tola kanatii malo um
you are the little girls

puki tola kana pii wala poi pana pena la tummotanikii pani tumkatani malo
many will go to the river your mama will make you grow and then you will look for
    water at the river

ua pipi soe malettii um
you will grow up and fish

pa pika u kachi pa kini nana nai kucha malo
you were in the hammock in the arms of your mama

ai pani kormakke nai maloyo
you were crying in the hammock

pani pi na pani kormakke nai malo
you were wandering around

[ma] chi tola pipi maloye um
when you were young

nana peka uu malo kpaa nukko pe maloye
mama was washing the clothes

pani tumkutani malo
mama was raising you

nana pipi maloye
mama's little one

pani poa pani poa malotii
you are in the house to cry

ak paa pipi sasi pee nai maloye um
[no translation]

tule puuna kola pipi malo pani kpaa pani poa pi maloye
they will be crying with the girl of the neighbor

ua pipipii
little baby fish

pani nukku pake pani poe pii maloye um
you will be crying in the arms [of mama]

tule puna kola pipi malo
the little neighbor's girl

nukku tani malo um
you are growing up

poe pipi poe pii poe pii pani nukku pake pani tai maloye
the little baby is crying in the arms of mama

naa pe o tummotanimalo um
mama raises you

poe pii poe pii paniko pani tai maloye
you are crying your character is to cry

um makkati kpa wale kpa
when the boys grow up

ua kpa saetii maloye
they will fish far out to sea

na peka ua kpa puna maloye
mama will eat their fish

machi tola kanapii maloye um
when the boys return

wala kpa paa machi tola konapii naa pe o tummotani maloye um
the boys without brothers will grow up alone

## Lullaby 39, Leticia Fernández

nana pe mesoke nana nai malo e ye ye
when mama leaves for the mountains

pani pina pani poe ma i e
you will cry for her

pani sola pani pani nana kola poe pii maloye
you will cry for your mama

nana pei mette nao e ye
mama will leave without knowing about her children

punolo pipii
little girl

kani machi tola pipii
little boys

poe pii poe pii pani tola maloye um
always crying for your mama

nana peka nai maloye
mama is with you

nana peka mani e kua pina koormake pati maloye
she works to earn money for you

pani sola pani pani poe kwatii maloye um
you are crying in the arms of your sister

nana peka nai maloye
mama loves you

pani poe tii malo puna tola kana tola ye
little girl I carry you in my arms

pipi pani pe o tummopale maloye um
you are growing up

pani to pani na o e
when you grow up

ua kuaa nukkuatii
you will go fishing

nana peka ua pipi kuaa soke pati kute maloye e
upon returning mama will clean the little fish

pani pina pani poe tii tai pani nukku pati pani nukkuatii
you are crying because you want to be in your mama's arms

nana kpaa pina pani kormakke tii maloye
for their mama they cry

ipi pani pe o tummowale nai
little one you will grow up

mani nukku wati mani nukkuetii maloye
you want to be in mama's arms

nana pe mette si nana osetotepati
mama left you and went to work until late afternoon

nana kuetii pani nana kala pani poe tii kpa
you will cry for your mama but mama sees sadly because she cannot come

nana kuake nuetii e ye um
yes mama sees sadly

papatii ani peka muu makati pa onokue na o e
papa goes to fish he goes very far to fish

papa anii pe malaka kuetii maloye
he goes for you who are living in the house

puna tola kanati malo
all my little girls

nai pe o tummowale maloye
I am raising you

puna tola kanatii maloye
all my little girls

pani nukku wapina pani poe kua tii maloye
you are crying because you want to be in mama's arms

nana pii pemette
but mama left you

nai maloye
they come

nana sola pani poi pi
the babies come crying behind mama

nana pei soketii suli maloye
but mama will not listen

pani an po nana pe me nae maloye
mama left you

kuatii walakua nukupati
you will be about the house

nana pei suki na o e ye
while mama is working

nana kuetii ye
mama is working

pani sola pani pani poe nai antukkut
and you are behind her crying

nana pinsa e pi suli ye
mama does not think anyone will comfort you

nana pemelo metsoke
[no translation]

osetotewati pai e um
it is late afternoon


nana pei sei
mama will come

ani papa nanikki
papa will come

pani nukku pakue pani siki so kuetii um
the little girl waits for mama to get her

puna pii ani sola pani poi nai antukut nana pinsae pi suli maloye
mama thinks that when she returns the baby will be crying behind her

pani to pani poe pa tii maloye
you are crying

puna tola kana suli kpa yopi
if she were not a little girl

pani poe kutii ka
she would not be crying in the house

nana ipi sa le sokele
when mama comes to do the housework

nani koe sii pani nukkue poe tii
you will be crying

nana peka ipi saetii maloye
mama will do housework

pani puna tola kanati maloye
she will do housework for you who are all small little girls

## Lullaby 41, Leticia Fernández

machi tola kanarkii maloye
you are all little boys

pani sapur urkua pale pani wake yala pale arpayeti malo waye um
you will go with your father to the mountains to work

machi tola kanarkii pani walaka pani tumputani maloye
you are the boys who will grow up

waka yale tanikii maloye
at the side of your father you will go to the mountains

papa ani peka sapur urkua pale waka arpayeti maloye
papa will teach you to work in the mountains

ya pani papa yala kale pani sapi wala kaka maiti maloye
at the side of your father you are cutting small trees

puna tola kanati tule neka piniti maloye
and your sisters in the house will be thinking of you

pea pini tii papa yeti maloye
they will always greet you upon returning to the house

puna tola kanapii ani peka uu mola koe nukkati maloye
your sisters will wash your clothes that you use for working

peki pani tule sapur urkua tanikki maloye
you [in my arms] are to work in the mountains

pani tumpu e pa tanikkii maloye
because of this you are growing up at the side of your father

kpapa yale tanikkii sapi wala kakae ti maloye
at the side of your father to cut small trees

pani tumpo e kua tanikkii maloye
for this you are growing up

wala pa kua pani machi tola kanapii malo
alone you grow at the side of your father

kuaa pani peka nu makati kpa pali ua kuaa e pi e kua nai pani kuse maloye
quickly and for you the little river girl will go to look for fish and thus she will
    always help you

nana tii pea pini ua kua sasike maloye
upon returning mama will greet you and clean the fish

pani wala papa tumko pani ua kpa so yeti maloye
you fish only for me

nana ye nana petakke maloye
mama will always be observing you

ua kua ti pani o kuneti maloye
the fish you bring will be to eat

yo nape pai yenikote kala
immediately you will be happy

ila tola kana neka pale pani meke pani nai maloye
when you go to the house of the devils [Panama] you will leave me

wala kua kua pelaye
when you go alone

pani mete pani nai maloye
you will leave me alone

nana pepa ipi nikuue kala nana peo tummotani maloye
your mama hopes that you will bring back presents and mama who made you grow up

nana pinsa carta malokua
mama thinks of always sending you letters

karmi ye nai nana peka kute maloye
[no translation]

pani tumkuturpala
and always mama thinks this: [she begins now to sing to the girls]

pani tumkuor tii
will you grow up or not?

nana pinsa ye
mama thinks

ye pani yaa kua kute mala sokele
when you are young girls I say

nana wala purkua nana pena lakua yepi puto ye
you will stay with mama

ani purkua ani kormakke tii puto ye
you will go everywhere with mama

nana tia titu yo purkui te mala sokele
and when mama dies some day mama will die

ani purkua pani ipi saiti pani kute ye maloye
we do not know what we will do

machi tola kanati
the sons will go

ila tola kana neka kakaliti
they will go to Panama

mani kuakua o nueti ye
to work in order to earn money mama thinks

nanatii pe malakale
they will send mama things

pe malakua seka nanatii
they will send mama things

ipi nukkuowele
when the sons are in Panama

nana pinsatii nana puto eye
mama always thinks this mama is always thinking

ani kala mimmi kanati
my little sons

ipi takkoe le nana pinsatii kuto e ye
you will go to Panama and send mama presents

pani tumkutani maloye
you are growing

yo pani kala pani
the boys

sapur urkua pali panii arpaiiti maloye um
you will work in the mountains


yo pani kala pani machi kpa mileti maloye
you will go to plant plantains

kola soka yala tanikkii maloye
you will be working at the side of your father

puna tola cantina
your sisters

ani yala palikkii malatii
for the boys who come at the side of papa

peka uu mola kue nukkati maloye
your sisters will wash your clothes

puna tola kanati
your sisters

tiiwala nukukua pali
just your sisters will go to the river

iikua sue tii maloye
to fetch water

puna tola kanati na ye
your sisters and mama

nana tii pe mala kpa pinni
they are here to greet you

nana ti ulu kpa e ti e ti maloye
mama will greet you and help to bring in the cayuco

nana tii na ye
mama is busy

nana pe malo tummotanikki kpa ye
mama is busy raising you

pani tumkortani maloye
you are growing up

pani mukku e kpa ye
when you were small

ipi pana pe malo tummotali kua
you grew and cried in the arms of mama

nana pinsa e kpa ye
mama thinks

nana pekpa ipi ni kue nakati nai
one of you will become important and will send mama presents

## Lullaby 48, Angélica Burges of Nalunega Island

tule puna tola pipi um
little girls

ani puna tola kana wala po po
you are my daughters

tuma ue tanikki maloye um
you are growing up in the house

ilu mala mana pinni nukati maloye
and you will serve to receive the visitors

ilu mala mana machi o e ye
the visitors will be men

na maka pulaye
mama only has daughters

puna tola kana walaa po po
little girls

na ma u e taniki maloye
I wanted that you would be girls

puna tola kanapi soke pu o e
girls that you are

tola puni kana wala kaki maniakua mie kua ti maloye
only the girls will walk about the house

puna tola kana kana um
like girls they should be

ilu mala kana pinni takkoe
they are born to receive the visitors in the house

ilu malo miku mala pole piki pu puto e ye
and to call on them

ilu mala machi kanapi maloye
the visitors will be men

io pana puna serkun wala kpo kpo ye
when you are older and unmarried

pani kilu mana kua mako e ye
you will sew clothes for them and greet them

pani kilu mana pio mako e ye um
you will sew clothes for them and greet them

pani kilu mala moo pili pali oko mako e ye
when the visitors come, upon arriving

niki olo kana io ko e ye
let them drink do not make them suffer

puna tola kanapi nana pe pua ye um
you are the women little girls

ilu malapa ipo mala yo kani pako e ye um
when you greet them do it happily do not let them suffer

ilu tule punapan terkan tu kuoe ye
they are older visitors

i wala nokele yeti maloye
do not leave them without full cups

tpi wale wala ki puu ye ti maloye
you will always be at their side

ilu wala ipu wala e ko peke nana kana peke ti puto e ye um
pay attention to what they say

ilu mala ilu maloye
you will always be at their side

ii mani manie malo e ye
what will you do?

puna tola kana soke puo e
mama has only daughters

nana peka nana pipi tili makoe
mama is looking for a turkey

nana pekoe noko pipi mani puke malo e ye
mama is looking for a turkey

puna serkun ti nana nana pipi nana perke ye um
you are still young girls and mama is happy

pani pirmako maki o e ye
happy that you are already older

tilu mala wala tapuka mola kala aki ko ko e ye um
you are old enough to cook and wash the clothes of the visitors

pani machir kanti maloye
you will greet the men

pani tule machirkan pinaye
you will greet the married men

pani tola petako e naye
you will greet them

pani tola aye piki ipuo ye na ye
you will always be happy

emi tii pani imalo tola puto ye
happy since you are women

## McCOSKER COLLECTION NUMBER 74.1 MADE IN 1974

The translations of three lullabies are given here as paraphrased by Víctor Pérez, a Cuna
Indian from Ailigandi.

### Lullaby 11, Eloisa Morres of Arretupo Island

Mario is the only son in the house
I do not know when he is going to grow up
brother, when are you going to call for help?
brother, when you grow, the uncles will call you to fish with them
when you are older, you will call me to wash the clothes
soon you will go with your father to work in the mountains
you are growing little by little
when you grow you will visit various places, we are girls who cannot do what boys
   do, we stay in the house to work

little sister
I am going to tell you, soon we will call our brothers
when they go to work, they are fishing for us
Mario, when you grow
we the girls stay in the house; when you grow up the uncles will call you to go to the
   foreigner's house to work
we the girls are going to work in the house
little sister: you are growing alone
the uncles are staying a long time in the foreigner's house
I am a girl, I am living with the family
we are girls and little sister, here you are growing up alone
Raquelita is a girl, and soon she will be helping her brother
the brothers are growing up and soon they will call us
Mario, soon you will grow and bring fishes to eat in the house
if the uncles were here, it would be good to find you

### Lullaby 12, Eloisa Morres of Arretupo Island

you are a boy who is going to grow and become a man, your father sees you
I was given a boy who will grow for me
when you grow, it will be for me and you will work for me, for the house
Mario, you are crying for your mama
soon you will not be with us when you grow up
I am a girl, I am with you and you are boys who are going to grow up
they are going to grow, they (the girls) are going to stay in the house, they (the
   boys) are going to work in the mountains

Eloisa Morres is about six years old. She is singing to Raquelita, her younger sister, about
Mario their brother, who is about five years old.

## Lullaby 13, Puna of Arretupo Island

small child, you are growing up to receive your brother who comes from fishing and to clean the fish that he brings

you are a boy who is going to grow and going to fish; your grandmothers are thinking that you will bring fish to the house. He is a boy; he will be a man and always he will be working, and the little girl is always in the kitchen

mama is watching you (the little girl), the uncles are going to call you to go fetch water in the river

mama is always attentive to what you do and what your needs are (the boy)

mama is doing the housework and she cannot attend to you; you are crying but mama cannot help you

mama is thinking, when you grow up you will be like the elders, working (the boy)

the grandfather is going to the mountains; you do not know the work that he does in the mountains, but you will receive him to see if he has brought something for you (the girl)

when the grandfather arrives, when he is in the house, because you are a girl, mama thinks that you will be well dressed, your mama always thinks this

mama is thinking of the other person: you will not bring him sadness, you will serve him well; the grandfather is always working in the mountains for the girls

mama will call you soon, where are you?

mama is always washing the clothes of the people

the people are coming; you will always receive them because they come with hunger

mama is thinking that you are my companion in housework and all that you will do

mama is always thinking, if the uncles in Panama will think to remember you by bringing you something

mama is always in the house waiting for when the uncles will return to the house; she is always in the kitchen working

the uncles will go to the house of the devil to learn to work and to learn to speak Spanish

the baby is crying and you will pick it up into the hammock and sing to it

you (the boy) will grow up and will go to Panama to work

soon the neighbors think that they too will have sons and they will work in the mountains; they will give them *madun* to drink, a drink for boys

the uncles are already men; they are always working in the river; he knows what he is doing because he is a man

you are a girl who is growing to receive the family

to receive the uncles when they arrive and to give them a drink

small little girl who is growing up

the uncle is always working in the mountains and you are here to receive him

come here, mama sees that the uncle is coming so that you can receive him

the uncle arrives with his boat and with the things that he brings from the mountains, and he calls you to help him bring up his boat on the beach

you are a girl who grows up beside your mama

you will cry for things that your mama cannot give you, your mama is working so that she can attend to you

your brother will be working in Panama like his cousin Roberto

mama sees you growing up to receive the visitors

## NILS HOLMER COLLECTION MADE IN 1951

("Cuna Chrestomathy," *Etnologiska Studier* 18:177–185)

### *Lullaby (a), related by Olobiginapi, the third chief of Ustuppu*

Napeka tula selekenaie uukachi kineye,
I am swinging briskly for you in the hammock,

Napeka uukachi ki tula aipanenaie taleku.
I am moving briskly to and fro for you in the hammock, it seems.

Emiti pani kwarukwa takkenye,
Now you are my little child, you see,

Unni nu pinale unnila pani po takkenye.
All you do is crying for the breast only, you see.

Nanti pe mettenatele sappur pali pani muchup poeta takkenye nu pinaleye.
If your mother goes to leave you for the woods, you will cry again and again all the
time for the breast.

### *Lullaby (b), Ammasippor of Ustuppu*

Susukwa, pani tunkutanikki, pani tummolo kusale,
Baby, when you come to grow up, when you have become a grown-up man,

Muupilli pali pani nanatakoe, pani muupilli pali manesaulu kine nanatakoe.
You will go sailing on the sea, you will sail on the sea in your canoe.

Pan ipemuutulekala pina pani soiti nanatoye.
For the sake of fish you will want to go sailing.

Em pani susukwa takkenye, pani nalusoet takkenye,
Now you are my baby, you see, you will go fishing porgy,

Pani nanatpaloe sappur pali macheret kuetteeye.
Again you will go to the woods, because you are a man.

Peti pani macheret takkenye, ipewaikwakwa arpatoe, Tata Ipeler onatoe.
You are a man, you see, you will go working (at planting) the corn until the sun
goes down.

Emi pani ipemimiryo naka osuilimakke takkenye.
Soon you will clear plantations below, you see.

Emi pani susukwa takkenye pap itu.
Now you are my baby, you see, until your father comes.

Pani sokto karson pinale nanatoe.
You want to go about wearing pants.

### *Lullaby (c) related by Efraín Castillero López, a son of Nele de Kantule, Ustuppu*

Uukachi ki anti peka polomakkenaie;
In the hammock I sit swinging for you;

Mimmie, melle poeye, ipika posapinsaeye?
Baby, don't cry, why do you want to cry?

Anti peka polomakkenaie.
I sit swinging for you.

Papati peka arpanaeti, peka okop tiknat insaye.
Father is going to work for you, believe [me], he has gone to plant coconuts for you.

Yoo tunkupiele [okop] ki matu kunnoye.
Soon, when you will grow big, you will eat bread and coconuts.

Yo(w)eche pe sappin kusale niakan nei se naoe,
Later on when you have become a young man, you will go to the negroes' houses,

Uumor pakkeka ku takkenye, punmar wiletaitinanaoe.
You will buy shirts, you will go about taking care of your sister.

Pan walikkachur takkenye, pani macheret ku takkenye, pe nan ka ieket takkenye.
You [will be] far away, you see, you will be a man, you see.

## Lullaby (d), related by Efraín Castillero López, a son of Nele de Kantule, Ustuppu

Yoo tunkupiele anka pe tii suo takkenye,
Soon when you will grow up, you will fetch water for me, you see,

Na punolo nape tummotanikki.
When I come to bring you up to be my little girl.

Yo[w]eche susmal apintaitinaor.
Later on you are going to take care of your brothers.

Pap ka nol enukkey, tat ka mas yoeka kue takkenye.
You will wash the clothes for your father, you will roast plantains for your grandfather, you see.

## Lullaby (e), related by Daniel Crespo, a son of Nele de Kantule, Ustuppu

Paniti kilumarkat takkenye,
You [will belong] to the uncles, you see,

Nape otummatanie, kilumar yarpali arbakutakkenye,
When I come to bring you up, you will come to work with the uncles, you see,

Tata ipelele onakkwetanikkoku pani nekaposumpa iekenae takkenye.
When you will come to pass the day [working outside], you are going to forget your
home, you see.

Nape otummotani takkenye, kirmar ka uasoet takkenye,
[When] I get to bring you up, you see, you [will] fish for the uncles,

Kirmar mas amiet takkenye.
You will fetch food for the uncles.

## Lullaby (f), related by Horacio Méndez of Ustuppu

Nanasailati peka naikualie,
Mother is sitting for you in the hammock,

Tulati aipanenaie, tulati selekenaie.
Moving briskly, swinging briskly, to and fro.

Uukachi ki peka tulati selekenaie, tulati aipanenaie.
I sit swinging for you briskly in the hammock, moving to and fro.

Nanati punator sokekuye, nanati punator sokekuye,
Since your mother is a woman, since your mother is a woman,

Uukachi ki peka tula na selekenaie, tula na aipanenaie.
She sits swinging briskly for you in the hammock, moving to and fro.

Nanti peka posumpanikapii kinatakketii, kinatakketii.
Mother goes about taking care of the house for you, goes about taking care.

Nanati, nanati peka wakkulukwale peka ipemimiryopi takkenaie.
Your mother, your mother prepares food for you in the morning.

Ani ukkule nape pinsaeye; napeka sasur sokeye, pani ukkuti mestao takkenye,
I think you are hungry; if I don't make [food] for you, you will suffer hunger,

Pani poetipi kutako takkenye.
You will just get to crying, you see.

Napeka Tata Nakipelele onakkwiali takkenye,
I spend the day for you, you see,

Ipemimiryo peka okusa takkenye,
Preparing food for you, you see,

Pani ipemimiryo ki pani puklusatokuye pani welikueti,
When you will eat food, you [will be] happy,

Pani kutokuaye pani totoeti.
When you grow up, [you will be] playing.

Pani kutokuye weki pani tummakutenakatinye, kwenatti impakine totoeti;
When you grow up, may it happen that you grow big here, playing with your
    brothers and sisters;

Pani kutoeti, pani kutosuliwalie.
Growing up, you will grow up, won't you?

Totoeti pani kutoenatte, pani tumma kuchokele,
You will grow up playing, won't you, [and] when you grow big,

Muu makattiti pa pupa aiprietie, pani kutosuliwalie.
You will go about on the sea, you will grow up, won't you?

Nanati wile pe tai takkenye,
Mother is looking after you, you see,

Pete muutulekala nikka ilekukwichi, pani kutoenye,
You are fishing [where] there is fish, if you grow up[?],

Pani tulemacheret sokekueye,
Since you are a boy,

Tata Ipelele apikaetieye, pani kutosuliwalie.
You receive [the heat of] the sun, you will grow up, won't you?

Wakkulukwar nape pinsaetii, anti kutosuliwalie.
In the morning I go about thinking of you, I will get there, won't I[?].

Muukunapilli kine nape apitakkekwichikutoe, nape apitakkekwichikutoe.
[While] on the sea, I will stand watching for you, I will stand waiting for you.

Nanati tulepunator sokekuaye posumpaneka kine pup aiprieti, anti kutosuliwalie.
Since your mother is a woman, she is going about in the house, I will get there, won't I[?].

Anti punator sokekuye, anti tulemacheret sokenaie,
Since I am a woman, I am saying [you are?] a man,

Teki nanti ipetiniki ulukwale pup aipriekwichi na epinsa takkenye.
And mother thinks [you] are walking about in the woods, you see.

Nanti punator sokekuye nanati naikusaye; anti niptola pa tanikki takkenye.
Because your mother is a woman, your mother is sitting in the hammock; I am the one who has come from above, you see.

Machipipie, pe papti an susa takkenye.
Little boy, your father took me, you see.

Anti Maniniiswalatola, anti neka se paraoteye par pinsasuli takkenye.
I am an inhabitant of the silvery star way, I cannot think of returning home again, you see.

Nanati peka tula na selekenai, tula na aipanenaie, tula na aipanenaie.
Mother sits swinging briskly for you, moving briskly to and fro, to and fro.

Nanati niptola pa tanikki takkenye, anti olokoetutu impapali, olokoelikitutu an neka takkenye.
Your mother has come from above, you see, as for me, my house is among the golden koetutu-flowers, the golden koeliki-flowers, you see.

Anmala neka wichulimalatti, oloniiswalatola, oloniiswalatola.
We are such as do not know the earth, inhabitants of the golden star way, people of the golden star way.

## Lullaby (g), Sia (wife of Mandiomaidiguini) of Ustuppu

Punolo pipie, napeka uukachi ki polomainaikuali, napekala posumpa yakkine;
Little girl, I sit swinging in the hammock for you in the house;

Punolo, nape otummoali pampakkati, pam pentakketi, matun tueti, nei turmieti.
Little girl, when I have brought you up, you [will be] always with me, helping me, cooking food, sweeping the house.

Petina tulepunatola takkenye, kwenatkan apintakket, kilumar apintakket.
You are a girl, you see, watching the brothers, serving the uncles.

Wakkutar papatina kwichikute, immal aminate pemar kala, pemarti punatol nanai takkenye.
In the morning your father got up, he has gone to fetch you things, you see, you are girls, you see.

Iwar yalapali uumol enukket takkenye, tii sumalat.
Washing clothes in the river, you see, fetching water.

Petina punatol takkenye; nape otummoalimarya,
You are girls, you see; when I have brought you up,

Tumma kualile neka ki uumot makkesioe;
When you become big, you will sit sewing clothes in the house.

Peti punatola sokkutinye, uaya nikka: nape otummoalina napirinye.
Because you are girls, listen: when I have brought you up, you must be good.

Pippikwa umpi an walikti; yoo tunkupi[e] sokele anitu pankutoe.
As long as you are little, you are about me; soon, when you will grow up, you will become separated from me.

Punormarye, susmalti peka sunnamakkali: "Napeka muumakatti pali nakweloe,
Girls, the brothers are saying to you: "We will go for a while sailing on the sea,

Muutule ilekunae, muumakatti pali naikusa, manisaur aipirenai.
Going to fish, stopping out at sea, turning the canoe,

Muutule nikka, ilekuenai."
There are fish, [we will] stop to fish."

Punamarti, nekaposumpati apitakket takkenye.
Girls, you are watching the house, you see.

Muumakatti pa neka palisokenai; Tata Nakipelele ulu onakkenai,
Out at sea, they are thinking of home; when the sun declines[?],

Manisaulu neka sikki aipiliali, uumol ainakkiali,
They are turning the boat homeward, hoisting the sails.

Mu apalisa ki opetanikki, neka se tokenonikki.
Getting wet from the waves, they return home.

# BIBLIOGRAPHY

Arauz, Reina Torres de
   1970   *Human Ecology of Route 17 (Sasardi-Morti Region, Darien Panama). Bio-environmental and Radiological Safety Feasibility Studies. Atlantic-Pacific Interoceanic Canal.* Felix Webster McBryde, trans. and ed. Columbus, Ohio: Batelle Memorial Institute.

   1972   "The Anthropology of Eastern Panama." *Bulletin of the Biological Society of Washington* 2:229-246.

Costales Samaniego, Alfredo, and Piedad Penaherrera de Costales
   1970   *Human Ecology of Route 25 (Atrato-Truando) Region, Choco, Colombia.* Maps and Drawings by Angel Barriga. Felix McBryde, trans. and ed. Columbus, Ohio: Batelle Memorial Institute.

Holmer, Nils M.
   1951   "Cuna Chrestomathy." *Etnologiska Studier* 18:1-183.

Kramer, Fritz, W.
   1970   "Literature among the Cuna Indians." *Etnologiska Studier* 30:1-166.

Loukotka, Čestmír
   1968   *Classification of South American Indian Languages.* J. Wilbert, ed. Reference Series, vol. 7. Latin American Center, University of California, Los Angeles.

Mason, Alden J.
   1946   "The Languages of South American Indians." *Handbook of South American Indians* 6:157-319.

McCosker, Sandra
   1974   "The Lullabies of the San Blas Cuna Indians of Panama." *Etnologiska Studier*
         33:1-190.

Nordenskiöld, Erland
   1938   "An Historical and Ethnological Survey of the Cuna Indians." *Comparative Ethnological Studies* 10:1-686.

Reverte, José M.
   1968   *Literatura oral de los indios cunas.* (Primer Premio "Ensayos," Concurso Miro, 1967). Panama.

Stout, David B.
   1947   *San Blas Cuna Acculturation: An Introduction.* Viking Fund Publication in Anthropology, 9. New York.

Wassén, Henry
   1949   Contributions to Cuna Ethnography, *Etnologiska Studier* 16:7-139.

# 2

# Cooperativism and Enculturation among the Cuna Indians of San Blas

NANCY BRENNAN HATLEY

## Introduction

A controversial approach taken by policy makers in attempting to develop areas of Latin America has been to encourage cooperatives, especially by the Agency for International Development (A.I.D.) and the Peace Corps as instruments of U.S. foreign policy. Among the underlying assumptions in that approach was that most indigenous communities provided a perfect environment for cooperatives because the Indian has a tradition of accomplishing certain projects on a communal work-force basis—Indians are described as "naturally, or at least culturally, cooperative." Recently, however, the cooperative movement in the Indian communities of the developing countries of Latin America has been considered a failure. When the establishment and functioning of cooperatives did not progress as planned, it was concluded that the idea of a tradition of cooperation among Indians was but a myth.

What follows is an examination of a successful Cuna cooperative in the community of Río Tigre. In this case the success may be directly attributed to two factors: (1) the preexisting organization known as the *sociedad,* which provides a firm foundation for the development of a cooperative, and (2) socialization and child-rearing techniques that precondition a Cuna for successful cooperative behavior. The sociedad has provided the Cuna with the organizational and basic business skills, while socialization and child-rearing techniques have created and nurtured an environment conducive to working cooperatively and collectively—both of which are vital to the success of the sociedad and the cooperative.

The Cuna inhabit a territory in northeastern Panama which begins at Punta San Blas and ends at the eastern side of the Gulf of Uruba. The vast majority of the Cuna (approximately 24,681) live on some 45 of the approximately 375 offshore coral islands of the San Blas archipelago, at a distance of about one mile from the mainland. The islands are small, densely populated, and less than three feet above water at high tide.

The Cuna are fairly recent residents of the islands, having moved to the coastal region of San Blas around the 1850s. The gradual move to the islands came shortly thereafter and for two major reasons: (1) the development of the coconut and tortoiseshell trade and (2) the islands provided a welcome relief from insects, snakes, and disease.

Although the Cuna have been in contact with Europeans and African blacks since the sixteenth century, they have maintained an extraordinarily low level of intermarriage and cross-cultural trade, exhibiting a strong sense of pride in their racial identity. As a consequence, the Cuna are one of the few surviving aboriginal tribes in Central America and northern South America who have managed to preserve much of their cultural traditions intact.

Most of the literature written on the island Cuna tends to generalize and to draw unwarranted similarities between them and those living on all the islands because of the obvious difficulty involved in studying each of the forty-five inhabited islands and because on the surface they seem to be identical—especially to the foreigner. But they are not and I wish to emphasize that the following article refers specifically to those people living on Río Tigre.

## The Sociedad

The sociedad is the organizational structure used by the Cuna of Tigre to perform most of their cooperative business activities. The basic premise of a sociedad is the same as that of a cooperative: the desirability and/or necessity of cooperation to attain a common goal. The Cuna, judging from their present organization of labor, strongly believe in the desirability of cooperation. They have realized the need for many people to work together to accomplish what many people working individually cannot do. In addition, the Cuna seem to realize it is easier, quicker, and more enjoyable to cooperate and work collectively than it is to work alone.

The rationale of cooperation for the traditional labor organization provided the foundation for the sociedades and for the Mola Co-op. The sociedad is basically an extension of the indigenous organization, but more sophisticated in that it calls not only for cooperation on the level of labor but also in the accumulation of capital. For example, one man alone could never have accumulated the capital necessary to buy a fishing net, a launch, or the goods to stock a *tienda* whereas a group of men and women could and did. The functions, management, employment, income, capital, and founding and liquidation of the sociedad are described below.

## Functions

The sociedad consists of numerous members, each owning an equal share of the assets and an equal right to the profits. The organization generally uses the contributions of the members as its major source of initial capital. Sociedades are either public—that is, composed of most of the people on the island and having open membership—or, private and notably smaller than the population of the island and having closed membership (e.g., Ukupa, whose membership is limited to relatives of the "founding fathers"). In addition, membership may be mixed or limited by sex. Among sociedades whose membership is limited to men are Ukupa, Abya Kuna, Ayuda Mutua, and Changuinola. Although only a male may hold title to membership, related women (i.e., the wife, sister, mother, daughter) may participate in the sociedad by right of the man's membership. Ukupa is primarily a farming sociedad. The Abya Kuna owns and operates a launch, sells goods wholesale and retail, runs a lottery, and distributes gratuitously—or at a discount—flour and plantains. Ayuda Mutua and Changuinola are fishing sociedades with important secondary functions. For example, Ayuda Mutua has a tienda, an insurance plan (for members only), a lottery, and a club house where the men can play dominoes, smoke, and talk. Changuinola is not as diversified, but like Ayuda Mutua, it is an important contributor to community functions.

Sociedades whose membership is mixed include three tiendas—Rancho, Panamá, and Colón, the restaurant, and the dance club, Noga Koppe. Of these Noga Koppe is the only sociedad that performs more than one function. The main function of the sociedades is putting on the weekly dances held for the town's entertainment. These dances, completely indigenous to San Blas, were begun and developed on Tigre, and for that reason Tigre is the annual host to a dance competition held annually on October 12. Additional functions include making and selling bread, selling sugar and coffee, and running a lottery. They also contribute, like Ayuda Mutua and Changuinola, to town functions.

Finally, there are three women's sociedades: Hilda Lutter de Durán, Augustín Serrano, and Solano, named after the person who founded the sociedad or a prominent member of the founder's household. The functions are the same for each: selling kerosene and gasoline, running a lottery, and primarily buying a pig and fattening it to host a feast for the island.

To get their activities started the sociedades require money and/or manpower from more than one household. All the activities were set up so that the initial investment, whether debt or shares, was repaid. Examples of repaid investments include the launch, restaurant, tiendas, and finca (i.e., land owned and farmed by Sociedad Ukupa).

## Management

Major decisions that will affect the long-term operations of the sociedad are made by a vote or a consensus of all its members. In the town sociedades, the vote is generally taken at the congress. In the smaller sociedades the vote is taken at a meeting of all the members. The members also elect the officers of the sociedades, usually annually. In most cases, the general votes are merely approvals of the recommendations of the *voceros* in the public sociedades, or of the *junta directiva* in the private ones.

All votes are usually preceded by considerable discussion. Examples of the decisions that would be submitted to the groups as a whole are those to make changes in the pay of employees, the investment of the profits, or the distribution of the profits. The advice of the junta in the smaller sociedades is more often solicited than is that of the *voceros* in a public sociedad.

Despite the ultimate power of the members and the strong influence of the recommendations of the officers, the key leader of the sociedad is the manager. He makes all the daily decisions and thus has a great effect on the operations of the sociedad. Even though the managers are not paid, most have to spend a great deal of time doing their job. Generally a manager is elected for a term of one year, and during that time, he is expected to run the sociedad as well as fulfill his traditional responsibilities to the family and participate in the town workdays.

This kind of management pattern seems to exist regardless of the size or function of the sociedad. The most traditional public sociedades have the same structure as the new private ones. The sociedades that build houses have a manager who is not paid and is responsible to the voceros. The same pattern holds true for the Chicha feast and other town functions. The town sociedades that run businesses with a more constant flow of activities such as the launch and restaurant are also managed in this way.

The smaller private sociedades have also followed this pattern. The tiendas generally rotate the job of manager among the members. Because of the small number of members in the tienda sociedades, however, they generally do not have juntas directivas. The larger sociedades, such as Ukupa and Abya Kuna, follow the town pattern much more closely, having a manager elected by the members and a rather powerful junta directiva to which he is responsible.

Although it is difficult to be certain of the origin of this, or any other structure, it seems that this one has its base in the older town sociedades that were organized to carry out projects in the town. In these, the manager resembled more a foreman of workday groups and consequently did not have to put in much more time than the others. Because being leader was an honor, the job of manager was probably accepted rather willingly. As the sociedades began to perform functions other than the mere project-oriented activities such as running the feasts, building houses, or maintaining the mainland roads, the job of manager became more demanding and more constant. Because operating the launch, the restaurant, and other activities is not limited to days when all have to work, constant supervision is required. The demands of the jobs have changed drastically, but the structure of management has carried over. Even the rather sophisticated private sociedades seem to have retained this structure.

This structure carries with it the obvious disadvantage of a lack of continuity in management—as soon as the manager really knows his job, he leaves. Also an unpaid manager cannot give his full effort to his sociedad, though he will generally do his best to make it run well because he is elected, subject to the members as a whole, and there is a good bit of social pressure on him to do well. In general, one could say that the advantages favor the small sociedad, small not in number of members but in activities. The smaller ones cannot pay a manager and rely on commitment. The larger sociedads require more consistent management to see through long-term investments and to keep the operations running smoothly, demand more time, and have trouble with part-time management.

## Employment

The most important single characteristic of employment is that all the jobs are passed around among the members, a rule that holds true for the paid jobs as well as for the nonpaid ones. This principle is seen most clearly in the sociedades that depend on town workdays for the labor, such as the town coco fincas. In these sociedades, all members of the town are required to work on the project on designated days. In sociedades that need a steady work force, such as the launch, the principle is modified though basically the same. Here the "unskilled" jobs are rotated among all the members. In the Abya Kuna, where the jobs were unpaid in the beginning (before the debt was repaid), all members were required to take their turn at work. Now the workers are paid, though the jobs are still passed among the members in the same fashion. Even the "skilled jobs," such as the restaurant cooks and the launch captains, are rotated among all those who are considered skilled enough to perform them.

Associated with the concept, or principle, of sharing the work are two firm beliefs. The first is that among the "unskilled" members of the sociedad, everyone is capable of performing the basic skills. Although certain members may be more skilled than others, all have an equal obligation to work when there is no pay, and all have an equal right to the jobs when they are paid. Second, the time needed to train people is not very important and everyone can learn to do the job. This belief causes the managers to have a great deal more patience with the fast turnover of employees than one would expect. The inefficiency of the new people and the mistakes that come with newness are not considered a major concern.

The basis for the job rotation system seems to be in the older sociedades that were performing tasks so basic that any able-bodied person could do them. As the functions of the sociedades changed, the basic practice of sharing has not changed as fast. Adaptations have been made through necessity, such as removing the skilled jobs of captain and machinist from the general pool of jobs; but, even here, once the jobs were removed from the general category, they were put on their own rotation system for those with the ability.

A second aspect of the rotation system may have its origin in the way the fruits of the coco fincas are distributed. In these fincas, all those who have a share are entitled to the harvest over a certain period of time. The sharing of the paid jobs may be like sharing the fruits of the finca. The salary is fixed, much like the coco yield. The benefit of the yield is given to the members by allowing them a certain amount of time or, for example, a month's salary. The salary may then be considered a dividend or a share of the profits just as a part of the coco production is a share of the profits from the finca.

The members very rarely receive any cash income from the society. Many of the tiendas distribute some of their profits at Christmas time, generally amounting to about ten to fifteen dollars per member. Most of the profits are kept within the sociedad and are used either to improve the business for which the sociedad was formed or to acquire an asset to be shared by the group. This could be a fishnet with a limited life or a coco finca that is quite secure. Most all of the successful sociedades have used some of their profit for a finca or several fincas.

In all of the sociedades, the income is used to repay the debts incurred in starting the sociedad before any money is used to expand the present operations, to buy other assets, or to be distributed. This seems to reflect a strong feeling of obligation to repay debts. Although the obligation to repay debts owed off the island is stronger than the obligation to pay within the island, most debts of one sociedad to another are repaid promptly. On these internal debts there is often no interest charged—or at most 10 percent. There is no due date for it is assumed that the debt will be repaid as soon as possible.

The desire to repay debts is closely associated with the desire to reinvest the profits, for the Cuna understand quite clearly that the value of their sociedad is the value of all the assets, which is usually the money invested, less the amount of the debt. Therefore, by repaying the debt, they are increasing the value of the asset they own. This increase is the same as what would come from reinvesting the profits in other assets of the sociedad.

There seem to be two major factors that have motivated the members to increase the value of the sociedad through reinvestment and debt repayment. First, traditionally there was little on which one could spend his money. Housing and dress were socially, if not "legally," restricted through tradition. One could not lead an easy life and use his income to buy mountain products and fish because tradition dictated that these products could not be sold (what was produced and not needed for the family was to be shared rather than sold). As a result of these traditions, there was little motivation to accumulate income. An income of coco, however, did have value because this could be traded; but since it was not traded for the basic items, this income was only supplementary.

The second major motivational factor is the importance of wealth to pass on to one's heirs. It is especially important to the Cuna that they pass on coconuts. Therefore, since the shares of a sociedad can be passed on they represent wealth to those who have them. If the sociedad has used its profits to buy coco fincas, the wealth represented by shares in coconuts is considered to be that much more secure. One might compare an investment in coco to an investment in bonds. The value is quite secure historically and good over a period of time. Though production is not great, it is steady, much like the dividends from a bond. Therefore, a sociedad will put its profits in coconuts much as a conservative organization that wants a secure place for its money will buy bonds.

## Capital

The sociedades generally acquire their initial operating funds from the sale of shares; this is supplemented by debt repayment. By most standards, the percentage of money that comes from debt is very high and the value of shares is quite low. This generally means that there is a huge debt to be repaid at first and a large membership base.

One would think that with such a small financial interest in the sociedad the members would not take a very active role in its affairs. The result, however, is just the opposite. Most members do participate, and when they stop participating they withdraw.

The initial small capitalization seems at first to be a definite weakness; but owing to the diligent debt repayment and reinvestment of the profits, this generally does not continue as a weakness for very long. This fast repayment is more certain than would be normal because the sociedades that still have debts outstanding generally keep their labor cost artificially low by not paying all of their employees, or by paying them at a rate below what they will receive once the debt is repaid.

## Founding and Liquidation

In the history of almost any sociedad one can discover one man, or a small group of men, who initially promoted it. Often with the larger private sociedades as with the public ones, he was a chief, a member of his direct family, or at least a vocero. These promoters continue to be very important in the life of the sociedad. Their importance is even greater in the new type of sociedad which requires more constant attention. These promoters frequently retain positions as officers or members of the governing board. Some of the more dynamic and effective managers are those who were among the initial promoters, or at least who were very close to the promoters.

When a member feels that a sociedad is beginning to decline or that his share is not enough to warrant the work he has to give it, he can withdraw (except from the public sociedades). When he wants to leave, all he has to do is indicate his desire, and he is paid his share of the assets of the sociedad. This ability to withdraw keeps the share from becoming so small that each member is left with but an insignificant part of the whole.

Just as one withdraws when shares get too small, members withdraw when the sociedad starts to do badly economically. Therefore, once the function for which the sociedad was formed has been performed and the profits decline, the sociedad begins to disintegrate and its membership dwindles. As a result, members are more likely to withdraw from a sociedad and let it die, and in turn start a new one with a different function, than they are to try to adapt the weak one that exists. This practice tends to keep sociedades limited to a single function.

## The Mola Co-op

The basic premise for any cooperative is the need to cooperate, the need for a group of people to work together rather than individually to accomplish an end. The collective labor organization among the Cuna calls for cooperation primarily in the area of labor. The sociedad calls for cooperation in both labor and the accumulation of capital. The Mola Co-op, however, extends beyond these two indigenous structures in that it requires cooperation and participation in the area of decision making as well as in labor and the accumulation of capital. The indigenous democratic political organization was instrumental in providing the women with the expertise in this decision-making aspect of the Mola Co-op, just as the labor organization and sociedad provided the expertise in the cooperation of labor and accumulation of capital.

The women were attracted to the Mola Co-op because it offered them a market for their goods,[1] a steady income, the opportunity to learn machine sewing skills as well as administrative and leadership skills, and a means of socializing. These advantages were sufficient to offset the time, effort, and money the women had to devote to membership.

What is known today throughout the Comarca as the Cooperativa de Productoras de Mola was merely a sewing school in 1965. Women on Nargana and Corazón de Jesús, under the direction of a Peace Corps volunteer, learned and practiced on borrowed treadle sewing machines and by the end of the year had begun to make "mola dresses" (hand-stitched molas incorporated into machine-stitched dresses) for sale. With the success of sales in Panama and a corresponding enthusiasm on the part of the women, the desire to participate spread to other islands. In September AID contributed twelve treadle sewing machines and with the distribution of these machines, the Co-op began to expand. Eight islands became involved in this sewing and selling.

For about a year these groups functioned more or less independently from one another with no unifying organization, even though all products were being channeled through the same market. And although it was neither formal nor legal, all the women were part owners of the store that was selling their products in Panama.

By 1967 certain standard sewing skills had been acquired and most of the island groups had a firm organizational structure. There was an obvious need for contact and communication on all levels. Certain responsibilities were becoming apparent, and the women felt these responsibilities should be shared by all equally. The store began demanding certain quality and standards. Consequently, many women saw the need for information and education.

The formation of a cooperative became one of the goals of the organization. The first step was a meeting of temporary representatives from all involved islands. In May 1968 all the islands convened for the first time. The purchase of a $5.00 share was required of any woman interested in becoming a member. Thus, no member was admitted without full payment for one share. Several more unofficial meetings were held before the Consejo de Administración (Board of Directors) met in July. This directive board consists of one representative from each of the member islands. Share money collected on the individual islands was presented to the treasurer. The share money was initially used to buy the material for making the mola products, which by this time had diversified for various reasons. Mola dresses were no longer being made, but rather stuffed pillows, table mats, napkins, stuffed animals, aprons, hats, and the like.

By May 1969 the Co-op had its own store and products were being sent in on a fairly regular basis. Because the store financially was barely "breaking even," however, the women were being paid on a consignment basis and some women had not been paid for more than a year. Then the store changed management and moved to a better location. The new manager began cutting back on costs, selling products wholesale, and exporting. Consequently, by May 1970 all the women in the Co-op had been paid in full and the Co-op was finally making a profit. In fact, the Co-op was making enough profit that a fund was established for the sole purpose of buying material. In addition, the women were being paid on a cash basis; as soon as the goods were received by the store the woman was paid at the next general meeting (held monthly)—regardless of whether or not her article had been sold.

The result of the economic progress was that the women took more interest in the Co-op. They began to realize it as a means of a steady income and thus began to produce more. They also took more interest in the monthly meetings, evidenced by better attendance and greater participation in the meeting itself. The Ministry of Agriculture[2] also began to take greater interest and assigned a Co-op agent, Eugenio Walter, a Cuna, to assist the women in Co-op education and thus initiate procedures for legalizing the Co-op. By May 1971 a great deal of progress had been achieved: a Panamanian woman was managing the store with the assistance of a Cuna woman; business was being conducted on a profitable basis; monthly Co-op education classes were being given by Walter; and membership was up to approximately 350 members with the addition of the socias from Ustupo (making a total of eight islands participating in the Co-op).

The prestige of the Co-op had also risen, as shown by the cooperation the Co-op received from the *sahilas* (chiefs who represent the various islands) and the launches. The sahilas of the eight member islands had recognized the need of Co-op women to travel and had made travel permits easier to obtain when the purpose for travel concerns the Co-op. The launches have agreed to extend special cargo rates to the Co-op when transporting their products and material. The Comarca in general also began to recognize the importance of the Mola Co-op by including its business on the agenda of the annual Congreso General.

The organization of the Mola Co-op consists of a junta directiva, chosen by the representatives from each of the eight islands. Meetings are held once a month and the location alternates among the eight participating islands. Those attending include the junta directiva, the representatives from each island, the store manager, the Co-op Agent, and important officials of the town in which the meeting is being held. The representatives from each island (usually around five or six) include the president, vice-president, secretary, and alternates. The alternates are an important carry-over from the sociedad; attendance at a Co-op meeting is considered a privilege to be enjoyed equally by all members and therefore must be rotated among all the members.

The manager of the Co-op attends every meeting and, apart from the payments, is responsible for submitting a report to the Co-op, which includes earnings, expenditures, and possible future projects which must be discussed and decided on by the socias, or members of the Co-op.

The Co-op Agent is responsible for educating the socias and seeing to it that the meetings and business conform to Co-op specifications. His job is a difficult one, for the majority of the socias are illiterate and do not speak or understand Spanish. Therefore, much of the Agent's time and effort is involved in translating and explaining what the manager, who speaks only Spanish, has said. His job would be vastly facilitated, of course, if the manager were Cuna and, at present, this is one of the primary goals of the Mola Co-op.

The sahilas, voceros, and other important town officials are invited to attend the Mola Co-op meetings as a matter of courtesy. This policy has definitely proven advantageous for the Co-op in that the better informed the town officials are, the more willing they are to cooperate with and assist the Co-op. In addition, these officials—because they have been chosen for their wisdom and knowledge—frequently offer the socias valuable advice and help.

It is in the monthly meetings that productivity policy is determined. Individual island problems are discussed in the meetings and the socias have recognized this to be most helpful in solving problems that could not otherwise be solved by the island group alone.

The individual islands are responsible for the bookkeeping and quality control. They are responsible for (1) judging the quality of the articles sent to the store (and seeing to it that a socia reimburses the Co-op for the value of the material in the event that her article is rejected), (2) packing and mailing finished articles to the store in Panama. In addition, each island is responsible for making a periodic inventory of supplies and placing an order for replenishment with the manager.

The Mola Co-op, like the sociedad, consists of many members, each having an equal share of the assets and an equal right to the profits. But the similarities between the cooperative and sociedad extend beyond these basic principles and can best be illustrated by analyzing the Mola Co-op—as was done with the sociedad—in terms of its functions, management, employment, income, capital, and founding and liquidation. In addition, the differences between the two organizations are also discussed to distinguish the Mola Co-op from the sociedad.

## Functions

The Mola Co-op is a production and marketing cooperative whose primary purpose is to make money. The principal functions include sewing mola products and sending them to the store in Panama City to be sold. Secondary functions include teaching fellow socias to sew by machine, running a lottery, and occasionally selling gasoline and/or plantains.

Compared with the sociedades on Tigre, be their membership mixed or not, the Mola Co-op is distinguished primarily because it markets its products in Panama City. The Mola Co-op, an all-female organization, is distinguished from the women's sociedades because it is a sophisticated business organization rather than a "hostess" organization whose main purpose is to provide a feast for the town.

## Management

Like the sociedades, major decisions affecting both the long-term and short-term operations are made by a vote or a consensus. The primary difference between the sociedad and the Co-op is that Co-op decisions are made in the monthly Consejo meeting by the junta directiva and representatives of the various islands. This has the effect of redistributing responsibility in the decision-making process but has not proven a major obstacle to the functioning of the Co-op. When a controversial decision must be made, the procedure is to present the issue in one meeting and decide on it in the following meeting. This allows the representatives to discuss it thoroughly with their individual island group. Naturally, when an issue calls for an immediate decision, the junta directiva and representatives are held accountable.

Another primary difference between the two organizations is that the manager in the Co-op receives a salary and the job is not rotated among the members. Surprisingly, however, there have been no problems created by this variation. This may possibly occur because the store operates in Panama City (a place where life is considered by the Cuna to be complex and difficult) and the women have an appreciation for the difficult duties of the manager. The manager is, nevertheless, held accountable to a great degree for the financial success of the Co-op—like the manager of a sociedad.

Although the manager of the Co-op lives and works in Panama, she does have a counterpart on the islands in the person of the secretary. The secretary's duties in the Co-op are roughly comparable with those of a manager in a sociedad. The secretaries in Tigre not only keep the books but they also conduct the sewing classes, attend the monthly Consejo meetings, conduct meetings on the island, and are in charge of the weekly lottery.

## Employment

Unlike the sociedad, the Co-op has no employees other than the manager in Panama. Each socia is responsible for her own work from the initial cutting of the pattern to the finishing touches made by hand or machine. There is, however, close cooperation among the socias in teaching various skills related to machine sewing or in any other steps involved in making a mola product. In fact, it is not unusual for an island to accept an order from the store which entails cooperation throughout each phase of production. For example, Tigre has accepted orders for molas so large that it would take one woman six months to fill them. By sharing the work the order was completed within a month. The pay, in turn, was distributed among all those socias who helped make the molas.

The only job rotation which occurs in the Co-op and which may be compared with the sociedad is that of the suplentes, the alternates who attend the monthly Consejo meetings. It is an attractive job, simply because of its social character, for there is no salary involved.

## Income

Like the sociedad, the establishment of the Mola Co-op necessitated an initial investment of $5.00 for a share. And again, like the sociedad, this initial investment was eventually repaid to each socia. In fact, by comparison, the Co-op has proven quite successful in terms of earnings on the initial investment for there is not a single socia in Tigre who has not earned at least double her initial investment of $5.00. Furthermore, unlike the sociedad, the members of the Mola Co-op receive a regular monthly income based on their production. They have not yet received interest on their investment, however, because the Mola Co-op has not accumulated sufficient profits.

As for investments other than the initial one, the only investment made by the socias on Tigre was for the construction of a sewing house. To finance the construction, the socias applied for and received a $150.00 loan from the junta directiva,[3] at a 10 percent interest rate. In order to repay the loan, the Mola Co-op on Tigre charged each socia $2.50 and the remainder was acquired through the sale of lottery tickets, gasoline, and plantains. The entire loan was completely paid off within six months.

Another similarity between the sociedad and the Mola Co-op which contributes to the success of the Co-op among the Cuna is the disposition of shares. The shares of the Co-op may be passed on to a member's heir. This factor probably played a role in attracting membership owing to the importance the Cuna now place on passing wealth to one's heirs.

## Capital

The Mola Co-op, like the sociedades, accumulated its initial operating funds from the sale of shares, but without the usual supplement of a loan. The shares were used to buy material and sewing supplies to be shared among all the member islands. The sewing machines were supplied through a contribution from CARE and AID.

## Founding and Liquidation

The Mola Co-op was initially the idea of a Peace Corps volunteer, but it gained momentum and popularity as the result of the strong leadership of such people as María Hernández de Escobar of Tigantiki—who became the first president of the Co-op—Adela López de Tejada of Tupile, Rosaura Navas of Tigre, Adela López of Playón Chico, and Rosalía Chiari of Corazón de Jesús. These women have provided strong leadership on their own islands and have held or at the time of this writing were holding positions as officers or members of the junta directiva.

Withdrawal from the Co-op is as easy a process as it is in the sociedad. To withdraw a socia need merely indicate her desire to the board of directors on her particular island, who must then relay the message to the junta directiva. The junta directiva is then responsible for returning to the socia her $5.00 *acción,* or share.

Fortunately, I can only discuss the liquidation of the Co-op in hypothetical terms, for the Co-op, to date, has proven a success for the women of San Blas, judging by its growth from 20 members on two islands to approximately 350 socias on eight islands. Liquidation, in any case, would probably parallel that of a sociedad in that the socias would simply request the return of their shares and let the co-op die.

The basic organizational structure of the Mola Co-op, then, is so similar to that of the sociedad that in some areas it is identical. This similarity was one of the major factors influencing the decision to develop the "sewing groups" into a cooperative. Another major factor was the belief that by forming the organization into a cooperative as opposed to a sociedad, the members could then be eligible for the support and protection afforded any business organization legally recognized as a cooperative by the Panamanian government.[4]

## Child-Training Techniques

Children are without a doubt the most valued element in any Cuna community. They are a source of pride and unlimited attention. To examine the techniques used by the Cuna in child rearing is important and relevant to understanding the success of the Mola Co-op for what it embodies is cultural specific education toward cooperative behavior— that is, the development and reinforcement of such behavior. The agents of child rearing, the techniques of socialization, and the behavior systems are the three areas upon which the following discussion is based.

### Agents of Child Rearing

An agent of child rearing is any person charged with the responsibility for the care, training, or discipline of the child, such as near and/or distant relatives, peers, neighbors, or special disciplinarians. These agents are responsible for socialization of behavior systems and are primarily the parents of a child and other children in the household. There are four categories of agents: caretakers, teachers, passive agents, and disciplinary agents.

Caretakers are most necessary for the very youngest children in that the younger the child[5] the less it is able to take care of itself. Usually for the first two years the main responsibility for caring for the child rests with the mother and about 75 percent of her time is devoted to that task. When she is unable to care for the child, the responsibility is delegated to another member of the household. As the child grows older the responsibility for care is increasingly delegated to the female children in the household. (Boys are usually not held accountable for care of a younger sibling, except to protect and comfort it.) Failure to take responsibility for caring for a child usually involves no more than a scolding. One might attribute this to the very positive feelings the Cuna have toward children; it is considered an honor and a means of enjoyment to care for a younger child and therefore children rarely shirk that kind of responsibility. In like manner, the child is not considered the sole "privilege" of the mother—by the mother or by anyone else. In other words, from the time it is approximately one week old, a baby is, in a sense, the common property of the village. It is carried from house to house, usually by another child (who is not necessarily a relative), so as to share the joy that a newborn is certain to evoke. In addition, the town is also responsible for caring for that child if it is ever in need and a member of its family is not available to care for it.

There are very few tasks that might take a mother, or chief caretaker, away from the child because it is generally acknowledged by the town and the household that a mother of a young child (up to three or four years) should be excused from those tasks that would necessitate her absence from the child for any length of time. When this absence does occur, however, the child—who by now has become quite accustomed to being cared for by a plurality of people—is then put in the care of another relative until the mother's return.

After a child reaches two or three years it is increasingly cared for by an older child in the household, who then becomes responsible for the child. Naturally, the mother is the principal "teacher" as far as weaning and the initial stages of toilet training are concerned. After that, the other children in the household play an increasingly important role, especially in teaching such skills as walking, talking, and even working. The mother and other adults then simply become overseers to assure that the child is being taught correctly by the children.

More role models are available for female children than for male because women rarely leave the island or even the house and when they do they take their children with them whenever possible. The adult men spend at least half the working day away from the island and the boys do not accompany them until they are about twelve or thirteen years old. As far as the boy's role around the house and island is concerned, there are two kinds of models. When an adult male model is absent (usually from 6 A.M. to 2 P.M.), the boy is taught his role by the women through a process of exclusion. That is, the women and girls in the household exclude a boy from specific tasks and roles that are considered the domain of women and improper for a boy to perform. Once the father or men in the household return, the boy is usually included in whatever the men may do—unless he is too young (i.e., not yet weaned from his mother).

During this early period lullabies are especially important, for a boy hears daily what will be expected of him as a man (see chapter 1 above).

Until a boy is old enough to accompany adult men, his principal models are his peers. Thus he spends most of his day playing with his siblings and neighbor children. As he grows older he is increasingly expected to play with other boys rather than girls.

Many of the games children play are derived from what they observe during such ceremonies as the Surba Inna, Inna Suiti, and Inna Mutiki. Children are welcome and present at any and all occasions—except perhaps for the Piba Uwe ceremony, a religious ritual the purpose of which is to purge the island of evil spirits. (For more complete information, see Nordenskiöld, 1938:496-499.) The participation of children in ceremonies and festivities is limited primarily to observation, although there is no such restriction as "be seen and not heard."

As children grow older their siblings and peers increasingly gain in importance as passive agents because of the time spent together in attending school. Also, as a child grows older it is expected to take on more community responsibilities (e.g., in the form of cooperative work projects) which are performed with one's peer group.

The authority to punish a child's deviations is left to the parents, grandparents, aunts, or uncles, in that order. If one of these disciplinary agents is not present, then the oldest person present (even if the difference in age is only a couple of years) is understood to have the authority to discipline a child. Men and boys, however, act as disciplinarians only when there are no women present. In the event a person in authority fails to control a child, that person or the parent is held responsible. This rarely occurs, however, and when it does a child's deviance is often dismissed because "children will be children." There is much leniency in disciplining children, and a parent—or anyone else, for that matter—can be chastised by the community for being too severe with a child. Conversely, if a parent or relatives are neglectful, the town has "policemen" who are authorized to discipline a child who is misbehaving in public. This usually consists of no more than a verbal scolding or, at most, threatening to tap the child with a much feared thorny stick called *dakke*.

## Techniques of Socialization

To control the behavior of children and to transmit to them rules, values, beliefs, and skills, various techniques are used by socializing agents: rewarding, inciting, distracting, instructing, disciplining, and specifying rules.

The most frequent reward techniques observed were tangible and intangible in nature. When a child is very young it is rewarded with affection, symbolizing love, acceptance, nurturance. But as the child grows older (betwen the ages of two and seven) material rewards in the form of food, toys, and pets are used. When this technique ceases it is supplanted with that of granting privileges. The idea of rewarding by granting privileges is actually a technique used very early with the child and as it grows older this becomes increasingly important. Rewards symbolizing prestige or achievement, however, are very infrequent.

Inciting is a technique used in conjunction with the reward of material goods. It takes the form of promises of reward contingent on "good" behavior. It is most frequently used with younger children although it is occasionally applied to older children when promising to grant a privilege.

Distracting is reserved almost exclusively for babies and very young children. Usually its purpose is to keep a child from crying and in this case often overlaps with inciting.

Young children are constantly being instructed. Parents usually are the agents when structuring situations for teaching purposes. For example, a mother will tell her young child upon leaving the house not to cry, to be friendly with other children, and not to quarrel or fight. Coaching and demonstrating, however, are done primarily by an older sibling or child in the house, although all members of the household will participate in this technique at some time or other. The occasion for this technique is usually to teach a child some skill and for very young children it is frequently in the context of play. For example, a common toy among the Cuna is a small wooden canoe with a paddle, carved by the father or other member of the household. While playing, an older child will invariably show a younger child the correct seating and paddling procedure. In this way, both boys and girls are introduced at a very early age (about three years) to a skill they will undoubtedly use for life.

The instruction in discrimination of cues is a technique less frequently used. The occasion for its use, however, is often to instruct a young child in self-protection—as against fire, never going alone to the ocean, and generally to stay close to home or other people who can protect a child from any accidents. This technique is frequently used when teaching a child to discriminate between personal possessions that are shared and those that are not. As a child grows older and more sophisticated, he or she receives instruction from the community at large through the medium of the nightly Congreso meetings. In these meetings the sahilas and the elders in the town instruct the people as to proper Cuna conduct and behavior—by means of fables or singing of any one of the numerous Cuna mythologies.

Another means of instruction that deserves mention is lullabies. Whereas an adult or older child receives formal instruction in Congreso, babies and very young children receive more informal instruction from lullabies. They narrate what the expected future of a child will be, as well as the future of other children in the household. They are particularly specific as to traditional male-female roles in life and one's responsibilities to one's elders.

Discipline as a technique of socialization takes four forms: physical injury, ridicule, denial of privilege, and withholding of support. Physical injury as a means of discipline is most important because of its absence and also because the Cuna place so much importance on suppressing it. According to the Cuna there is no justification for disciplining a child (or anyone else, for that matter) by injuring him physically. Andrew Salazar explained it in this way: "A child is a very precious thing and to hurt it or abuse it in any way is to bring about one's own sorrow and hardship in old age. For who will take care of one if not one's children? And what child, if abused in its youth, will have love and want to care for such a parent?"

Ridicule, by contrast, is undoubtedly the most frequently used form of disciplining. It is a technique used by people of all ages, both sexes, and in any and all occasions. Teasing is not only the most common form of ridicule and discipline, but it is also the most commonly used technique of socialization. Sometimes the teasing can be quite intense. But regardless of the intensity, the object of the teasing must show good humor lest he or she suffer the consequence of ostracizing or denial of a privilege.

Denial of a privilege is less frequently used to discipline because the Cuna consider it relatively severe. When a child is very young and the object of this type of discipline, the denial is usually little more than a threat since disciplinary agents are so lenient with children. As a child grows older, however, these threats, though less frequent, are more real. The agent of discipline begins to change from primarily household members to the community at large. Finally, when the transgressor is an adult the agent of this kind of discipline is the town council, which uses the following measures for denial of privilege: revoking a person's right to travel for a period of one year; barring a person from either membership or active participation in a sociedad for one year; and, when applicable, removal from office and/or prohibition from holding office in any organization for one year. The causes for imposing such strict sanctions are usually related to transgressions of a moral nature or to overt displays of anger.

Withholding support is a more complex means of discipline which is used frequently in response to a child's deviation. The occasion for imposition of such discipline is usually when a child misbehaves in public (i.e., cries, has a tantrum, or displays aggressive behavior). Rather than discipline a child publicly, however, the agent will usually wait until they arrive home and then scold the child, saying that such behavior is shameful and that people will look poorly on the child and probably ostracize it for such behavior. If a child persists, the agent of discipline may threaten not only public ostracizing but also withholding the support of family and relatives. Again, however, this means of discipline is infrequently enforced because of the general leniency toward children. As a child grows older the threat of ostracizing by peers and the community becomes an important means of social control. Living conditions (e.g., close quarters, small island, and high priority placed on cooperation) make this form of discipline a serious concern and one to be avoided.

Rules of conduct are clearly specified during early childhood and are repeated continuously throughout one's lifetime, especially at the nightly Congreso meetings. A common scolding for a young child is as follows: "Who told you to misbehave? You misbehaved and therefore you suffer the consequences."

## Behavior Systems

A system of behavior is a class of responses and the response tendencies associated with a given type of motivation or general category of response (Whiting et al., 1966:43). The behavior systems examined here are nurturance, sociability, self-reliance, achievement, and responsibility. Nurturance tends to influence sociability; and training in self-reliance tends to influence achievement striving (ibid., p. 15).

These particular behavior systems were chosen because they are most conducive to creating a cooperative personality. Behavior systems that would stand in opposition to cooperation would be aggression, and an excess of self-reliance, of achievement training, and of competitiveness.

*Nurturance.* —Nurturance is behavior directed at caring for the needs of others who are more helpless. It is likely to be exhibited in interaction with another person who is behaving succorantly, as in taking care of a baby. A highly nurturant person, however, may exhibit nurturance also in relation to another person who would be perfectly able to take care of his own needs. In interacting with a more helpless person, nurturance is the opposite of aggression. Thus, there is a distinction between the mere absence of aggression—refraining from hurting the more helpless person—and positive nurturance—actively helping him (ibid., p. 48).

In childhood, nurturance is most conspicuous in one's behavior toward younger children—and not exclusively toward one's younger siblings. This may be in part because of the concept among the Cuna that a child is the joy and responsibility of the entire community. A young child, perhaps from about three to seven years, may be rewarded with praise for showing nurturant behavior toward another child, but as the child grows older, the attitude shifts. It is then expected to be nurturant and therefore rather than being praised for such behavior, a child, or anyone else, is punished for the absence of it.

Another important means for expression by socializing agents of beliefs, practices, and values associated with helping people in need is found in the religious beliefs manifested in the mythology and historical accounts related in the Congreso. Several nights each week are devoted to counseling the men in proper behavior as prescribed by ancestors, gods, and mythological characters. This advice relates the benefits of helping others in need and of the necessity for the Cuna to live in harmony with one another—to cooperate, not quarrel. In addition, daytime Congreso meetings are called monthly specifically for women to give them similar advice—probably in deference to their important role of imparting to their children the desirability and necessity for nurturant behavior.

Another factor influencing nurturant behavior is the intrinsic rewards of such behavior, examples of which include the companionship that results from caring for another child and—not to be underestimated—the privilege of access to more food (e.g., bread and sweets, which, when available, are given without reserve to young children). Conversely, intrinsic punishments for absence of nurturant behavior include a lack of companionship and playmates—in fact, a kind of ostracizing by one's peers. Not only are there no inhibitions to nurturant behavior, but in fact, only encouragement.

*Sociability.*—Sociability is behavior that consists of making a friendly response to other people and enjoying friendly interaction. It implies an expectation of reciprocity, and is most likely to be seen in the relationship of people of approximately equal status. Sociability may also be manifested toward superiors and the response expected of the other party is a similar friendly response rather than a response more characteristic of the superior or inferior position (ibid., p. 60).

Sociability is an extremely important aspect of life on Tigre and most Cuna babies are initiated into it within one week after birth. They are taken (usually by a sibling or another child) from the mother and to visit from house to house where they are passed from one pair of arms to another. An infant is never left alone, not even while sleeping.

A child's propensity for friendliness is very important and probably for that reason the Cuna interpret a baby's first smile and laugh as a positive indication of sociability. As Sra. Hilda Lutter de Durán expressed it, "When a baby smiles or laughs for the first time, it means it will be friendly with all."

The sociability of the older child toward others is usually rewarded by including the friend (or friends) in trips to the river or by giving gifts of food to the friend and/or to the friend's family, for example, fetching water for the friend's family when a trip to the river is made.

The only occasions for punishing a child's sociability are when it is obviously interfering with the child's tasks, or when the sociability with the opposite sex of a girl who has reached puberty threatens her chastity. Otherwise children are punished only for a lack of sociability, such as withdrawing or being aggressive when friendly interaction would have been possible.

The high value placed on sociability is reflected in several ways: the emphasis placed on cooperative work efforts; the fact that most tasks are performed on a group basis; and the number of sociedades that serve both a social and economic function. The nightly town meetings and the importance parents place on their children's having friends are also indications of the value of sociability. Finally, all the women interviewed were active in at least two or more sociedades.

The very fact that almost all activities in Tigre are carried on collectively rather than individually influences intrinsic rewards for sociability. This is related to the many rewards, such as food, that are associated with social functions. Examples of a few of the group activities in which the participants are offered food and/or drink are weddings, funerals, special Congreso meetings, the three puberty celebrations, housebuilding, the annual dance festival on October 12, Christmas, and New Year's Eve.

Conversely, the factors influencing intrinsic punishments for sociability are almost nonexistent in Tigre. There is a marked absence of opportunity aggression, of aggressive rejection, and of castes and classes whose social regulations might lead a young child to be punished for friendly advances across barriers not yet discriminated. The primary factor influencing intrinsic punishments for lack of sociability is that life in Tigre is so arranged that the child who withdraws is deprived in many ways.

Finally, sociability behavior is reinforced simply because of the ease with which a child who tries to be sociable succeeds in being so. It owes this in part to the widespread friendly mode of response so prevalent among the Cuna children and to the general absence of rules restricting friendly interaction among children in close contact.

*Self-reliance.*—Self-reliance is behavior that consists of taking care of oneself, of being independent of nurturant assistance from other people to supply one's needs and wishes. It involves a definite orientation toward meeting one's needs oneself but is not to be confused with isolation or withdrawal from sociability. Self-reliance is distinguished from responsibility to the extent that it involves independence of method in reaching one's own goals, whereas responsibility relates to the acceptance of orientation toward goals set by one's status position (ibid., pp. 52–53).

In general, the Cuna places much less emphasis on training in self-reliance than on training in succorance, nurturance, and sociability. For example, in infancy and early childhood, a child is encouraged to depend on others to fulfill its wants and needs. For the first three years or so when a child is never left alone, the youngster is encouraged to play with others so that even in play they can attend to his slightest wants and needs. Even when being toilet trained, a child is not pressured toward self-reliance but is trained to go to either a sibling or to another child to accompany him in relieving himself. In fact, a boy usually is not trained to be completely self-reliant with respect to toilet training until he is about five or six, and a girl until she is about seven or eight years of age.

Evidence of self-reliance in connection with hunger and thirst does not appear until late in childhood. It is not until a boy reaches manhood, that is, goes regularly to the mainland to farm and thereby contributes to the food supply of the household, that he is allowed to enter the kitchen house without the consent or knowledge of an adult and help himself to whatever prepared food is available. This is essentially true also for girls. They may start preparing some of their own food at about the age of eight or nine, but must have the permission of another woman in the household. To prepare food without someone else's consent, a woman usually must be considered an adult, that is, married or at least past puberty.

Boys are treated differently from girls in respect to their freedom to play away from home. Boys are encouraged to show self-reliance and independence in this regard at about three and a half to four years of age, when a child has obviously mastered the skill of walking and identifying his whereabouts. A girl, however, is not allowed to leave the house alone until she is about six years of age, the age at which most girls enroll in school.

As for rewards and punishment for self-reliant behavior and their relation to inhibiting or encouraging such behavior, there is a distinct tendency to punish self-reliance. This kind of training is evidenced, for example, in the reproof a child receives for getting his own food between meals or—for a girl—for leaving the house alone.

The training of the socializing agents is reinforced by physical and social factors. For example, the economy and natural resources dictate that one can function best on a group or cooperative basis, not on an individual basis. In addition, because of the unpredictability of meals (anywhere from 12 noon to 6 p.m.) self-reliance may often mean missing out on meals and going hungry.

*Achievement.*—Achievement is a system of behavior that consists of "evaluating one's behavior and that of others by referring to standards of excellence, and striving to behave so as to merit as high a place as possible on a scale of excellence" (ibid., p. 55). Achievement motivation includes competition with others for the highest place on some recognized scale of attainment, and though it may be the most important form of achievement striving, it is not the only one. Where competitiveness is restrained there may be a vigorous striving to attain individual standards of excellence. Achievement motivation, however, should not be equated with social mobility. In addition, "achievement-oriented behavior, and training for it, will often be encountered in situations which are also relevant to responsibility and self-reliance" (ibid.).

During infancy and early childhood very little concern is expressed with respect to achievement motivation or striving. There is more quantitative evidence of evaluation of children than qualitative. But even this is rarely voiced or discussed. In fact, there is very little pressure applied toward achievement striving in childhood.

As a child grows older there is more emphasis on achievement striving with respect to those skills that are aesthetically important, such as a woman's ability to make molas or hammocks and a man's ability to make baskets, wood carvings, and canoes. Apart from these skills, however, the Cuna view a man's ability to be a good fisherman or an eloquent speaker, for example, as a gift one is born with or has acquired by means of medicine.

Reward is given not so much for achievement-oriented behavior as for industriousness. This may, in part, be attributed to the firm belief among the Cuna that everyone is equally capable of performing the same task. In fact, achievement-oriented behavior is minimized to the extent that everyone, children and adults, is severely criticized and teased for boasting about their achievements. The principal goals set by the society are such that they are attainable by all and therefore, to the Cuna, it is improper for someone to boast about his achievements. Furthermore, competition is so discouraged that an individual who is successful in competition may be ostracized by unsuccessful competitors. This seems to be based in the belief that no one should make any gain at the expense of another and that everyone is equal.

*Responsibility.* — Responsibility is behavior that consists of performing tasks, duties, or routines expected because of one's status in the community or family. Included are economic tasks, collecting food and fuel, carrying water, cooking, washing clothes, attending school, and participating in rituals as an obligation. They are duties thought of as required for the good of the family or community (ibid., p. 50).

Responsibility training begins quite early in a child's life, although the extent varies between girls and boys. At about four years a child is expected to help the other children in the household care for the chickens, feed them in the morning and put them in their baskets or cages at night. This responsibility is so common that at times it seems to be a community task, that is, young children from various households run playfully around in a group gathering up the chickens at dusk.

At this age children are expected to start helping other children. This applies more to girls than to boys because girls are given more responsibility at an earlier age as they are expected to do more chores around the house. For example, at the age of about eight a daughter is given the responsibility of seeing to it that her father's supply of bath water is always full. This daughter is perfectly within her rights to ask another younger girl in the house, four or five years of age, to help her fetch the water. The daughter may not scold the younger girl for failing to help, however, since everyone recognizes that the responsibility belongs to the older girl and not the younger.

Children are encouraged to take on certain responsibilities by associating the task or chore with adulthood and special privileges. Responsible behavior is often rewarded, then, with a special privilege.

Responsibility is also rewarded with praise, though in a rather indirect way. A child often hears—in the home, at Congreso meetings, and even at school—that children who help their parents by performing chores and tasks for them are good and a source of pride for their parents and that those who do not must not love their parents.

A show of lack of responsibility may bring a quick reprimand. Usually, the cause for such punishment is tardiness in performing a task or evading it altogether. If the cause for punishment seems to warrant more than a mere reprimand, for example, if a young man shirks a responsibility that may result in a shortage of food for the family or community, the parents or head of the household may threaten the child with taking him before either the town council or Congreso for public censure. In the most severe cases a young man may be forced by the town to perform special tasks for the town, but this rarely occurs.

The Cuna place a high value on industriousness and have contempt for a lazy person, as reflected in the often-repeated saying that one who rises and bathes after the sun has risen is lazy and will age before his time. Parents will also caution a son against sloth by saying no woman will want to marry him, or that once he does marry, his father-in-law will not be so kind with him as before, for he will make him work very hard.

Several factors influence the intrinsic rewards for responsible behavior: the food supply is directly dependent upon the man's performing his duties as a farmer, fisherman, and gatherer of food; many of the tasks performed are considered pleasurable in themselves (e.g., going to the river to fetch water and wash clothes); and, as one grows older and takes on more responsibilities, there is a corresponding increase in opportunities for one to socialize since many of the responsibilities are of a cooperative nature.

Children are gradually introduced to their prospective tasks and responsibilities and therefore there is little opportunity for one to be frustrated when trying to be responsible. Another important factor influencing a child's attempts to be responsible is that the assignment of tasks is well adjusted to a person's skill level as a function of age and individual differences.

## Conclusion

The success of the Mola Co-op is directly related to its minimal demand for modifying the social and economic relations between individuals. The similarity between the sociedad and the cooperative added to the child-training techniques that provide the Cuna with the background so necessary to a successful Co-op are the primary causes.

The child-training aspect is vital to understanding the perpetuation of cultural values and institutions. In examining the different behavioral systems and socialization one can understand why the Cuna cooperate so successfully. The agents of child rearing are of course important elements in the process of socialization because they give guidance and serve as models for the perpetuation of cooperativism. The techniques used by the agents are the means used for controlling the behavior of children and for transmitting rules, values, beliefs, and skills to them. Thus, Cuna childhood training has prepared Cuna adults to participate in a community where cooperation is the modus operandi, and the institutions of the society reinforce and reaffirm that training.

The success of the Mola Co-op may be attributed not only to the relevant experience and preparation that the Cuna acquire through the sociedad and child rearing but also to the needs that it fulfills: the Co-op provides an income for the women which they would have no other means of acquiring, and it provides the Cuna an attractive and valuable socializing medium.

## NOTES

1. The mola consists of two rectangular pieces of appliqued cloth sewn to a yoke or bodice for neck and sleeves. To make the mola, a woman takes several pieces of cotton fabric of different colors and bastes them together along the outer edges; then working from the top layer down she cuts through the various layers to create the various designs. As the shapes are cut out, the edges of the openings created are turned under and sewn to the fabric layers underneath. The color showing through the openings depends upon the number of layers which are cut through in a particular place. Depending upon the amount of time a woman

can devote to sewing, and the care taken, a mola requires from two weeks to several months fo finish.

2. The Department of Cooperatives is under the auspices of the Ministry of Agriculture.

3. The junta directiva has its own "Emergency Fund" derived from a monthly 25¢ per socia contribution.

4. Some of these benefits include eligibility for government loans, the aid of a Co-op Extension Agent, and the advice and help of accountants and auditors.

5. There are basically six recognized age levels among the Cuna: (1) *coe*, or baby, which refers to those children who are still suckling the mother's breast; (2) *mimi* (f.), *machigwa* (m.), children who vary in age from 4 to 12 years; (3) *tungu*, a girl who is nearing puberty; (4) *yawgwa*, a girl who has started to menstruate but who is still a virgin and unmarried, and *machi sappingwa*, her male counterpart; (5) *ome* (f.), *macheret* (m.), an adult, usually applied to those who have married; and (6) *mu* (f.), *dada* (m.), terms used in reference to grandparents or simply old people.

# BIBLIOGRAPHY

Agencia para el Desarrollo Internacional (A.I.D.)
1972    *Cooperativas agrícolas.* Mexico and Buenos Aires: Centro Regional de Ayuda Técnica.

A Committee of the Royal Anthropological Institute of Great Britain and Ireland
1971    *Notes and Queries on Anthropology.* Oxford: Alden Press.

Contraloría General de la República
1970    *Censos nacionales de 1970.* Vol. I, Lugares Poblados de la República. Panama: Dirección de Estadística y Censo.

Foster, George M.
1967    *Tzintzuntzan.* Boston: Little Brown.

Hilger, Sister M. Inez.
1966    "Field Guide to the Ethnological Study of Child Life." *Behavior Science Field Guides,* vol. 1. New Haven: Human Relations Area Files.

Holloman, Regina E.
1969    "Developmental Change in San Blas." Ph.D. dissertation, Northwestern University.

Kramer, Fritz W.
1970    "Literature among the Cuna Indians." *Etnologiska Studier* (Göteborg) 30.

Murdock, George P., et al.
1971    "Outline of Cultural Materials." *Behavior Science Outlines,* vol. 1. New Haven: Human Relations Area Files.

Nordenskiöld, Erland
1938    "An Historical and Ethnological Survey of the Cuna Indians." *Comparative Ethnographical Studies* (Göteborg) 10.

Oviedo y Valdes, Gonzalo Fernández de
1944    *Historia general y natural de las indias, islas, y tierra firma de la Mar Oceano,* vol. 4. Asunción: Editorial Guarnia del Paraguay.

Panama
1972    *Constitución Política de la República de Panamá.* Panama.

Puig, Manuel Maria
1948    *Los indios cunas de San Blas.* Panama.

Requejo Salcedo, Juan
1908    *Relación histórica y geográfica de la Provincia de Panamá.* Madrid.

Romoli, Kathleen
1953    *Balboa of Darien: Discoverer of the Pacific.* New York.

Stavenhagen, Rodolfo, ed.
1970    *Agrarian Problems and Peasant Movements in Latin America.* Garden City: Doubleday.

Stout, David B.
1947    *San Blas Cuna Acculturation: An Introduction.* New York: Viking Fund Publications in Anthropology.

Torres de Ianello, Reina
1957    *La mujer cuna de Panamá.* Mexico: Instituto Indigenista Interamericano.

Wafer, Lionel
1934    *A New Voyage and Description of the Isthmus of America.* L. E. Elliott Joyce, ed. Ser. 2, 73. Oxford: The Hakluyt Society.

Whiting, John W., et al.
1966    *Field Guide for a Study of Socialization.* Six Culture Series, vol. 1. New York: John Wiley.

Wolf, Eric R.
1966    *Peasants.* Englewood Cliffs: Prentice-Hall.

# 3.

# "To Fly as Birds": Myth and Ritual as Agents of Enculturation among the Huichol Indians of Mexico

PETER T. FURST AND MARINA ANGUIANO

## Introduction

It was Carl Lumholtz, Norwegian pioneer ethnographer of the Indians of the western Sierra Madre of Mexico who, in a classic monograph, *Symbolism of the Huichol Indians* (1900), first told the outside world something of the extraordinary children's ceremony he called "feast of the green squashes." Conducted annually by the shaman of the local community at the time of the ripening of the first fruits of the fields, he wrote, the feast was dedicated to a female deity, the goddess called Mother East-Water. Because his primary interest was in the material objects associated with Huichol ritual,[1] Lumholtz's attention was drawn to this ritual especially because of the important role played in it by the thread cross, a magical-protective object of apparently great antiquity and wide distribution in the New World as well as the Old World, which the Huichols call *tsikúri* (*tsikuli*) and which since Lumholtz's time has come to be popularly, though inaccurately, known as "eye of god."

Lumholtz (1900:154) described the tsikúri as follows:

> An "eye" is a cross, of bamboo splints or of straw, interwoven with variously colored twine or yarn in the form of a square, which is set diagonally. The string is wound around the sticks from the centre outward, the loops being so placed that one side of the square is smooth, while on the reverse side of it the sticks are plainly noticeable. Occasionally one stick may show on one side of the square, and the other on the other side.

Some of the large "eyes" are made with a double weaving, so
as to present a smooth surface on both sides. The colors used
vary according to the god for whom the "eyes" are made.
Sometimes the sticks are of equal length; but generally one
stick is much longer than the other, for convenience in tying
the "eye" to the head of a child or to an arrow, for transfixing
some object that may be tied to an arrow, or for placing the
"eye" upright in the ground. Those in which the sticks are of
equal length are hung to arrows or to the roofs of god-houses,
and are attached by the free end of the string from which the
object is made.

Lumholtz was given to understand that the thread cross was a symbol
of the power to see and understand unknown things—the shamans of
old, he wrote, used it rather in the manner of a magical mirror to see the
Mothers, meaning the feminine deities. One of his informants told him
that the moon was originally called tsikúri, in the sense of mirror. Finally,
he wrote, the thread cross represents a prayer, specifically asking that
the god to whom the object is addressed rest his or her eye on the
supplicant.

While the meaning of "eye" ascribed to it by Lumholtz appears to rest
on a misunderstanding—hardly surprising considering the formidable
barriers to mutual understanding faced by both ethnographer and
informants, who shared neither a common mother tongue nor a common
system of classification and of codifying reality—the tsikúri is indeed,
like so much else in Huichol ritual, a veritable symbol complex, endowed
with a multiplicity of simultaneous meanings that extend from the living
to the dead (Furst, 1975:62–64). What is correct is Lumholtz's emphasis
on the crucial role played by the thread cross in the lives of children, and
its prominence in the ceremony of the first fruits. The tsikúri is, in fact,
preeminently a sacred protective symbol for children. About its place in
the squash ceremony, he wrote:

> "Eyes" are especially used at the feast of the green squashes,
> being tied to the children's heads in an upright position by
> means of a hair-ribbon. They are thought to ensure the health
> of the children. A shaman's plume is stuck underneath the
> same hair-ribbon. At this feast, some "eyes" are also placed
> upright in the ground near the squashes, and express prayers
> for health and luck and plenty to eat.

At this feast, he continued, the thread cross represents a male squash
flower, but as the flower could not evolve into a squash it became the

"eye" of Mother East-Water, for she is the creator of squashes and of all flowers "and takes special care of children." She was also considered to be the mother of the culture hero Káuyumarie, the Divine Deer Person. Káuyumarie, apart from his other attributes, is the shaman's spirit helper and companion animal as well as guide and protector of peyote pilgrims. In the mythic first times he helped the First Shaman, Tatewarí (Our Grandfather), the divine Fire, put the world in order. Káuyumarie also made the first thread cross for the protection of children.

Considering the wealth of firsthand factual information and insights that abound in Lumholtz's writings, it is regrettable that he was able to give us only a glimpse at the children's ritual, mentioning the lengthy chants of the officiating shaman but not providing any of their content or meaning.[2] The feast, he writes, (pp. 155–157),

> is called wima'kwari ("to beat the drum"). It is held in October. The men run deer and gather the squashes. In the mean while the shaman, seated in his armchair, facing as usual the door-opening of the temple, (east), beats his drum and sings from early morning until sunset. On the same day the women bring the children to the temple, and place them on both sides of the shaman. Tied to each child's head are a shaman's plume and an "eye." At this feast the children are called tuwai'no. They carry rattles in their hands; but if a child is very small, the mother holds the rattle for it. The rattle, is called kai'tsa, is made from a hard fruit resembling a small gourd, that grows on a certain tree found in the country, for instance in the cañon of San Juan Peyotán. The rattling noise is produced by small stones, which are picked from ant-hills and put inside.

> The children stand on each side of the shaman so as to form a row, which extends toward the door-opening. At the end of each row stands a shaman called Ver'ika[3] (the rabbit sun) to guard them. The men return from the deer-hunt after sunset, and corn-cakes and native beer are offered to the children, the "eyes" and the rattles having first been taken away from them by their parents. During this ceremony the children stand together on both sides of the shaman, and the people form a semi-circle in front of him. The guardians of the children stand at the ends of the semi-circle, next to them. To the right of the children is a heap of squashes which are to be cooked, and to the left are the jars to be used for that purpose.

The children are then carried to their homes, while singing and dancing continues in the temple all night. The next morning the children are brought back. Before sunrise, the squashes, which have now all been cooked, are taken out of the jars, and first given to the children, and then to the grown people. At this festival the adults drink hi-kuli (peyote), but native brandy is not allowed. During this feast, ancient girdles are hung up next to the squashes. They are supposed to keep the children from getting tired when "they go yonder where the water springs forth." This expression is taken from the song used at the feast. . . .

It is noteworthy that the feast is accompanied by much noise of the drum and the rattle. Once upon a time, so the myth relates, the squash was a girl whose name was Riku'ama, the name referring to her as making a rattling noise with bells (riku'a) or some other object. Perhaps this was originally suggested by the rattling noise which the dry seeds make inside of the squash when shaken (pp. 155-157).

This ceremony, for which until recently we had only this barest of descriptive outlines, persists to the present time virtually without modification. It plays a more or less crucial role in the transmission from generation to generation of some of the essentials of the indigenous intellectual culture. It is thus in a very real sense decisive in the process of enculturation.

Enculturation, needless to say, is a continuous process, hardly dependent upon a single event, however important. There are many other occasions in the crowded ceremonial calendar and many minor rites and observances, as well as just ordinary, everyday living, through which the child learns, without being specifically told, what "being Huichol" is all about. Nonetheless, it is particularly in the ceremony of the shaman's drum and the green squashes, as the one drama specifically focused on young children, in which they participate annually for the first five years of life as actors and thereafter as participant observers, that the young Huichol boy or girl learns "how one goes being Huichol."

For despite its superficial resemblance to the harvest festivals or thanksgiving rites of other peoples—for example, neither the young squashes nor the tender new ears of maize are supposed to be eaten before the ceremony has been conducted—its primary purpose is not to foster appreciation of the first fruits of subsistence agriculture. Rather it is to impregnate the young minds with the peyote tradition and a kind of subjective map of the geography of the sacred, through the device of a metaphorical celestial journey to the home of the Mother Goddess and, beyond it, the place of the Divine Deer-Peyote, the magical land called Wirikúta, which lies some 300 miles to the east of the present Huichol homeland in the north-central high desert of San Luis Potosí.

It is this crucial aspect of the drum and new squash ceremony, which the Huichols call Tatéi Néiya,[4] (var. Neirra), literally "Our Mother Ceremony," that Lumholtz seems to have missed; at least he failed to emphasize it in his writings. But, as Myerhoff (1974:113–116) notes in her recent book on the peyote hunt and the deer-maize-peyote symbol complex, the purpose of the ceremony actually is to relate, in lengthy chants, the essentials of the peyote origin myth, which stands at the very center of Huichol intellectual culture, and to provide an " 'inner map,' a cognitive and spatial plan transmitted from one generation of Huichols to the next."

## Huichol History and Acculturation

The country the Huichols today call their own consists of five separate, and, from the Indian point of view, self-governed regions, or *comunidades,* on occasion antagonistic toward one another, each with its native authorities under a *gobernador* (Huichol: *tatuán*) elected by the elders of the *comunidad.* Terms of office range from one to three and sometimes even more years, the changeover from the old to the new administration being known as *cambio de varas* (changing of the staffs). The ceremonies attending this important event are held in the civil-religious ceremonial center, which has few permanent residents, becoming crowded with people from the surrounding country only on certain festive occasions (cf. Anguiano, 1974:169–187). Apart from the Indian government the comunidades fall within the jurisdictions of different Mexican municipalities, located outside the Sierra proper, but to all intents and purposes the latter exercise only minimal control over the political life of the comunidad.

Published references to the Huichols as a "tribe" are wholly incorrect; no central tribal authority over and above the authorities of each of the five comunidades exists, and although the most important shrines, the sacred cave at Teakáta, are located in one of the five comunidades, that of Santa Catarina, neither it nor any of the others is recognized as the seat of an overall authority. Likewise it is incorrect to label the residents of the different comunidades as tribes or subtribes. In contrast, the people residing in the different regions of the Huichol country do feel and express an intense emotional bond with their particular part of the indigenous environment and, as noted, they are sometimes quite hostile toward a neighboring comunidad. As one might expect, this is so especially where there has been a history of boundary disputes, or where portions of one comunidad were added to another through intervention from the outside. The degree of non-Indian economic or ideological influence in one or another comunidad has also added to friction between some of them.

In any event, all Huichols speak the same language, identified by linguists as belonging to the Coran subfamily of the Aztecoidan branch of the Uto-Aztecan stock, the Coran languages (Huichol and Cora) being most closely related to the Nahuatlan subfamily of any of the Uto-Aztecan languages (Spicer, 1969:779); but there are dialect differences between several of the comunidades. Most important, Huichols have no doubt whatever about their own ethnic identity: when speaking Spanish they call themselves proudly, not to say aggressively, Huicholes, and when speaking their own tongue, they identify themselves as Wixárika,[5] their (apparently) aboriginal term for themselves. Their self-definition as Wixárika is not only very firm, it also extends outward into the classification of objects and other material and even nonmaterial phenomena in the native environment. These are assigned their place according to whether they are considered to be Wixárita—that is, aboriginally a part of Huichol culture—or of alien origin, borrowed from non-Huichol Indians, called generically *tewitéri* (sing. *téwi*), or from Spaniards or Mexican mestizos, referred to as *teiwárixi* (sing. *teiwári*—not to be confused with the reciprocal kinship term *tewarí,* meaning grandfather, grandson).

Anthropologists—especially those more concerned with acculturation and culture change than with cultural conservatism and the persistence of tradition, or with economics and sociopolitical organization (sectors in which there certainly have been marked changes) than with the indigenous religion—may have different ideas of the implications of "being Huichol" than the Indians themselves. Certainly the trained outsider perceives that "Huichol culture" is characterized by a degree of heterogeneity, and that its different subsystems, no less than different regions of the Huichol country, have become differentially acculturated to the outside world. To think of the culture as a whole, or even any of its subsystems—including world view, religion, and ritual—as "pure," in the sense of its condition at the time of European contact, would of course be romantic nonsense. It is nevertheless true that more than any other sizable indigenous Middle American population, the Huichols have successfully resisted Christianization of their religion and ritual life. In that sense their intellectual culture is without question a "traditional" one, just as their sizable pantheon is mainly Indian, with numerous major and minor deities that are either aboriginal or borrowed from some other Indian source, and a rich ceremonial cycle that is almost wholly free of Christian overlay or flavor.

Even so, we must recognize that however "traditional" or non-Christian it may be, the subsystem that comprises world view, religion, mythology, and ritual is also a product of recent history, reflecting not only actual prehispanic survivals but also successive reformulations and reinterpretations of these survivals. One would expect these to have occurred at different times and in different places—and with different degrees of intensity—not only under the impact of contact with, and borrowing from, other Indians, such as Central Mexicans transplanted to the western frontier by the Spaniards, and with the Spaniards during the early missionary period, but also after the church gave up its efforts—in general unsuccessful—at sustained Christian instruction and conversion and abandoned the Sierra Indians to the very shamans the clergy naively assumed to have been vanquished forever with the end of Cora resistance in 1722.

This is not to say that the church made no lasting impression of a sort. The Huichol ceremonial calendar does include observances that originated with the missionaries (especially Holy Week). But these ceremonies have been greatly modified by indigenous beliefs and practices (as they have also among the Coras). And, in any case, they have added to, and not replaced, the great corpus of traditional ritual, just as Christian deities and saints, while they may be acknowledged and included in religious recitations by shamans even outside the Catholic-derived rituals, have not displaced, but only augmented the multitude of indigenous supernaturals. Only in the case of the Virgin of Guadalupe, whom the Huichols consider to have been an Indian woman, has there been a kind of synthesis of old gods and new, inasmuch as many Huichols think of the indigenous sky deity, Our Mother Young Eagle Woman, and the Virgin of Guadalupe as one and the same.

While regional and to some extent individual differences must be acknowledged, especially in the way some rituals are performed and myths recited, it is nonetheless essentially correct to speak of a common Huichol *Weltanschauung* that transcends these differences, as well as a common religion and a common intellectual culture. Likewise, most Huichol-speakers share in a common socioeconomic system based on swidden or slash-and-burn agriculture in which maize—still planted by most Huichols with the traditional digging stick—is the mainstay, nutritionally as well as ideologically, with beans and squash as secondary crops grown in community-owned but kin-group-worked *milpas*. Animal husbandry, increasingly facilitated by government assistance, especially through the Instituto Nacional Indigenista (INI) and the general development plan known as Plan Huicot, is of growing importance in many parts of the Huichol country. Farming of the formerly uncultivated *mesas* with

the aid of tractors and plows also promises to augment the bare subsistence yield of the traditional farming methods. Still, modernization
directly affects—and will probably continue to affect for some time to
come—a relatively small proportion of the population. Huichol culture
will of course change, but it will probably survive; which means that
however many of them will be taught to read and write, in their own
language and in Spanish (and their number is constantly on the rise),
most young Huichols will continue to be enculturated as Indians, not
as members of a larger society. And they will assimilate what "being
Huichol" means through increasingly active participation in a traditional
lifeway, world view, and ceremonialism that are, by common agreement,
accepted as uniquely Huichol, however heterogeneous the sources may
appear to the outsider.

   While the territory settled by speakers of Huichol was formerly far more
extensive than it is now, the Huichols were evidently well established
wherever they live today when the first Spanish missionaries reached
them, presumably in the mid-1600s, or possibly somewhat earlier—but
in any event substantially before 1722, when their linguistic and cultural
cousins, the Coras, were conquered. We can also be certain that some
missionaries appeared in the Huichol country considerably before the
Huichols were at least nominally pacified. The time of Huichol "pacifi-
cation" is as yet uncertain, but Spanish *congregaciones* were established
in some parts of the southern portion of their territory—for example, at
Huaximic—by the mid-seventeenth century. Actual submission, however
nominal, of the Huichols may have taken place at the end of that century
or at the beginning of the eighteenth, that is, roughly twenty to thirty years
before the conquest of the Coras (Anguiano, 1975).[6]

   The latter almost certainly have resided in the Sierra for a long time.
Early Colonial sources speak of two Cora populations, one in the foothills
and lowlands between the Sierra and the Pacific Coast, the other in the
Sierra. Preuss (1912) thought an ancestral Cora population might have
been responsible for the well-known shaft-and-chamber tombs and the
funerary art characteristic of Nayarit and thus referred to the ancient
culture as "Old Cora." To some degree ideological links can be recognized between the Coras and Huichols and the subject matter of shaft
tomb art dating some two thousand years ago; likewise there are sug-
gestive similarities between Cora-Huichol themes and myth and ritual
among the Pueblo Indians of the Southwest, as well as similarities between
the symbolism of the latter and the funerary art of west Mexican tomb
cultures. At least the Huichols, if not the Coras, have a mythic tradition
in which a spider identifiable as a tarantula or trap-door spider (the
animal form of the Puebloan Spider Grandmother) constructs for the first

people, the Hewi, a tunnel tomb resembling a typical deep shaft-and-chamber tomb—again suggesting historical links both to the Southwest (which also has some tombs of this shape) and possibly to the ancient tomb cultures of Nayarit and Jalisco (Furst, 1974a, 1974b). If Preuss was right and at least the ancestors of the modern Coras lived in the general region where they are now some two thousand years ago, Huichol ancestry is singularly obscure, and probably more ethnically diverse than Cora ancestry. All things considered, some of these ancestral Huichols might have been seminomadic hunter-gatherers originating in or near the self-same north-central peyote desert to which Huichol *peyoteros* still travel on their annual pilgrimages. Other groups contributing to Huichol ancestry may have arrived from the coast and other areas adjacent to the Sierra. Once in the mountains, the various small-scale populations, which presumably shared certain linguistic and cultural traditions, gradually coalesced, becoming to some degree acculturated to the sedentary Coras. Just when this might have occurred is likewise difficult to estimate, but significant movement of Indians fleeing from the lowlands and foothills into the relative safety of the Sierra is reported to have followed the so-called Mixton War, the great rebellion—ultimately unsuccessful—which native shamans led against Spanish rule in western Mexico in 1541/42 after the departure of Coronado from Compostela on his quest for the Seven Cities of Cibola.

In any event, the considerable delay in the establishment of Spanish administrative control in the Sierra—among the Coras, at least, not until fully two centuries after the fall of the Aztecs—and the continued relative isolation of the Huichols from the mainstream of Mexican colonial and postcolonial life thereafter, help explain the remarkable degree to which the Indians have clung to a traditional ideology. For even after some missions were established and the Spaniards had introduced the present system of native government, the Huichols quite successfully resisted any real conversion except on the nominal scale. Likewise, whatever attempts the Spaniards might have made to "reduce" some Huichols into larger communities (the so-called *reducciones*), where native beliefs and rituals might have been suppressed with more success through force and sustained Christian indoctrination, proved unavailing in the face of stubborn refusal to relinquish the still characteristic settlement pattern of widely scattered *ranchos* (farmsteads) inhabited by close kin under a headman or elder. Typically these elders were also family shamans, as they are to this day, just as each *rancho* continues to have its own guardian spirit(s) who function in the manner of a "household god," apart from, or alongside, the native pantheon proper.

That the Huichols remained free of alien control over their lives at least for the first century to a century and a half after the conquest of Mexico, and were largely able to go their own way into modern times, is not to suggest that they also remained impervious to European traits. Particularly in the realm of material culture and economy, alien innovations, from domestic livestock and metal tools to musical instruments, were assimilated early on. It is interesting, for example, that many unaccompanied songs, or those played on such native instruments as the reed flute, the drum, or the musical bow (the taut string of which is beaten with the tip of a hunting arrow) sound completely prehispanic. Joseph E. Grimes (personal communication), who lived among the Huichols for a dozen years, thought that music played on the Huichol versions of the violin and guitar had the distinct flavor of sixteenth- and seventeenth-century Spanish round dances adapted to the native musical tradition. These stringed instruments, on which many Huichols excel, are now an indispensable part of every Huichol ritual, including the peyote ceremonies.

The uniquely Huichol still, which Lumholtz (1902:183-185), who thought it might be pre-Columbian,[7] described and which closely resembles a primitive still native to the Philippines, may also have reached the Huichols as an innovation at a comparatively early time, possibly by way of the Manila Galleon, the first of which crossed the Pacific between the Philippines and Acapulco in 1565. The arrival of these trading vessels from the Orient to Mexico's Pacific coast was always the occasion of great *ferias,* which attracted thousands of Spanish-Mexican merchants, as well as many Indian traders, to Acapulco from many parts. The Huichols themselves were well known as long-distance traders who exchanged products of the interior (including peyote, highly valued then as now for therapeutic properties) for salt and other commodities of the coastal lowlands. The strikingly Filipino design for the Huichol still might thus have been passed into the interior by a traveling Huichol, or even by a native of the Philippines who deserted the Spanish fleet and sought refuge (as black slaves sometimes did in different parts of the Americas) with the Indians. It would be surprising indeed if such contacts with the outside world even before the establishment of military outposts and Franciscan missions did not enrich or modify at least what might be called Huichol folklore, if not the more important sacred traditions. There is also evidence for linguistic borrowing early on in the history of Huichol contact with the new colonial power. Tim Knab (1976, and personal communication), while doing research on linguistic acculturation and borrowing in the Sierra Madre Occidental, recorded several Nahuatl loan words in the Huichol language. Knab believes that such loan words (e.g., *calihuey,* from the Aztec *huey* = big, *cali* = house, meaning temple, the term Huichols use for their indigenous temples as a rule only when they speak Spanish, *túki* or *tukípa* being the indigenous Wixárika word) were borrowed early in Colonial times from Tlaxcalan allies of the Spaniards who had been resettled on the western frontier as a buffer against the still unpacified Indian populations of the Sierra Madre Occidental. Knab believes that Christianized Tlaxcalans were also one source for the Indianized versions of the Christian myth cycle among the Huichols and that very likely at least some of the correspondences between certain Huichol myths and deities and those of Central Mexico are similarly a result of early contact with Tlaxcalans. Of course, some similarities could also be ascribed to common historical sources—e.g., a common proto-Uto-Aztecan substratum ultimately traceable to the putative point of origin of the Uto-Aztecans in southern Arizona and northern Sonora. Knab suggests, and we believe he may be correct, that differential acculturation, in particular the differential degree to which some of the Christian mythology became assimilated in different parts of the Huichol country, is directly related to proximity or distance of the sixteenth-century population of parts of the Sierra to such Spanish colonial settlements as that at Colotlán, Jalisco.

In any event, whatever the degree of sixteenth-century Central Mexican influence on the oral traditions of different Indian groups in the still unconquered Sierra Madre Occidental, the fact is that the Huichols, Cora, and Nahua-speaking "Mexicanos," such as those at San Pedro Jicora among whom Preuss recorded texts in 1906/07 (cf. Preuss and Ziehm, 1968), share some myths that are virtually indistinguishable from each other, while also bearing some resemblance to traditions among Nahuatl-speakers in central Mexico. One thinks here especially of stories of the deluge, the dog as female ancestor, and the origin of maize. Those originally recorded in Nahua-Mexicano by Preuss and translated into German by Elsa Ziehm, after she had checked the original manuscript material with informants at San Pedro Jicora, are remarkably similar in form and content to descriptions of the same mythical events obtained by us from Ramón Medina[8] and other Huichol informants; likewise they strongly resemble the material published by Zingg and Lumholtz on the Huichols, and by Preuss himself on the Coras. Unless all three happened to retain very similar versions of traditions that originated in a common older stratum, there must have been considerable borrowing back and forth among the different—but linguistically related—peoples of the Sierra, if all three, in fact, did not receive these particular myths from the same foreign (but again linguistically related) source.

The Huichol myth of the birth—more correctly transformation—of Tayaupá, Sun Father, falls into the same category; certainly it bears a striking resemblance to the Central Mexican tradition of the fiery self-sacrifice of him who was to become the Sun. This myth is of special interest here in that, like the bird-children's flying journey and the peyote pilgrimage itself, it involves travel from west to east—below ground by the Sun and above ground by the people—with the ultimate destination the sacred hills in Wirikúta. The ancient people who attended the birth of the Sun are identified as Huichols, but by appearance and behavior they merge with the primordial Héwi, the mythic predecessors of the Huichols, inasmuch as they are anthropomorphized animals or, more correctly from the point of view of the Indians, animals and people at the same time. So, for that matter, are some of the first peyote pilgrims. Actually, the distinction in the mythology between the predeluge Hewíxi (pl.) and the postdeluge Huichols is often vague, it being characteristically uncertain, even in the narrator's mind, whether a particular event took place before or after the drowning of the earth.

Be that as it may, the Huichol flood myth not only clearly belongs to a much wider, pan-Amerindian (not to say virtually worldwide) deluge tradition but is closely related to Central Mexican cosmology with its characteristic successive world eras, or Suns, each with its own full complement of terrestrial life, that came into being and were destroyed before the appearance of the fifth and present age. In Aztec tradition, as recorded by the early Spanish chroniclers, the Fifth Sun appeared after the destruction of the earth by water in a universal flood. As it survives today, Huichol history compresses and simplifies these successive "creations" and destructions (actually, transformations): for example, where the Aztecs have the first era being devoured by jaguars, the Huichols tell of but a single Héwi girl ("Oh, she was so plump, so fat and beautiful, that poor little Héwi girl") whom a jaguar, a transformed shaman-sorcerer, stalked and devoured—not, as one might expect, because he was hungry but rather because he required a *female* soul to "complete himself."[9] The other cataclysms of central Mexican mythology, destruction of the world by fire and wind, respectively, are incorporated as ordeals in the travels of the goddess Nakawé and the Indian called Watákame, Clearer of Fields, to the four quarters of the flooded earth.

Nakawé, Great-grandmother, the "little old one," is the fundamental earth-creator goddess who put the world in order and by magical acts of transformation restored life to the earth after its destruction by water. Nevertheless, Tatewarí, Grandfather, the primordial guardian shaman who is conceptually merged with the divine Fire, is widely considered to be the principal deity in the extensive pantheon of male and female *kakauyaríxi,* another generic term for the supernaturals that dwell in sacred locales within and near the Huichol country, as well as in more distant places. Noteworthy among the latter are the desert springs and water holes of Our Mothers—the Mothers of terrestrial water and of rain—that lie within sight of Wirikúta. The level desert between the

Wirikuta range and another sacred range called Tsinuríta is sometimes referred to as "Patio of Our Grandfathers and Grandmothers." That the order of importance of some of the deities varies from one part of the Huichol country to another (e.g., some Huichols think of the Sun Father, rather than Tatewarí, as the principal god, others hold them to be of equal rank, and still others put Tatewarí ahead) is surely due again, at least in part, to the different influences that impinged upon the indigenous system from outside sources.

Many Huichol gods clearly embody natural forces, others in essence are the "Masters" or "Owners" of different animal species that are so characteristic of the religions and philosophical systems of societies on the socioeconomic level of hunting and gathering. The gods are typically addressed by ritual kin terms, for example, Our Grandfather (Fire), Our Mother, Elder Brother, Great-grandmother (Nakawé), Our Father (Sun), and so on, or generically Our Grandfathers, Our Mothers, and so on. Just as there were, for example, four Tezcatlipocas, each identified with a different color and cardinal direction, in the prehispanic central Mexican pantheon, so in Huichol cosmology there are male deer deities and Mothers of Water (terrestrial as well as celestial) of the different directions. Not surprisingly, rain is of uppermost concern to the Huichols and much ritual, including the peyote cycle, from the celebration of the new squash through the peyote pilgrimage to the ceremony of the parched maize that precedes the clearing of new fields, has as its basic aim the procuring of rain. In contrast to central Mexico, there is no male deity with the attribute of rain. Rain has its origin in the sacred springs, water holes, and other bodies of water that are the abodes of the Mothers; it is they who rise into the sky in the form of clouds from which the terrestrial water returns in the form of rain to water the thirsty earth, Our Mother, in a never-ending cycle that requires the fulfillment of ritual obligations to complete itself. If we may permit ourselves a gross simplification of Huichol *Weltanschauung,* we may say that it is essentially shamanistic, magical, and animistic, in some aspects typical of incipient subsistence farming societies but in some of its underlying assumptions more so of hunters and gatherers.

## Style and Content in Religious Recitation

In the first decade of the twentieth century the German ethnologist Konrad Theodor Preuss also paid an extended visit to the Indians of the Sierra, spending the first half of 1906 with the Cora and the second with the Huichols. Commenting on the obstacles to recording and understanding Huichol sacred texts, he wrote:

The transcription of religious songs presented great difficulties. Whereas the cantadores (singing shamans) of the Cora always provided a lively dictation of every song, here it took a long time before the three singers at my disposal allowed themselves to be persuaded to give me word for word information. Initially and with much wasted time they gave me only an extract with occasional supplements, which moreover was so aphoristic that the content was barely more than a listing of the names of deities and objects. And then they could not be persuaded to repeat the same text in more explicit form. Only after numerous attempts—two of them never did come to do this—did I succeed in obtaining a literal version, from beginning to end, and now to my dismay it became clear why the others could not be talked into it. Because here the chants do not repeat themselves at different ceremonies as they do among the Cora. Also there aren't separate songs, each with its specific content; rather a single song is carried the whole night through, another the entire following day, if the ceremony lasts that long. That can be done only through the broadest elaboration of every single thought and its application to each of the many gods of the four to six world directions. Nonetheless there is no repetition *per se,* so that understanding always requires the complete chant. So what we get is veritable monsters of chants that are only somewhat shortened in that the chorus, by immediately repeating each of the singer's sentences—allegedly to keep him from tiring himself—takes up half his available time. . . .

The content of the songs consists mostly of a dialogue of the gods with the messenger of the fire deity Tatewarí, the trickster Káuyumarie, who is deer . . . or with Tatewarí himself. Who speaks here are natural objects, whose deeds are recounted at the same time, bird feathers, arrows, and other ceremonial gear, in short, it is a magical world that continues to correspond completely to the contemporary world view of the Huichols (Preuss, 1907:188).[10]

Eventually Preuss broke the code, so to speak, and began to understand just what it is the singing shaman relates to his audience, however epigrammatic his rendition. With some few exceptions, he writes (1908:374–375), every song cycle begins with the calling of Káuyumarie from his house at the eastern end of the world. First the singing shaman holds a conversation about the nature and purpose of the ceremony with Tatewarí, who has emerged from his home in the earth beneath the hearth in the center of the temple and who manifests himself in the ceremonial fire. Tatewarí, however, informs the shaman that he is unable to work alone, and through the shaman he dispatches two ceremonial arrows with pendant feathers to Káuyumarie. The arrow messengers find Káuyumarie asleep in the dark in his house, which is magically enclosed by feather wands, and guarded by jaguars, mountain lions, and snakes. The arrows touch Káuyumarie on his feet. But he is reluctant to come to the ceremony: he says he is sick, he has a fever, he has a cold, or his feet hurt, and his wife also reinforces his desire to stay home. Finally he agrees to go but cannot find his shamanic feather sticks; his wife equips him with everything he needs for the journey and reminds him also not to play around with other women along the way. Following these familiar scenes, which a good singing shaman always elaborates greatly for the entertainment of his audience, Káuyumarie eventually reaches the temple, traveling through the required levels and stages of the world. At the temple he at once initiates negotiations with the gods, calling them one by one by name and presenting them with the specific circumstances of the ceremony and negotiating with them about the removal of whatever negative forces or evil might threaten the social group. Káuyumarie is also the last to leave the ceremonial area. But this must be before sunup, because he fears the Sun, and if the ceremony lasts beyond dawn he must ask the Sun for permission.

None of this, Preuss notes, is acted out; instead, everything is related in the characteristic abbreviated and aphoric style in a single monotonous religious recitation of great duration, and with minimal gestures—for example, lifting the plumes, turning to the four directions—to underscore a particular phrase, and with little attempt to adhere to a specific sequence of words.

One or the other of us had occasion several times to listen to this introductory discourse of the shaman with the Deer Person Káuyumarie, who, although sometimes functioning almost as a trickster, is nonetheless the shaman's essential spirit helper and companion. Even in the context of curing, the singing shaman might delight his audience by stringing out his evocation of Káuyumarie with humorous references to the latter's well-known sexual predilection: for example, Káuyumarie might inform the shaman that he would rather play with his attractive deer-wife than make the long and arduous journey from the end of the world to the rancho, the shaman in his song relaying to his listeners Káuyumarie's words, those of his flirtatious wife, and his own urgent summons in sometimes explicit, sometimes allusive form (for example, "If that is how it is, being as he is he does this thing.") The native audience, of course, possessing as it does the requisite prior knowledge with which to flesh out the more cryptic passages, understands and chuckles appreciatively at lines that mean little to the uninitiated outsider.

That is the sort of situation that Lumholtz had to deal with during his sojourn with the Huichols in the 1890s, and that would have confounded us with respect to the children's ceremony, as it frequently did on other occasions, without whatever published data were available (as they were not to Lumholtz) and the literary narratives of the late Ramón Medina. In the case of the Tatéi Néiya rite, described in extenso in these pages, we had his text, "When the Drum Is Beaten and the Mara'akáme Flies the Children to Wirikúta" in which mythic time and actual events, past and present, are merged, and which he invested with some of his own experiencs as well as hopes and expectations for future pilgrimages. As noted, and as is shown below, the actual style of the lengthy song cycle as sung in the context of the ceremony itself contains enough "shorthand" passages as to be at times nearly incomprehensible to all but an indigenous participant in the culture—unless one had some knowledge of the peyote pilgrimage and the peyote origin myth of which the pilgrimage is the reenactment, and patient collaboration and translation by a willing and knowledgeable informant from metaphoric and poetic language into that of the everyday world, "footnoted" where necessary so that strangers to the culture might learn what the sacred story is all about and, beyond that, how it fits into the process of becoming Huichol.

The Huichol child, of course, learns all these things by slow accretion, as crucial elements are added and become clearer in the course of hundreds of hours of singing and storytelling, rather than as did we, in this instance, through the medium of a verbal drama that for our benefit was endowed by a gifted and perceptive narrator with a beginning, middle, and end, in which the actors were clearly identified by name, performing actions that were more or less explicitly described and located in time and space, and, eventually, by having the privilege of participating in an actual pilgrimage, in the course of which reference was made repeatedly for our benefit to events on the bird-children's flight.[11]

It should be noted, however, that while Ramón's narrative of the magical flight of the bird children, recorded in 1966 by Myerhoff and Furst, is far more explicit and descriptive than would be the purely religious recitation through which the shaman weaves his measured way through most of one night and the following day, Myerhoff (1974:114–115) is right in suggesting that the chanted version as well is generally less allegorical, less obscure, and more precise than many others in the sacred repertory, and that this difference is determined by its purpose. That, as noted above, is to provide his young audience with an "inner map" on which the sacred places and events of the peyote pilgrimage are indelibly etched. By their vicarious (but in their own minds, those of their relatives, and of the shaman, nonetheless real) flight as transformed birds in each of the first five years of life, the young Indians become increasingly prepared for direct participation in the sacred pilgrimage, which Huichols, whether or not they have themselves traveled to Wirikúta, tend to view as the sine qua non for the survival of their culture (Furst, 1972a:136-184; 1972b:109-196; Myerhoff, 1974). In a very real sense it is just that, not only because ideally to assure survival one should as faithfully as possible follow the ways of the ancestors (it was Tatewarí who established, and led, and many of the male and female supernaturals who participated in, the primordial peyote hunt), but also because it is in the ecstatic-visionary dreams triggered by the divine hallucinogenic cactus that the novice pilgrim (*matewáme*) comes to see for him or herself the truth of what the elders have been passing down. Ancestral deities manifest themselves, traditional lore is confirmed, and the validity—indeed superiority—of the indigenous lifeway established. As the peyoteros sing:

> We are all,
> We are all the children of,
> We are all the sons of,
> A brilliant colored flower (peyote),
> A flaming flower.
> And there is no one,
> There is no one,
> Who regrets what we are.

In short, one sees not only "how one goes being Huichol," but that "being Huichol" is the correct way to travel.

However important in and of itself to the process of "becoming Huichol," the Tatéi Néiya rite of course should not be lifted from the larger context of myth, ritual, and daily life, all of which in any event tend to merge, with no clear boundaries between them. For that reason we wish to present here in outline form at least some fragments of the ideological environment in which the child grows up. Common threads and themes tie the myths and rites to each other and to daily activity. Everything is alive, all phenomena, including those we would call inanimate, being endowed with a life force; objects in everyday use are as likely to have had a previous form as animals or, better, animal-people, as did people themselves.

"Myth" is often contrasted to "history" as though the former were by definition imaginary and the latter fact. Ramón made no such distinction: in Spanish he called all Huichol traditions, including those that explain the origin of the natural phenomena in terms of magic and transformation, *historias de nosotros,* our histories. To cite Preuss (1907: 191–192) again:

> From the start all tales are conceived as absolute truth: that is how it was in ancient times. In ancient times the roots, plants, flowers, fruits, trees, animals, mountains, water, and other natural phenomena that act and talk in the narratives were persons, which is why *tewíari,* persons, is often added to the name of the natural object. Man as such occurs but fleetingly in the myths, although he is apparently frequently the hero. Stories about this and that are always launched into with gusto without it being explained which animal or natural object the tale is all about. Only if one inquires directly can one sometimes find out what is meant. Noteworthy here is also the concrete in the whole world view. For example, if I remark that this person appears to symbolize water, the narrator replies, "One says it is Water Person." On the other hand many objects are animals. Only when one is convinced that there is no human being in these stories, and one knows, or, as the case may be, suspects, which object is meant, is an understanding of the nature of the subject possible.

Characteristically, the gods have their animal forms: the Mothers, for example, are snakes. Although the gods have their own distinct personalities and functions, including those that are essentially aspects or manifestations of one another rather than wholly separate beings, and are associated with or symbolize different world directions (e.g., Mother East Water and Mother West Water, or the deer deities of the cardinal points or quarters), there do not seem to be many petitions or prayers that are specific to only one or another deity; it is our impression, rather, that all gods are receptive to all kinds of requests, provided the proper ritual obligations are observed. While it is generally true that the male gods are associated with the dry season and the female with the rainy, or growing season, and that these male and female deities appear to function in a system of complementary opposition, we cannot agree with Zingg's dry season–wet season "war of the sexes" interpretation of the Huichol pantheon (Zingg, 1938); rather, we have been continually impressed with the emphasis in Huichol life—daily as well as ceremonial—on unity, "being of one heart," as the quintessential precondition for health, fertility, and survival itself, not only of the individual but society as a whole, a concept that extends from the physical to the supernatural environment.

Although certain myths and narratives and, even more so, religious recitations or chants are specific to particular ceremonies, what Ramón used to call "our histories" may be fitted wholly, or in part, into some other occasions. Of course, the recitation of the song of the bird-children belongs peculiarly to Tatéi Néiya, but allusions to this magical event can be found elsewhere in the peyote cycle, just as the chant itself may be expanded to include such fragments of other "histories" as an individual shaman may consider to be of moment. It is significant that where custom in some other traditional societies may dictate faithful and accurate adherence to a particular myth, with no word or sentence permitted to be out of place, the Huichols generally value and enjoy poetic elaboration on the basic themes of their mythology: the better a *mara'akáme* can sing in this respect, the higher his prestige.

As Preuss himself noted, no two Huichol shamans ever agree completely on the correct version of a myth or chant, and four different shamans even from the same region are as likely as not to produce four different variants of the same religious song. The basic themes, the essential core, however, are firmly embedded. Despite the passage of time, regional differences, increasing influences from the outside, and the idiosyncratic aspects of Huichol shamanism, the few peyote pilgrimages that have been witnessed by non-Huichols essentially conform to that described by Lumholtz (1900:17–20) on the basis of informants' statements, just as many other salient aspects of Huichol intellectual culture as they appear today to the outside observer remain remarkably consistent with the descriptions published by the early pioneers of Huichol ethnography.[12] Below, by way of illustration and of necessity greatly abbreviated, are some highlights of the "histories" of fire and sun, abstracted from our own field notes but, insofar as early published versions are available, very similar to the latter.

## Yéuxu (Opossum) and the Theft of Fire

The first beings in the world were not Huichols but Héwi and Nanáwata, who were animals and people at the same time. The Nanáwata lived somewhere near the edge of the world in the four directions, while the Héwi made their home near the center hole from which they had emerged and where they had settled after wandering to the four quarters in search of their proper place. Great-grandmother Nakawé was already in the world, looking after the animal people and the plants and other things on which they lived.[13]

At that time no one knew anything of peyote. Also, there was total darkness, the sun not yet having appeared. Nor was there fire, so the Héwi were unable to cook their food and there were no hearths by which to warm or orient themselves. Actually there are two separate traditions to account for fire. In one, the headman of the Héwi (or else the old goddess Nakawé) caused fire to appear by rubbing two sticks of wood together. This fire was named *tái*, the generic Huichol word for fire. Another tradition, far more important in the Huichol scheme of things, has it that fire was unknown in the Upperworld until Yéuxu, Opossum, who had a special connection with the Underworld and the dead, ventured below and managed to steal fire from its terrible guardian. Previously considered by his fellows as of little value, despised for his foul smell and his affinity for carrion, Opossum succeeded brilliantly where four prior attempts by other, more esteemed, animal-people had failed. This was because he was able to snatch a live coal from the center of the smoldering Underworld fire with his prehensile tail (for which reason today opossum tails are hairless) and hide it in the pouch on his belly before his deed was discovered by the Owner of Fire, who rushed after Opossum and, cutting him up into little pieces, flung him in the four directions on the five-level stairway leading to the Upperworld. "After a while," continues the tradition, "Opossum reflected on this and put himself back together again," in what can be recognized as true shamanic fashion. Whole once more he returned to the Upperworld and gave fire to the Héwi, which is why Huichols today must honor Opossum, holding him to be a powerful and sacred personage and refraining from eating his meat. Indeed, as every Huichol child is told by his elders, however hungry one may be, eating Opossum meat during one's lifetime is a sure way for one's soul to be crushed after death in a stone trap, which an Underworld Guardian Opossum operates and which blocks the path from this life to a happy afterlife in the rancho of one's dead relatives (Furst, 1967:70-71). It is noteworthy that to this day, when breaking camp on the peyote pilgrimage the officiating shaman and some of his principal companions remove a small live coal from the sacred hearth (the manifestation of Tatewarí), and place it in a woven medicine pouch worn around the neck. In any event, as might be expected, the gift of fire by Opossum radically transformed the lifeway of the ancient Héwi: in a very real sense it marked the transition from nature to culture.

## The Great Flood and Dog Woman as Ancestor

Some time after this crucial event, a Héwi named Watákame, meaning "Clearer of the Fields," was girdling and cutting trees and brush with his stone axe in preparation for planting maize, beans, and squash. Each evening at sundown he returned bone-tired to his home, leaving behind the many trees and bushes he had leveled and planned to burn when they had dried, in the manner of slash-and-burn digging-stick agriculture as it is still practiced by the Huichols. But each morning, upon returning to his place of work he discovered all the vegetation back in place, alive and growing as before. Puzzled at first and then increasingly frustrated and angered as the days wore on and the process of regeneration repeated itself, he asked what could be happening here. Whereupon Great-grandmother Nakawé appeared, carrying her magical *kwarére* staff. The kwarére is a long section of bamboo with the roots, modified into a conventionalized bird, left on and forming a kind of handle at the top. Bamboo is the oldest plant on earth, say the Huichols, and Nakawé is its owner, having made it before there was any other vegetation on the surface of the world (the Hopi say that the fast-growing bamboo was created by Grandmother, the old earth goddess, as a passageway for the first people to climb up from the Under- into the Upperworld).

Watákame discovered that it was with her kwarére that Nakawé herself had each day regenerated trees, as a sign to the Héwi that it was no use trying to plant—this world was soon to be drowned in a great lake that would cover the earth from east to west and north to south. Watákame alone was to survive, Nakawé told him, in the company of a small black bitch dog with a white spot on her neck. She showed him how to cut down an amate tree (*Ficus* spp.) and carve from its trunk a watertight box. As the waters rose, she sealed Watákame and his canine companion inside. Seating herself on the lid she paddled or poled successively to each of the four quarters of the world. Wherever they came they found the people drowning, although the Nanáwata women, even in their last hours, were playing a curious throwing game with balls of *ixtle* (agave) fiber string to a tune that Huichols still sing or play on the reed flute, the violin, or on the string of the musical bow.

When the waters had subsided, Nakawé landed the box and set about bringing plants and animals back to life with her magical staff, her woven snake girdle, and her triangular cape, which also had magical regenerative powers. Watákame and his dog set up residence in a rock shelter, from which he set forth at dawn each day to begin clearing a new field in which to raise maize from the five kernels he had managed to save from the great flood. Not having a wife, Watákame was lonely and he wondered who would make his tortillas and his atole (maize gruel).

To his surprise, each night upon his return he found atole and tortillas and other kinds of food whose preparation is normally woman's work.

"What could be happening here?" he asked himself, "How can this be when I am all alone, with this little dog as my only companion?" He resolved to ask Nakawé, and at dawn the next day, having patted the dog farewell and watched her run back into the cave, he called on the old goddess to explain the mystery. The following morning, at her direction, he again watched the little dog disappear inside but instead of continuing on his way he concealed himself behind a tree. After a time, to his great wonderment, a naked young woman emerged from the cave, carrying on her head a jar with which she disappeared down the slope in the direction of a stream. "How can this be?" he asked.

Again following Nakawé's advice he entered the rock shelter and there, next to the hearth, he saw the skin of the little black dog with the white spot on the neck. Beside it were the things a woman used to make tortillas—metate and grinding stone and the whitish *nixtamal* water in which sprouted maize is soaked with lime prior to grinding. At Nakawé's direction he cast the dog skin into the fire. Hearing the woman outside cry in pain, "You are burning me, you are burning me," he quickly poured the soothing nixtamal water over her body.[14] That, the Huichols say, explains why Indians are neither black nor white but an intermediate brown, the result of the black color of the dog skin mixing with the nixtamal water with which Watákame cooled down Dog Woman's body.

From the union of Watákame and Dog Woman, now permanently transformed into human shape by the burning of her skin, came the new race of people—the ancestors of the Huichols—that populated the earth after the drowning of the Héwi and the Nanáwata. Watákame, being a powerful shaman, also caused people to appear magically from the ten fingers of his hands. Inasmuch as they reckon their descent from Dog Woman, the Huichols, then, can truly be called Chichimeca, literally "Lineage of the Dog," the generic term applied to a number of desert-dwelling peoples who in prehispanic times lived north of the northernmost extension of Mesoamerican civilization (the Aztecs themselves claimed Chichimeca descent). Many of the so-called Chichimeca groups do in fact share a similar dog-as-ancestor tradition with the Huichols, and the noted Mexican ethnohistorian, Wigberto Jiménez Moreno (personal communication), for one, feels that the name is derived from this mythic descent tradition.

## The Birth of Tayaupá (Sun Father)

The Huichol origin myth of the Sun is so similar in several respects to those of central Mexico at contact time as to suggest diffusion, if not of the entire tradition, at least of the strikingly Aztec-like theme of human sacrifice. In contrast, it is possible that both the central Mexican solar myths and that of the Huichols derive ultimately from common roots and that the basic elements of the story of the birth of the Sun, as recorded in the sixteenth century in central Mexico and more recently among the Huichols, were present already in an older Uto-Aztecan substratum ancestral to both the Aztecs and their far-flung linguistic cousins. Again much abbreviated, the Huichol version reads as follows:

In ancient times (it is not clear whether before or after the great flood), although the people had fire (Tatewarí), night and day were indistinguishable, all being darkness, for there was as yet no sun. The (animal) people asked Great-grandmother Nakawé, their chief, what they should do so that the sun might be born. After lengthy council it was decided that one of their number would transform himself into the Sun Father through autosacrifice. As in the case of the theft of fire, there were four volunteers, but each failed ignominiously. Finally, a fatherless youth noted for his self-contained behavior, his lonely vigils, and his solitary games, especially his favorite, which was to shoot arrows at a hollow disk or hoop made from a large flat cactus leaf,[15] declared his readiness to perform the essential autosacrifice by which he would be transformed into the Sun. The boy's mother was none other than the earth and maize goddess 'Utuanáka. The goddess did not want to see her son die and she pleaded with him to let someone else become the Sun Father. But he spoke of his wish to help the people have their Sun Father and flung himself into the same fire that had previously rejected the others (another version, narrated by Ramón, spoke of a lake or inlet that turned fiery-red—i.e., into fire or blood—at the moment of impact) and descended down the five levels of the underworld, where dangerous animals, including a great double-headed serpent that encircled the earth disk, were waiting to devour him. Nakawé and Tatewarí placed their ears to the ground and told the animal people to follow the youth's subterranean path to the east, where they would attend his birth as Sun Father from a mountain called 'Unáxu (Cerro Quemado, Burned Mountain, highest point in Wirikúta). All the people hurried eastward to Wirikúta, although it was not yet known to them that one hunted the Deer-Peyote in that sacred land, for the peyote pilgrimage had not yet been established by Tatewarí.

The animal people hid themselves in fear when the sky turned red and the ground began to tremble, and they wondered out loud what appearance the newborn Sun Father would have and what he should be named. When finally he burst from his Mother, the earth, it was in a great shower of fiery rocks and sparks. Of the animals that had speculated what he should be named, it was Turkey who by calling out *tau-tau-tau* gave the Sun one of his proper names, Táu. Ever since, Turkey has been the Sun's companion.

The newborn Sun Father's birth was not to be a smooth ascent to the top of the sky, however. He was exhausted from his long subterranean journey from the west and his struggles against chthonic monsters and sorcerers that tried to devour him or otherwise block his path. Instead of climbing straight up the five levels of the Upperworld he not only sank down again and again but brought the whole sky down with him, until the earth began to scorch, plant life withered, and the animals came close to death in the terrible heat.[16] Some burrowed frantically into the ground or sought shelter beneath rocks and in the roots of trees. Thus was established the behavior of species that typically shun the intense rays of the noonday sun.

To facilitate the fatigued Sun Father's proper ascent, the great Mara'akáme, Tatewarí, caused three things to be done at once: (1) to raise the sky and the sun to their proper height, he caused five brazil trees to be erected, one in each of the four quarters and a fifth in the sacred center;[17] (2) with Káuyumarie's help he showed the people how to construct for the tired Sun an 'uwéni, the characteristic Huichol basketwork chair on which shamans and headmen are seated during rituals, thereby establishing for the future the custom of making such chairs in miniature effigy for the supernaturals; and (3) he sacrificed a child so that its life blood might nourish the Sun Father and restore him to sufficient strength to travel south and west through the sky at the correct distance for lighting up the world and causing maize and other food plants to ripen, but not again to threaten the very survival of the earth.[18]

It can be seen that such traditions, chanted at great length and with much repetition (albeit typically in the shorthand style discussed above) at rituals from which children are never excluded, as well as recounted in more explicit form as tales, provide the charter for all kinds of customs and beliefs in the world in which the Huichol child grows up and that together make up the content of "being Huichol." Apart from the requirement of making 'uwéni chairs for the gods, which range from very small miniatures left as offerings in sacred places to larger ones that are placed on altars in the small xíriki or oratory on the rancho, or in the larger tukípa or temple, the solar myth explains why certain animals require or prefer shade or the dark of night, why blood (animal, not human) is essential for the feeding of the supernaturals in an unending cycle of reciprocity between the people and the gods, and why tukípa and xíriki represent microcosms of the four-quartered universe with its supporting trees of the four directions and the center (another myth that tells of the construction of the first temple under the direction of Tatewarí reinforces the latter).

Most importantly, there is the constant experience of the mara'akáme's essential role as mediator, weather prophet, guardian, and interpreter of the traditions, and above all, curer, something that cannot help but impress itself indelibly on the young as they observe many of their fathers or, more commonly, grandfathers (occasionally also mothers) functioning on one or another level of shamanism. For Lumholtz was quite right when he wrote (1900:5-6) that a great many of the adults—fully a third, he said—are at least curing shamans, surprising as that may seem in the context of a sedentary agricultural society. Indeed, for many of the young it is a given that Tatewarí himself is alive and well in their very midst— and this not merely in the sense that fire (especially the ceremonial hearth) is his physical manifestation, or that on the peyote hunt the leader is addressed as, indeed becomes, Tatewarí.

Rather, there is something of the essence of Tatewarí in every mara'a-káme, however low-level. The prototypical shaman, Tatewarí, stood between the people (as semidivine animal ancestors themselves considered to have been shamans) and the hostile powers of the universe, including the potentially destructive forces inherent in the Sun Father (another great shaman). That of course is precisely the role of any shaman, be he headman of a local kin group, or one of its members, or, on the upper end of the prestige scale, one of the select leading shamans of great charisma and power whose renown extends far beyond their own immediate social environment to the very boundaries of the community, and occasionally even beyond. Such men may, in fact—as was the late great shaman of San Andrés Cohamiáta, Colás—be thought of, addressed, and referred to as "Tatewarí," a merging of a living person with the Great Mara'akáme, primordial shaman, and principal deity, ordinarily reserved for the peyote pilgrimage.

What is especially interesting here is the conceptualization, explicit and implicit, of fire as mediator par excellence between the earth and the capricious solar deity, as well as other potentially destructive forces. Fire can be manipulated and controlled by man, whereas the sun is beyond human reach.[19] Of course, as every Huichol knows, fire can also get out of hand, as it sometimes does when the felled trees and brush are burned before the planting of the maize and the uncleared forest beyond the milpa catches fire. But by and large Grandfather Fire (as Lumholtz called him) is benevolent, cleansing and transforming and, above all, despite (or perhaps because of) his origins in the underworld, the earth mother's womb, providing nurture, warmth, illumination, and protection against the ever-threatening and mysterious forces that abound in the dark of night.

Nothing could make the shaman's protective and mediating role vis-à-vis the Sun Father more explicit than the former's position in the temple during the rituals. As Lumholtz noted, the doorway of the tukípa faces east, and the mara'akáme is so seated that he looks out of the door toward the rising sun. But there is more to this than that. Between himself and the doorway of the temple, and beyond it, the emerging Sun Father on the eastern horizon, is the ceremonial hearth, at once the seat of Tatewarí and his manifestation. From the point of view of the shaman as master of fire, then, the protective power of Tatewarí, the deified Fire, stands between himself as guardian of the social group and a god who is generally beneficient and always essential to life, but who also has the potential for catastrophe, for the individual in illnesses that, like smallpox, are particularly associated with the Sun, or on the cosmic plane by failing to be reborn or not rising to the proper height.[20]

At this juncture we wish to reemphasize that all Huichol "history," be it the myth of Opossum as Bringer of Fire, the birth of Sun Father, the construction of the first temple, or the origin of *hikuri* (peyote), is absorbed by the children on ceremonial as well as secular occasions, in different versions, and in different narrative styles. They might hear of Opossum's adventures, for example, in a folktale told by the grandfather, in which case actors and actions might be more or less explicitly identified and perhaps a moral drawn (as it is in the myth cycle relating the origin of maize, which, by relating in one instance how the Mother of Maize, in her animal form as Dove Woman, retrieves Maize Baby from its neglectful foster parents, and in another, how Blue Maize Girl, having been shamed and ill-used by her mother-in-law, magically empties the storage house of all maize and returns to her rancho, reinforces the exalted place of the plant as sacred mainstay of life [Myerhoff, 1974:204–214]). Or, again, Opossum Person and his crucial role in giving fire to the people may be brought up in relation to death and the afterlife, in the context of the mara'akáme's chant that relays to the survivors the adventures of the soul on its way to the rancho and dancing ground of the dead relatives. For, as we recall, Opossum operates a chthonic stone trap (one of several Huichol variants on the well-known theme of the dangerous or paradoxical passage in funerary, heroic, and shamanic mythology in many parts of the world [cf. Eliade, 1964]) that threatens to fall and crush those who violated the taboo against eating opossum meat (Furst, 1967:39–106).[21] Or, again, portions of the fire myth might appear within a lengthy prayerful recitation of the deeds of the ancestors. In that event, the form would certainly be allusive and allegorical, not requiring, for either the sacred business at hand or intelligibility, what we would consider definition or "logical" sequence. Instead of explicitly recounting how Opossum made his way into the underworld and, pretending to be asleep, proceeded to snake his long, prehensile tail into the smoldering fire of its guardian in order to make off with a live coal, the shaman might sing, "He caused it to enter there, saying as he did, 'If I do it well, they will receive it there. Thus he did this thing,'" or some such fragmentary language, leaving his audience to fill in the proper details from their accumulated store of traditional knowledge. This audience, it should be noted, customarily includes not just kinfolk and neighbors but also the ancestors, that is, the very actors in the drama he is describing and whose personal attendance and assistance in procuring rain, crops, livestock, health, children, and general fertility and well-being and other good things he invokes with his magic songs and power objects. That is always the first order of business on sacred occasions: to summon Káuyumarie and the divine ancestors so that they might join in the festivities and complete the circle between the living and the dead, present and past, this world and the other, and between nature, culture, and the supernatural. For with his chants of the traditions, the shaman does more than relate what was. Rather, he transposes the mythic past into the present and the present into the past, thereby merging "real" time and mythic time. Typically he does this also when he cures, for in mythic time, the time of the ancestors, when Tatewarí himself was curer, everything was possible.

It can be said that most of the traditions, major and minor, that account for the origin (typically always by transformation rather than creation *ex nihilo* in the Judeo-Christian sense) of the different natural and cultural phenomena that make up the physical and metaphysical environment are eventually absorbed by the Huichol child in the two complementary modes, the one more or less explicit and the other allusive. As noted earlier, this includes the momentous myth that provides the charter for the pilgrimage to Wirikúta and the hunt for Elder Brother, the divine hikuri that is at once peyote, deer, and maize and that manifests itself initially as Deer.

The chant that relates, to the beat of the *tépu,* the hollow-log, three-legged upright drum, the adventures of the bird-children, and their joyful reunion with their divine Mother, Tatéi Niwetúkame, is not what the Huichols would call—as Ramón customarily did—"history," inasmuch as it describes not a past event but what is supposed to be happening in the here and now. Here also, as in the course of an actual peyote hunt, present time and mythical time flow together, the shaman acting as mediator who, by his special magical powers, the assistance of Káuyumarie, and the sound of the drum, succeeds in lifting himself and the children out of the everyday context into a nonordinary, magico-mythical temporal and spatial environment.

Below we describe in some detail the ceremony which the Huichols sometimes call Tatéi Néiya and sometimes To Beat the Drum. We also reproduce passages, footnoted where necessary, from the chanted version of the celestial journey of the bird-children, recorded in 1971 by Ramón and his wife Lupe in Huichol and subsequently rendered by them into Spanish. It is from the latter that the English translation here used was made. Although already available in print (Myerhoff, 1974:179–184), we also reproduce the narrative of the magical journey recorded for us in 1966 by Ramón, which includes some explanatory language that he inserted for the benefit of the ethnographers but which would be super-fluous in a strictly native version. There are many layers of meaning, of course, and to make some of these more easily understood we will first reproduce in its essential details the myth of the peyote hunt of the divine ancestors, that prototypical magical event that every peyote hunt is supposed to reenact as faithfully as possible and from which is drawn the cognitive map of the sacred geography the child is expected to assimi-late on his magical flights.

## The Primordial Hunt for Elder Brother

In ancient times, it is said, after Tatewarí and Nakawé had put the world in order with the help of Káuyumarie and had assigned the different gods to their places, the Great Mara'akáme called the ancestors together to hold council. They were gods, those ancient ones, the same gods we Huichols have today, some great, some small, some important, others not. Some came from the four directions, some entered through openings in the roof, others through the doorway that faced east. Some climbed to the surface of this world from a sacred hole in the center of the tukípa, which is why the floor of the temple has such a hole today. All of the ancient gods were complaining of many ills. One suffered from pain in the stomach, another's chest ached, a third was beset by stiffness of the legs, yet another by a pounding in his head. "What can this be?" they asked Tatewarí. "We have come to you to be cured, for you are the great Mara'akáme, who makes and unmakes."

With his power Tatewarí divined that their illnesses were caused by failure to follow the ways of the ancestors. He told them they had been made sick because they had not gone to Wirikúta to hunt the divine híkuri, and that only by doing so would they find their life.[22]

After making their preparations, which included, as they do today, the making of many prayer arrows and votive gourds, strict fasting[23] and abstinence from salt and sex, ritual washing, and among many other requirements the collection of specially consecrated firewood ("Food of Tatewarí") so that the kinfolk who remained at home might properly tend the sacred hearth until their return, the primordial peyoteros took their assigned places and in single file followed Tatewarí, with the antlered Káuyumarie as guide, on the long trail to Wirikúta. Behind Tatewarí walked, each in his proper place, carrying bow and arrows, baskets and shoulder bags, Sun Father and Elder Brother Deer Tail, the old one known only as Great-grandfather, and the other male "Owners" of different species of animals. The trail was hard and with the heat of day and the bitter cold of night, the lack of food and drink, the long hours of walking at the rapid pace set by Tatewarí, the many wakeful nights filled with dancing and singing and listening to the Mara'akáme's teachings, it is not surprising that some of those ancient ones remained behind, preferring, like Rabbit, to settle "in their spot." Stopping here and there, to rest, make their offerings, cook tortillas, or grind the yellow face paint from the desert shrub called úxa, they established the sacred places that must be properly acknowledged when one travels to the peyote.

After many days, fatigued beyond feeling and near death with hunger and thirst, convinced they could endure not one more step, they arrived at the edge of a lake. Here they found a rancho, and from the rancho emerged Huichol women bearing gourds of sacred water and tortillas for the exhausted pilgrims. Those Huichol women were Our Mothers, owners of rain and of the water on and under the earth. They live there at that place to this day, in the springs called Place of Our Mothers. From there one travels to the field of flowers that is the home of Our Mother Niwetúkame, Mother of all the children, who gives the child its sex and soul when it is born. From the place where Our Mothers Live (Tatéimatiniéri), the ancient ones were given their first sight of Wirikúta, there on the distant horizon.

After drinking the sacred water of Our Mothers and washing their heads, all those ancient ones, the men in front and the Mothers following, all in single file, each according to his place, all being of one heart, traveled together in unity. There, on the first altar (mesa), in the distance, Tatewarí espied the divine Deer, Elder Brother who is called Wawatsári, the Principal Deer (deer deity of the South), and by other names. First they saw his tracks and then they saw him. Though he tried to escape, from the first altar to the second, and though he transformed himself, he could not. Setting up their snares, those ancient ones, Tatewarí and his companions, ran him down and they saw that where he left his hoof-prints grew peyote. As he lay dying at their feet they prayed and honored him, so that his soul would not leave them for the top of the mountain ('Unáxu, birthplace of the Sun). They saw that he did not die but was peyote. They cut off his antlers and ground them on a metate to make a drink, but really they were drinking peyote. Feeling refreshed they sang and danced, seeing beautiful things in many colors. When they collected his hooves to make a rattle they saw that these too were peyote. All his flesh and his bones, all were peyote. Then they climbed to the top of the mountain to place their offerings. On the fifth day, wearing the clothing (skin) of deer, they turned west toward their homes, baskets and bags heavy with the flesh of the divine Deer that was peyote, their gourds filled with sacred water from the springs of Our Mothers. When they arrived, they made a circuit of the sacred places, especially Teakáta (the cave of Nakawé), and hunted deer with their snares, all as Tatewarí had arranged it. In that way they returned to where they had started, but feeling well, as Tatewarí had told them.

## The Tatéi Néiya Ceremony

Just as the peyote hunt is derived from a mythological prototype, so is its allegory, the magical flight of the children to Wirikúta. Zingg (1938:546–548) published one version of the origin myth of the drum and squash ceremony which, though somewhat sketchy, nonetheless serves to give the ritual its necessary ancestral dimension.

As Zingg tells it, the primordial first fruits ceremony had as one of its primary purposes the curing of sick children. The parents in the mythological event were the son and the daughter of a personage called Duck Boy, who had become transformed into Duck when he dived into the primordial waters to catch fish whose blood was needed by Nakawé to anoint the votive gourds of the Rain Mothers. Although Zingg seems not to have realized it, Duck Boy, whom he called TumuSauwi, is none other than Watákame, Clearer of Fields, who with Dog Woman fathered the new race of people after the destruction of the world by water; in another of Zingg's narratives (1938:542), the name Watákame is in fact attached to Duck Boy by Tatewarí as he transforms him temporarily into a deer.

Duck Boy's sons and daughters had to marry one another because there were then no others of their race. The taboo against incest was overcome with rituals: the boy had to kill a female deer, whose blood was used to anoint his paraphernalia,[24] and to shoot eagles with his bow and arrows. The girl had to catch lizards with a crooked stick, their blood being needed to anoint the ceremonial paraphernalia of Nakawé.

The brother-sister couple had many children. When they fell ill the parents asked Káuyumarie to divine what they should do. He told them to carry offerings to the home of the Goddess of Children in the peyote country. Failing that, they were to take them to her sacred cave near Santa Catarina in the Sierra.

Following Káuyumarie's instructions they found a sacred hollow log from which to carve a drum, and nearby, a ceremonial disk (*tepári*) on which to make the fire for tightening the drumhead. The people carried the log with great care to the rancho, for it was very "delicate." When the shape of the drum was complete, they set up lasso traps to catch the deer from whose skin the head was to be made. When deer fell into the traps Káuyumarie told them this meant long life for the children. Then the people made rattles and such other paraphernalia as were required for the first fruits ceremony, and laid out new maize ears and squashes. The first night the singer sang the sacred chants and at dawn he beat the new drum. The faces of the children were painted with peyote designs, and shaman's plumes, thread crosses, and new ribbons were put in their hair. The shaman then sang to all the gods *in order that the children might learn* (our italics). In the afternoon again deer had to be killed to obtain blood for anointing the ceremonial paraphernalia. Thus the cure was effected.

According to Zingg's version of the myth, it was now safe to eat the fruits of the fields, for "the green corn has had bad arrows taken out of it in this ceremony. In the same fashion is the squash treated" (1938: 549).

Actually, the meaning is somewhat more complex. "Bad arrows" refers to the concept that most sickness has a magical origin and that the physical symptoms of disease are brought about by magical projectiles—"arrows of sickness"[25]—propelled into the victim's body by a sorcerer, perhaps, or a supernatural displeased over a taboo violation or failure to heed a vow or ritual obligation. The *elotes* (green ears of maize) and squashes that play a part in the children's ceremony are more than just the first fruits of the milpa: they are themselves the participating children in another form. In the context of the mythological ceremony, then, extraction of the arrows of sickness from the maize and squash signified not only that henceforth they were safe to eat but that the sickness had been removed from the children for whom the ritual was first established. As every Huichol is aware, curing or, at the very least, what we would call "preventive medicine," is, after all, an important aspect of ritual. This myth, then, like that of the origin of the peyote hunt and others, is one more reminder that health and well-being, for the ancestors as much as for people today, is dependent upon proper regard for the ancient customs.

Three different but complementary versions of the children's ceremony follow: (1) Ramón's rendition, recorded in 1966; (2) ethnographic notes on a Tátei Néiya in 1971; and (3) portions of a shaman's chant narrating the magical flying journey to Wirikúta, again by the late Ramón Medina:

*The View from Within: Ramón's Narrative*

### When the Drum Is Beaten and the Mara'akáme Flies the Children to Wirikúta

Here I speak of the ceremony of the drum, of the squash, of the hikiri (elotes, ears of green maize). The new squash, the new maize that is roasted on the ear, the tender maize. It is the ceremony of the children. One calls it Beating the Drum. I will tell you of what the mara'akáme sings there.

The new maize, the new squash, they are sacred. They are purified, they are anointed with the blood of the deer. It is hunted because it is sacred, so that we may eat. We spend the time of the rains, from May to June, to July, to August, even to September, to the last days of September, without food, without maize from the fields, without squashes, without anything. Just old, dry maize which has been stored to make tortillas. Some of us do not have even that. This is a time of great danger to us, much hunger, much pain. We are hungry. But it is dangerous to eat of the new fruits before the ceremony. Before the drum is beaten. Before the deer has been hunted. Then we go and track the deer. Many of us go, the men go. The women stay to sing and to pray. Many go and between us we beat the drum, as it was in ancient times. All those go who have families, who have children. If there are ten men, or twelve, all of them go. The head of the drum is the skin of the deer. Tatewarí gives it the proper sound. The mara'akáme sees that it has the right tone. The drum is beaten and everyone fasts before they go to hunt the deer. The *nawá* (maize beer) is ready. It has been strained. Everything is ready.

All night the mara'akáme sings in the túki where Our Grandfather (Fire) burns. Our Grandfather, Our Father, Our Mothers, Our Great-grandparent, Our Grandmothers are in their places. Their votive bowls are in their places. Their arrows are in their places. Their *nieríkas*[26] are in their places. The mara'akáme has spoken to them about the ancient times. He has told them how Our Grandfather, Our Father, Our Mothers, Our Elder Brother, all of them arose, how the maize came to be, how the deer came to be, how the peyote came to be. Now the children will go on that journey, to Wirikúta, to the peyote country. The mara'akáme takes them. All pray there, very beautifully, sitting in the circle, in their places. Then the deer is hunted so that our food, our life, may be anointed with its blood. Without the deer we cannot gather, we cannot eat. That is why it is so beautiful.

The next day, in the morning, it begins. The mara'akáme sits there in his chair. On one side are little boys, on the other side little girls.

Very pretty all of them. They are adorned, very beautifully. They wear the tsikúri (thread cross) in their hair, they wear the sacred arrows. And then he tells them, the shaman tells them, "Look, my little ones, we are going to make this ceremony, so we can eat hikiri now, so we can eat squash now, so that we may be able to feed ourselves. Because now we have nothing to eat."

All right. Everyone is carrying their little candle, their sacred staffs, the incense burners with the sacred incense. All of them happy. Contented. They carry rattles so they can sound them while the shaman is singing, while he is beating the drum. While he tells them of the ancient times so that they may come to know the heart of the Huichols. So that they may know how it was. So that all the new food, the new squashes, the hikiri, will be purified.

"Look," he tells them, "it is this way. We will go over this little mountain, we will fly over this mountain. We will travel to Wirikúta. We will go where the sacred water is, where the peyote is. In the direction where Our Father comes up."

And from there they fly, like bees, straight, they go on the wind as one says, this way. As though they were a flock of doves, very beautiful, like the singing turtledoves. They fly evenly, you can see that they become as little tiny bees, very pretty. They continue from hill to hill, they fly from place to place as the shaman tells them. The mara'akáme goes with Káuyumarie, Káuyumarie tells him everything. He protects them all. A little girl is missing a wing because the father or the mother have committed many transgressions. If they are missing a wing, the mara'a-káme puts it back on. Then she flies with the rest of them. She says, "Oh, how good is Tayaupá, how good is Tatewarí." She says, "Thanks to them our mara'akáme has the power."

So they continue to travel. As they come to a place, the shaman points it out. "This place is called such-and-such, that place is called so-and-so." So that they will know of it, how it was in ancient times, how it was when Our Grandfather, Our Father, Our Greatgrandparent, Our Mothers, when they went this way, when they crossed over there, when they went to Wirikúta. When Tatewarí, Tatutsí (Greatgrandfather), Tayaupá (Sun Father), Tamátsi Máxa Kwaxí, (Elder Brother Deer Tail), when all of them crossed over there. When the children of the first Huichols went there so that they became cured, when they became well.

That is what the drum says. When it is beaten. There I will fit in. To the south, to the north, to the east, up above, thus I speak to Our Grandfather, Our Father, Our Mothers, Our Greatgrandparent, all of them. Thus speaks the mara'akáme. The arrows that cleanse, they fly and land in the growing maize field. They fall where 'Ai Xuríta (Red Cliffs) is, where the children fly, where he leads them on the wind. They land on one of the rocks. It is as though they were clinging to the rock, like a little animal holding fast. They do this as he speaks to them, as he goes explaining to them. Then they rise again. And the mara'akáme says, "Let us go, let us travel together once more." The shaman tells them, "Look, children, you are not familiar with these paths. There are many dangers, there are many animals that eat children, that threaten people. That is how it is on this road." The shaman tells them everything. "You must not separate," he says to them. "You must stay close together, all of you." And the children are very glad, very happy. They smile and laugh because soon they will be able to eat hikiri, squashes, everything.

They fly on to Tsánakuxári, where the Amate stands. Then they fly to where they say Takútsi, the one who is called the Hermit of the World, the ancient one with white hair who stays by herself alone, passed by in the time of the Great Flood, when the earth was softened by the water. She passed by here and you can still see the tracks she made. That is why this place is called Takútsi Kakái, Our Greatgrandmother's Sandals. The Sandals, it is called, the footprints she made. And so the mara'akáme goes explaining everything to the children. How she made the Flood. How she unmade it and put the trees and all these things back into the earth after it had dried out. About Watákame and the dog, the little black she-dog in the canoe. How the seeds of the maize, of the squashes were saved. Everything, everything the mara'akáme explains to them.

> Eagles on the south, you eagles on the north, you eagles in your places, fly like that, go down there on the south, go down there on the north.

So he speaks to them. He requests this of them. So he speaks, so he tells them.

They fly on to Tekuári, to Where the Arrows Are. They fly past there. *Xiuwa, xiuwa, xiuwa,* so goes the sound of their flying. Their wings. They arrive at Teakáta, The Volcanic Place. There, among the cliffs, they get to know the place. It is the place where in ancient times, the First Mara'akáme, Tatewarí, blessed the sacred water in the caves, so that everyone could go there, our relatives, the Huichols, everyone.

They arrive there when the mara'akáme says, "Look, children," and proceeds to explain everything. "Look," he says, "here, this water, it is sacred, it has been blessed by our ancestors." And then he takes a gourd bowl and with it sprinkles the sacred water over them. He blesses them and tells them, "Look, let us do this thing, here you must be blessed, here you are cleansed, all of you." They bring one of their number close to him and he is sprinkled with the sacred water, he is cleansed. And then another, and another. He tells them, "I bless you with the water from the sacred caves which Our Father and Our Grandfather placed here. I bless you in the Four Winds, to the right and to the other side, to the north, to the south, and up above, all of it very well, so that you can walk wherever you wish." And then he says, "Come, children, we must leave, because we are not just going here, which is close, but very far away, to Wirikúta."

So they learn the place where Our Grandfather is. They get to know where Our Father is. They get to know where Our Greatgrandparent is. They get to know where Our Mothers are, where our Grandmothers are. He tells them this. After they have been there, they go on. On they go. "We have learned how one stands," he says to them. "We finally know how to make an offering to the south, how to make an offering to the north, how to make an offering to the east, how to make an offering up above. How one gives offerings." So he says to them. So I say as I fit in there, as I take my place. He prays:

> Let us feed them. There where Our Grandfather is, there on the south, there on the north. Where you all are, you all to whom I make this offering. Here it is. You, Our Aunt, Our Mother who are there. You, Kumukíte, who are there, gather yourselves together. You, Our Grandparents, who are kept in our houses as rock crystals, and you who do this, gather yourselves together. You, Our Grandparents who are given offerings, gather yourselves together. You, Our Grandparents who are given offerings, gather yourselves together. Your votive bowls are sitting here like that, your votive bowls are in their places, there they are.

So he speaks to them. Thus the children, the children who fly with him over there, learn everything. Then he sings:

> Just on the north
> When he had made an offering to you all on the north
> When he had made an offering to you all
> When he had laid down an offering to you all
> He offers to you all to the south
> He offers to you all to the north, on your left
> He offers to you all in the east.

There it is.

> When he had made an offering to you all
> He offers to you all in the south
> He offers to you all in the east

Where you dwell, Xutúri'iwiyékame
Where you are, 'Utuanáka
You did it—you are the one
Accept your offering.

That is what he says. He gives them their offerings.

Where you are, Scorpion Girl
You who did it
Their Mother is like that.

Thus he sings and makes his offerings to them. He offers them on his right, he offers them on his left, he offers them to his east, he offers them above. Also he offers them to his west, where Our Mother Haramára (the deified Pacific Ocean) dwells, also to where Our Mother Hamúxa dwells. He makes his offerings to them. Where he lands, where they come to rest, there he makes offerings to them.

So at last he says, "We will fly on." He tells them, "Let us fly away from here to over there." He rises. They land at Wakanaríxipa. There they land. There is a terrible mountainous country. Here the mara'akáme explains to them, "On this road where we are traveling, this is the path our ancestors traveled. That is our custom. That is the road they traveled in ancient times and which we have not forgotten. That is the way we must travel, the symbols we must follow. For when someone dies, there is always someone who comes after. And he travels the same path and follows the same symbol." That is what the mara'akáme tells all of them.

So I speak. That is why the story comes to us from many years ago, from ancient times, and I cannot tell you how long ago that was. Ever since the earth was born. from that time on we have followed this path, our custom. As I tell it to you now, so the mara'akáme tells it to the children. Then he flies on. The children participating fly on. They fly to Where The Star Lives. Then they fly to a place they call Hukúta (La Ocóta, Pine Grove, The Place of Kindling Wood). Now they say, "Mara'akáme, tell us, how will we cross that river there?" "Well," he says, "I know how." And he takes them, safely. Then they fly to a place called The Lake. There they stop and he says, "Look, here there are very fierce animals which might eat you." We love the water, the water is sacred to us, but we do not love the animals which are in the water, those that are dangerous, those that try to devour Our Father as he travels through the water. So the mara'akáme tells them.

Off they go again. They come to Kuyetsariépa. From Kuyetsariépa they fly on, to the place called Where a White Scrub Oak Stands. It stands between rocks. He sings, "I will stay in that oak tree, no, I cannot place my offerings there." So he sings, so that they will know how it happened there in ancient times that the Caterpillar Person could not cross over there to Wirikúta, because he was tired. Because he was hungry and thirsty. "I will stay in that oak tree," so he sang, as in ancient times.

"At last," he prays, "All you who are in Wirikúta, those who are eaten as peyote, we are going there. We are on our way to Wirikúta." He says to them, to those children, "We are going," looking off to his right, to his east. He says to them, "Act and feel like eagles. You will go there on your wings." They give instructions to one another, they learn. One tells the other, "Light your candle," and he answers, "Yes, very well." The mara'akáme takes tinder, he takes flint, he takes steel for striking fire. They do this five times and they light the candles and worship there and go on their way. They travel and come to a place they call Las Cruces, Where the Cross(road) Is. They exclaim "Oh, look, we really have come far, yes, we have come far. And how will we be able to go on?" And they say, "Well, it is because we are going to Wirikúta, where the peyote grows, where our ancestors traveled. We have to get rid of our sins, everything."

They fly on and arrive at Huejucar. They do not linger there for long because that is a pueblo full of Spaniards, and they do not wish to stay there for more than one minute, one moment. They just pass the place and continue on their way and say, "No, here we cannot stop, we cannot linger, because the Spaniards here are mean, they can do us harm. It is best to go on our way." This the mara'akáme tells them. The mara'akáme, he travels with Káuyumarie, who is the Sacred Deer. He is the companion of Our Grandfather, Our Father. The mara'akáme travels with his help. Káuyumarie, he leads them all, he is the one who is taking care of them all.

They do not linger here in Huejucar because of the bad Spaniards and they fly on to the rancho called El Tepetongo. Here in ancient times they made 'isi (petates-mats) from the sotol cactus. They fly to the place called The Serpents because in ancient times there were many dangerous snakes here. And since there are many dangers in that place also they do not linger there. They travel to Irons Flying Up and after they have passed there they arrive at Tepári (decorated circular votive stone disk), Where Tepári Is. It is the Tepári of Káuyumarie. They get to know it in the daylight. Here Káuyumarie grinds his face paint, they grind the roots for the colors with which the Huichols paint themselves, paint their faces. It is the paint that they get from the roots they find growing in the country of the peyote. The yellow root. That is how it is. To get to know that place, that is why Our Grandfather, Our Father, take hold of us. This is where they painted their faces, those travelers to Wirikúta. There, where the Tepári is, where the ceremonial disk is, is what that place is called. There they painted their faces. There they picked up the root, to carry it with them, so that they bring it to their homes. Our Grandfather passed by here in ancient times; it is he who placed it here. It is in ancient times that it was given its name, when Our Grandfather passed by here, when Káuyumarie passed by here. It is a very beautiful place. Very sacred. So they learn all that from the mara'akáme.

From here they travel on, flying, after they have instructed one another in all the things they must do. They inspect all their offerings, everything, for now comes the most mysterious thing of all the great things on that journey. They arrive at the place called Xapimukáka, Where the Vagina Is, where it is called La Puerta, the Door, the Gate, in Spanish. Káuyumarie opens it with his horns. He pushes the door aside with his horns and he tells the shaman, "Here, the way is open, we may proceed." It is a very sacred place. Where they (the peyoteros) sat in their places around Our Grandfather, close to Our Grandfather.

They travel on to the place called Hinárimayáka, Where the Penis Hangs. Here the shaman speaks to Our Mothers, Our Grandparents: "Let us see what the deer tail plumes say." There too he will speak to Our Grandfather. Their life can be found here. Our Grandfather speaks to him.

They fly on. They come down at San Miguel. After they come down at San Miguel they pass on to The Orchard. After they pass through The Orchard they go to Mayutekúta. After they leave Mayutekúta they come to Where the Red-tailed Hawk Roosts. After they leave Where the Red-tailed Hawk Roosts, they come to Tsauwírie. They come to Hainamári (Enclosed Clouds). "See," the mara'akáme says, "Our Mother stands in that place. The one who sends rain down to us. The one who makes us grow is over there," he says to them. He takes his arrows. He holds them out on the right, he holds them out on the left.[27] Finally, at last, he tells them, "you can do it." They do it. "All right," he says again. "You are all to pay attention, pay attention." They do it. They stand close. They fly on again, to the place called 'Urutsáta, Among the Arrows. He tells them about this very clearly, so that they will know. They continue on their way. They descend holding on to one another. This place is called The Breast of Our Mother. That is the name it was given in ancient times. There, they go on. Then to Wítsexúka, where they sit in a circle. "What is this place here named?" he asks the children. So they learn. He goes on and on, until all can sleep there.

Then they come to the place the Huichols call Ramúxa, which the Spaniards call Tierra Ramos. Then comes Téi Ki Húta, he calls, "Oh, where Our Mother is, oh, where Our Mother 'Enuíxi is." He takes his votive bowl from his bag and makes it go *kará*! The earth reverberates: *Xiawawawawawau.* "See that it is so," he says, "look out for it all. This deer tail plume of yours, your face paint design, these sandals of yours, this wristband of yours, this life of yours." So he speaks. "This is your life, this is why we make this journey."

We are not eating anything to speak of on this journey. Just a few watermelons, squash, green roasting ears of maize, just something, one thing and another. Oh, we carry a real load of life! If Our Mother is thus, if Our Father (Sun) there is thus, they will give it to us, they will feed us. You, Our Mothers, Our Father, you will give it to us. That is what will happen. When the Mara'akáme has said this, he will make his offerings, he will place the sacred things on the ceremonial shelf. Once, twice, three times, four times, placing it for Our Mother 'Utuanáka. When he has placed the offering on 'Utuanáka, when he has placed it on Our Mother Xutúri'iwiyékame, then he says, "Now at last I have fulfilled my obligations. I have spoken to you, My Mothers. I have fulfilled my obligations. There, as it is like that, as the smoke emerges upward." So the mara'akáme speaks, so the children learn.

He looks toward Tsinuríta.[28] He flies on to Dead Man's House, which we call Mu'úqui mayáka. They fly on, to Há Matíwe, the place that is called Falling Water. When they have flown to Falling Water, they come to Tsinuríta. There he stands, extending his arrows to the Mothers and Fathers in various directions.

"You have all seen it, where we are, where our place is." So he speaks. "You too are in your places." And he goes on, traveling, saying, "We are on our way." To the place where Wirikúta lies, which they call Real de Catorce, there they travel. He beats the drum.

It is almost noon. Then afternoon. He beats the drum. As it gets dark they travel on. They have gone to Tsinuríta. They go by Wiki Hápa (Place of the Bird). They go by Tupína Hápa, where the Hummingbird Person lives flying from flower to flower since ancient times. After they have been there, they go on to 'Aitsaríka (declivity with sacred caves). Then they come to Máxa Tekúta (Mouth of the Deer) and when they have passed by Máxa Tekúta they come to Máxa Huxíte (Eye of the Deer). Here they place the offerings of Our Mothers and Our Fathers. It is where their ceremonial staffs stand, where their *kunuári* are, where it is called Kunuaríta. From here they fly to Yu'ítsu (Blue Staff).

Where it is called Wirikúta, where Peyote dwells, there they arrive. When he has gone there, when he has beaten the drum, when he has stood by the sacred pools, where it is called Tatéi Matiniéri, when he has spoken to the Mothers and the Fathers, to Our Father, to Our Grandfather, to Our Greatgrandparent, when he has laid his offerings down, when their votive bowls are in their place, when their arrows are in their place, when their wristbands are in their place, when their sandals are in their place, when all is in its place, then it will be good, then we will have life. If I can do it, I will do it, there, in its place.

The children are happy, all, they are contented. All because now they can use the hikiri (elotes, green ears of maize), the squashes, everything. Because now they are blessed. They have gone their way until they arrive at this place, where the peyote is, where the deer is, where Our Mothers, Our Grandfathers are. The offerings are made, the deer tail plumes are in their place, the arrows are to the south, to the north, to the east, up above. He holds them out. The horns the deer has, they are there, in their place. They say, "Oh, it is the mara'akáme, the mara'akáme is here with them." He says, "Oh, Our Father, Our Grandfather, Our Mothers, you all who dwell here, we have arrived to visit you, to come and see you here. We have arrived well." And when they arrive, they kneel and Our Father, Our Grandfather, Our Elder Brother, embrace them.

"What did you come for, my children?" they ask. "You have come so far, why did you travel so far?"

They answer, "Oh, from this place and that, this way and that, we came to visit you so that we will know all, so that we will have life."

"All right," they say, "it is well." And they bless them. And there they remain but ten minutes, a very few minutes, to speak with Our Father, with Our Grandfather, with all of them there. After ten minutes the mara'akáme says, "Let us go now, my children, because we are not from here, we came to visit Our Mother. Mother, we are leaving, give us your blessing." And then the Mother gives them the blessing and they leave.

Ah, I am worn out from beating the drum. I have taken them around, flying, to show them the places, being as I am. I will certainly be able to do this. I will fly straight out. I will fly along, *paupaupaupaupau,* one day, two days, three days, four days. On the fifth day I will arrive. See, I say, I have a good heart. He says to them, in the south, in the north, to the east and up above, "See, I have a good heart."

## The View from Without: Tatéi Néiya at El Colorín, Nayarit

In 1971, the authors were invited to attend a Tatéi Néiya to be conducted in September or October by Ramón for children of the settlement of El Colorín, Nayarit, in the foothills of the Sierra Madre Occidental. Though outside the boundaries of Huichol territory as such, El Colorín can nevertheless be considered to be traditional Huichol, inasmuch as its inhabitants number some eighty Huichol-speakers and only two families of mestizos. The people of El Colorín observe the ancient customs and several, including women, have participated in peyote pilgrimages.

Unfortunately, in June of that year Ramón was fatally wounded in a shooting fray during a fiesta to celebrate the clearing of new milpa land at a rancho he had established for himself in the foothills, and only one part of Tatéi Néiya, mainly limited to a naming ceremony for children one year of age, was held, with José Ríos, an uncle of Ramón's widow Lupe, as officiating mara'akáme. Himself a traditionalist with a considerable command of esoteric knowledge, José Ríos, with his wife Eusebia and three of his sons and their wives, had been a participant in the 1968 peyote pilgrimage under the leadership of Ramón, for whom it was his fifth. Since five pilgrimages are required to become a full-fledged singing shaman, it was on the successful conclusion of the 1968 hikuri hunt that Ramón, until then an apprentice shaman, regarded himself—and was recognized by his kin—as being "completed." He was to make two more pilgrimages before his death in 1971, one, in the early spring of 1970, entirely on foot, a ritual obligation Lupe and he undertook in payment for her cure from an attack of rheumatoid arthritis.

One reason given for not going through with the entire Tatéi Néiya ritual at the proper time of year was that none of José Ríos's close kin had recently been to Wirikúta, so that no peyote, an essential ingredient, was available. By December, several members of the family had made such a pilgrimage, and with sufficient peyote now available, it was decided to complete the rite before any more time elapsed. Anguiano was able to attend on this occasion at the invitation of Ramón's widow and her uncle José Ríos.

That Tatéi Néiya could have been delayed in this manner without dire consequences requires some explanation. The ceremony's crucial role in the enculturation of the young, as emphasized throughout these pages, notwithstanding, the "first fruits" aspect should not be underrated, it being quite true that one is not supposed to eat of the new harvest of maize and squash until after these two most important cultigens of Huichol subsistence agriculture have been properly consecrated and the gods themselves offered their nourishment. Obviously, this taboo was violated for to go without the fruits of the milpa would have meant starvation. That this could be done without having the children fall ill and even die, as devout Huichols believe they surely would in the absence of the required rite (one recalls the curing aspect of the mythological Tatéi Néiya), is because a good mara'akáme can always propitiate the gods by offering a quid-pro-quo arrangement: the gods allow themselves to be manipulated in exchange for some extra effort in their behalf. In an instance such as this, the shaman would explain to Máxa Kwaxí and the Mothers, through the medium of Káuyumarie, why the ceremony could not be held in time and, promising to conduct it with special care and offerings at an early opportunity, ask that the people, in particularly the children, be allowed their vital sustenance in the meantime without being made ill. A special pilgrimage to Wirikúta would be typical of the kinds of ritual obligation people assume in such cases.

The Ríos-Medrano rancho consists of eight independent nuclear family dwelling units, each with sleeping room, detached kitchen, and storage house or granary. In addition, there is what Lumholtz called a "god house," the xíriki, the dwellinglike sanctuary or household temple found on most Huichol ranchos. Commonly the xíriki serves as repository of all sorts of ceremonial paraphernalia and images of different deities, noose or lasso traps for the ceremonial deer hunts, stores of fresh peyote brought back from Wirikúta, bottle gourds and more modern containers filled with sacred water from sacred springs in the Sierra or at Tatéi Matiniéri, and so on. It is often also within the xíriki that the women prepare nawá, the ceremonial maize beer that is known elsewhere in Indian Mexico by its Aztec-derived name, *tesgüino* or *tejüino*,[29] and that is indispensable to Huichol ritual as the preferred beverage of the living as well as the dead (for whom special bowls of nawá are set aside, lest they tumble into the nawá pots of the living and spoil the drink).

The most important occupant of the sanctuary—indeed, the principal reason for its existence—is the *'urukáme*, a ceremonial arrow (*'urú* = arrow) to which a very small and very sacred medicine bundle has been attached. The little bundle, barely two inches long and perhaps half an inch thick, consists of an outer covering of specially woven and sometimes embroidered cotton, inside of which is a small length of hollow bamboo. The bamboo conceals a tiny rock crystal inside a wrapping of soft Bombax cotton; fibers from the same tree also close off the two ends of the tube. The Huichols conceive of this translucent stone as the crystallized skeletal soul of a deceased shaman or other person of superior knowledge, whose desire to return to earth to dwell among his or her kin as supernatural guardian has manifested itself, through an illness or some other sign, to the shaman-headman of the extended family. The *'urukáme*, also known as tewarí, Grandfather, is retrieved in the shaman's dream journey from behind the sun (Furst, 1967). A xíriki may house several *'urukáme*. José Ríos's xíriki faced toward the east, the direction of Wirikúta and the birthplace of the Sun Father. With the ceremonial hearth of Tatewarí, the sanctuary forms the sacred center of a small ceremonial plaza enclosed by several of the houses that make up the extended family rancho; it is here that ceremonies such as Tatéi Néiya are customarily conducted.

Children participating directly rather than as spectators in Tatéi Néiya are collectively called *tevainuríxi*. They are fitted out in their best clothes and miniature tsikúri (thread crosses), one for each year of their age, ceremonial arrows are stuck in their headbands, and they are given small gourd rattles whose sound, said to represent the rustling of their wings, accompanies that of the drum on whose vibrations the shaman and his spirit helpers lift them magically into the sky. As a rule, the young participants range in age from one to five only; in this case six-year-olds were also integrated by their grandfather, the officiating mara'akáme, "so that they too will see our life." The ceremony, whose description below closely follows the field notes taken by Anguiano, augmented with explanatory material by Furst, was to last three days, from the night of December 22 through December 24.

## First day, Wednesday, December 22, 1971

The night's proceedings will consist of the mara'akáme, José Ríos, requesting permission from the gods, through the medium of five chants, to commence traveling to Wirikúta on the following day with the assembled children. All participants are more or less closely related to one another.

10 P.M. One youth, not dressed in characteristic Huichol clothing, tunes the drum, called tépu[30] in Huichol, by holding its open lower end over the fire, to tighten the deerskin drumhead. The action also blackens the underside of the drum, with some of the smoke emerging from its "mouth," a small rectangular opening about halfway down from the top. The soot from the body of the drum is considered to possess magical therapeutic properties and is sometimes used by mara'akáme to decorate the faces of people participating in a ceremony, the designs intended to protect them against harm, or, alternately, assist in curing them.

The singing shaman, José Ríos, and his two assistants, called *kwina-puwáme,* take their places around the sacred fire, Tatewarí. The singer is quite old, as is one of the two assistants, the other being a mature man. Off to one side, as the preparations for the ceremony proceed at a leisurely pace, a group of people listens to Mexican music on a transistor radio.

The tépu will be pounded by a youth, who receives from the mara'akáme the designation of "keeper of the drum" and who seats himself on a typical Huichol seat of tule and wood.

The mara'akáme ceremoniously lifts the cover from his palmfiber *takwátsi* and removes from it various ritual objects:

1. Four *muviéri* (shaman's plumes).
2. A candle, decorated with a red flower. Candles, of Spanish origin among the Huichols, are commonly called *katíra* (from *candela*); the ceremonial candle is also known by a more indigenous term, *háuri.*

3. A special kind of muviéri that has fastened to it the rattles of a rattlesnake, *xáye*. The complete name of this especially potent shaman's plume is *muviéri xáye káitsa makavíye* (*káitsa* = child's gourd rattle).

4. A species of tuberose with a small medallion of a Catholic saint attached to it.

The takwátsi is placed on the ground on a piece of *costal* (sacking) lying in front of the singer and his assistants. The objects named above are arranged as follows: one of the four muviéri remains inside the shaman's basket. On the lid, from left to right, lie (1) the rattlesnake muviéri, (2) one muviéri, (3) tuberose, (4) candle, (5) another muviéri. The fourth muviéri is in the shaman's hand. Also lying on the sacking are two small gourd rattles, called *káitsa*, and four multiple tsikúri, thread crosses, belonging to the children. The tsikúri consist of different numbers of connected thread crosses, depending on the age of the children. The form of these thread cross arrangements differs to some degree from those seen in other Huichol communities. Several packs of cigarettes also lie beside and around the takwátsi. Four lighted candles are placed at the singer's feet.

The same youth who is to play the drum now sounds a trumpet (*awa*) made from the horn of a bull (in Lumholtz's time the Huichols still used conch shell trumpets; these are now extremely rare, having been replaced by cow, bull, and goat horns).

The singing shaman is seated on a sacred bench, *ne 'ipári*. On either side of him, on the ground, are the assistants (kwinapuwáme), all face toward the xíriki. The men of the rancho form a circle around the fire, Tatewarí. The women remain seated to one side.

The preparations completed, the sacred songs are about to begin.

*First song.*—At 10:30 P.M. the horn is sounded again, followed by the opening lines of the first of the five songs, the Keeper of the Drum accompanying the mara'akáme. Normally, the shaman would keep the muviéri in his right hand; because José Ríos's right hand is missing, he holds his muviéri and the muviéri xáye in his left as he sings, accompanied all the while by the pounding of the drum. The assistants repeat the last stanza. Another Huichol, who has remained standing, sounds the awa (horn) for some moments. The mara'akáme sings softly, head tilted, hat covering most of his face. He has his eyes almost closed.

One of José's sons, who serves as the adjudicator or judge in the governing structure of El Colorín, stands up before the singer and his assistants, holding the káitsa (gourd rattles) and tsikúri (thread crosses) in his right hand. He shakes the rattles rhythmically to the beat of the drum. The technique and tempo are as described by Lumholtz (1900: 32); the drummer hits the deerskin head with the palms of his hands, lifting the right one high up and bringing it down once, while the left makes two rapid beats. The effect at a distance is almost that of equal beats, because the corresponding beats of the left and right palms are almost (though not quite) synchronous.

The mara'akáme now places the muviéri on the drum, and his son follows suit with the thread crosses and rattles. This marks the completion of the first song, in which the singing shaman, echoed by the assistants, has announced to the gods that the children are going to be traveling tomorrow to Wirikúta, under the tutelage of their mara'akáme. The song was directed to various deities: Tatéi Wérika 'Uimári (Our Mother Young Eagle Girl), Tatéi Haramára (Our Mother the [Pacific] Ocean), Our Mother Niwetúkame, Elder Brother Káuyumarie, Tatewarí.

There is a break of a little over ten minutes to give everyone a rest. José Ríos and the others engage in small talk and much joking—typical behavior in a ritual context.

*Second song.*—At the outset, the tsikúri and rattles are again arranged upon the costal cloth. The drum begins to sound, accompanying the principal singer, who invokes Máxa Kwaxí, the assistants repeating the last verses. The mara'akáme again holds the muviéri and the muviéri xáye (rattlesnake rattle plume) in his left hand.

His niece, Lupe Ríos (Ramón's widow) arranges two vessels and a bottle containing nawá (tejüino).

The Keeper of the Drum has been relieved by another youth.

The muviéri that remained in the takwátsi has now joined the rest of the ritual objects on top of the shaman's basket.

Elder Brother Máxa Kwaxí, the deer deity, has asked the singers for nawá to drink.[31] They and the drummer offer a little of the fermented maize drink to the gods of the five cardinal points (east, west, north, south and the center) and subsequently drink it themselves.

As in the first chant, José's son, the judge of El Colorín, sounds the rattles, which he grasps in one hand together with the composite thread crosses. Then he lays them on the drum, and at the same moment the shaman also places his muviéri on the drumhead. The singer asks the gods for permission to embark on the sacred quest to the peyote country, Máxa Kwaxí asks for a drink of nawá and the song ends with the information that the gods are getting ready to agree to the children's pilgrimage.

Once again the singers rest, the break lasting for fifteen minutes. The people chant, smoke, joke, and drink.

*Third song.*—As before, after having arranged the tsikúri and rattles in their places, the singing shaman, muviéri in hand, begins the song, to the pounding of the tépu. José Ríos invokes Máxa Kwaxí and the horn is blown four times. On this occasion it is the assistants who bring the song to an end; evidently, agreement has not yet been given to commence the journey.

*Fourth song.*—Before the singing is resumed the drum is tuned again; the deerskin drumhead being first wetted down with water and the drum then held over the fire to dry and tighten the head.

The mara'akáme begins the song by again invoking Máxa Kwaxí. The horn is sounded repeatedly throughout. The Keepers of the Drum take turns, without missing a single beat. The rhythm changes. From time to time the mara'akáme waves the muviéri from left to right as he sings. The name of Máxa Kwaxí recurs again and again in the song. As before, the song ends with the mara'akáme arranging the muviéri, and the judge the tsikúri and rattles, on the drumhead.

The Huichols ask us for cigarettes and for mezcal (distilled agave liquor), made in Oaxaca, which we had brought as a gift and which the Indians simply call "Oaxaca." They say Máxa Kwaxí now needs to smoke and drink.

*Fifth song.*—In this final recitation of the opening cycle, the mara'a-káme sings for the first ten minutes without the muviéri in his hand. Subsequently he takes them up and with them indicates that the judge should commence shaking the rattles. As in the previous chant, the mara'akáme gestures from left to right with the muviéri as he sings.

The majority of the women have now left to lie down, only three remaining to observe this initial phase of the ceremony.

It is during this fifth and final chant that the horn is sounded most frequently; it is also blown vigorously to signal the song cycle's conclusion. Máxa Kwaxí has been invoked. Now the gods have begun to give their agreement, having been convinced by the mara'akáme and Máxa Kwaxí that tomorrow's magical journey can be carried out as desired. The ceremony ends at 12:40 A.M., about two hours and forty minutes after it began. Each song lasted about twenty minutes, with breaks of up to fifteen minutes each between them. The gods had been invoked and fed, permission been requested and finally granted for the sacred journey of the *tevainuríxi* to begin on the following day.

## Second day, Thursday, December 23, 1971

The drum, with the rattles and the tsikúri on top, was kept all night in one of the sleeping huts. "Since yesterday," says the mara'akáme, "the gods, Elder Brother (Máxa Kwaxí), Káuyumarie, Tatewarí, and the others, are inside the drum, waiting to carry the children flying to Wirikúta, on this very day."

7:30 A.M. Rising we find everyone is already well into preparing for the ceremony. The mara'akáme has put on new clothing, beautifully embroidered.

The women are busy preparing *tétsu* (meat in a spicy sauce wrapped in maize dough and steamed in dried maize husks, known as *tamal,* from the Aztec *tamalli,* in Mexican Spanish. In the rest of Mexico the tamale is a popular dish; for the Huichols it is strictly ceremonial). The tamales will be eaten later.

By about 9 A.M. what the Huichols call an *'utá,* bed, consisting of reeds laid upon a wooden framework, has been arranged in front of the xíriki. On it they have placed green maize and squash; two rattles; the multiple thread crosses; six candles; three tin pots containing nawá; two plates with four thick maize tortillas called *papaturíxi (papá -te =* tortilla, *turíxi =* children) each; a box of chocolate; flowers; four gourd bowls each containing five tamales; a small gourd filled with nawá; a bottle of nawá; three small platters with six miniature leaf-shaped tortillas; and another platter with a number of tamales. Four lengths of reed grass, tied together into a rectangle, form a kind of headboard for the "bed." Various ritual objects have been tied to it: two shaman's plumes; one large tsikúri with only a single thread cross; three ceremonial arrows to which small bundles containing rock crystals have been fastened (the supernatural guardians or household gods known as 'urukáme or simply as tewarí, Grandfather) described above; a special ceremonial arrow of Tatewarí, large in size, with feathers at its base and a green paper flower as decoration, that has been carried to Wirikúta and back on a peyote pilgrimage; another arrow without feathers that is to be left as an offering to Tatewarí in the peyote country, and lastly a votive arrow for Our Mother 'Utuanáka. The whole back of the 'utá is decorated by Lupe with purple flowers.

The "bed" functions as a kind of altar and accordingly is called *niwetári,* the name of the ceremonial shelf in the túki (temple) and xíriki that holds all manner of ritual paraphernalia. In front of the niwetári, at a distance of about five meters, the drum is set up, girdled around its upper half by a woven belt decorated with two kinds of flowers: the *puwári,* a species of marigold (*Tagetes erecta,* Aztec = *cempoal-xóchitl*) that is considered sacred (as the flower of the dead) all over Mexico and which is believed by some people to be capable of affecting perception), and the *teurári,* a small red flower called *madroño* in Spanish. Two muviéri have been inserted in the woven belt.

An arrow representing the shaman has been stuck into the ground in front of the drum. From the arrow to the head of the niwetári runs a cactus fiber cord (*wikuxáy*) to which a total of twenty-one small balls of cotton (*kwiamúxa*) have been tied. The string is said to be supported at one end by Máxa Kwaxí, at the other by the shaman's ceremonial arrow. Its symbolism is explained as follows: in each little cotton bundle travels the spirit of one of the children, twenty-one in all, who will be flying to Wirikúta. Deer—that is, Elder Brother Máxa Kwaxí—and shaman are the ones who will bear the string of children. Actually, only sixteen of the twenty-one children who are to make the magical journey are physically present; the other five could not attend but are nonetheless included in absentia.

The singers—mara'akáme and assistants—arrange themselves before the drum, facing east. The mara'akáme himself is seated on an old school bench, which he has invested with the power that adheres to the 'uwéni, the characteristic circular chair with woven arm and backrest and a deerskin border encircling the seat that is reserved for shamans and elders or headmen of ranchos. The assistants are, in fact, seated on two such 'uwéni. In front of them on the ground is a length of costal, on which they have placed several rattles, some of the children's thread cross symbols, and a dish filled with violet flowers.

José Ríos removes his muviéri and the decorated candle, katíra, from his takwátsi and arranges them together with the rattles and the tsikúri. Two shaman's plumes are tied to the back of his bench, as they would have been to the customary 'uwéni. The drum is tuned again by holding the open lower end over the fire.

The people gathered for the symbolic journey to Wirikúta form a sort of rectangle that is closed on one end by the three singers and on the other by the ceremonial shelf, niwetári. The cord with the cotton balls in which the souls of the children will travel is in the center of the rectangle. To the left of the singing shaman and his assistants, four boys, one girl, and one mother with her small daughter in her arms have seated themselves on sacks. The greater number of participants, five boys, three girls, and two mothers with infant daughters in their arms, is on the right. Thread crosses have been stuck in the ground in front of the boys on the right-hand side. The majority of the nine boys and seven girls participating are old enough—between three and six years of age—to be able to sit by themselves and shake their rattles. The mothers of the littlest ones take them by the hand and shake the rattles for them.

Several mestizos watch from the sidelines, but as tolerated observers, not as participants.

The mara'akáme and his assistants and the Keeper of the Drum begin the chant. Violet flowers have been scattered over the ground around them. Also on the ground right in front of José Ríos a small twig has been placed, almost entirely hidden by the tail of a deer—symbol of Elder Brother Deer Tail, Máxa Kwaxí.

The chant drones on. The Keeper of the Drum is relieved by a companion. The children shake their rattles without letup. The women assist, accompanying the assistants and repeating the last stanzas sung by the mara'akáme, thereby greatly drawing out the already lengthy recitation.

Lupe has passed out candles among the participants. A gourd bowl containing an ear of red maize, one of the five sacred colors, has been placed upon the niwetári. Platters containing a candle, an apple, a mandarin orange, a cooking banana (*plátano*), and crackers have been put in front of each of the sixteen children.

The children's grandmother, Eusebia, dances by herself. For a long time, a Huichol-made violin and guitar accompany the shaman's singing as well. The mothers participating in the ceremony as well as the grandmother have painted their cheeks with a red circle. Some have added a small blue cross in the center of the circle, others have drawn a blue circle within the red one.

Catarino Ríos, one of the sons of José and Eusebia (and also one of the members of the 1968 peyote pilgrimage in which Furst participated), dances with his mother, their arms placed over each other's shoulders.

A small pot and a glass containing peyote juice, two packets of cigarettes, and a whole peyote cactus are placed in front of the mara'akáme. Ground-up peyote has also been poured into pots on the niwetári. From time to time the mara'akáme and his two assistants take a sip of the liquefied peyote. Platters of fruit, a box of crackers, a gourd bowl with a slab of cooking chocolate, and the violin and guitar of the musicians are added to the other things on the niwetári.

From time to time the mara'akáme takes some of the violet flowers from the dish in front of him and flings them into the breeze. They fall within the square of the participants. This is explained as follows: On the path to Wirikúta, as the children alight in the various sacred places, they pick flowers and scatter them—this to divert them and make them happy, "lest they stray and linger on that road."

Many times during the chant mention is made of Máxa Kwaxí. Catarino relives the Keeper of the Drum. José gestures with his muviéri and the muviéri xáye to the cardinal points, addressing himself to the gods that dwell there. This completed he places the muviéri and the muviéri xáye on the drum. It is time to rest for a while.

For the moment the principal singer is the only one to rise; the other "travelers" remain in their places. We are told, "Up to this moment, they have already passed through different places—Teakáta, the sacred cave of Greatgrandmother Nakawé in the Sierra, where they did not stop; Jerez; Las Víboras (Serpents); San Miguel; and Zacatecas. But still they have not glimpsed a single god. They are resting now so as to be strong when they arrive at the sacred gateway, Haikitéme, a place where they will run great risks. Soon they will arrive in Wirikúta to look for the hikuri (peyote) which they will be taking.''

Once again Lupe fills the pot with ground-up peyote and returns it to its place in front of the mara'akáme.

Two horns sound, signaling a dance. There is to be dancing during this rest period, just as one does on an actual pilgrimage to Wirikúta. Two men play the violin and the guitar and three others begin to dance. The rest shout out their pleasure. Lupe sings for a short while, in step with the music and the dancing. She stops singing but music and dancing continue. Two new songs are sung by a youth. Two horns sound and a group of adult men and women, holding one another two by two (men with women, men with men, women with women), commences dancing in a circle to the right of the rectangle formed by the "travelers." Everyone jokes and chats freely—clearly everyone is feeling good about the ceremony.

Eventually the drumming and the chanting resume; this time it is initiated by the assistants, followed by the mara'akáme. Again the women repeat the last stanzas. Tamales are placed in front of the singing shaman, and the violin and the guitar are again added to the other objects on the niwetári.

We have been informed that Káuyumarie has told the mara'akáme, José Ríos, that when they all arrive at Tatéi Matiniéri, the place of the Mothers this side of the peyote country, we, the invited visitors, should participate in the customary offerings there by giving some money as a gift to the takwátsi (the shaman's basket in which Káuyumarie himself is manifested). This is communicated to us by Lupe, who tells us to make the offering when she advises us of the right moment.

The children and the mothers rise and, helped along by one of the assistants and instructed by the mara'akáme, make a ceremonial circuit around the fire, Tatewarí. In this way, they are told, the Mara'akáme (meaning Tatewarí) will care for them and help them to arrive safely at their destination.

The drumming has stopped to give the Keeper of the Drum time to tune the instrument by the heat of the fire.

The chant continues with the women participating as before. The horn is blown twice. One of the daughters of José and Eusebia, who has served as one of the principal assistants in the chanting, lights the candles in front of the participants.

Now Lupe advises us that the time has come to place the money and a candle, asked for by Káuyumarie, before the shaman. It is done.

For some time now the word Wirikúta has recurred in the chant, indicating that the travelers have at last arrived to be received by the Mother. The chanting stops for five minutes. The following occurs during the next twenty minutes—the length of time the children are to remain in "over there" (that is, in the sacred peyote country).

A green ear of maize is placed on the cloth in front of the shaman. A glass is filled with coarsely ground maize, the food of Káuyumarie. The singing starts again. Hikuri, peyote, is symbolically harvested. The mara'akáme passes two muviéri first over the heads of the children seated to his right and then along the length of the cord, in the direction of the drum. Then he addresses himself to the children on his left. The two muviéri are first passed over their heads, and then once more along the cord from the direction of the niwetári toward the drum. In this way, we are told, he is starting them out on the return journey from Wirikúta to El Colorín. Two mothers go to the niwetári and revolve the green ears of maize and the squashes so that they face in the opposite direction— again symbolizing that the children are now homeward bound. The sound of drum and chanting dies away.

The platters of food (fruit, crackers, and tamales) are passed out among the people. Eusebia carries to her husband, the mara'akáme, who has remained seated, a plate with tamales and a vessel filled with peyote juice. From the latter they both drink, offering it first to the gods. The other women also offer tamales and peyote to José. A little later the mara'akáme passes the same things out among the participants (peyote is also ritually exchanged among the participants in an actual pilgrimage). The children are given fruit and crackers.[32] But neither the mothers nor the singers—the principal shaman as well as the assistants—are allowed to eat; they must fast until past midday. Only the children are permitted water since the sun is strong. They also eat from the plates in front of them. This part of the ceremony has a special name, translatable as "We Are All Going to Eat."

12:15 P.M. The "return to Colorín" is about to commence. Once again the drum sounds. The principal singer now is Catarino, who has been trained by his father, the mara'akáme. The women continue to echo the assistants. The chant proceeds until the pilgrims are said to have arrived on the banks of the Río Chico, on their way to the Sierra Madre Occidental.

José removes one of the muviéri from the back of his seat and moves to the front of a line formed by the children, carrying their rattles, and by their mothers. They are to go on a ceremonial circuit of the rectangle formed when they were seated. One of the boys carries a green ear of maize and one of the girls a squash, the first fruits. After passing close to Tatewarí (the ceremonial fire) they arrange themselves in front of the niwetári, shaking their rattles. There the mara'akáme, José Ríos, addresses himself to the gods of the five directions, gesturing with his muviéri toward each. Everyone prays at the same time, under the direction of José. Lupe becomes emotional and cries. Music and chant have not stopped for a single moment.

All make another ceremonial circuit around Tatewarí, pause facing the fire, and José again acknowledges the deities of the cardinal points. Everyone prays in unison. A candle is lit and placed in the fire. José and other adults direct the children to lay squashes and green ears of maize near the fire. Eusebia, grandmother of the children, moistens the heads and faces of her grandchildren with a flower that has been dipped in sacred water she is carrying in a small vessel. In the same way she purified each of the children who did not themselves participate in the ritual.[33] Finally she sprays water over her own head with the same flower, after which she burns some copal incense near the niwetári.

During the last fifteen minutes of the recitation of the children's progress toward their homes, a violin and guitar accompany the shaman. Now "they are arriving in El Colorín." Catarino and one of the assistant singers (kwinapuwáme) rise, each taking up some of the tsikúri and several rattles, which they shake. Then they place them on the drum to signify the end of the journey. It is now 2 P.M.

All of the offerings are gathered up from the niwetári. With great care Eusebia unties the cord with the little cotton balls and rolls it up. The green ears of maize, tamales, peyote juice, crackers, and nawá are distributed all around. Drum, thread crosses, rattles, and muviéri are stored in the xíriki.

## Night ceremony, December 23

At 8 P.M., preparations begin for the ceremonial cooking of the green ears of maize, and for the dance that gives thanks for the rains that have been received from the Mothers. Appropriately the rite is called Tatéi Néiya, Our Mother Dance.

The mara'akáme and his assistants arrange themselves facing the fire. The assistants now are not the same as those who sang last night and this morning. Now they are two young men: the one to the left of José Ríos is his nephew, Andrés López, the one to his right Julián García, first cousin to the mara'akáme. The other assistants have set out for their own homes, some distance away. On the ground before the singers there is a piece of costal, and on it the takwátsi, his shaman's basket, closed now and covered with a red cloth. Two muviéri lie across the takwátsi. In front of these objects, set upon a small stone, is a lighted candle. In his left hand the mara'akáme holds one ordinary muviéri and the special plume with the pendant rattlesnake rattle, the muviéri xáye.

8:15 P.M. José begins to sing and the seconds follow suit. At times some women also help the assistants along by repeating the last stanza. On this occasion there is no playing of the drum. Several women advance toward the xíriki.

Fifteen minutes later the horns are sounded several times, announcing the dance. All the attendants shout happily. First they make a ceremonial circuit around the fire, carrying lighted candles and dancing slowly. In front go one man and two women arm in arm. Again the horn sounds. The singers do not stop chanting. The dance clearly follows a plan: the dancers circle the fire, making one turn forward and one backward. From time to time they turn in place. Most of the dancers dance alone, others in pairs. Presently they form two lines, the men closer to the fire, the women on the outside. Lupe has not once stopped singing. Everyone is either yelling or whistling or both, with obvious pleasure. Jokes are made; during the dance, there are shouts, "Forward, you old mule!"

From time to time the horns are blown. The mara'akáme directs which dances should be danced. The first is Hikuri Teukái Nenéi, meaning, according to our informants, "let us dance the dance of peyote." Another is Tatéi Néiya, Dance of Our Mother. The dancing, always around Tatewarí, the ceremonial fire, lasts in this case about an hour, in an atmosphere of great elation and camaraderie.

Customarily in the Feast of the Drum the dancing goes on all night, but this time it was cut short because everyone was anxious for us to hear the interpretations of a musical group, made up of the Ríos Medrano brothers, of Mexican folksongs and *corridos* that are sung in the mestizo villages of the states of Nayarit, Jalisco, Zacatecas, and Durango. The group includes a bass, a violin, a *guitarrón,* and a guitar, under the leadership of Catarino Ríos, and it was impressive. Huichols appreciate and enjoy Mexican folk music and like listening to it on transistor radios; thus far this has not led to any noticeable deterioration of the indigenous musical style.

## Friday, December 24

7:30 A.M. All of the green maize and squash has been cooked in preparation for distribution. Today's ceremony is called *hikiri kumíxa* meaning, roughly, "the elotes (green ears of maize) are going to be eaten."

9 A.M. Two youths are vigorously playing the Huichol guitar and violin accompanied by singing and dancing. Lupe sings a song in Huichol, which was translated as follows:

> "When I had my sweetheart,
> "I loved him very much,
> "And he loved me very much.
> "We were new (virgins).
> "He told me we should go (ahead),
> "I told him no.
> "But still, I had desire."

A young man in the group of dancers answers her jokingly, "Even I would like it, let us go now, since you are desirous." Everyone enjoys the joke.

At the same time, three young men, Catarino among them, dance to the beat of the music, each moving about separately. Lupe stops her singing but dance and music continue. Eusebia and some of her daughters also dance. All this serves as introduction to the ritual of the invocation of benefits on the first fruits and their conveyance into the xíriki.

Within the xíriki, the green maize, the squashes, and a vessel containing water and wild flowers are arranged on the costal. The mara'akáme, José, enters the xíriki and with his muviéri "cleanses"—that is, cures—the green maize and the squash so that they will not harm those that eat them. Next, he takes a piece of squash and offers it, accompanied by prayers, to Tatewarí. Seated before the first fruits, the mara'akáme cleanses each of the children with his muviéri.

Women and children now make a ceremonial circuit around the fire, the children bearing in their hands a piece of squash and a piece of green maize. José purifies everyone and everything with his muviéri. The mothers pray together with the shaman. As on the previous day, the children are purified with wild flowers dipped in sacred water from the receptacle kept in the xíriki.

Since the gods have now eaten, the first fruits are passed out. Lupe herself distributes to everyone equal shares of all the presents we had brought to El Colorín.

Lupe turns to us, saying, "It is done well." No great thing is made of the end of the ceremony: after three exhausting, emotionally charged days and nights the ceremony is over. The children have been flown to Wirikúta and they have returned safely; in another year, probably, they will hear it all again, and again in the following year. The sacred places will be named, the ancient landmarks pointed out. By the time they

embark on their own pilgrimage, they will travel along a road they have
long since learned by heart.

## Shaman's Chant of the Magical Pilgrimage

Notwithstanding its length and its more or less sequential progression
from a starting point in the Sierra to its goal, the peyote country and the
place of Our Mother Niwetúkame, by way of the venerated places where
the gods rested or where significant events occurred on the primordial
pilgrimage, the text reproduced below, in translation from Ramón's and
Lupe's own Huichol-to-Spanish rendition, represents perhaps a fifth of
the actual narrative substance of the first half of the chant, each passage
of which is customarily repeated from two to four times by the singer's
two assistants and the children's kinfolk. The second half, not included
here, narrates the adventures of the children on their return flight from
Wirikúta, which also includes a ceremonial circuit that takes in the
birthplace of "Our Mother the Drum," and sacred caves and other
abodes of the gods in the Sierra, especially Teakáta, the cave of Nakawé.
According to Ramón, the return flight from east to west does not precisely
follow the trail from west to east any more than does the return journey of
the actual peyote pilgrims. The location of other localities made sacred
because the ancient ones stopped there on their way home with their
burden of peyote must be learned as the singer sets the bird-children down
in one named spot after another and lifts them up again into the sky on
the vibrations of his drum.

It will be seen that the chant stresses the reception of the children by
the Mother Goddesses, especially Niwetúkame, considerably beyond what
is found in the narrative above. Niwetúkame is said to be the divine
Mother who is "special for children" and who is said to determine the
baby's gender. It is also she who places the kupúri—a term that literally
refers to the fine hairs on the infant's head or those in the center of the
spineless peyote cactus but which is employed as metaphor for soul or
life force—into the child's skull at the point of the fontanel; indeed,
fontanel and kupúri are conceived as one and the same (Furst, 1967). The
other Mother prominently mentioned in relation to the arrival of the
children is Xutúri 'iwiyékame, a fertility goddess said to reside in a field
of many-colored flowers (xutúri = paper flower). Both Niwetúkame and
Xutúri share attributes with the young Aztec Mother Goddess Xochi-
quetzal, who in turn corresponds to the Huichol earth, maize, and
fertility goddess, Our Mother 'Utuanáka. Again, one should not make
too much of the apparent separation between two different Mothers of
children and fertility, or between them and 'Utuanáka herself: along with

other Mothers of the earth, maize, and fertility in a general or a specific
sense, they are closely related personifications of the female mana in the
universe, with personalities and attributes specific to particular states
or planes but in the final analysis, like their Aztec counterparts, manifestations or aspects of the same fundamental goddess (Toci [Grand-
mother] among the Aztecs; Nakawé, "the little ancient one, she who put
the world in order," among the Huichols.)

According to Ramón, what the singing shaman describes in the chant
is what Elder Brother Máxa Kwaxí (Deer Tail), the deer god who travels
as guide and guardian through the sky with the shaman and his flock,
relates to him through the agency of Káuyumarie, the shaman's helper.
Káuyumarie is also Deer, but unlike Máxa Kwaxí or Wawatsári (the
"principal Deer") not always to be relied upon, because he has the nature
of a typical trickster and in ancient times sometimes behaved so badly
that Nakawé had to "tame" him. Since they are not sharply defined as
separate personalities, however, and even their names tend to be interchangeable, it is not always clear which of the several supernaturals
conceived as Deer play what specific role in a particular tradition or ritual
(a problem obviously of more concern to the outsider than to the Huichols,
whose system of ordering reality does not require that everything fit neatly
into its own narrow slot). To quote Ramón:

> Understand this well. The mara'akáme sings and it is re-
> peated, repeated, repeated, repeated. But it is Máxa Kwaxí
> who is saying these things, in secret (magically), and the
> mara'akáme who hears it, who interprets it. Máxa Kwaxí,
> Káuyumarie, Wawatsári, and the mara'akáme, they are the
> same (that is, act in concert). And Káuyumarie is the muviéri
> (shaman's plumes) and he is takwátsi (shaman's basket); Tak-
> wátsi Káuyumarie is what it is called.[34] Káuyumarie carries
> his muviéri on his head; his horns, his antlers, those are the
> muviéri. With his muviéri he hears the secrets of Máxa Kwaxí.
> In this way Máxa Kwaxí tells it to Káuyumarie, and Káuyu-
> marie tells it to the mara'akáme. And the mara'akáme inter-
> prets everything correctly, so that they will learn it well.

As previously mentioned, Ramón and his wife Lupe recorded the chant
on tape, which was then played back for them to translate from Huichol
into Spanish. The English version follows Ramón's own Spanish reasonably faithfully:

> Look, you tevainuríxi[35]
> Surely we are going to where the peyoteros have gone
> On the pilgrimage of the peyote.

Who knows if we are going to arrive or not,
Because the journey there is dangerous.

One must fly in order to walk over the wind
Light as the air,
To fly as birds.
We will make camp
There under the highest trees
That you see there
And one sees them . . .
One hears the whirring of their wings.

Máxa Kwaxí gives them direction
There, there is the name of where they are going to fly,
To enter there.

Now about the tevainuríxi
They rise as though they were a string of shiny beads.
And then he says,
How pretty this pilgrimage is,
So says Máxa Kwaxí.

And then they rise from there,
And they are given other (signs)
And there they see where the pool of water is
But it is not water.
It is an atole that is called *tsinári*.
That is what that camp is called
And that is where they have to stay.

They rise up, there from the Water of the
Sour Atole.
And then they send them on
Toward Las Lajas, where there are
Stones which are *lajas* (slabs or flagstones).

They continue walking,
So one hears the sacred tevainuríxi walking
And paying their (ritual) obligation.
One hears the sounds of them
You must realize it is as though one heard the sound of
Sacred water.

One hears a sound as of branches rustling
They go through a little bit of darkness
Because the clouds envelop them in the wind
But the tevainuríxi don't ever stop walking
One hears a rippling as though they were a cataract.
They are going to know
Where Tatéi Niwetúkame lives.
The goddess of family life.

They told them once again where
There were traveling
Where they were going
They are going through where there are many ocotes (pitch pines),
Where there are many ocotes, in the *ocotsári* (ocotal)
They say to the poor tevainuríxi,
Because they were going with much humility,
And they are tired.

Now they have arrived where they told them, at Ocotsári
They are resting a little bit
Then they rise again from there
They told them here you go straight to where that tall oak stands
    (*muyéwe*)
They have to tell you, from there you will go next to To Enter In.

How pretty the rattles sound
They sound very pretty
And the tevainuríxi keep on walking.

One hears it even in the middle of the drum's sound,
Why is it this way?
It is because they are very sacred.

They told them again where they were going
They gave them the directions
That there Where the Cross Is they could get
Information. It is a cross, an ancient cross (i.e., not Spanish)
This is the name of the place,
Of the encampment where the tevainuríxi go, entering.
One hears the rustling when
They make their encampment, where they told them
When they folded their wings, the tevainuríxi.

They rise up from there
And they told them again where
To stop once more.
And they said to them there where it is called
Huehukawána.

They rise from there,
And then they start traveling again,
And they told them, there where it is called Kumayáka, the Snakes,
They enter again.

Again they continue traveling,
The tevainuríxi,
They are very sacred,
They go walking very happy, with much joy, very contentedly.

They rise up from there
And then they went and they told them where to go
to settle in Teapári mutimáni,
Where one grinds úxa.[36]

Again they travel, travel,
One listens to the pretty rustle of their wings.
Why is it that I never heard this thing before?
You who are the oldest, Eagle,[37]
Try hard to get them to rise up,
In order to travel faster.

Again they travel,
And they continue on the trail to the camp of the Petates (woven
     mats).

Again they travel,
Traveling toward where they are going.
It is certain that we are going to know that place,
Though a good long journey still remains ahead of us.

Again they travel,
And they told them to continue traveling,
In order to arrive at Jerez.
Teapúa matewúa (Jerez).

Máxa Kwaxí goes traveling
Among the tevainuríxi on this journey

Because they do not know,
Only Máxa Kwaxí knows.

From there they rise and continue traveling
Towards San Miguel.

Again they go traveling,
They rise up to go to it, to San Miguel,
They travel and travel
And now they are getting tired.

They rise up from San Miguel
And they continue traveling
And then Máxa Kwaxí tells them
We are going to arrive at Green Fields.
Harahuerta.

You, Máxa Kwaxí
Who know it well,
Go watching over the sacred tevainuríxi,
So that they shall not take away their 'úxa,
Here there are many spirits that can take away their 'úxa,
Or that can make them blind.
You, Máxa Kwaxí, you know how to take care of them.

You go watching the four winds, so that they don't take
Away from you a single one.
You are taking care of them
So that one continues to hear the rustling of their wings.

They rise again over the plain,
They go flying, flying, very low, low, low,
Because it is a very green, green plain,
And it makes them happy.
They go traveling with the wind.

Máxa Kwaxí knows that another one goes behind,
Another mara'akáme.
He says to him, oh, you are drunk,
Why are you walking falling down,
Don't drop one of the *xukúri* (votive gourd),
Don't drop a child,

Because if you do it is a grave offense.
He tells him this.

Don't lose your votive gourd,
You know it very well.
We continue to travel,
Don't worry, my children,
Don't worry
Máxa Kwaxí alone takes care of you.

They continue walking
Seeing to the offerings,
Keep on walking, always keep up.

Weríka 'Uimári,[38] don't stop walking,
And give encouragement to the other companions
Who are tevainuríxi.

They arrive at the encampment with the name of the mountain lion,
Mayemuyéwe.
And he arrived at this camp, because
Here in times past the gods gave it its name.
They are arriving where Mayemuyéwe is.

They rise up from this camp and
Continue to travel to where the Mescal is.
Mai muyáka.
On the right side, and on the left, so that it opens,
In order to open it.
So that they can enter, the tevainuríxi.[39]

Let us go enter where the danger is,
With much care, to see Weríka 'Uimári (Our Mother Young Eagle
    Girl).
They continue traveling, they continue traveling,
In order to climb up the divide.

They climbed up,
They arrived at Tsauwiriwana.
And they continue to travel.

And then have now entered,
And they go traveling through the clouds,

Inside them.
They are traveling through Haikiténi (through the clouds).

Take good care of your companions, who are tevainuríxi.
Take care of them because here we are going through danger.

They continue traveling and one hears the pretty
Rustling of their wings as they continue to travel.

They rise up from where it is the Mescal,
And then they tell them, they are going to
Arrive at Xuráwe muyáka, the Morning Star,
The camp of the Morning Star.

Let us go to Hauriyápa, Tatéi Matiniéri.
We are going to know, you who go as the very first ones,
Máxa Kwaxí says to the tevainuríxi.

And then they say, let us arrive at the Place of the Bird
Because there is a hummingbird, a little hummingbird
That doesn't have wings and cannot fly,
There is the bird, where we put Tsauwíri below,
There I am going to give you wings, so that you can fly.
And from there so that we can climb up Tsauwíri (the divide or pass).

Then they told them where the Place of the Bird is,
They named it,
So that they could arrive there.

Máxa Kwaxí says to it how we are going to give you wings
So that you will be able to fly well.

You who are able to take out all this,
Take it all out, so that it may be given to the tevainuríxi.

So then he says, now we have arrived where
It is Hainamári, where the doorway is.
You who can, Máxa Kwaxí, make the gate hold
Because here there are those who take away their face paint,
Those who can take away úxa,
For that reason they must guard them well.

Now they have arrived where the main gate is (because there are five)
So says Máxa Kwaxí.
Now yes, Máxa Kwaxí says, now we will open it on the right
In order to enter 'Uru Tsáta, Where the Arrows are.

You who can, Máxa Kwaxí,
Now open the doors.
Now he is opening the doors,
On the left side,
On the right side he opens it,
He opens the main gate,
And then all the tevainuríxi go inside

One hears the pretty rustling,
Because they are now going inside the cloud gates,

Be very very careful, Máxa Kwaxí, with those who are going for the
     first time
Because they don't know anything

Right now we are going through much danger
There are many arrows of sickness that can make us fail,
Let us go to Kútsaráupa Háuriyápa, where Tatéi Matiniéri is
Mu'úquimayáka (house of the dead man), Xukuríta (place of the
     Offering Gourd)
Tupína Hapa (place of the Tupina Bird), Hinárimayáka (Penis),
     Xapimukáka (Vagina), Xutúri (place of the Paper Flower). All
     these places they fly to.
All this they learn well.

Then they said, you who can and who know well
How to protect us, place yourself by our side,
So that there will be no problem.
So that as far as there are problems, I don't want any tevainuríxi to
remain behind,
Here among the spirits of those who failed I do not want them to fail
in their sacred undertaking.
For there are many here who can make us fail.
Kakawáme, you who never run out of words,
Be here with me to help me.

They continue to travel,
Continue traveling where they are going
They go very contentedly,
They continue to travel.

They continue to travel,
And he with his power
Continues to travel,
And to the back of them Máxa Kwaxí closed the gate.
And so they continue traveling.

He goes traveling
And they have told them where to walk.
Guadalupe Ma'ayéwe.
They go traveling in order to arrive at that camp.

They continue traveling
One hears the sounds, the pretty sounds of the tevainuríxi,
As they travel on the wind.
They go traveling and circling where it is
The little tsikúri (thread cross).

They continued to travel,
Like little birds.
Then they got up from there
And continued to travel,
Those tevainuríxi
To the point of Paxtúri.

They go traveling very slowly, very carefully,
With much care
Because they are going Among the Arrows ('Uru Tsáta) where there
    are offerings
There is Guadalupe Mayéwe, where the offerings are,
Where the offerings are that the ancient ones left there.

Always travel with great care,
All are traveling,
The tevainuríxi, with much penitence,
Because they are going very sacred
With their muviéri, slowly, slowly,
They make a little noise, a little noise,
As though there were drops of water.

All the offerings, the gourds, the arrows,
The offerings travel among the tevainuríxi.

They go traveling, they go flying,
As if a little tiny thing were flying on the wind.
They are seen on the wind.
They pass over a little lake,
But little by little, in order not to
Fall into the water.

They marked the place, Tsinuríxka, that is the
Point at which they are going to enter.
Tsinuríxka they call the offerings the Wixárika (Huichols) left.

They said to them, you are going well
In the right direction,
You are going to land at
Mukunyúwe, where the offering of the knotted cord is.[40]

They go descending and ascending
As if they were a little bit heavy.

They go along the string (with cotton puffs)[41]
Keeping well together so they don't fall,
Hanging on tightly.
They go traveling along the *wikuxáu* (string),
They travel along in order not to make an error,

Mayenúe, they rose to travel to Mayenúe,
They rise up from Mukunyúwe, where the sacred cord is.
Then they began to travel again until they arrived at
Mayenúe, having been where the little sacred cord is.

The shaman is taking care of the children
Whom he is taking along
He is cautioning them
So there will be no problem.

All the companions arrive at Weríka nuítsi,
Who is the eagle deity
Which you know well.

Also Tsikuáquikáme (ceremonial clown) is among the tevainuríxi,

In the form of a tiny tender calabash,
They go along playing very contentedly,
Traveling along.

I too am going to Parikutsi,
With great happiness and pleasure I am going.
Says Tsikuáquikáme.

Let's go where lives Weríka 'Uimári,
Let us go where Our Mother 'Utuanáka is,
Let us go where Niwetúkame is.
All of them, in order to know where Our Mother is.

Let us go where the one who embraces us is,
The one who loves us much.
The one who is Our Mother,
Máxa Kwaxí tells them.

The ones who are here for the first time,
The little children, you don't know,
We are going there so that you will know,
Máxa Kwaxí says to them.

They rose up from there and then
They gave them more directions.
Now you are going to land on that mountain.

They land on the mountain called Witséxka tsíye[42]

There one heard the little tiny, tiny noise
Because they were going little by little
On the journey.
And they landed on
On the mountain of Wítsekatsíye.

They said to them again, only the Sun
told them, there is another place,
So that you can go and rest.

There is Uxáta (Punto Zacatongo)
There is the path that leads directly to it.

They continue traveling,
Traveling very contentedly
All the hummingbirds go traveling very happily.

They are traveling along very happily
And from here on they are going to be
Traveling even more happily, because
They are throwing them flowers, the orange marigold,
The red madroño, the flowers they are throwing them.

They are going along with much happiness
With their tsikúri, on the heads of the children,
They go along happily because
They are going to find out where they are going.

They rose up from Uxáta
And went flying again
They are flying right now on the wind.

They go traveling and traveling
And arrive at Kiaráka, (Tierra Ramos),

They rise up from Kiaráka
And they entered Ramúxa (Ramos) which is the town,
And they continue traveling in order to land.

They are traveling along in
Order to arrive at the divide
That separates them from Tatéi Matiniéri.

Uxipíta is where they rested,
Where Our Grandfathers rested,
Where the Sun rested,
Where Our Grandfather (Fire) rested,
In the encampment of The Drum.

This is where they rested
in ancient times
when they came here on the pilgrimage
Máxa Kwaxí tells them.

Be very careful, my sons, my children,
because now we are going to arrive at Hauriyápa, (where we leave
    the candles and offerings)
Where we leave the offerings, the candles,
We are going to arrive at 'Útzaráupa, Tatéi Matiniéri.

We are all going to return well,
Without any problems,
Because we are going where is Tatéi Wérika 'Uimári,
Tatéi Kúkúrú 'Uimári, Niwetúka tukamáte, Tatéi Niwetúka is Our
    Mother,
'Utzaráupa is Our Mother.
We are going there to know, to understand.

Máxa Kwaxí does not hesitate,
I am the one who will lift you high,
If something happens to us I am the one who
will return you to your encampment.

We are going to pass by where Kúkúrú 'Uimári is
Who is the Mother of Maize (in the form of a dove),
We are going to pass by there,
Máxa Kwaxí says to them.

The tevainuríxi continue traveling
Very contentedly because
They are going to know Wirikúta
And understand.

They all go walking very contentedly as
If they were playing.

They continue traveling
To where stands the 'úxa tree (for grinding face paint).
They arrived at the encampment of the úxa tree.
And the camp of The Lion.
They arrived.

They continue traveling,
One hears the rustling, little by little.
Slowly, slowly,
As if they were drops of water.

They go traveling, they continue
Traveling, on the wind,
Very slowly they go flying.


Now we are getting closer to 'Utzaráupa, Tatéi Matiniéri,
Don't stay here, don't linger here,
Because here there is a danger.


Now we have arrived at Hauriyápa,
Where Xutúri[43] is,
Where there are children
Where children come to bathe.
Now we have arrived at Hauriyápa.


Finally they arrived at Tatéi Matiniéri (Place of the Mothers),
Now they are seeing what Wirikúta is all about.
Everything that is there in Wirikúta.


Máxa Kwaxí gives them life,
Kupúri to everyone.
He says to them, let us see, let us have
Kupúri for these children,
Who come here to know you.


Here this place is called Kutzaráupa
This place is called Tatéi Matiniéri,
Those who don't know, who are new ones,
Who are first ones (matewáme, -te = novice peyotero).


Here is where one presents the nunútsi (baby) to the gods
There is one who will name the child,
To give him to the gods who are here at Kutzaráupa.


Give the child who comes, the matewáme,
To the four winds.


Pray as should be done,
Because they are the child's father and mother,
You can pray so that the gods, Sun, Fire,
Kutzaráupa, Tatéi, will become aware of this.

Now they have fulfilled everything,
Now they are aware of the fact that here is a child matewáme.
He says:

Tatéi Matiniéri, Tatéi Kutzaráupa,
Everyone here, it is that this child has come.
Do we not wish,
Do we not wish,
His fathers and his mothers,
To present him to the four winds?
Embrace him well, take hold of him,
So that he will not fall ill,
Tomorrow or the next day.
Kupúri is our life,
Give them life.
Kutzaráupa, give them life,
Tatéi Matiniéri, give them life,
So that one day he will come
To arrange the offerings.

They continue traveling from there
But they had already fulfilled their obligation.
They continue walking
And they told them that at such and such a place,
There is a little door,
Through which you have to go,
In order to be able to continue walking.

They continue walking
But very carefully, over the offerings,
To where the xukúri are, the offering gourds
And he goes walking little by little with his xukúri family.
With his children he goes walking little by little.
Slowly, slowly, he is going amid the offering gourds
If he were to go fast or clumsily, there can be problems,
And for that reason he goes carefully, carefully, slowly, slowly,
With his wings, little by little,
In order to tell the children where they are going, in order to see.
Where they are to place their feet,
To see how they are going to emerge without any problems.

Now he is going over Tsinuríta,
Over to the Kakauyaríxi, the ancient gods,
Tsinuríta is flowers, the *cempoal* flower, madroño, *azucena*,[44]
*Xuxúri, tsáuye, tsuwíri*, lots of flowers,
That he is watering at Tsinuríta.
It is called that because it is very flowery, very pretty.
They are attending to them
Because the tevainuríxi are traveling here.

Now they can drink nawá (fermented maize),
So that they will realize that we also bring *ma'awári* (offering),
    which is nawá.

The shaman says to them,
He who has a son or a daughter
Should be careful how they are named,
How they are told (taught),
What work we have
What (ritual) obligations we have,
As a woman, and as a man.
The man giving tobacco to the other men,
Those who came to the fiesta,
And giving them nawá to drink,
And the woman, there, next to the shaman, lighting candles,
Distributing (gifts) to the shaman,
So that tomorrow and the next day they will say,
Ah, that woman has heart,
That man has heart.
So the shaman says to them.

He says this never ends,
This is about our heritage which our
Grandfathers left us.

The shaman says to them.
I don't remember where I was,
In what state I went,
And his wife responds to him,
Well, you know, only you know where you went,
In what encampment you were,
His wife tells him.

For that reason many singers do it this way,
and have problems within their family,
Things don't come out well,
The family gets sick.

Let's see, I am going to see in which encampment I was,
To see where the family is,
I am going to see,
Let's see if it's the same as it was (in ancient times).

He continues traveling.
Tsinuríta, Tsinuríta.
He rises up from Tsinuríta,
And continues walking there, on the clouds.
Little by little, he leads them there.

Ah, now yes, now I have discovered that there is peyote here.
Now let us all take some,
How pretty the peyote is,
It is like a sacred flower.

He continues walking,
But with his flowers,
Eating, nourishing himself,
With his úxa, with his sacred food,
With his whole family.
All his family goes along very happy,
Happily eating *tutú* ( = flower, i.e., peyote).

They continue walking,
They told them you have to arrive at the passage of the clouds,
And they arrived there.
They told them you have to arrive at the úxa tree.
And they arrived there.
They told them you have to arrive at the camp of the Lion.
And they arrived there.
They told them you have to arrive at Tatéi Matiniéri.
And they arrived there.
They told them you have to arrive at Tatéi Matiniéri.
And they arrived there,
Little by little,
The rustling of their little wings,

Flying on the wind.
Wherever they said,
They arrived there.

They continue walking, walking, slowly, slowly,
They were going to arrive at the pass of the clouds,
With great care, very carefully,
Remember well where we are going.

Because we are going over the offerings.

We are approaching Paritekua
In front of Wirikúta
We are getting there.

Now he is beginning to perceive from afar,
'Unáxu, where the Sun Father came out
Above Wirikúta.
Now we are getting closer.

They went up from the pass of the clouds
And they continue walking.

They arrive at Chakíra (Bead Necklace).
That is what that ancient encampment is called.
They arrive at the encampment of Chakíra.
And they continue traveling.

They continue walking
And they arrive at the encampment of darkness.
They arrive there and they continue walking.

They continue to walk
Slowly slowly, flying, flying,
The tevainuríxi go very well
The tevainuríxi go without problems.

They continue walking,
Until they climb up Tsauwíxika,
As when one grabs hold of something, like vines
In order to swing yourself over.
In order to climb up to the sky.
They arrived at the sky.

They continue traveling,
They left there and continued walking,
To Eye of the Deer.
Eye of the Deer is the name of that camp.

They continue walking
They arrive at Tukitsáta (at the *túki* = temple)
Where fire is born, from the firebrands.
Teakamutemáne tatéima,
Where Tatewarí was born.

They continue walking,
They rise up from there
They went up from Tukitsáta
Slowly, slowly, and flying happier than anything.

They told them that they were going to arrive.
Wiru'uíma, Wiru'uíma,
Let us arrive at the Wiru'uíma,
That high mountain (in Wirikúta).
They arrived there.

I say to them, this is Wiru'uíma.
I say that to the children,
To all those who are *matewámete* (novice pilgrims).

Wiru'uíma embraces them, Wiru'uíma, the mother of the drum,
Wiru'uíma embraces the children.
Because they are going to visit with much pleasure.

She asks them, where do you come from,
Where do you come from?
What pretty children who come here from so far away to visit me.
So far they come to visit me,
I do not know why.
Where do they come from,
Who are their relatives?
So says Wiru'uíma.

Now we have arrived,
Where Niwetúkame is,
The one who has an offering gourd of the children,
The very Mother of all the children.

He says to her, look, I bring you your family.
We have never come here before,
We don't know anything,
We came here to see Niwetúkame,
To see her,
We came to see.

Here is where Sun Father burst forth,
Here where remained our Mother
Who is Niwetúkame.

He takes out a very pretty thing
Which is xukúri (offering gourd). He holds it out to them,
He says to them, sit down on it very happily,
With much sadness, with feeling like they are going to cry,
He says to them, they come so far,
And I do too.
I never knew them, says Niwetúkame,
I have never seen them,
Now I am very happy, I am very content.
So speaks Niwetúkame.

I will give them life,
I give their life to them so that they will go happy.
I give them flowers.
She throws flowers at the feet of the children,
Marigold, madroño, cactus flowers, and many others.
She puts out nothing but her flowers for the children,
Because they go so sacred they are well taken care of.

She embraces them with great pleasure,
She embraces them,
Look my children, I am the one who embraces you,
I am the one who releases you from here,
And you go there.

Do everything with great care,
In all matters guard the kupúri
In everything.
I don't know where they come from.
In truth I do know well where they come from, but I want them to
    tell me.
So speaks Niwetúkame.

There also comes Tsikuaquikáme (ceremonial clown).
Tsikuaquikáme arrives very happy.
Now light the candles,
You children, everybody light your candles
Because you are with your Mother Niwetúkame.


Here we are now, very happy, very content,
They embrace their Mother Niwetúkame,
We are at 'Unáxu, where Sun Father burst forth,
And we know everything,
We know where Sun Father burst forth.


One sees the ocean, very pretty,
Some little bits of foam that emerge
It is very pretty, I would like to arrive there,
For its secret (i.e., magical power) is good for one.
We already came,
We have seen everything,
Of Our Mother Niwetúkame,
We have learned everything,
Where Our Mother is,
Where the xukúri is,
Where the flowers are,
Where the Kakauyaríxi are,
Which are Our Grandfathers, Our Grandmothers.
There in their places,
Where the Deer is,
Where Our Mother Peyote is.
Now we have arrived here,
Resting, resting.


Now we have come,
Now we have seen them,
We have seen their places,
So that we return well, taking the drum,
To where it was born.
There by the edge of the sea,
There it was born, there we will return it,
There, far away,
We will follow our steps,
There we will follow the rustling of the wings,
The wings, the steps, of the tevainuríxi.

The above, of course, tells only half the story. Still to come was the narrative of the homeward flight of the tevainuríxi and their obligatory ceremonial visit to all the sacred places in the Sierra. Eventually, the sacred geography firmly fixed in their minds, the tevainuríxi would physically embark on the same ceremonial circuit following their return from Wirikúta as initiated *hikuritámete,* companions on the hunt of the divine peyote.

It had been Ramón's intention to narrate this important second portion on a future occasion. Alas, this was not to be. Only three months later, on the occasion of a fiesta to celebrate the clearing of forest for a new milpa, Ramón died of gunshot wounds before his relatives could get him out of the foothills of the Sierra, across the Río Santiago, and to a hospital in Tepic, Nayarit. The fatal shots were fired by another Huichol during an argument; what it was about is not known, but eyewitnesses said there had been the usual heavy drinking that is customary, not to say obligatory, on such festive occasions. The killer tried to escape into the hills but was apprehended by Lupe's relatives, who delivered him, wounded but alive, to the authorities in Tepic. They said the man had been "crazy, crazy with jealousy."

Apart from its personal meanings to his wife, Lupe, to his relatives, and to those of us who knew and valued him as a friend, Ramón's death dramatizes the other side of the coin of Huichol life. The cultural ideal, the valued norms, are unity, balance, harmony. Especially on the sacred occasions one is expected to lay aside all feelings of hostility toward others: as Ramón himself often remarked, "All must be unity, all must be of one heart." He said this in relation to the peyote pilgrimage, but it applies no less to other ceremonies and behavior as a whole. But in the real world, the Huichol culture, no less than any other, has its built-in share of contradictions and disruptive elements, and there is frequent violation of ideal behavior. Needless to say, forces beyond the Huichols' control, impinging daily on the different sectors of the traditional lifeway, if not actually undermining its very foundations, have tended to further disharmony and aggravate interpersonal and intercommunity conflict.

That said, there is a special pertinence to some of Myerhoff's conclusions about the underlying significance of the maize-deer-peyote symbol complex to the survival of Huichol culture. In Wirikúta, she writes (1974:260–264), there is no time, with its compartments and limitations, nor are there conflicting claims and intrusions of the social reality into the subjective, individual domain. All the negative aspects of the human heritage—discord, jealousy, ambivalence, contentiousness—are removed, and the distinctions between the real present and the mythological past disappear: all is immortal, all is harmony. Further, the symbol complex takes up the problem of moral incoherence, because by

making possible the retention of the past as part of the
present, it eliminates the need for dealing with the question
of why the world changed, why the beauty and freedom of
former times has passed away, why man lost touch with the
gods, plants, and animals, why the Spaniards steal Huichol
land, and why it is no longer possible to pursue "the perfect
life—to offer to the gods and chase the deer."

During the peyote hunt in Wirikúta, she continues, the major symbols

make the imaginary life the real life, and provide that fusion
of the "lived-in" with the "thought-of" order which Geertz
describes as one of the major tasks of religion. Wirikúta is
not an imaginary place. The pilgrims need not speculate as
to what it might be like. Through their own will, dedication,
and virtue, they are truly there and even those who never go
know it from the reports of other peyote-seekers. They touch
the earth, feel the hairs of the gods brush their faces, feel the
warmth of the fire as it sears their past away, taste the waters
from the sacred springs, turn the peyote over in their mouths,
and watch with their own eyes as the surrounding world becomes a luminous and vivid place of magic animals and plants
and flowers. . . .

These people envy no one, at least that is their ideal. They have
in abundance a culture's greatest gift—an utter conviction of
the meaningfulness of their life. As Ramón was fond of saying,
"Our symbols, the deer, the peyote, the maize of five colors—
all, all that you have seen, there in Wirikúta, when we go to
hunt the peyote—these are beautiful. They are beautiful
because they are right."

As stated earlier, Tatéi Néiya should not be seen in isolation from the
whole of Huichol intellectual culture. In a narrower sense, its principal
function is clearly within the maize-deer-peyote symbol complex, and
obviously cannot be understood apart from it. Nor should Tatéi Néiya be
overvalued, especially in the context of this paper: enculturation proceeds
along many paths simultaneously. Nevertheless, as Myerhoff has emphasized, the maize-deer-peyote complex and its associated traditions lie
at the very heart of the Huichol lifeway. In that sense Tatéi Néiya is indeed
crucial to that lifeway's endurance: more than any other ritual, it assures
that each Huichol child, almost literally with its mother's milk, begins
practically from birth to absorb some of the essential truths of Huichol

traditional culture, long before it ever embarks on an actual peyote pilgrimage, and, in fact, whether or not he or she will ever physically visit Wirikúta.

## NOTES

*(Unless otherwise indicated, the notes are by Furst.)*

1. Lumholtz's main objective during the two extended visits he made to the Huichols in the last decade of the nineteenth century was to describe Huichol ceremonial art and technology in its cultural context, to learn insofar as possible its symbolic content, and to make a documented collection of Huichol material culture and symbolic art for the American Museum of Natural History. His fieldwork in the Huichol country and his other extensive travels among the Indians of western and northern Mexico resulted in an additional monograph for the American Museum of Natural History, *Decorative Art of the Huichol Indians* (1904), and a two-volume travel account, *Unknown Mexico* (1902), among other publications.

2. These and some other shortcomings in Lumholtz's pioneering work aside, three quarters of a century later one cannot help but be continually impressed by his scholarship, courage, perseverance, and humanity. In his time there were virtually no means of communication in western Mexico; where we have the benefit of roads and airstrips, he could only walk and climb, sometimes for weeks on end. Conditions were hard, the Indians not always friendly, the barriers to mutual understanding formidable, and prior knowledge of the culture nonexistent. Under the circumstances, in this instance as in others, it is grossly unfair to hold such pioneers accountable by the standards of contemporary scholarship. It, after all, owes much to their early endeavors. The modern student of the Huichols has the work of Lumholtz from which to proceed; Lumholtz, being first, had nothing but his own respectful curiosity.

3. Wérika (vérika) actually means eagle but the term is also applied to the hawk, a very sacred bird associated with shamans. The role of the hawk or eagle shamans as guardians of the children's flanks will become clear below. There is also a Huichol deity called Tatéi Wérika 'Uimári, Our Mother Young Eagle Girl, who nowadays is sometimes merged with the Virgin of Guadalupe and who is depicted in Huichol ritual art as a bicephalic eagle; a similar bird with two heads is found also in Aztec art and is thus not, as was once thought by students of Huichol symbolism, an adaptation of the double-headed Hapsburg eagle that was introduced into Mexico with the Conquest.

4. Orthography follows McIntosh and Grimes (1954).

5. The term is translated by Lumholtz as "doctors" and related by him to the high percentage of curing shamans among them. Lumholtz's rendering is doubtful, but no other explanation exists. The word "Huicholes" may be a Spanish corruption. It has been suggested that it derives from Guachichil, a now extinct language formerly spoken east of the present Huichol homeland. As early as 1653, however, Bishop Juan Ruiz Colmenero referred to a *nación de los quisoles* and to its language as *quichola*. This Indian *nación*, then still unconquered, was said by him to live in the eastern part of the Sierra del Nayar, in a portion called Sierra del Tepic, west of Tlaltenango and Colotlán, Jalisco (Santoscoy, 1899:ix). (Anguiano)

6. As late as 1783, however, such Huichol *comunidades* as San Sebastián, Santa Catarina, and San Andrés Cohamiata (also spelled Camiata, Coamiata, and Coamata in

early Spanish documents) were still considered as the "extreme frontier" of the Spanish cabecera of San Luís de Colotlán. The inhabitants of the Sierra were described as hunters, traders in salt and fruits, with little knowledge of Spanish and generally ignorant of the Christian doctrine (Carmen Velázquez, 1961). (Anguiano)

7. Alcoholic beverages of many kinds were in wide use in the Americas prior to European contact, but these were fermented, never distilled. No native distillation of alcohol is known from the New World prior to the Conquest.

8. For six years one of the principal Huichol contacts for Furst, as well as for Dr. Barbara G. Myerhoff and others interested in Huichol traditional culture. Our association with this extraordinarily gifted artist, narrator, and shaman (mara'akáme) goes back to 1965, when Ramón was commissioned to create a group of wool-yarn "paintings" illustrating Huichol myths for the ethnic arts collection of the University of California, Los Angeles. Initial contact was through Father Ernesto Loera Ochoa, a Franciscan priest at the Basílica de Zapopan, near Guadalajara, Jalisco, who befriended many Huichols and who popularized their arts and crafts through a small museum and crafts shop maintained by him at his church. Ramón at the time was one of his principal artists. Understandably cautious at first, and given to subtle distortion of Huichol traditions so long as he was not wholly certain of his questioners' intentions toward the native culture, Ramón eventually became not only a valued friend but sufficiently convinced of the value of accurate recording of the traditional culture, as he saw and interpreted it (to some degree idiosyncratically), to insist on, more than invite, actual participation in the peyote pilgrimage, without which, he said, it would be impossible to understand anything of Huichol culture. At the time Ramón and his wife Lupe occupied some land, squatter-fashion, on the outskirts of Guadalajara, growing the traditional crops of maize, beans, and squash and relying for cash income on their copious production of imaginative and colorful yarn paintings. Eventually they moved to Tepic, the capital of Nayarit, and in 1970 Ramón reestablished a more traditional rancho in the foothills of the Sierra, on the edges of the Huichol country proper, clearing land for the sort of subsistence milpa agriculture that forms the basis of Huichol life. It was here that he died in 1971, having been fatally wounded in a quarrel with another Indian (see concluding paragraphs, below).

9. In narrating this tradition Ramón explained that had the jaguar been female, she would have had to devour a male Héwi, so as to achieve that essential male-female balance or unity that in Huichol thinking is sine qua non for the continuation of life itself. The theme of jaguars devouring a woman, elaborated in Central Mexican cosmology into the destruction of the first world era, is also found in Amazonian mythology.

10. This passage was translated from the German by Furst.

11. Furst participated with Dr. Barbara G. Myerhoff in a peyote pilgrimage in December, 1966, the first to have been witnessed by anthropologists, and subsequently, with his late wife Dee Furst, in a second pilgrimage in December, 1968 (Furst, 1972a; 1972b).

12. The content of some Huichol myths or folktales as told nowadays to outsiders by sophisticated informants may have been somewhat, though not crucially, affected by the writings of Lumholtz and more recent ethnographers. Certainly Huichol commercial folk art has not remained unaffected by various publications. Lumholtz's *Unknown Mexico* (1902) has long been available in Spanish translation, and although few Huichols are literate, it is known that his descriptions and, above all, illustrations of Huichol culture as he saw it at the turn of the century have found a small but appreciative indigenous audience. It may also be that his photographs and drawings of traditional Huichol art have at least helped old patterns to survive into the present, just as the detailed accounts of North American Indian ritual by early anthropologists have proved useful to tradition-alists seeking to keep the old ways alive. A more recent publication by one of the present authors, on the yarn paintings of the late Ramón Medina, issued in Spanish by the Mexican

Ministry of Education (Furst, 1972c), inspired much imitation of Ramón's style and subject matter, as did an earlier publication in English on the same topic published by the Los Angeles County Museum of Natural History (Furst, 1968), which found its way into the hands of Huichol artists after Ramón's death in 1971. None of the above should be understood to imply that traditional Huichol culture is not full of vitality sufficient to assure its survival without the impetus of outside interest; nonetheless, the growing appreciation of things Huichol by outsiders in recent years could not help but affect at least some of those Indians who for one or another reason had drifted away from the indigenous culture into the no-man's-land between "being Huichol" and becoming Mexican. This includes especially a few gifted urbanized Huichols who as artisans seeking to interpret the traditional culture in an alien environment found themselves moved to reenter, if not the geographical, at least the spiritual Huichol world, as indeed Ramón himself had done following a period of emotional and physical displacement in the 1960s.

13. The origin tradition of the Héwi bears a marked resemblance to that of the Hopi.

14. In addition to the obvious cooling effect of the nixtamal, the fact that sprouted maize soaked in it gives it a regenerative and therapeutic quality. Likewise *masa,* the maize dough ground on the metate after the soaking, is considered to be therapeutic: e.g., the mother or grandmother of a pubescent girl places masa against her vagina on the occasion of her first menstruation. This act derives from the maize origin myth, in which Blue Maize Girl, having been unjustly scolded for supposed laziness by her mother-in-law, becomes despondent and commences grinding herself into masa on the metate and stirring herself into atole in a clay jar.

15. Obviously a version of the well-known North American hoop and pole game, which takes diverse forms but manifests an underlying unity across its enormous distribution area, which extended north of Mexico from the Pueblos to the Eskimos, and from California to New England. In general the game consists of throwing a javelin, arrow, or dart at a moving or stationary ring; in some instances, counting sticks are associated with it. With variations of the dice game, that of aiming a projectile at a hoop was the most popular and widespread of all American Indian games; like most others, however, it was probably nowhere wholly secular. In fact, there is good evidence that in many places both the implements and the game itself had sacred meanings (e.g., among the Zuni the netted gaming hoop is an adaptation of the magical spider web spun by Spider Woman, mother of the Twin War Gods and symbol of her protection; among the Sioux the hoop was marked with symbols of the four sacred world quarters; the Dakotas used the gaming wheel and throwing sticks in the Ghost Dance and among Plains Indians generally the wheel or hoop represented the Sun [Culin, 1907:420–527]).

16. In Aztec cosmology the collapse of the sky upon the earth occurred in the context of one of the cyclical destructions of the world.

17. Cf. page one of the Codex Fejervary-Mayer, depicting the central Mexican conception of the four quarters and sacred center, each with its specific tree.

18. Ramón added the detail of the child sacrifice on another occasion, when his wife, Lupe, was out of earshot. This was because at the time of the original dictation, Lupe cut him off at this point, saying that she did not wish to hear of such things and that in any event, someone must have told the story wrong because Huichols love children too much to sacrifice one even for such an important reason. The sacrifice, she thought, must have involved an animal, not a Huichol child. There are, nevertheless, persistent reports in the Sierra of occasional child sacrifices in times past, during a prolonged drought, for example, or to alleviate some other natural disaster.

19. Sun Father is one of the great deities in the Huichol pantheon, to the point of being the equal of the old fire god, Tatewarí, or following just behind him in rank order. Many Huichols, however, are somewhat ambivalent about the solar deity, who is said to be

capable of arbitrary or capricious acts toward the people. He may, for example, send "arrows of sickness" into a person for no apparent reason, whereas other deities—especially Tatewarí—tend to use illness as punishment for ritual transgression or as reminders of neglected sacred obligations, such as an unfulfilled promise to undertake a peyote pilgrimage. Huichol ambivalence toward the deified Sun would appear to be a function of the Sun's relative uncontrollability as compared to fire, for example. See note 20, below.

20. The obsession with the maintenance of the proper distance between earth and the destructive potential of solar fire is very widespread, as are myths and rituals concerned with this theme. The Brazilian Sherente, among other tribes of the widespread Gê family, for example, attributed droughts to the Sun's anger with the people and for that reason, and to keep the Sun at a safe distance, held great ceremonies, lasting over several weeks, that included long periods of chanting, fasting, and enforced wakefulness; many of these tribes shared with others (including some in Mexico) a myth of a burning headdress which, dropped by the Sun, causes a conflagration in which all the animals perish (Lévi-Strauss, 1970:289-292). Because of the similarity of these beliefs to those of the Huichols, particularly with respect to the role of terrestrial or hearth fire and of the shaman, the master of fire, as mediator between earth and Sun, Lévi-Strauss's analysis of the larger meaning of Sherente belief is of particular interest:

> Celestial fire must not enter into conjunction with the earth, because if they come into contact, they would cause a general conflagration of which drought constitutes a moderate, but empirically verifiable, initial symptom. Nevertheless, primitive humanity used to enact in mime the conjunction of sky and earth—and may even have believed that such a conjunction actually occurred—before cooking fire, which is doubly "domesticated," appeared to act as mediator between the sky above and the earth below, since it manifests the qualities of celestial fire here below but spares man its violence and excesses; and at the same time moves the sun away from the earth, since their proximity is no longer required for the purpose of heating food (1970:293).

Among the Huichols one of the important duties of the mara'akáme is to see to it "with his power" that the Sun Father is properly reborn each dawn and makes his customary celestial journey across the sky; to the same end a number of deceased shamans also travel with the Sun in the form of celestial rock crystals. Not every shaman is required to attend the solar birth rite, however, since Huichols consider it sufficient to know that somewhere in their country a mara'akáme is making the appropriate ritual gestures (Joseph E. Grimes, personal communication).

21. For significant comparative data from South America on Opossum's relationship to the origin of fire and, hence, the transition from nature to culture, and at the same time to the loss of man's immortality and to death and the afterlife, and taboos against opossum meat, see the chapter, "The Opossum's Cantata," in Lévi-Strauss's *The Raw and the Cooked* (1970:164-195). Almost all Tupian tribes, for example, share the myth of the theft of fire from its Vulture Guardian by a demiurge who feigned death and putrefaction—in other words, Opossum; related traditions are present also among the speakers of Gê languages. While it is true that opossum ecology might by itself generate certain common North and South American mythic themes, the striking similarity between some of these, and the fact that they are found especially among people in both areas that have retained a strong component of preagricultural, hunting-and-gathering ideology, at least suggests common historical roots for these and a whole series of other common mythic themes in a very ancient shared substratum predating perhaps even the early peopling of South

America by hunter-gatherer bands from the north. For other cross-cultural data on the opossum see also Wilbert (1974:82–83).

22. One suspects that here we are dealing with more than myth. Considering that the sacred peyote country lies within the old colonial Spanish silver mining district of Real de Catorce and that in the first two centuries after the Conquest such mines exacted a fearful toll among Indians enslaved to extract the precious ore, it is likely that for a time few Huichols ventured from the safety of the Sierra into territory in which capture and enslavement into the mines was a very real possibility. The mythological event described may thus in part be a historic memory of the resumption of traditional travel to Wirikúta when the dangers were no longer so acute. The historic element is quite explicit in the narrative of the bird-children's flight, where the shaman warns at several points of "bad Spaniards" whose pueblos must be avoided lest they bring the pilgrims to harm.

23. Ritual fasting before, during, and after the peyote pilgrimage is said to help summon and retain in their midst the divine ancestors, whose personalities and names the pilgrims themselves assume (cf. Dundes, 1963:213–220).

24. Another example of male-female complementarity.

25. "Arrows of sickness" are the negative counterpart of the ubiquitous ceremonial or prayer arrows which, as Lumholtz (1900:84) notes, are inseparable from every aspect of Huichol life as the most common expression of prayer for all "the wants of the Indian from the cradle to the grave." The supernatural sickness projectiles are extracted with the characteristic techniques of shamanic curing—e.g., sucking, spitting, blowing, brushing (with the muviéri, or shaman's plumes), fumigating with tobacco smoke, massaging, and so forth. Sucking vigorously at the affected part the shaman eventually produces from his mouth for all to see the illness-causing foreign object, which may take the form of a cactus spine, thorn, twig, fish bone, cotton thread, seed, or pebble. Removal of the physical symptom is insufficient in and of itself for a complete cure, however. Rather, the shaman must also divine the supernatural origin of the sickness and the reason for which it was inflicted, and the patient must agree to fulfill certain ritual obligations; in the event that the source is identified as a human sorcerer the curing shaman may magically reverse the direction of the projectile or, at the patient's behest, shoot his own magical arrows at the enemy. Any shaman has this power to cure and conversely, to inflict illness, but few would willingly gain the notoriety of sorcerer.

26. "Appearance," or "face," ceremonial shield or disk decorated with designs specific to the different deities.

27. This refers to Káuyumarie employing his antlers ("arrows") to hold back the clashing cloud gates that threaten to close on the pilgrims from either side as they attempt to pass from "this world" into "that other world." Hainamári, the Enclosed Clouds or Gateway of Clouds, then, represents the mystical divide on the other side of which lies the sacred land of the ancestors. It is thus again the "dangerous" or "paradoxical" passage through which, as Eliade (1964) has pointed out, only those who have become spirit can safely pass. That, of course, applies to the children as magically transformed spirit birds, as it does also to the participants on an actual peyote hunt, since they, having shed (by fasting, ritual obliteration of adult sexuality, and other purification rites) their ordinary selves, have assumed the personalities of the supernaturals who initiated the peyote pilgrimage in ancient times.

28. Sacred mountain range that faces the Wirikúta range.

29. *Nawá* means fermented beverage in general rather than only the drink made by fermenting maize. The Huichol term relates to the Pima-Papago *nava* or *nava-it*, an intoxicating ritual drink made by these Indians of Arizona and northern Mexico from fermented cactus fruits.

30. The upright three-legged cylindrical tépu of the Huichols resembles a similar vertical drum, called *huehuetl* by the Aztecs, in wide use in pre-Columbian Mesoamerica, including west Mexico, as shown in archaeological art from as much as two millennia ago. Oddly, however, the Huichol word for this drum, *tépu*, relates to an entirely different type of prehispanic drum, the *teponaztli*, a horizontal cylindrical wooden instrument whose top was slotted in the shape of a capital H to form two tongues. Both the huehuetl and the teponaztli were strictly ritual instruments; likewise the tépu, which is presumably later among the Huichols than what they call the "bow-drum," meaning the hunting bow used as a percussion instrument, the taut string being beaten with the tips of two hardwood arrows while the curved back is held down with the foot on an inverted hollow gourd bowl. This is clearly a more complex adaptation of the hunting bow as musical instrument than that described on an earlier page (one end of the bow held against the mouth while the player taps the taut string with a hunting arrow). Interestingly enough, Lumholtz (1900:34–35), who did not see a musical bow among the Huichols, noted the striking similarity between the sound of the tépu as played by the Huichols and the Cora bow-drum: "The tempo (of the tépu) is the same as that produced on the musical bow of the Cora with the two sticks, and the sound of the two instruments is somewhat similar, especially at a distance, though the bow is by far the more musical."

31. Not only the living and deceased relatives but the gods and sacred animals require and enjoy nawá and are included in the ritual drinking. When a deer has been brought into the rancho or ceremonial center from the ceremonial hunt it is carefully laid down on embroidered cotton cloth, in particular the Huichol version of the characteristic triangular poncho-like garment called *quechquémitl* by the Aztecs and *xikúri* in Huichol, the people ask it to forgive them for having killed it and feed it symbolically with its favorite foods and with nawá. There is a special song Huichols sing which names the five kinds of grasses that deer prefer and which, along with maize beer, must be offered to the deer that has temporarily surrendered its life to the hunters for the ceremonies.

32. Customarily, the mara'akáme feeds small amounts of real or symbolic peyote to the young participants in Tatéi Néiya during their brief "sojourn" in Wirikúta, just as he gives their first taste of the sacred cactus to his companions on an actual peyote hunt. Bits of tortilla or crackers are frequently employed as metaphoric peyote, especially for the youngest tevainuríxi, but there is no prohibition against children trying the real thing. In fact, they are carefully watched for their reaction to the often exceedingly bitter and acrid taste. If they seem to enjoy it, it may be taken as a sign that they will grow up to be gifted shamans. But no stigma attaches to expressions of distaste. An infant only seven days old, a two-year-old, and a boy aged ten—all grandchildren of José Ríos and Eusebia Medrano— participated in the 1968 peyote pilgrimage led by Ramón Medina, but only the oldest actually ate peyote (in prodigious amounts and with no noticeable ill effects); Ramón only touched the faces of the two younger children with a piece of "the flesh of Elder Brother," although he intoned the customary exhortation, "Here, eat this, so that you will see your life."

33. The same ritual is performed by the peyote pilgrims following their return from Wirikúta.

34. It is this conceptual merging of the takwátsi of the mara'akáme with his spirit helper Káuyumarie that differentiates it from the ceremonial baskets of ordinary men, rather than any formal differences, such as raw materials, shape, or basketry technique. In the context of a ceremony the identification of the takwátsi with the divine Deer may be underscored by placing antlers on or close to the basket. I stumbled on this aspect of Huichol symbolism by way of art: in one of his "yarn paintings" (wool yarn designs impressed into a base of beeswax spread on plywood or composition board) Ramón depicted one stylized takwátsi

without and another with deer antlers; the latter, he explained, "had antlers growing from it because it was Káuyumarie, the *"takwátsi Káuyumarie"* of the shaman; in ancient times, he said, takwátsi was deer, just as, for example, the tobacco gourd was snake and tobacco hawk.

35. The name given to the children who participate in the magical pilgrimage to Wirikúta. They are said to fly there as birds; which species is meant is unclear, Ramón saying that their little spirits shimmer like hummingbirds but that they are not hummingbirds as such.

36. Yellow dye ground from a root, used for face painting by peyoteros. Cf. Lumholtz (1900:196–203).

37. One of the shaman's assistants, who as guardian eagle helps protect the bird-children on ther flight or possibly Tatéi Weríka 'Uimári, Our Mother Young Eagle Girl.

38. Our Mother Young Eagle Girl, usually depicted as a bicephallic eagle.

39. Hainamári, the gateway of the clashing clouds, is the dangerous passage through which one enters the sacred land of Our Mothers, the divine Ancestors, and the Deer-Peyote. The Huichols say it is the divine Deer who wedges his great antlers into the opening between the cloud gates, so as to hold them back while the pilgrims slip through, one by one, in single file. On the actual peyote journey this is pantomimed by the mara'akáme, whose muviéri, or plumes, are identified with the antlers of the sacred deer. On the 1968 peyote hunt Ramón led the pilgrims through the symbolic gateway playing his hunting bow like a musical instrument by holding one end to his mouth and tapping the taut ixtle (maguey fiber) string with the hardwood tip of a composite arrow. The resulting music, it is said, has a magical effect; like the beat of the drum at the first fruits ceremony, the sound of the bow string lifts the pilgrims into the sky beyond the reach of potentially hostile influences. The musical bow appears to be very ancient among the Huichols; there is a whole repertoire of songs, many dealing with the adventures of the mythological pre-Huichol Héwi and Nanáwata people, for which bow music is said to be the only proper instrumental accompaniment.

40. Three knotted cords play an important role in the peyote pilgrimage. One is the so-called calendar cord described by Lumholtz (1900), on which the length of the peyote pilgrimage is represented by knots, one for each day, which are untied one by one as the days pass. Another is for the ixtle string into which the officiating mara'akáme ties knots representing the adult extramarital sexual experiences of each of the pilgrims; at the end of a ceremony at which the peyoteros publicly profess these experiences naming each partner by name, the knotted cord is burned, symbolically returning the pilgrims to a childhood state. A third, and in some ways most important, cord is that into which the pilgrims are knotted, one knot for each peyotero, thereby tying the participants to one another and to the shaman along what can be seen as a symbolic umbilicus; the knots are untied after the peyoteros return (cf. Furst, 1972b:159–161).

41. Ixtle string on which small balls of cotton woollike filaments from the fruit of the *Bombax* tree have been arranged to represent the children. One end of the string is usually attached to a ceremonial arrow stuck into the ground near the shaman's drum, the other to a miniature shaman's chair decorated with thread crosses and deer antlers, representing Elder Brother, or, as in the ceremony witnessed at El Colorín, to a ceremonial shelf with offerings and symbols pertaining to Máxa Kwaxí.

42. *Wítse* = a small predatory bird.

43. Xutúri 'iwiyékame, Goddess of flowers and fertility.

44. Day lily or madonna lily.

# BIBLIOGRAPHY

Anguiano, Marina
1974   "El cambio de varas entre los Huicholes de San Andrés Coahamiata, Jalisco."
       *Anales de Antropología* (Mexico) 11:169-187.
1975   "La cultura huichol y su participación en la sociedad nacional." *Trabajo Social,*
       2d ser., no. 9. Mexico, D.F.: Escuela Nacional de Trabajo Social, Universidad
       Nacional Autónoma de México. Pp. 23-26.

Carmen Velázquez, María del
1961   *Colotlán: Doble frontera contra los Bárbaros.* Cuadernos del Instituto de
       Historia, no. 3. Mexico, D.F.: Universidad Nacional Autónoma de México.

Culin, Stewart
1907   "Games of the North American Indians." *Twenty-fourth Annual Report of the
       Bureau of American Ethnology.* Washington, D.C.: U.S. Government Printing
       Office. Pp. 29-846.

Dundes, Alan
1963   "Summoning Deity through Ritual Fasting." *The American Imago* 20(3):
       213-220.

Eliade, Mircea
1964   *Shamanism: Archaic Techniques of Ecstasy.* Bollingen Series 86. New York:
       Pantheon Books.

Furst, Peter T.
1967   "Huichol Conceptions of the Soul." *Folklore Americas* 27:39-106.
1968   "Myth in Art: A Huichol Depicts His Reality." *The Quarterly* (Los Angeles
       County Museum of Natural History) 7(3):16-25.
1972a  "To Find Our Life: Peyote among the Huichol Indians of Mexico." In *Flesh of
       the Gods: The Ritual Use of Hallucinogens.* Peter T. Furst, ed. New York:
       Praeger Publishers. Pp. 136-184.
1972b  "Para encontrar nuestra vida: El peyote entre los Huicholes." In *El peyote y los
       Huicholes.* Salomón Nahmad, Otto Klineberg, Peter T. Furst, and Barbara G.
       Myerhoff, eds. Mexico, D.F., Secretaría de Educación Pública. Pp. 109-196.
1972c  "El mito en el arte: Un Huichol pinta su realidad." In *Mitos y arte huicholes.*
       Peter T. Furst and Salomón Nahmad, eds. Mexico, D.F., Secretaría de Educa-
       ción Pública. Pp. 114-125.
1974a  "West Mexican Art: Secular or Sacred?" In *The Iconography of Middle
       American Sculpture.* New York: The Metropolitan Museum of Art. Pp. 98-133.
1974b  "Some Problems in the Interpretation of West Mexican Tomb Art." In *The
       Archaeology of West Mexico,* Betty Bell, ed. Ajijic, Jalisco, Mexico: Sociedad de
       Estudios Avanzados del Occidente de México. Pp. 132-146.
1975   "House of Darkness and House of Light: Sacred Functions of West Mexican
       Funerary Art." In *Death and the Afterlife in Pre-Columbian America,* Elizabeth
       P. Benson, ed. Washington, D.C.: Dumbarton Oaks Research Library and
       Collections. Trustees for Harvard University. Pp. 33-68.

Knab, Tim
1976   "Huichol Nahuatl Borrowings and Their Implications in the Ethnohistory of the
       Region." *International Journal of American Linguistics* 42 (33), 261-264.

Lévi-Strauss, Claude
1970   *The Raw and the Cooked.* New York and Evanston: Harper and Row.

Lumholtz, Carl
  1900   *Symbolism of the Huichol Indians,* American Museum of Natural History, Memoirs 1, no. 2. New York.
  1902   *Unknown Mexico.* Vol. 2. New York: C. Scribner's Sons.
  1904   *Decorative Art of the Huichol Indians,* American Museum of Natural History, Memoirs, 3. New York.

McIntosh, Juan B., and José Grimes
  1954   *Vocabulario Huichol-castellano, Castellano-huichol.* Mexico, D.F.: Instituto Lingüístico de Verano y Secretaría de Educación Pública.

Myerhoff, Barbara G.
  1974   *Peyote Hunt.* Ithaca and London: Cornell University Press.

Preuss, Konrad Theodor
  1907   "Die Hochzeit des Maises und andere Geschichten der Huichol-Indianer." *Globus* 91:185-192.
  1908   "Die religiösen Gesänge und Mythen einiger Stämme der mexikanischen Sierra Madre." *Archiv für Religionswissenschaft* 11:369-398.
  1912   *Die Nayarit-Expedition. Erster Band: Die Religion der Cora-Indianer.* Leipzig: B. G. Teubner.

Preuss, Konrad Theodor, and Elsa Ziehm
  1968   *Nahua-Texte aus San Pedro Jicora in Durango I: Mythen und Sagen.* Quellenwerke zur Alten Geschichte Amerikas IX. Berlin: Ibero-Amerikanisches Institut Preussischer Kulturbesitz.

Santoscoy, Alberto
  1899   *Nayarit, colección de documentos inéditos, históricos, y etnográficos acerca de la Sierra de ese nombre.* Guadalajara, Jalisco: Documentos Curiosos.

Spicer, Edward H.
  1969   "Northwest Mexico: Introduction." In *Handbook of Middle American Indians,* Vol. 8, Part II. Austin, Texas, 1969. Pp. 777-791.

Wilbert, Johannes
  1974   *The Thread of Life: Symbolism of Miniature Art from Ecuador.* Studies in Pre-Columbian Art and Archaeology Number 12. Washington, D.C.: Dumbarton Oaks. Trustees for Harvard University.

Zingg, Robert
  1938   *The Huichols: Primitive Artists.* New York: G. E. Stechert.

# 4.

# The Context of
# Huichol Enculturation:
# A Preliminary Report

E. RICHARD SORENSON, KALMAN
MULLER, AND NICOLAS VACZEK

From research film records of Huichol Indian daily life and social interaction, we have begun to examine the dynamics of transmission of the culturally molded patterns of human behavior that characterize this traditional way of life. While it is still too early to make definitive statements about the dynamics, the context in which the behavioral patterns emerge can be described.

Huichol habitation in the Sierra Madre mountains of northwest Mexico is primarily at higher elevations, along the tops of ridges in a deeply dissected topography, usually in association with the pine and scrub oak stands seen in these upper montane regions. Here childhood experience is associated with an indigenous economy based on subsistence maize agriculture predating the Conquest. The Huichol world view is still deeply tied to this ancient agricultural practice as well as to a still older hunting tradition. Numerous animalistic images and beliefs are interwoven with agriculturally oriented myths that apparently arose as the Huichol became sedentary farmers. These myths provide a basic cosmological setting for the Huichol way of life and thus play a role in the cognitive development of the growing child.

Maintaining an integrity traceable to pre-Columbian times, the Huichol mythology, ritual, and symbol have been augmented, but not fundamentally affected, by "Christian" and "Christo-pagan" influences (see Furst, 1972). In testimony to the persistence of their belief system there is a Catholic mission church at San Andres abandoned by earlier missionaries. Here members of the surrounding ranchos gather for ceremonies; but the Christian elements associated with it have been so incorporated into the Huichol cosmogony that outside priests are not even allowed to participate.

Exposed to acculturative forces since the early missionary contact in the eighteenth century, the Huichols have long resisted external influences. Most of the exposure to Western culture has been through personal experiences outside of the Sierra, although recently increasing numbers of non-Huichol Mexicans have begun to reside in the region bringing new ideas and practices relating to agriculture, commerce, education, medicine, and government.

Although mobility in the Sierra still remains limited essentially to foot or horse, there are now a number of airstrips throughout the Sierra. San Andres, a major focus of this study, is the beneficiary of the largest airstrip, providing access to the outside in an hour instead of the week usually required for the overland journey to Tepic and other towns.

Although aspects of the material culture and socioeconomic structure of the Huichol milieu have been discussed by a number of scholars (Myerhoff, 1974; Weigand, 1969, 1973; Furst, 1967; Furst and Myerhoff, 1966; Grimes and Hinton, 1961; Zingg, 1938; Lumholtz, 1902), there is as yet little data on the behavioral development dynamics in the everyday social and cultural setting. We have therefore focused our attention on this aspect of the Huichol way of life through filmic observation concentrating on child behavior and social interaction in the natural social and environmental setting.

Each rancho (or group of households) maintains dispersed cultivated plots, usually situated on the steep sides of communally owned barranca land. More recently, however, plowed hilltop fields have also begun to appear. The ranchos are for the most part socioeconomically autonomous—self-sufficient in terms of production and consumption of goods. Each typically comprises an extended family and is essentially independent of surrounding households except for participation in the large religious gatherings. It is at the rancho level that the most important activities in everyday Huichol life take place, including many religious functions, usually in full view and often involving the participation of the young children. Social regulation also operates primarily at the rancho level, along with self-government and socialization, even though shifts of household units from one rancho to another within the same kindred are not unusual. Thus, from the point of view of the growing child, what goes on and what is believed to be important is carried on largely in the extended but basically familial setting of the rancho.

Indigenous ceremonial centers, or *tukipas*, focus religious and ceremonial life at a higher community level extending beyond the rancho. Households come together at these sites to participate in seeking the help of and enjoying their tribal deities. Babies and children become a component of this ceremonial milieu, with their participation developing informally as their childish attempts to join in are tolerated.

The Lophophora or peyote cactus (called *hikuri* or *hikuli* by the Huichol), widely used in daily life and for religious purposes, is esteemed for both its spiritual and medicinal qualities. This hallucinogen is used in social and religious gatherings in which children participate.

Transmission of a culture's characteristic patterns of behavior takes place as the growing child's nervous system interacts with and is differentially patterned by his experiences. Different milieus provide dissimilar typical situations that may expose the infant and young child to quite different languages of sensory input, different patterns of behavioral experience, different gestalts of emotional organization, and different focuses of perception and cognition. Patterns of behavioral response, social interaction, and human organization assume characteristics typical of a way of life or culture. Work in New Guinea (Sorenson, 1968a, 1971, 1976; Sorenson and Gajdusek, 1966) has shown that it is easier to unravel these patterns when we examine how children adopt the forms embodying their culture as they grow up.

The culturally specific patterns of behavior exhibited by an individual are molded primarily during infancy and childhood. The divergent paths along which such human development may proceed are divided by such basic human experiences as touch, kiss, caress, and embrace; smell, taste, nursing, and feeding; sound, voice, story, and myth; gesture, rhythm, music, and dance; and manners, morals, etiquette, and kinship.

To study such expressions of human behavior in changing and vanishing cultures requires that we deal with observations which are transient, aperiodic, nonrecurring, and unreproducible. A reliable phenomenological record is needed not only to permit detailed and lengthy statements, but also to substantiate findings. For this reason we turned to film records of naturally occurring daily social behavior as the basic research resource.

In earlier studies of human behavior, visual records have proved valuable, in some cases critical. The use of film to discover and demonstrate culturally specific patterns of behavior on Bali by Mead and her colleagues (Bateson and Mead, 1942; Mead and McGregor, 1951) clearly illustrated the value of visual data in anthropological inquiry. More recently, Birdwhistell's (1952; 1972) discovery of subtle, visible components in communication from film records showed that film was indispensable in detailed analyses of human interaction. This was further supported by Hall's demonstration of cultural difference in nonverbal human interaction (1959). The study of patterns of human movement in dance and work (Lomax, Bartenieff, and Paulay, 1968; 1969) and their relation to social and economic evolution (Lomax and Berkowitz, 1972) would not have been possible without access to a growing body of anthropological films containing retrievable data not necessarily sought or recognized by their filmers.

We are all enculturated beings and embody, therefore, culturally specific patterns of awareness and understanding. Culturally bestowed ideas of value screen human sensory input and structure cognitive appreciation. We recognize, conceptualize, and express in terms of the precepts, categories, and habits bequeathed by our own culture. We perceive and talk about what we encounter in other cultures through the colored spectacles of our own culture.

Film provides a means to penetrate this cultural barrier to obtain human behavioral data not limited to that recognized or categorized by the culturally molded cognitive organization of the human mind. Because the light sensitive emulsion of film produces an objective chemical facsimile of the pattern of light falling on it, it preserves a phenomenological record of that pattern of light received. Because of this, film preserves information not just of what has been "seen" and "selected" by the culturally programmed mind of the filmer but also what has not. It preserves a deeper record of passing human events than is possible by relying on any person's perceptive and descriptive capabilities. We used the camera to obtain much of our data because it provides a wedge by which these cultural barriers to perception, understanding, and data collection may be further penetrated.

The deeper phenomenological record made possible by film records permits reexamination of a past event as often as needed and as new knowledge leads us to ask new questions. It also makes possible careful examination and reexamination of details and relationships which may be too subtle, fleeting, or complex to be detected in the real time of daily life or under the demanding conditions of fieldwork in other cultures. Film records thus reveal "fossils" of the evolution of human behavior patterns and social interaction which would otherwise vanish without a trace.

Using methods worked out in the study of the protoagricultural way of life of the Fore people of New Guinea (Sorenson, 1967, 1968a, 1971, 1976; Sorenson and Jablonko, 1975), we have completed a preliminary examination of the film records obtained to date of naturally occurring behavior in traditional Huichol Indian communities.

The importance of religious belief and practice is clear. Unlike the Fore of New Guinea, Huichol enculturation is imbedded in a religious ceremonial context which governs a large body of belief and action. Although some striking similarities between Fore and Huichol early child handling and training make these cultures more like each other than either to our own Western culture, the religious component in the Huichol way of life separates it from the Fore way of life by a wide gulf. Like the Fore, the Huichol provide their children with a socially benevolent community life. But unlike the Fore, a ceremonially rich, indigenous religion emphasizes personal contact with drug-induced deities in powerful social and ceremonial contexts.

Traditional hunting and agricultural practices combine with religious understanding and the use of peyote to form the symbolic complex underlying the Huichol way of life. Children participate in the ceremonially related cultural expressions, and also participate in the religious appreciation of peyote-induced hallucinogenic experiences. Similarly, shamanistic interpretation and treatment of problems, often performed in the presence of children, follow the peyote-influenced indigenous religious beliefs.

From birth, integration into Huichol culture is marked by sacred events and beliefs. An infant is the focus of ceremonial attention, usually directed by a local curandero. For a short period that begins three or four days after birth, the shaman is intensively involved with the family, giving advice and taking measures to insure the safety and health of the child. Physical handling of the child by the shaman at these and other times early in life is usually gentle. The day-to-day care, handling, and protection of the young child is assumed by members of the extended family in a rancho residential setting which allows continual interaction with a variety of guardians. For the first few years of life the child is a center of concern and attention. This diminishes, however, as the child grows older.

The molding of child behavior in daily life tends to be nondirective, with young children participating in what is going on about them according to their own interests and attractions. Tolerance of childhood spontaneity is the rule. For the very young the arena in which this spontaneity is exercised is close to or in rancho huts. The territorial reach is gradually extended, however, as experience and confidence increase. Initially exploratory activity is usually near parents engaged in their normal daily activities. As the children grow older, involvement in adult economic and ceremonial life becomes more formal without being regimented. Youthful responsibility is granted and easily received early in life. Participation in social and economic events is not so much a matter of meeting adult expectation but of cooperation and contribution to shared goals.

Competitiveness among peers does not seem to develop, and play is usually gentle enough to permit participation by children of different ages. Children are not usually forced against their will either by adults or age mates. Bullying is rare. Aggressive tendencies in play might gain parental attention, but such expressions are usually left to subside of their own accord without parental intervention. In one of our film sequences, a young girl lightly kicks a boy who is kneeling near an adult female. As she moves on, stepping behind him, the girl anticipates playful retaliation and turns to defend herself from the boy. He turns throwing a mild punch as he rises. A short period of playful tussling ensues, and the pair part, smiling at each other and at the woman who has finally raised her head from her work. From film records of such events we expect to learn more about the degree to which this type of interaction sequence is representative of cultural patterning, and what role it might play in Huichol solidarity.

Development of the human faculties that lead to solidarity and coordination within the community takes place during the enculturative process. Along with stylized maneuvering in ceremonial situations, everyday Huichol social experience seems to be marked by a rich awareness of bodily movement and interaction. Filmed examples indicate that certain types of conduct or modes of expression may receive quick sanction or disapproval by eye contact and/or movement. In one sample that we examined, a boy is hopping near his guardian, from whose hand an uncapped beer bottle hangs by a string. As the boy turns toward the adult male in his hopping, he notices the bottle and swoops it up for a drink, which lasts about two seconds. The boy's attention then shifts and his free movement continues. From repeated viewing of such sequences and examination of hand and mouth micromovements, we may determine the manner of restraint exerted by the adult to limit the quantity of alcohol consumed. In this particular case it appeared that the boy took and yielded the bottle in synchrony with the expression of consent by the adult.

Children are introduced to ceremonial activities early. Although they often sit or stand about in decorations they have been given, considerable leeway is given to their unsophisticated inclinations. They are rarely coerced or disciplined as they attempt to join in or watch the proceedings in their own way. At other times, when their involvement must be more structured, adult guidance is affectionate and often accompanied by humor. It is in this participatory way that Huichol children come to learn many of the behavioral and ceremonial forms and tasks which characterize the Huichol way of life.

The role of peyote in enculturation is not completely clear. Within a community, its use ranges across all ages, hierarchies, and situations. It is used in medicinal contexts, both orally and by direct application to wounds. Even toddlers are given subhallucinatory doses of peyote, both in ceremonial settings and in daily life around the house, where it may be ground into the tortilla batter. Hallucinatory doses, even very large ones, are typical in initiation ceremonies, particularly during those associated with the annual peyote pilgrimage. Before the pilgrimage commences, confession of sexual affairs is required to avoid disharmonious contact with the peyote deity—in our terms a "bad trip." Children as young as ten years of age can be asked to join in these recitations. Even a child of seven days may be carried on the pilgrimage (Furst, 1972). It is not clear yet what part the confessions play in social solidarity, but on the surface they do not seem disruptive.

The increasing contact with European influences is transforming socialization processes among the Huichol so there is some urgency to completing the film sample for this study. In San Andres a school and carpentry shop have been established and a road linking the village to the outside is nearly completed. Under the guidance of government specialists agricultural practices are beginning to change, modern medical services are reaching more and more individuals and commercial interests are venturing deeper into the mountains.

Our study also seeks to document shifts in Huichol behavioral dynamics that may be related to these modernizing influences. The visual data we are obtaining represent a transition period for a culture whose way of life can be traced directly to pre-Columbian origins. The pattern of disappearance of these remnants is not fully predictable. These preliminary observations dealing with Huichol enculturation are based on initial review of approximately 60,000 feet of research film material: 20,000 feet taken by Dr. Kalman Muller, and 40,000 feet by John Lilly, Jr., both of whom have collaborated with our cross-cultural Study of Child Behavior and Development in Cultural Isolates. Further film analysis is under way, and research film sampling of naturally occurring behavior in Huichol communities continues.

## BIBLIOGRAPHY

Bateson, G., and Margaret Mead
   1942    *Balinese Character: A Photographic Analysis.* Special Publications, vol. 2. New York: New York Academy of Sciences.
Birdwhistell, R. L.
   1952    *Introduction to Kinesics.* Louisville: University of Louisville Press.
   1972    *Kinesics in Context.* New York: Ballantine.
Furst, P. T.
   1967    "Huichol Conceptions of the Soul." *Folklore Americas* 27 (2): 39–106.
   1972    "To Find Our Life: Peyote among the Huichol Indians of Mexico." In *Flesh of the Gods.* Peter T. Furst, ed. New York: Praeger. Pp. 136–184.
Furst, P. T., and B. Myerhoff
   1966    "Myth as History: The Jimson Weed Cycle of the Huichols of Mexico." *Antropológica* 17:3–37.

Grimes, J. E., and T. B. Hinton
1961 "Huichol and Cora." In *Handbook of Middle American Indians*. E. Z. Vogt and R. Wavehope, eds. Vol. 8, Part 2, *Ethnology*. Austin: University of Texas Press. Pp. 792-813.

Hall, E. T.
1959 *The Silent Language*. New York: Doubleday.

Lomax, A., I. Bartenieff, and F. Paulay
1968 "Dance Style and Culture." In *Folk Song Style and Culture*. A. Lomax, ed. Publication 88. New York: American Association for the Advancement of Science. Pp. 222-247.
1969 "Choreometrics: A Method for the Study of Crosscultural Pattern in Film," *Research Film* 6:505-517.

Lomax, A., and N. Berkowitz
1972 "Evolutionary Taxonomy of Culture," *Science* 177:228-239.

Lumholtz, C.
1902 *Unknown Mexico*. Vols. 1 and 2. New York: Scribners and Sons.

Mead, M., and F. MacGregor
1951 *Growth and Culture: A Photographic Study of Balinese Childhood*. New York: Putnam.

Myerhoff, B. G.
1974 *Peyote Hunt*. Ithaca: Cornell University Press.

Sorenson, E. R.
1967 "A Research Film Program in the Study of Changing Man: Research Filmed Material as a Foundation for Continued Study of Non-Recurring Human Events." *Current Anthropology* 8:443-469.
1968a *Growing Up as a Fore*. Paper and film presented at the Postgraduate Course in Pediatrics, Harvard Medical School, September 10, 1968.
1968b "The Retrieval of Data from Changing Culture: A Strategy for Developing Research Documents for Continued Study." *Anthropological Quarterly* 41:177-186.
1971 "The Evolving Fore: A Study of Socialization and Cultural Change in the New Guinea Highlands." Ph.D. dissertation, Stanford University.
1976 *The Edge of the Forest: Land, Childhood, and Change in a New Guinea Proto-agricultural Society*. Washington, D.C.: Smithsonian Institution Press.

Sorenson, E. R., and D. C. Gajdusek
1966 "The Investigation of Child Behavior and Development in Primitive Cultures: A Research Archive for Ethnopediatric Film Investigations of Styles in the Patterning of the Nervous System." Supplement to *Pediatrics* 37 (11): part 2.

Sorenson, E. R., and A. Jablonko
1975 "Research Filming of Naturally Occurring Phenomena." In *Principles of Visual Anthropology*. Paul Hockings, ed. The Hague: Mouton.

Weigand, P. C.
1969 "Modern Huichol Ceramics." *Meso American Studies*, no. 3.
1973 "Cooperative Labor Groups among the Huichol Indians in Jalisco, Mexico." *Meso American Studies*, no. 7.

Zingg, Robert
1938 *The Huichols: Primitive Artists*. New York: G. E. Stechert.

# 5.

# To Learn for Tomorrow: Enculturation of Girls and Its Social Importance among the Guajiro of Venezuela

MARIA-BARBARA WATSON-FRANKE

## Introduction

The issue of education intrigued the early anthropologists in their studies of the family (e.g., L. H. Morgan, E. B. Tylor). And yet, at that time traditional man was often presented as an irrational, childlike creature, who was unable to control either himself or his offspring (e.g., Todd, 1913). Many of these scholars contradicted their own denials that traditional education existed by actually describing the practices and attitudes displayed by "primitives" in bringing up the new generation (e.g., Monroe, 1906). The concept of "education" was measured one-sidedly against the standards of Western society, a practice that has remained alive for a long time in anthropological writing. Thus, Karsten wrote in his book on the Toba Indians (1923:25) that "the Tobas educate their children in complete liberty. Parents are never seen punishing their children for disobedience or faults committed. This is partly due to the fact that *the sense of what is proper and permissible is not among the Indians developed in the same way as in civilized societies* [italics mine]."

It is for such reasons as these that Spindler's remark (1963:54) about educational anthropology being a "pioneer's" field can still be considered valid, though we have now reached the point, it seems, where this situation is about to change. Nevertheless, our interest in and our attitude toward the education *of girls* is not changing at the same pace and is still dominated by the values of a male-oriented society. The situation presently is not too different from that thirty years ago when the *American Journal of Sociology* published a series of papers given at a symposium entitled

"Education and the Cultural Process" in 1943. Of the fourteen papers presented, not one dealt with the education of girls. Only Herskovits in his contribution, "Education and Cultural Dynamics," referred to female education, and he did so only in passing. And Watkins (1943), for example, in his discussion of bush schools (in his paper, "The West African 'Bush' Schools") dedicates three and a half columns of his paper to the schools for girls, whereas ten and a half columns are given to describing and evaluating the bush schools for boys! A detailed account of the girls' schools is considered unimportant by the author: "No great detailed consideration of it seems necessary here, for in organization and operation the *sandi,* or 'society for girls,' is parallel to the *beli* school for boys" (1943:673). Watkins reports that the boys "are proud" of their bush-school days, but he omits any information pertaining to the girls' attitudes toward *their* education. The style of presentation makes the girls' experience appear as less significant, and the reader is left wondering if the girls' education is regarded as less important by the girls themselves and their society, or if this is simply the author's view.

A recent article by Baily (1972), discussing the importance of women's education for society, also follows the old conventional road, with the author mentioning only the traditional roles of woman as mother and homemaker as justification for improving female education:

> Special attention needs to be placed on education for girls
> and women, because women take care of the homes, and their
> skills level largely determines the quality of life in the family.
> In addition, women are usually responsible for the pre-school
> training of children; they are bearers of culture (1972:38).

Earlier writers, like Fénelon in the seventeenth century, had already argued along similar lines, making woman's "natural" abilities the basis for her education.

What is needed, actually, is a *cultural* approach to woman's education. We must ask if a society displays beliefs in a strong sexual dichotomy and then, if so, determine how this is expressed in education. What, for example, is expected of girls and which role do women themselves have as educators? Moreover, how far does a culture permit women to become self-reliant, independent personalities?

We cannot take one cultural view, such as the male-oriented Western view, for granted as "natural" (cf. Mead, 1935) and argue from there.

In the following sections, the education of girls in a matrilineal society of South America is discussed. The socioeconomic consequences of education for the woman's position in Guajiro society is examined and briefly compared with data from a patrilineal society of New Guinea to shed light on some of the questions mentioned above.

## The Example of the Guajiro Indians

The Guajiro are a cattle-herding tribe who inhabit the arid, windswept Guajira Peninsula in northwestern South America.[1] They have a matrilineal social organization, and a strongly developed social class system.[2]

## Childhood

This study centers mainly on that phase of education that begins with the onset of puberty, since this is the critical period that serves to determine the girl's successful transformation into an adult woman. Detailed data relating to the earlier phases of education and the socialization process of boys and girls in general can be found in other studies (Watson, 1966; 1968). For our purposes here, a short summary of childhood education will suffice.

Very early childhood is a permissive time in Guajiro culture. The baby is fondled, fed, taken up, comforted whenever he[3] shows signs of distress, hunger, or a desire to play. Although contact between mother and child is close during the nursing period, the child is nevertheless required to accustom himself from the beginning to physical separation from the mother: even the small infant, for example, sleeps in his own hammock, which is slung next to the mother's. The baby may also be cared for by other females in the house in case the mother has to do some routine errand; the mother, however, is usually reluctant to be separated from the baby for long periods and she will take him with her if she has to go on a protracted journey (Watson, 1966).

Weaning is accomplished abruptly by smearing the nipple with a bitter substance or by slapping the child. Sometimes, at this stage, the child is taken to another relative's house "so that he will forget the breast." But, whatever the methods used, the infant's crying and tantrums are ignored by adults present. At this point, the permissive phase of childhood ends, perhaps too early and too painfully to be remembered later on in life; Guajiro Indians, for example, do not recall childhood as a "golden age," and there is no glorification of the happiness of childhood as is so frequently found in our culture.

The child now is treated increasingly like a small adult. Children are given tasks like holding or carrying objects and chasing animals away from the rancho (i.e., tasks that they can easily manage). As a rule, children are not given tasks which they are unable to do or which pose a challenge to them, for this might have "negative" consequences. Gua-jiros—children and adults alike—are expected throughout their lives to effectively and dutifully carry out duties that are appropriate to their sex, age, and abilities. Play, or any behavior associated with idleness, is discouraged. One day I saw a four-year-old girl dance to the music of a transistor radio. It was an unusual scene and I took a picture of it which captured the little girl's charm and self-indulgence. When I showed it to my interpreter, a very serious, proper Guajiro woman, she made only disparaging remarks, saying that little Anna was not good for anything.

At the age of about five, the activities of life begin to separate boys and girls. Girls stay close to their mothers and other adult female relatives, while the boys start going out to the pastures with the men. Both boys and girls are socialized to show respect toward others and to carry out their duties responsibly and effectively. Also, both are reminded constantly that their behavior is crucially important in determining whether or not they and their families will be respected by others.

At about the age of ten, boys and girls are often sent to live with other relatives. Boys often go to stay with the maternal uncle (MoBro); whereas the girls usually go to live with the maternal grandmother (MoMo), who seems to be the preferred relative, or with a maternal aunt (MoSi). These new living arrangements help children to learn how to deal with important matrilineal kinsmen outside their immediate family and to develop feelings of responsibility toward the extended matrilineal kin group.

## First Menstruation

When the girl reaches puberty her life changes drastically. She is isolated from society and kept in seclusion for about two to five years, depending on the socioeconomic position of her family. The institution is usually called *encierro* or *blanqueo* in Spanish, or *michi* ("in the house") in Guajiro. Here I use the term *encierro* since this was used by my interpreter in her Spanish translation.

When I asked about the first occurrences of this dramatic change of life, Guajiro women usually gave me one of the following versions:

"When I became a señorita, they put me into a tiny *chinchorro* high up under the roof."

"When I developed,[4] they cut my hair very short and gave me cold baths; and I had to take much medicine."

"When I became a señorita, they put me in a small hammock which was highly uncomfortable; and I was not given anything to drink or eat."

Everything the women mentioned happens to the girl, but detailed research has shown that the correct *sequence* of events is different, as I reconstructed it. The literature available on this topic also does not seem to report the exact succession of events. While the initial statements of my informants do not take cognizance of the exact sequence, however, this very lack is of great importance to us since it shows us which particular events are emphasized by the Guajiro women themselves. All of these women gave more or less lengthy accounts of the discomforts, unhappiness, and even humiliation they had felt when these things happened to them. But only further questioning in long sessions, demanding patience from the informant as well as the anthropologist, revealed the correct sequence of single events within the encierro.

As soon as the girl detects the first blood she must inform the female adult in charge of her and she is rushed *at once* to a separate hut or to a section of the rancho separated from the rest of the house. This new living space has usually been prepared for her in advance so that there is no delay in isolating her from the family group. The girl may spend all her years of seclusion in that closed-off-section of the house, or, she may—in case the separate hut is not ready for some reason—be transferred to this hut when it is finally finished. This must be done at night, however, because once the girl has started menstruating no one is allowed to see her except the woman who is in charge of her, or her teacher, if her family has hired one (see below). After she has been confined for some time, the girl may be allowed to receive short visits from older, trustworthy women; special care must be taken, however, that she is not seen by men or that she does not set eyes on men herself. The hut is small with a very low entrance so that a woman can enter only by crawling on her knees, and it has no windows. But informants added, sometimes with a concerned smile, that there were usually some peepholes in the hut through which the men attempted to get a look at the girl.

Once the girl has entered the hut she is told to lie down on the floor on her stomach without moving. This is necessary so that she will not give birth soon after she marries. One informant said that this was done to control pregnancies.

The girl is also given a medicine around midnight, right at the beginning of the encierro. The majority of women claimed that this medicine caused the girl to vomit and that she was thus cleaned inside by the time they put her into the small hammock (see below). Some women, among them an especially well-educated Guajira, maintained that this did not necessarily happen and that only "bad" girls vomited on this occasion. This medicine, called *huawapi,* is designed to control and space pregnancies so that she will have three, or, at the most, four children during her lifetime. During the first month of her encierro she will be given this medicine three times daily. Later, as a married woman, when she gives birth, she will take this medicine again, for three days after delivery, but for no longer, for if she does she will become sterile. This, like other medicines, has become known to the Guajiros through dreams.

The above information refers to girls who start menstruating at night. But when the girl starts menstruating during the day, for example, the time she must lie on the floor is shortened or even eliminated, although the medicine is administered as before.

Once she enters the hut or the enclosure, the girl is spoken to very seriously by her caretaker and reminded of her duties in her new life as an adult. One woman, who took care of her enclosed granddaughter, told the girl:

"You must learn for tomorrow, so that you will be able to fulfill your duties, and become a good woman like your mother. You must learn to weave hammocks and bags for your husband and for your family. You must behave well. Do not look around. Don't walk around, sit down and weave. Be considerate of others. Later you must be a good hostess; you must behave like your mother. Treat all equally well, otherwise people will call you pretentious.

Now your life will change, you will no longer act like a child, you will no longer laugh and do silly things. Now you must take responsibility; you must be considerate. It is no longer the way it was when you were a little girl; now you are a woman."

In the morning, the girl is put into a small *chinchorro* (a loose-meshed hammock) which is so narrow and short that it does not allow a comfortable position for sitting or lying. This chinchorro is usually made by a particular relative, usually by the girl's mother, but if the mother is dead or for any reason is unable to weave it herself, the maternal grandmother seems to be the preferred person to prepare the chinchorro for the new señorita. It should be blue and white or just white; colorful chinchorros with designs are not acceptable. Everything the girl comes in contact with must be simple.

After the girl is put into the small chinchorro, it is drawn up close to the roof. In this task the woman taking care of the girl may be assisted by another woman. Now the girl is instructed to lie absolutely motionless. If she moves her legs they will grow to uneven length. She is not allowed to scratch herself or she will get ugly skin. If she feels any discomfort she is allowed only to rub up against the hammock. She remains about three to six days high above the ground. (Obviously this tends to last the actual time of menstruation itself, although this was not spelled out or confirmed by my informants.) During this time, she is denied any food or drink except the medicine *huawapi* and other potions that are believed to make her beautiful and enable her to keep her youthful looks later in life. One of these medicines also helps her to fight the thirst somewhat. Women said that they had no need to urinate or defecate, so that this arrangement posed no problem. And if she needs to relieve herself, she is handed a little sand-filled box to use.[5]

When her hammock is finally lowered after three to six days, the girl is helped out of it and onto a stone for now she should *not* touch the ground *at all.* Moreover, the girl usually feels so weak that she can hardly stand up by herself.

The next step is very important and involves cutting the girl's hair. Customarily someone other than the girl's caretaker will cut her hair. The woman who does this gives the girl advice on how to behave herself in the future:

"At this moment I will cut your hair. You will lose all the hair, the hair of your childhood. So this does not exist anymore. New hair will grow, the hair of a woman. This hair of yours will be cut now because all the world touched it when you were a child. You are not a little girl anymore. Don't laugh like little girls do; your life will change now. Now you must take responsibility."

If the girl cries she will be severely criticized for her childish attitude and reminded of her new status as an adult woman who must exercise self-control.

One source mentions the maternal aunt (MoSi) as the one who cuts the hair (Pichón, 1947:159). But this may not be an absolute rule. What seems to be of utmost importance is that this woman have a high reputation. She is chosen carefully by the girl's family because of her virtues. She must, for example, be a successfully married woman, a woman whose family received a high bride price for her; she must be known as a hard and skillful worker, especially in weaving; and she must have a high reputation for being a good hostess and a faithful wife. Such a woman, it is believed, will bring the enclosed girl luck, and the girl will actually turn out to be as skillful and successful as the older woman. In contrast, if a woman of bad reputation were to cut the girl's hair, she would ruin the señorita's future, and the girl would turn out to have a "bad head," meaning she would not stay with her husband and would run around with other men. No incidents were reported, however, where the blame for an unsuccessful education was put on having chosen the wrong person for this occasion.

Some of the women commented on the humiliation they had felt when they lost their hair, but only informants in the city stated that this was done so that the girl would feel embarrassed about her appearance and would stay inside. Informants in the peninsula emphasized the magical power that the hair and the act of cutting the "hair of childhood" had for the girl's future life. If the hair were not cut, they felt, it would soon turn white; but if everything were done according to custom, the girl would have luck in life, would develop a good character, and would find a decent husband. The cut-off hair is carefully collected in a little bundle and is kept under a divi-divi-tree near the house or is hidden in a place near the ocean, that is, a place where nobody can find it. As one informant said, "This hair must be treated with care because the girl's luck depends on it."

Following the haircut the girl is helped out of the dress she wore while she was still a child, and she is given a bath. During the bath she is again reminded of the change in her life. The bath is supposed to give her beautiful firm flesh and is supposed to prevent her from becoming a loose woman: "the baths build a señorita's character." The water for the bath has been stored in four large jars that have been especially made for the girl's seclusion, since everything that touches the girl at this time must be "new." The water is stored overnight so that it is cold at the time of the bath.

From now on, the girl is given four baths a day, at least during the first month or so of enclosure. The frequency of the baths seems to vary from region to region and from family to family, owing to the differential scarcity of water in the Guajira, in general, and to the small variations of custom.

After the bath the girl is clad in a new dress that is different from the usual dress (*manta*) of female adults. It resembles more a shirt, having only short sleeves and reaching only to the knees. It is made of thin, white material; designs or bright colors are not acceptable in such a dress, "certainly not a scandalous color like red," as one woman expressed it. The girl will receive another dress for changing when this one gets dirty. She will not have more than two dresses, however, for an enclosed señorita should not have many clothes and everything she has must be extremely simple. Like other objects she comes in contact with, these shirtlike dresses have been made especially for her. According to Gutiérrez de Pineda (1950:51) and López (1945:37) the girl is dressed in a manta of the type worn by adult women. All of my informants contradicted this, however, and made it clear that the enclosed girl was always supposed to wear the small, shirtlike dresses.

Once dressed, she is led back to her hammock and given her first meal, which consists of chicha prepared without salt or sugar. She is fed by her caretaker, since she is not allowed to feed herself.

Meanwhile, relatives and friends of the girl's family have gathered to celebrate her entrance into adult life (the beginning of the encierro). The celebration starts when the hammock is lowered. People drink chicha, share a meal, talk, and listen to the sounds of drums and singers. After midnight the first singer rests, eats, and drinks while a second one takes over the singing until morning. They sing about the girl inside, the physical beauty she will acquire while being enclosed; they sing about her white skin and the long black hair she will have when she comes out again; they sing about the things she will learn inside, the beautiful hammocks she will weave, and the young men who will come and buy her weavings and will ask to marry her.

Informants' opinions about these celebrations differed. First of all, it seems, only well-to-do families can afford a big celebration. A family with only a few animals could not pay for the food and drink for so many people or for the services of musicians. Some well-educated women, whose families had seen better days when their herds were still large, called this celebration a bad custom that put bad ideas into the girl's head:

"Some people have men sing when the girl is let down. This is true. But my family did not do so. It is bad for the girl; she will become crazy, thinking about men all the time, since men are there to sing especially for her. Some families make a real fiesta on this occasion. But, again, this is very bad. The girl learns to enjoy singing, dancing, drinking, since all this is arranged in her honor. She gets used to these things and she will later change husbands many times." The informant quoted here was aware that the enclosed girl does not participate in the celebration, but she believed, like the Guajiro in general, that direct or indirect contact with bad behavior will lead to disaster. When I asked how it could "hurt" the girl when she really wasn't there, the informant replied: "But, didn't the girl *hear* the singing, laughing, and merrymaking all night?"

The following weeks, like the first days of menstruation, are still considered to be extremely dangerous for the girl. My informants would not put it in these exact words, but rather, would say: "The enclosed girl is very delicate; she needs special care, like a child" (female informant, 55 years old, Maracaibo). "The enclosed girl is sacred; she is something very special and utmost care must be taken so that everything goes right" (female informant, 65 years old, Guajira).

During this time the girl must observe very strict food taboos. The only thing she is allowed to eat this first month is the tasteless chicha. Even after twenty or thirty years, Guajiro women would still vividly express how much they had tired of this diet and had disliked the monotony of it. No explanation for the purpose of the custom was given.[6]

Significantly, the girl is still fed during this period, and she is not allowed to be fed with a spoon. Not eating with a spoon might point to the importance of a liquid diet as well as to the taboo against feeding herself. Her passive role is also reflected in that she is given baths instead of taking them herself, and because she must lie motionless without scratching herself, as in the very beginning.

Little girls talk about the upcoming encierro and the horrors it has in their imagination. There is much reluctance to approach the mother or other elder female relatives for explanations, and the girls receive their "knowledge" either from other girls who have not yet reached puberty themselves but who will in a few years, or from a girl who just "left" the encierro. More fantasizing than informing goes on this way, and the girls at times get increasingly anxious and apprehensive. One woman, when talking about her childhood, smiled when she recalled those days but she also remembered the deep fears she had felt:

"A girl older than myself told me about the life inside. She was already a señorita. When I asked her what she had done inside, she told me that it had been awful. 'You must drink much water in there, they treat you like a little goat,' she told me. When I inquired how she had liked all these baths one was supposed to take, she said to me: 'Oh no, no baths. They prepare hot water, with some herbs in it and put this in your anus.' Now I was really frightened. And when my cousin came out some time after that I decided to ask her and she told me that that girl had lied to me. But my cousin told me that she had suffered much hunger and that many baths were necessary. Then I quieted down."

Mothers and elder female relatives, when touching on this topic, only mention the positive side and they emphasize the new skills the girl will learn: the ability and knowledge she is going to achieve during her time of seclusion. The medicine, the baths, the severity of fasting in the beginning are not mentioned.

When the girl has thus spent her first month inside in quiet, inactive isolation, she enters a new stage. She can now eat certain foods, and instruction in weaving and related work begins.

After a month or so has passed, she is given her first full meal since leaving the outside world: a dish including meat. But it must be meat from a young animal. Especially good is a little white lamb with a pretty face; if the girl eats lamb meat she will become a beautiful woman with smooth skin and she will keep her youthful looks. In former times the best meat for this occasion was thought to be deer or *paloma del monte*, animals native to this region. But most women agreed that lamb was the best substitute if deer were not available. Goat is less desirable, but is acceptable. The girl, however, should not eat beef, which is taboo to her during the whole time of her enclosure. The almost stereotyped answer given for not letting the girl eat beef is: "If she ate beef, she would age soon; her flesh would become flabby and her skin wrinkled. She would not look youthful for very long."

Explaining this, one woman said that cows aged quickly once they had given birth, and therefore a girl should not eat a cow's meat. Another informant, also referring to the quick aging process in cows, pointed out that cows' noses were covered with lots of wrinkles: "Once a cow has given birth four times, she is old, therefore a girl should not eat beef." Other meats are placed under restriction, too, but no item in the diet is given such attention as beef. Here we must recall that the Guajiro in general do not eat beef except on special occasions. Beef has ritual power and importance: it is eaten at weddings, funerals, following successful shamanistic curing, at the coming out of an enclosed girl (see below), and at the graduation of a novice shaman who has just successfully ended her training. Outside such events the Guajiro usually eat sheep and goat meat, so that the taboo of eating beef in reference to the señorita is to be seen, I feel, as an extension of this general taboo in Guajiro culture. It is important, however, that the informants themselves never referred to this generally observed taboo concerning beef when talking about the encierro and its customs.

There are other food items that are tabooed to the girl. She should not drink milk, although some informants added that later in the encierro this taboo is not observed so strictly, that after some time she could drink milk every morning but the milk had to come from one particular cow, not just from any animal.

While some said that chicken was allowed, the majority listed it under the prohibited items. They explained that hens aged quickly and the girl would soon start to think of men if she ate chicken, and that she would soon get married. Others pointed to the ugliness of hens: "Hens have ugly feet when they get old, and so the girl would have ugly feet one day and her hair would become ugly." Also the high fertility of hens made them an undesirable food item, according to other informants: "Hens are not good for anything, they just have many little chickens; so, if the girl ate chicken, she would have many pregnancies."

But while practices like the baths or the taboo against scratching herself were always mentioned in connection with securing her physical beauty and the building of her character, some of the food taboos as such were seen to be associated with her weaving skill:

"If the girl inside ate beef, for example, the threads on the loom in front of her would all become chaotic, and she would be unable to weave the design correctly, and this would be really bad in the beginning of her isolation. Eating chicken would likewise have a bad effect on her weaving ability; her eyesight would fail and she would not be able to weave." Here the informant reminded the author of the hens' practice of always keeping their eyes close to the ground to find something to eat.

The enclosed girl should eat food prepared with only a little salt. Excessive intake of salt would cause her skin to become dry and be covered with white spots; her hair would become thin and would split. But if a señorita follows a low-salt diet, she will be rewarded with a smooth and shiny skin.

She should not eat roasted maize, for doing so would cause dandruff; and she should not eat much sugar for if she did she would get ugly teeth.

Asked for a general guideline for señoritas' meals, several informants stressed that only *known* foods should be eaten. Therefore, canned food is prohibited. With canned meat, for example, they pointed out that one could not even be sure what type of meat it was. Here, too, we might add that the Guajiro in the peninsula do not like canned food in general and believe that only freshly slaughtered animals give good, tasty, healthy meat. The girl in seclusion should not eat a plant that is not known, for it could be a plant that dried out quickly. She should avoid fish "since one does not know much about the life of fish," information that came from an informant from the central Guajira, far away from the coast; another woman who had spent her childhood near the coast said that fish was a good food item for the enclosed girl, since, as she put it, it was a "valuable source for energy." It is apparent from these remarks that strange influences over which one has no full control have to be kept away from the girl. Food is no exception. We can assume that some of these taboos are a result of contact with the Western world (e.g., prohibition of canned food), and that the adolescent girl had to be kept away from foreign influences, considered evil by the Guajiros.

## Learning

When the stage of inactivity ends for the girl, she starts her learning and working period in the encierro. Although Guajiro women nowadays buy their weaving thread in the market towns of Colombia and Venezuela, a señorita is still required to prepare the raw cotton and spin her own thread. The different stages of the work have been described in detail in another paper (Watson-Franke, 1974). It is important to keep in mind that weaving during the encierro is by no means the girl's introduction to the world of thread and stitches, for she starts her weaving very early in life. One can see small looms in ranchos where little girls are at home. The mother will set up a loom so that the little girl can practice the first and easiest weaving combinations. At this time, when she is about four or five, the typical girl is also practicing her first crocheting stitches. Some girls, in fact, are said to have learned to weave designs *before* being enclosed; they are believed to hold special promise.

The very basic tasks like processing the raw cotton require quick and skillful fingers and are usually taught to the girl by the woman in whose house she is enclosed, that is, her own mother, her maternal grandmother, or a mother's sister. To teach the girl the more complicated designs and refined work, families of some means usually hire a special teacher. The services of a weaving instructor are very expensive, so the period of intensive instruction for which such a teacher is hired depends on the family's financial capacity to pay her.

Great care is taken to choose a woman whose social reputation is very high. She can be a relative, like the mother (Pichón, 1947:159f.), a maternal aunt (Gutiérrez de Pineda, 1950:54), a paternal aunt (Polanco, 1958:132), or an unrelated woman known for her expertise. While the woman must possess excellent credentials as a weaver, she must also be known as a perfect hostess and wife. Success in teaching and learning depends on the context in which it takes place, that is, on the proper objects and people chosen to surround the girl. The Guajiro expect a teacher to be a fully experienced person, and that means she must be married. They look with doubt on a spinster teaching in the public or missionary schools. The Guajiro believe that a teacher should not expose the student to but one limited segment of society or experience (e.g., unmarried life) but bring her in contact with the whole female experience possible in the culture. It does not mean that the teacher should discuss with the girl details of married life, especially the sexual aspect of it; on the contrary, the enclosed girl should not see young girls or young married women, who would probably discuss sex with her. But the teacher should have a knowledge of life in order to be able to assist and guide the girl in the right direction toward womanly responsibility and maturity. This concept of the teacher and the attitude toward the Western style spinster teacher is not confined to the Guajiro; it has also been observed in other tribal societies as well (Read, 1960; Yeld, 1961).

Successful teaching and learning of weaving is of utmost importance to the girl's future (see Watson-Franke, 1974). Weaving skills give a woman social and economic prestige and security in society. To take but one example, if a girl is raped, which is a very serious offense in Guajiro culture requiring payment of damages, and if the family of the girl demands that the man pay them and make her his lawful wife, he can refuse to make the bridal payment on the ground that she does not know how to weave (Gutiérrez de Pineda, 1950:55). Weaving and crocheting are everywhere popular topics of discussion among Guajiro women;

Guajiras living in the city often defended their knowledge of tribal culture by pointing to their weaving knowledge; in contrast, some women who had only a very limited command of these traditional skills felt quite uneasy and insecure when the talk turned to these subjects.

The girl is taught that weaving is important but also enjoyable. Judging from informants' remarks, the girl finally learns to accept her solitude and to find satisfaction in her work. Demonstration and admonition, though, are not considered to be sufficient to make the girl a hard-working and skillful weaver. Older informants mentioned that a silkworm was put around the girl's wrist to make her a diligent worker. There is probably a connection here to the custom of wearing magical bracelets made up of little wooden pieces. The wooden cubes are believed to house a spirit that makes the girl work, gives her ideas about designs, and helps her to fight fatigue when she falls asleep in front of the loom. This spirit is thought to be female or male.

The products that the girl weaves during the encierro are sold by her family. The money or the animals received for the weavings become the girl's property. Frequently the interested clients are young men who show their interest in the girl in this way. The works of a señorita are considered to be of top quality. A young man is impressed when he purchases a well-woven hammock from an enclosed girl; indeed, one can truly say that a Guajiro girl first impresses her suitor by her skills rather than by her looks! Here a goal in Guajiro female education that is quite different from the Western model becomes apparent: the girl is not taught to catch a man's eye; rather she learns the skills that enable her to keep a man. So while the girl is inside, socially isolated, she still builds up a social reputation through her work which may stand her in good stead in securing and keeping an appreciative husband.

## "Coming Out"

The mother is usually the one who decides the length of the encierro. After a period of time ranging from two to five years the girl is told that she is ready to leave. As a rule, she knows about how long she will be confined when she starts the seclusion period. In tribal culture, only exceptional circumstances will end the encierro prematurely. The girl's serious illness or economic difficulties in the family requiring the girl's labor may lead to an early "coming out." Of course, it sometimes happens that a girl "breaks out" of her encierro, an absolutely scandalous act of behavior by Guajiro standards, but for which no concrete examples were given by traditional informants.

Once the girl has been outside and has been seen, a return is impossible and another enclosure would be of no value. Interruption of the encierro is highly undesirable and should be avoided at all costs. One informant who had lived in the city for about eight years at the time of the interview told me about the sudden end of the encierro of her second daughter whom she had enclosed some time after the family had moved to the city. The mother displayed confused amusement when telling me what had happened, but her story also revealed the shock, disgust, and helplessness she had felt:

"I enclosed one daughter when I was already here in the city. One day there was some commotion out in the street, an accident, I believe it was. Everybody went out to see what had happened. At that time my daughter had been inside for two weeks. I went out into the street myself to see what it was all about. When I looked around I saw my own enclosed daughter in the crowd! I couldn't believe what I saw. There she was, outside, among a crowd of people! I had wanted her to stay inside for a year. But now I had to take her out. Once the girl has been seen, she must leave the enclosure for good; there is no way to return and continue."

There is one exception to not confining a woman a second time: If a woman is a bad wife, her family may decide to lock her up once again, hoping that this new solitude will change the woman into a responsible person at last. One informant gave the following account of such an incident:

"A man bought a girl, but he already had a wife; she was my cousin. The girl came as a child into the house and the wife took care of her. She also taught her when she entered the encierro. At that time, when the girl became a señorita the wife became jealous of her. The wife was very ill, though, and after her death, the husband married this girl and lived with her. Then he left the Guajira and went to work in Santa Barbara. He sent her food to live. They lived like this for two years. She behaved badly, she was like a crazy woman, always running around with other men. Finally her uncle (MoBro) got angry with her because of her conduct and he enclosed her again. When she left the encierro she married another man who did not know her past, and she told him that she had lost her virginity in a rape case. With him she had children."

In the above case only some aspects of the encierro for pubescent girls are of importance, notably the effect of isolation, and food taboos, but there is no teaching of skills involved, as with the adolescent girl.[7]

If everything in the encierro goes according to plan, the family prepares a big fiesta in honor of the girl. In poor families, which cannot afford to entertain many guests, no such celebration is held.

Before sunrise on the day of the coming out the mother and other female relatives give the girl a bath. For this she may be taken outside her hut to a secluded area near the rancho where none of the visitors who arrive early can see her. After the bath she is clad in a beautiful new, brightly colored manta, and adorned with jewelry. The manta is short enough to show the golden bracelets around her ankles; her hair, which is now long, black, and shiny, is cut a bit shorter around her face to let the necklaces and earrings show. She wears rings and bracelets. Guajiro women, who are ordinarily reserved and rather tight-lipped people, sometimes get carried away when they recall the day "when they came outside": "Everybody was looking at me. Remember, they hadn't seen me for three years!"

When the girl is ready to meet the guests, the woman who took care of her during the years of isolation gives her a few gentle strokes with a small stick to encourage her to step outside into the world again and face all the visitors who came to see her. She is the center of attention on this day. The women present will wait on her. Prospective suitors are invited to help celebrate and take a look at the girl. Though it is a day of joy and pride for the young Guajira, it is also a critical moment, since the community is judging her and her family on the job they have done. Her looks and her poise are subject to critical appraisal.

The following days and weeks are used to reacquaint the "new" woman with the outside world. Although the Guajiro always strongly deny that the long isolation has put any strain on the girl, their actual behavior shows that they take the possible existence of such uneasiness and insecurity on the girl's part into consideration. During the following two or three days, she usually stays at home receiving visitors. Young women come to chat with her; young men visit under the pretext of seeing her family. After that she begins to accompany older relatives on visits to other ranchos and, finally, she goes on errands by herself, like fetching water or selling a woven item. The time for this adjustment was given as two or more weeks. The girls do not find it easy to reenter the world. Old informants described how they had gone to the waterhole with pounding hearts, not knowing what to do when they passed a man on the way.

Another indication that some girls fear the outside world and its demands is the extremely long period of seclusion which some enclosed women choose to endure. Several informants mentioned cases of girls who had been enclosed up to eight or ten years and did not want to leave and face the outside. The reactions of the families involved vary from giving less and less assistance to using forceful means to make her come out. In one instance the relatives did not do the necessary repair work on the hut so that the young woman finally had to leave a collapsing house.

A girl who prefers to stay inside will not be so strictly shielded from male visitors as she was during the early years of her seclusion. One woman told the extreme story of her cousin who was finally dragged out of the hut by her mother to meet her future husband. When she refused to cooperate they shut her up in the hut together with the man. While she destroyed everything inside, fighting a hopeless fight, family and friends outside celebrated the marriage of the two.

The Guajiro maintain that a girl has learned to be a hostess long before she is enclosed; as a small child she waits on visitors and receives training in housework. She does not forget what she learned in the early days; this knowledge stays with her and can be put to use once she comes "outside" as an adult. Housework is not done during the encierro. Reports to this effect must refer to highly acculturated contexts.

The girl who finishes her encierro without great conflict is now prepared to assume her role as an adult female and is prepared to marry.

## Knowledge and Social Position

Here we want to examine how education as a process through which one acquires knowledge and control of skills influences and shapes a woman's position in Guajiro culture.

*Knowledge is power*: This can be called a cultural universal. If a group of people is given a certain body of knowledge from which the rest of the group is excluded and which is important to the whole society, that group then holds authority and power because its members possess a *skill* (owing to the teaching itself) and also *control* its utilization (owing to the exclusiveness of the teaching). Of such a quality is the knowledge that the Guajiro girl receives during the years of her seclusion when she is made fully aware that she is a woman and that this is something she should be proud of. That knowledge, importantly, includes weaving, for as a weaver the Guajiro woman can successfully fulfill her economic role in life. Therefore, it is deemed necessary that she undergo a long and specialized training, and her teachers expect her to show high achievement-motivation. She is reminded again and again that through her weaving skills she will achieve the economic independence expected of a woman in Guajiro society, and that with this skill she may even achieve wealth and fame.

The Guajiro boy, in contrast, is not made aware of his manhood in the same focused fashion that the girl is made aware of her womanhood. The man does not learn a skill exclusively reserved for men. Men are responsible for the animals, but when they are absent in cases of visiting or feuding, the women are expected to take care of the herds. So it is not surprising that Guajiro women frequently would react with amused disbelief or strong disapproval when they were told that in conventional Western society the sons are favored over the daughters in receiving a higher education.[8]

Through her weaving the Guajira can enhance the social status and living standards of her family, by providing them with necessary articles like hammocks, bags, or belts; but she can also sell these things for cattle and money. I have seen that the first things she weaves in the encierro, such as the hammocks, are sold and she is allowed to keep the payment. Thus, through her own skill, a woman can attain ownership of the most highly valued objects in Guajiro culture—cattle. This means that her skill gives her access to the following interchangeable values: the woven products themselves, which are highly valued among the Guajiro; money; cattle; and/or jewelry, all of which become her property and which she alone disposes of as she sees fit (e.g., distribution to family, sale, capital investment). The educational process not only provides her with the knowledge of this skill, it also makes her aware of its importance. Guajiro women think very highly of their productive skills.

When asked directly, the Guajiras at first deny that they find women more important in their society; they bring up all sorts of arguments to demonstrate that they find the tasks of both sexes equally vital to the survival of the whole culture: What would a family do if there were no men to go and look after the animals? What would a family do if they had no women who did the weaving? A family is happy to have a baby girl, who will be a hard worker one day; but everybody welcomes a boy just as much. Once they had made their point that both men and women were necessary to keep the social order going, however, women often fell pensive and finally expressed a thought, something like the following: "Well, both work hard, but the woman gets the better education. She learns many things inside that a man will never know."

Which factors, precisely, give the Guajiro woman the strong position in her society? Data from other cultures can help us to clarify this problem. The group chosen for comparison here are the Mount Hagen people, horticulturists who live in the Western Highland District in Papua New Guinea.[9] While Strathern (1972) does not deal with education per se, she gives a detailed picture of women's abilities, responsibilities, and status in Mount Hagen society. This culture is of interest to us because, like the Guajiro, women in Mount Hagen society are producers: they plant, tend, and harvest the gardens, and raise the pigs that have high value in the exchange system. Unlike the Guajiro, the Mount Hagen people have a patrilineal social organization and follow a patrilocal residence pattern.

Social prestige and status in Mount Hagen society are not associated with production as such but with *exchanging* goods. During childhood girls as well as boys are encouraged to exchange food and small possessions, and the children refer to these activities as *moka*, as the exchange system of the adult is called. But later, in adult life, only the men are active exchange partners and the woman stays in the background growing the plants to feed the pigs with and taking care of the pigs themselves. The women look at the pig as an end in itself—the pig is food; the men see a pig as a means for obtaining other valuables like shells and for enhancing their status by the procedure of exchange itself. The men decide how garden land is allocated, a crucial decision affecting woman's work, for only a good plot will produce strong plants to feed the pigs well. The men prepare the pork at the ceremonial occasions and distribute it. They believe that "women lack the intelligence to judge when it is ready," and improper judgment of cooking time is considered to be a bad omen. Thus, the Mount Hagen woman produces the economic basis of her society without having any power to make vital decisions in its regard. The women express their resentment, but they cannot speak out in public. Women are seen as weak beings. Don't they leave their natal land when they marry? Isn't it only through the husband that they establish ties with the land? And people agree among themselves that a woman without a husband is nothing. A woman is always under the guardianship of a male and "hence has no explicit title to property of any consequence" (Meggitt, 1974:186).

The Mount Hagen woman does not possess so highly specialized a skill as does the Guajiro woman. The Guajira produces and owns a product she herself can exchange for other goods. And while the Guajiro men control money and cattle as well, she alone controls the woven products. The Guajira is economically flexible in contrast with the Mount Hagen woman who cannot exchange the pigs herself.

The lesson we learn here is valid for women in tribal as well as in industrial cultures: work as such does not help a woman to attain a high social position in her society, but the fact that the work is *skilled* does. The ultimate meaning is that an education that transmits skills and knowledge *highly valued by society* is necessary for the woman if she is to obtain a high status in her society. Theoretically, this type of education not only would transmit practical or technical skills, but also would transmit the values connected with these skills and would determine the high valuation of those who perform them. It is therefore necessary to study in further research the sociocultural factors (such as matrilineality, division of labor, beliefs connected with these complexes) underlying educational concepts and how and why these favor men or women in a given society.

## NOTES

1. If no other sources are indicated, the ethnographic data are derived from fieldwork in 1972 in the Venezuelan Guajira.

2. See Wilbert, 1972.

3. The following data apply equally to boys and girls unless otherwise indicated.

4. With these phrases the Guajiro circumscribe the onset of the first menstruation.

5. It might also be that the menstrual flow ceases soon. Gutiérrez de Pineda (1950:55) mentioned that the medicine causes the menstrual bleeding to stop during the whole time the girl is secluded. This was not mentioned by my informants.

6. To explain this as a form of baby food because the girl is treated like a newborn, helpless, innocent creature does not truly make sense, since she is not allowed to drink milk. Could it be that this diet contains certain elements influencing the hormone system and thus the physiological development of the girl, as research on the diet of pubescent girls in Australian tribal cultures has shown?

7. Interesting in this context is that the Guajiro also enclose people who have killed or seriously injured another person. The offender stays inside for weeks, months, or even one to two years, observing certain food taboos; such a person must be fed, must wear specially made new clothes, and must have only limited and selected social contacts. Here it becomes apparent that isolation is seen as an effective measure to deal with crises in life.

8. This concept that a solid education is very important for the girl does not change even under the impact of acculturation, as for example, when the family moves to the city. Only the motives change. Women in the peninsula explained the necessity of a girl's education in terms of a woman's social and economic responsibilities in Guajiro adult life. Women in the city stressed the importance of self-reliance in women, since the possibility of being abandoned by the husband was considered a great possible risk, one that had actually been observed or experienced by many; thus the girl had to be prepared to fend for herself and her family one day. Conflicts over this question arose as to how to do this most effectively, since in the city environment conflicting value patterns affected the parent (Watson, 1975a; 1975b).

9. All data referring to this region are taken from Strathern, 1972, unless otherwise indicated.

# BIBLIOGRAPHY

Baily, Wilfrid C.
   1972    "The Role of Education in Bringing about Change." In *Aspects of Cultural Change*. Joseph B. Aceves, ed. Southern Anthropological Society Proceedings no. 6. Athens, Ga. Pp. 31–48.

Fénelon, François de Salignac de La Mothe
   (1687)  *The Education of Girls*. Boston.
   1890

Gutiérrez de Pineda, Virginia
   1950    "Organización social en la Guajira." *Revista del Instituto Etnológico Nacional* (Bogota) 2(2).

Herskovits, Melville J.
   1943    "Education and Cultural Dynamics." *American Journal of Sociology* 48(6): 737–749.

Karsten, Rafael
   (1923)  *The Toba Indians of the Bolivian Gran Chaco*. Acta Academica Aboensis.
   1967    Humaniora IV. Oosterhout.

López Ramírez, T.
   1945    "Algunos datos sobre la menstruación, la preñez, el aborto y el parto." *Acta Venezolana* 1:34–43.

Mead, Margaret
1935    *Sex and Temperament in Three Primitive Societies.* New York.

Meggitt, M. J.
1974    " 'Pigs Are Our Hearts': The Te Exchange Cycle among the Mae Enga of New Guinea." *Oceania* 44(3):165-203.

Monroe, Paul
1906    *A Textbook in the History of Education.* New York.

Pichón, F. D.
1947    *Geografía de la Guajira.* Santa Marta.

Polanco, José Antonio
1958    "Notícias guajiras por un guajiro. Part 3." *Boletín Indigenista Venezolano* 6 (1-4):131-136.

Read, Margaret
1960    *Children of Their Fathers: Growing Up among the Ngoni of Nyasaland.* New Haven, Conn.

Spindler, George D.
1963    "Anthropology and Education: An Overview." In *Education and Culture: Anthropological Approaches.* George D. Spindler, ed. Stanford. Pp. 53-83.

Strathern, Marilyn
1972    *Women in Between: Female Roles in a Male World, Mount Hagen, New Guinea.* London.

Todd, Arthur James
1913    *The Primitive Family as an Educational Agency.* New York.

Watkins, Mark Hanna
1943    "The West African 'Bush' School." *American Journal of Sociology* 48(6):666-675.

Watson, Lawrence C.
1966    "The Guajiro Life Cycle." Ms. Venezuelan Indian Project. Latin American Center, University of California, Los Angeles.
1968    *Guajiro Personality and Urbanization.* Latin American Studies vol. 10. Latin American Center, University of California, Los Angeles.
1975    "Learning To Cope: Urbanization and Cognitive Adaptation among the Guajiro of Maracaibo." Ms.
1976    "Urbanization, Cognition and Socialization of Educational Values: The Case of the Guajiro Indians of Venezuela." Chap. 13 of this volume.

Watson-Franke, Maria-Barbara
1974    "A Woman's Profession in Guajiro-Culture: Weaving." *Antropologica* (Caracas) 37:24-40.

Wilbert, Johannes
1972    *Survivors of Eldorado: Four Indian Cultures of South America.* New York.

Yeld, E. R.
1961    "Educational Problems among Women and Girls in Socoto Province of Northern Nigeria." *Sociologus* 2:160-173.

# 6.

# The Inca *Warachikuy* Initiations

## DOUGLAS SHARON

Among the empire-building Inca aristocracy, adolescent initiation ceremonies for sons of the nobility were used to socialize future leaders into the beliefs and values of church and state. The rituals (Warachikuy) by which such internalization was accomplished have quite correctly been compared to the tests and ceremonies performed in medieval Europe to bestow knighthood on youths of noble blood. But the Warachikuy—although reinforcing state institutions—was of the same order as puberty initiations in simpler societies lacking political organization. In both instances the goal is the same: incorporation of the young into the roles and norms of adult society.

Rowe (1946:283–284, 308–311) summarizes the information and bibliography on Inca initiation ceremonies extracted from the ethnohistorical sources.[1] The most detailed and reliable accounts of these rituals are Molina of Cuzco (1947:chap. 6, pp. 91–119),[2] first written in 1572, and Cobo (1956:bk. 13, chaps. 25, 30, pp. 207–213, 219–220), composed in 1653.

In writing his account of the Warachikuy Cobo used Molina's data, as well as information gathered in the 1550s by Licentiate Juan Polo de Ondegardo. The bulk of Polo's material is now lost, so that Cobo's version of it is all we have. Thus, where Cobo's report differs from Molina's we know that these passages are based on the earlier and somewhat more reliable work of Polo. Even this earlier material was gathered about twenty years after the Conquest, however, and is based on the recollections of informants, not on firsthand observation. Unfortunately, so far as we know at this time, none of the eyewitness chroniclers of the Conquest—some of whom were direct observers of Inca rituals—wrote detailed accounts of the Warachikuy. It appears that we will probably never know all the details of this ritual.

Other chroniclers give abbreviated versions of the Warachikuy, or provide additional information on limited aspects of the ceremony. Thus, after discussing the Cobo and Molina versions, the reports of Pachacuti (1950, written ca. 1613), Garcilaso (1966, finished in 1609), Cieza (1959, written in 1551), and Fernández (1963, written in 1571) are summarized to develop the fullest account possible of these important state rituals. In accord with ethnohistorical methodology, each account is summarized using the same style, details, and chronological order as the original author. Also, key terms such as Quechua words and place names rendered in Spanish are replicated as found in the sources cited.

## Molina's Version

In Molina's report on the Inca calendar we are informed that in the month of *omac raymi,* which he correlates with September in the European calendar, the Indians of Oma, a town two leagues from Cuzco, performed what he refers to as the *guarachico* ceremony, during which young men were knighted and had their ears pierced. Meanwhile, in Cuzco the mothers of youths eligible for knighthood began preparations for rituals that took place in the Inca capital throughout the month of November. Women of the same lineage met together in each other's homes to drink and weave the clothing that their sons were to wear for the initiatory rites. The future knights were kept busy with tasks assigned to them by the Inca.

Molina claims that October was named *ayarmaca raymi* because this was the month when the Indians of Ayarmaca (Ayamarca) knighted their young men in ceremonies similar to those performed later at the capital. In Cuzco the *chicha* (maize beer) for the forthcoming ceremonies was brewed by a method called *cantaray.* Youths eligible for initiation made a pilgrimage to Guanacauri (Huanacauri) hill, on which was located the principal *guaca* (or *huaca,* sacred place, shrine, or object) of the Incas— considered to be the brother of the first Inca, Manco Capac. The journey was made to offer sacrifices at the huaca and seek its permission for the forthcoming rite of passage. The boys spent the night at the huaca, in imitation of their ancestors' activities during the migration to the Cuzco region recounted in Inca mythology. The next day the youths fasted, while returning to Cuzco bearing bundles of straw on which to seat their parents and other relatives.

November was called *capac raymi,* festival of the lord Inca, one of the three major celebrations of the year, according to Molina. During the first eight days of the month all of the parents and relatives of the knights-to-be prepared the necessary paraphernalia for their wards: sandals (*ojotas*) of special straw (*ooya* [*sic*], for *coya*), slings (*guaracas*) of llama leather, and black embroidery for special tunics (*chumpicacico*) of tawny llama wool over which were worn white wool capes (*supaya colla*) that reached to the knees and were tied at the neck with a thick woolen cord ending in a red tassel. On their heads the candidates wore black caps (*llautus*).

On the morning of the ninth day everyone gathered in the plaza. The parents and relatives of the initiates wore an outfit called *collca oncu*, tawny-colored capes, and a headdress (*quitotica*) made from the black feathers of the *quito* bird. After having their hair cut, the candidates for knighthood donned the outfits prepared for them by their relatives. Many girls aged eleven, twelve, and fifteen years were also present at the plaza, dressed in outfits called *cusca acsu* and *cochilliquilla*. Referred to as *ñusta callixapa*, they were from a principal lineage and served as chicha bearers during the festival.

After gathering in the plaza, the participants went to the Temple of the Sun to bring out the images or huacas of the principal deities (Sun, Thunder, Moon, etc.) of the Inca pantheon. These were carried in procession back to the plaza. The image of the Moon (*passa mama*), considered to be female, was carried by the women. When the cult icons were set up in the plaza, the Inca took his place beside the image of the Sun, and the young nobles passed in review, making the sign of *mucha* (blowing a kiss), the standard Inca gesture of reverence offered to sacred personages, objects, and places. They remained standing until noon, when they again saluted the huacas, and—after seeking permission from the Inca— departed for a place named Matagua at the foot of Huanacauri, where they spent the night. Each candidate, accompanied by his relatives, took one llama for sacrifice to the cult object on top of Huanacauri hill.

At sunrise on the tenth day, a day of fasting for everyone present, the party climbed up to the huaca accompanied by priests (*tarpuntaes*), who tore a little wool off each sacrificial llama. At the top of the hill the priests burned five llamas in front of the huaca and then distributed the torn wool among the initiates and their relatives. The latter blew the wool into the air while addressing a prayer to the Creator, Sun, Thunder, and Moon. After the prayer, at nine A.M. the priests gave the boys slings and bundles of straw, admonishing them as follows: "Now that our father Huanacauri has given you slings, be brave and sound and live as honorable people." The slings were made of llama leather and *chaguar* wood, after the fashion of the slings borne by their ancestors when they emerged from the sacred place of origin, Pacaritambo, during the Creation.

Descending the hill, the party came to a ravine named Quirasmanta where the initiates' fathers and uncles whipped the boys' arms and legs in the name of the huacas, addressing them in the following fashion:

"Be brave as I have been and a man of good; and receive the graces that I have so that you will imitate me." Then, while the candidates remained standing and holding the bundles of straw, their relatives sat down and sang a song (*taqui*)[3] called *guari* (or Huari or Wari after an ancient deity).

Upon completion of the song, the elders stood up and the company started back to Cuzco. On the road home they were met by a royal herdsman who was in charge of special llamas (*raymi napas*) dedicated to Inca festivals. He was accompanied by a consecrated llama (*napa*) dressed in a red tunic and wearing golden ear spools, musicians playing on seashell trumpets (*gayllaiquipas*), and an Indian bearing the royal standard (*suntur paucar*). When the two groups met a dance was performed, and the entire procession—led by the sacred llama and royal standard—went to the central plaza of Cuzco. The candidates continued to carry their bundles of straw while their slings were wrapped around their heads.

Back in the plaza, after everyone offered reverence to the principal Inca deities, the boys were again whipped by their relatives. There followed the taqui called guari performed by all. Then the youths served drinks to the elders who had whipped them. By this time it was nearly evening, so everyone returned to their houses to feast on sacrificed llamas, and the priests placed the cult images back in their temples.

For the next few days the boys rested in their homes in preparation for the remaining events of the Warachikuy. On the fourteenth day of the month they again assembled in the plaza of Cuzco with their relatives. (Here Molina digresses briefly to point out that the initiates had to be directly descended in the male line from the Inca aristocracy. In November provincial governors performed the same rituals in their territories as those carried out in Cuzco whenever they had sons who had come of age.) The images of the Creator, Sun, Thunder, and Moon, accompanied by their respective priests and the Inca, were once more set up in the plaza. Out of the stores collected from the people for the sun cult, the chief priest gave the candidates outfits called *misca onco*: red- and white-striped tunics and white capes with blue cords ending in a red tassel. Their parents gave them the special sandals made at the beginning of the month. The girl chicha bearers were given women's clothing of the same colors.

Once outfitted, the initiates hung their slings on palm wood halberds (*yauri*), which they brandished while offering reverence to the huacas of the Creator, Sun, Thunder, and Moon, and to the Inca. Just before this their relatives had whipped them with their slings on the arms and legs, while urging them to be brave and to render service to the huacas and the Inca.

The boys then went to an uninhabited place named Raurana (Yaurana?), one league from Cuzco, to spend the night in tents. They were accompanied by the girl chicha bearers, the sacred llama (raymi napa or *topa guanaco*) with the red tunic and golden ear spools, and the royal standard. When they had left the plaza, the huacas were returned to their temples and the Inca went home.

The next morning the group walked a little more than half a league to a ravine near the hill named Quilliyacolca, where they stopped for lunch. After lunch they decorated their halberd blades with fine straw (*ycho*) and white wool. Such halberds were called *topa yauri*. They walked to the hill of Anaguarque (Anahuarque), two leagues from Cuzco, to sacrifice at the huaca on its summit that gave the hill its name. This was the huaca of the Indians of Choco and Cachona. It was said that since the time of the Flood the huaca remained so light that it could run like a falcon in flight.

At the huaca the candidates offered it wool that they carried in their hands. The sun priests and priests from the other huacas (*tarpuntaes*) burned five llamas as sacrifices to the Creator, Sun, Thunder, Moon, and Inca. Relatives of the initiates whipped them on the arms and legs using the boys' own slings and admonishing them to be brave. Then, while the youths remained standing, the rest of the company sat down to perform the *guarita* (guari?) song accompanied by shell trumpets (this time spelled *guayllaquipas* by the scribe who copied Molina's original manuscript).

After the song, the girl chicha bearers ran back to where the party had spent the night. Here, waiting with chicha, they called out to the initiates to come quickly. At the summit the boys formed a line in front of the huaca. Behind them were two more lines: one of halberd bearers and another of assistants to help the boys if they fainted or fell. At a signal from a richly attired Indian, the youths ran down the hill. Some of the runners ended up with battered shins, others were killed in falls. At the bottom of the hill the thirsty contestants were given chicha by the girls who were waiting for them. The purpose of this race was to discover which candidates were the strongest. Each time the race was run, at least eight hundred youths participated.

Once back at the hill named Yaurana (the first time the scribe spelled it Raurana), the group performed the guari song. When finished, the initiates' slings were removed from their halberds so that the boys' relatives could whip them on the legs and arms. By this time it was about the hour of vespers, so the entire party returned to the plaza in Cuzco, led by the sacred llama and the royal standard.

As they entered the plaza the youths performed the mucha for the images of the Creator, Sun, Thunder, Moon, and for the Inca, who was seated with his court near the image of the Sun. The members of the two moieties of the city (Hanan or Upper Cuzco and Hurin or Lower Cuzco) sat in their respective sections of the plaza. Standing before the people of Cuzco, the initiates performed the guari song and then were whipped by their relatives. Since it was now evening, the Inca and his court retired to their respective homes.

That same evening the candidates and their relatives went to a place called Guaman (or Huaman) Cancha at the foot of Yauira (Yavira) hill, half a league from Cuzco, where they spent the night. The next morning at dawn the party climbed the hill to the huaca, where the Inca joined them to award the youths gold ear spools and red capes with blue tassels.

Here Molina digresses to inform us that the huaca was instituted by Pachacuti Inca Yupanqui as the place where knights were to receive their breechclouts or *guaras*. It was the major huaca of the Indians of Maras. Huascar Inca embellished the huaca by having two stone falcons placed on the altar at the top of the hill.

The *guacamayo* or priest of the huaca burned five llamas and offered libations of chicha, asking the Creator, Sun, Thunder, and Moon to grant that the new knights would be brave, unconquerable warriors, successful in every venture they undertook. Then he issued the youths' breechclouts (*guarayaros*) along with red- and white-striped tunics—both of which were collected as tribute from the Inca subjects. The boys also received gold ear spools, which were tied to their ears, as well as feathered diadems (*pilco cassa*) and necklaces made of gold and silver medals. After lunching at the huaca, the initiates performed the guari song for an hour—following which they were whipped by their relatives, who urged the youths to follow the example of their brave warrior ancestors who never retreated. When the whipping was finished, the party returned to Cuzco behind the royal standard and the sacred llama.

Molina tells us here that the guari song was given by the Creator to the first Inca, Manco Capac, when he emerged from the cave of origin at Tambo (Pacaritambo). It was to be used only for the capac raymi festival—the four ceremonies (at Huanacauri, Anahuarque, Yaurana, and Yavira) of which were instituted by Manco Capac with his own son, Sinchi Roca.

Back in the plaza at Cuzco the boys offered mucha to the principal huacas of the Inca faith, as well as to the royal mummies that had been brought out with the other cult icons so that the boys could drink with them "as if they were alive." The initiates also petitioned their deified royal ancestors to make them fortunate and brave.

When the youths were seated in their respective moieties, dancers dressed as felines appeared. On their heads they wore feline skulls decorated with attached golden disks, golden ear spools, and golden teeth replacing the originals. The skull was joined to the pelt at the neck, into which the dancer inserted his head so that the pelt hung over his shoulders. Golden bracelets were placed on the legs of the pelt. The remainder of the dancer's costume consisted of a red tunic with a red and white border, reaching to the feet. The tunic was called *puca caycho anco*. The feline dancers were called *hilla cunya chuqui cunya*, and the name of their dance was *coyo*. Invented by Pachacuti Inca Yupanqui, it was performed twice daily for six days to the beat of four drums, two from Hanan Cuzco and two from Hurin Cuzco. On each of the six days sacrifices of llamas, clothing, gold, silver, and the like, were made to the Creator, Sun, Thunder, Moon, and Inca on behalf of the initiates so they would be fortunate in war and in all their enterprises.

On the twenty-first day of the month the initiates went to bathe in the Calixpuquio (Calispuquio) springs behind the fortress of Cuzco, a quarter of a league from the city. At the springs they removed the outfits they had worn during their initiation, replacing them with others called *uanaclla*. The new outfits were black and yellow with a red cross in the middle.

After the bath the young men returned to the plaza in Cuzco to offer the customary reverence to the major huacas. Then they went to their homes to receive gifts from their kinsmen. Each new warrior received from his principal uncle a shield, a sling, and a club to be used in war. Then the other relatives gave the youth clothing, llamas, gold, silver, and so on. When delivering his gift, each relative gave the recipient one lash—along with a lecture to be brave, to never betray the Sun or the Inca, not to neglect the cult of the huacas, and to imitate the valor and bravery of his ancestors. When a future ruler was knighted, all of the officials of the region gave him similar gifts as well as herdsmen for his flocks. Once the gifts had been distributed, bundles of firewood were dressed with men's and women's clothing and burned, along with a llama and two birds (*pilco pechio* [*pishgo?*] and *camantira pechio*), as a sacrifice to the Creator, the Sun, and the Inca to request that the new knights be successful in warfare.

On the twenty-second day of the month the youths had their ears pierced in the agricultural fields (*chacaras* or *chacras*) or in their homes. If the ear split during the opening ceremony, this was interpreted as a bad omen for the unfortunate youth. After the ear was pierced, cotton threads were passed through the holes. These were replaced each day with increasingly larger threads to open up the holes to support large ear spools.

Molina includes material regarding rituals associated with the ear-piercing ceremony not contained in Cobo. Immediately after the ear piercing, on the same day, the priests of the Creator, Sun, Thunder, and Moon—and the herders of the state herds belonging to the Inca—counted the number of llamas in the herds of church and state. On this day began the rituals for the church flocks, conducted throughout the empire to guarantee the increase of these herds. The llamas were sprinkled with chicha and the herders were given food and clothing. Those whose flocks showed the most increase were given more goods, while those who showed no increase were punished.

On the twenty-third day of the month the statue of the sun (*huayna punchao*) was carried to the "houses of the sun" known as *puquin*, located on a high hill. Here for several days sacrifices were made to the Creator, Sun, Thunder, and Moon to guarantee that "the people would multiply and all things would be prosperous." During these days everyone drank and celebrated. Once the sacrifices came to an end, the statue of the Sun was returned to its temple in a procession headed by the royal standard, a golden llama (*cullquinapa*), and a silver llama (*curinapa*)—these being the Sun's insignias, which accompanied the statue wherever it went. With this procession capac raymi came to an end.

## Cobo's Version

Turning now to Cobo's report of the Inca calendar, we are informed that in the month of *homa-raymi puchayquiz*, which he correlates with October in the European calendar, the mothers of youths eligible for knighthood met in each other's houses to drink and weave their sons' outfits. In the meantime, the boys were kept busy with tasks assigned to them by the Inca.

On the second day of November (*ayamarca*) the future knights went to Guanacauri to ask permission to be knighted in December, since this was their principal huaca and the brother of Manco Capac. They slept at Huanacauri in imitation of the pilgrimage made to the site by their ancestors. The priests of the huaca gave the boys slings, lined their faces with llama blood, and then sacrificed the llamas that the candidates brought especially for the anointment and sacrifice. In the afternoon of the following day the boys returned to Cuzco, bringing a bundle of straw for their relatives to sit upon during the forthcoming celebrations. During the day they fasted and received fine tunics from their relatives. The candidates were also required to chew the maize used in the preparation of the chicha to be consumed during the December festivities. Their fathers and uncles brought the special water from the sacred spring of Callispuquiu to be added to the masticated maize. Relatives supplied the firewood and containers in which to prepare the chicha. During the fabrication process a woolly white llama was burned to guarantee the quality of the brew. The entire month of November was spent in preparation for Capac Raymi. Each day the candidates paraded around the central plaza with their elders, concluding with drinking and sacrifices performed to guarantee that the youths would be good knights. Outsiders were sent out of the city, since only the citizens of Cuzco were allowed to see these ceremonies. Cobo says this festival, called Ytu-Raymi, was also performed whenever there was pestilence or too much or too little rain. To end the month, each of the two moieties of Cuzco paraded and sacrificed four llamas. Then outsiders were allowed back into the city.

During *raymi,* the first month of the Inca year, which Cobo correlates with December in the European calendar, the festival of Capac Raymi (rich or principal festival) was celebrated. Cobo informs us that to be eligible for the knighthood ceremonies that dominated this festival, a young man had to be a direct relative and descendant of the Inca kings. Even the crown prince and his brothers, if he had any, had to be initiated. Although Cuzco was the major center for these ceremonies, provincial governors of the royal line performed the rites in their regional capitals for their sons and their sons' noble age mates. Boys between the ages of twelve and fifteen were selected to receive breechclouts and have their ears pierced.

At this point in his narration Cobo refers back to preparations made in previous months. He tells us that these preparations were begun well in advance of the festival. First, a large group of girls of noble birth from twelve to thirteen and fourteen years of age were selected to serve in the festival. A few days before it began, they were at the hill named Chacaguanacauri weaving the borders for the boys' breechclouts (guaras). While they were there, the huaca or idol of Huanacauri was placed on the hill. The future knights also went to this hill to collect straw with which to decorate their halberds. Leftover straw was divided among their relatives, who were responsible for providing the sacrifices, gifts, chicha, and outfits for the festival. Cobo gives exactly the same description of the outfits worn by the candidates and their relatives as that provided by Molina.

On the first day of December all of the leading nobles assembled in the plaza of the Temple of the Sun to organize the festival. They ordered all noncitizens to leave Cuzco until the festival was over. These people were assigned to dwellings located where the four major roads of the empire entered Cuzco. They were joined by tribute bearers from the four quarters of the empire, who waited to be received by state officials and priests.

This same day the knights-to-be were brought by their relatives to the plaza of the Temple of the Sun, where the images of Viracocha, the Sun, Moon, and Thunder were placed on golden benches decorated with feathers. The embalmed mummies of past Incas were also brought out for display in the temple plaza. (Such displays of idols and mummies were customary on all of the solemn occasions of each month.) The mummies were included so their descendants could drink with them as if they were alive, and, on this occasion, so the candidates could ask their ancestors to make them as brave and fortunate as they had been.

Once all had congregated, the Inca appeared, accompanied by the highest nobles of the court. He took his seat next to the image of the Sun, while his court sat around him in a tight circle. Then one hundred of the largest and healthiest llamas to be found in the empire were brought in. Their wool was long and their tails were raised and straight. After being led four times around the statues of the major Inca deities, the llamas were offered to Viracocha, on behalf of the Sun, by the chief sun priest. Thirty Indians were charged with sacrificing three llamas per day and four on some days, so that the one hundred would be consumed by the end of the month. The sacrifice was carried out by quartering the animal in four equal parts, which were subsequently added to a large bonfire. Great care was taken not to lose any blood or body parts when delivering the quarters to the fire. White maize, ground chile peppers, and coca were also thrown into the fire. The unburned bones of the llama were ground up and blown into the air to the accompaniment of an invocation. Left-over powder was placed in a hut in the Pomachupa district of the city, where it was kept with great veneration. Identical rituals were performed on the first day of each month.

On the second day of December, six old llamas called *aporucos* were led into the plaza by six herders carrying maize and coca with which to feed the animals. The aporucos were paraded in this fashion for four days, until by the fifth of the month the candidates and their relatives were ready to begin the actual initiation ceremonies. On the fifth day, after assembling in the plaza and offering reverence to the Inca and the assembled deities, the candidates and their relatives requested permission from the Inca to begin the ceremonies.

Permission granted, the party set off for Huanacauri hill with the royal insignias, a white llama (napa) and the standard called Sunturpaucar, in the lead. The white llama, believed to be the first of its species to appear after the Flood, wore a red tunic and golden earplugs. It was accompanied by two female priestesses who carried chicha for it to drink. It was trained to eat coca. Herds of these special animals were kept and venerated by the Inca. They were never killed, and were buried with great solemnity when they died. The royal llama was accompanied by the six old aporucos and six young llamas from herds owned by the state sun cult. The young Inca nobles carried the slings they had received in November in their left hands. In their right hands they carried cord made from the century plant.

The party slept that night at the foot of Huanacauri hill. The next day at sunrise they approached the temple and the huaca at the top of the hill. The boys delivered their slings to the priests of the shrine (the slings were returned the next day), who then bled the old aporuco llamas from a vein above the right leg while the candidates lowered their heads so as to be anointed by the spurting blood. When all had been anointed, the llamas' wounds were closed and they were dressed in tunics, earplugs being placed in their ears. Then clothing, sacrifices, the six young llamas from the flocks of the sun cult, and llamas brought by the initiates were all burned. Before being sacrificed, the six young llamas were bled while being led around the hill. On the spot where they bled to death they were burned. During the burning ceremony the initiates and their relatives blew tufts of the llamas' wool, torn from them by the priests before being bled, into the air while supplicating the huaca of Huanacauri to guarantee the health and prosperity of the Inca and to favor the youths in their endeavors. To conclude the rites on Huanacauri, six small earplugs of silver and gold donated by the Inca were buried in the huaca.

On the return to Cuzco the party—led again by the royal standard, the white llama, and the aporuco llamas—stopped at a ravine where the fathers and uncles of the boys whipped them on the legs and arms with the boys' own slings, while admonishing the initiates to be strong and good in imitation of their elders. After the slings were returned to them, the initiates performed a combination dance and song called guari.

Once returned to Cuzco, the group proceeded to the principal plaza where the candidates—after offering reverence to the major huacas—were once again whipped by their elders with their own slings. Then all present performed the taqui, or dance, called guari to the accompaniment of large seashell trumpets. When the taqui was finished, the boys offered drinks to their elders and the priests sacrificed the aporuco llamas, the fresh meat from which was served raw to the candidates. This ritual was believed to give them permanent strength. At last everyone returned home, and the priests replaced the major idols of the Inca pantheon in their places.

For the next six days the boys rested in their homes in preparation for the remaining tests of their initiation. At the middle of the month they returned to the plaza where, in the presence of the Inca, the principal priest of the sun issued them special clothing from the stores collected by the state from the people. Cobo's description of the boys' clothing, as well as that issued to the girl chicha bearers, parallels the Molina data. The boys received halberds (yauri) which they draped with wool, straw, and their slings. Then, brandishing their halberds like pikes, the boys saluted the major deities and the Inca before departing for another sacred hill, Anaguarque, near Huanacauri. This time the group included the girls from the nobility who had been selected to carry the containers of chicha for the rituals.

As on the previous pilgrimage to Huanacauri, the party was preceded by the royal standard, the white llama, six old aporuco llamas, and six young llamas. The llamas were sacrificed in the same manner and order as during the Huanacauri pilgrimage.

Tradition held that from the time of the Flood this huaca had been so light that it could run like a falcon in flight. Thus it was the site of a race to test the candidates. Once the group arrived at the huaca on the hill, the boys offered wool and the priests performed the same ceremonies and sacrifices as at Huanacauri. Then the elders whipped the initiates, admonishing them not to be lazy in the service of the Inca, advising them that they would be punished if they were, and reminding them of the reason for the ceremony and of the victories the Incas had realized as a result of the fortitude of the boys' fathers. This ordeal over, the boys stood with their halberds in their hands while the rest of the party seated themselves and performed the taqui called guari.

After the taqui, the maidens rose with their chicha containers and ran down the hill to await the boys' arrival. They called to the boys, admonishing them to hurry, as they were waiting for them. At this point the boys formed many lines with alternate lines of elders between them, so that each line of boys was backed up by the boys' respective relatives—who subsequently watched out for the safety of their wards. In front of the lines a richly attired official gave the signal, and the multitude was off. Some were seriously injured in the scramble. When the participants reached the bottom of the hill, the maidens served chicha first to the elders and then to the boys.

The group also went to Sabaraura hill, where six llamas were burned and others were buried, followed by individual sacrifices. Once again the boys were whipped, after which all returned to the plaza in Cuzco and rendered reverence to the principal huacas and the Inca. Then while the two moieties of Cuzco—Hanan or Upper Cuzco and Hurin or Lower Cuzco—sat in separate sections of the plaza, the initiates danced and sang the guari. Afterwards they were whipped again. Since by this time it was dusk, the Inca and his court retired to their homes and the boys and their elders left for Yavirá hill, directly across from Carmenga. The usual llama sacrifices were offered, after which the boys received their breechclouts and helmets along with gifts offered on behalf of the Inca (golden earplugs, which were tied to their ears, feather diadems, and necklaces of gold and silver medals). After performing the usual dance, the boys were again whipped. Returning to Cuzco, they offered reverence to the principal huacas.

Up to this juncture in the narrative both Molina and Cobo agree regarding the order and general details of each ritual, with Cobo providing more details on the llama sacrifices. From this point forward Cobo and Molina disagree as to the order of the remaining ceremonies performed at the end of Capac Raymi—although their descriptions continue to agree in many of the details.

The next ceremony described by Cobo is a bath in the springs of Calispúquiu, behind the fortress of Cuzco, approximately one mile from the city. After bathing in the springs, the youths returned to the plaza in Cuzco where their relatives bestowed gifts upon them. The first relative to do this was the principal uncle, who gave his nephew a circular shield, a sling, and a mace or club to be used in warfare. Behind him came the other relatives, who established the young noble's property base with their gifts. Each relative gave the youth one lash, accompanied by a short admonition to be brave and loyal to the Inca, and to take great care in revering the cult of the huacas. When an Inca prince was initiated, all of the principal chiefs from the empire were present to deliver rich gifts.

The last initiation ceremony for the young Inca nobles consisted of piercing their ears out in the chacaras (agricultural fields) of the Cuzco area. This was followed by public ceremonies and a dance in the plaza, referred to collectively by Cobo as Aucayo. For these rituals lumps of cornmeal were mixed with the blood of sacrificed llamas. On this day outsiders were again allowed to enter Cuzco, where they were offered these lumps by priests of the Tarpuntay lineage as a gift from the sun, to content them so they would not feel excluded from his festivities. This repast was served on great plates of gold and silver from the table service of the sun cult reserved especially for the purpose. As the recipients consumed what was given them, they offered words and gestures of thanks to the Sun. After they had eaten, the priests admonished them that this food of the Sun would remain in their bodies as a witness to report any heresies against the Sun or the Inca. Such would be revealed, and the offenders would be punished. The recipients were required to promise that they would not speak out against their benefactors at any time in their lives, as a condition for participation in this ceremony. Several days were spent dancing and drinking without rest. The music for the dancing was performed on four large drums of the Sun, each played by four Indian leaders dressed in feline garb. Cobo's description of their outfits corresponds with that of Molina in every detail.

According to Cobo, the dance opened with the sacrifice of two young llamas, performed by four old men. When the dance was over, thirty llamas were brought from the herds of the Inca and divided, along with thirty outfits, among the officiating priests, who were charged by the Inca with offering sacrifices in his name to all of the huacas of Cuzco. Thirty bunches of firewood were dressed like men and women and burned as an offering to the Sun on behalf of the new knights.

On the last day of the month the celebrants visited the plaza of Puquin hill bearing a large golden llama, a large silver llama, six young llamas, several dressed aporucos, thirty white llamas, six llamas of silver and gold, seashells, and clothing. Here everything, except the gold and silver images, was burned. With this ceremony, Capac Raymi came to an end.

Cobo closes his chapter on Capac Raymi with information about enlarging the holes in the knights' ears after piercing. His data replicate Molina's account.

## Comparison of Molina and Cobo

We cannot distinguish on which day of the month each ritual occurred because the combined information of Molina and Cobo is incomplete and contradictory. For example, Cobo has the candidates leaving Cuzco on the fifth day of the month after a series of llama ceremonies, whereas Molina places this event on the ninth day after eight days of final preparations on costumes. Cobo places these final preparations before the beginning of the Warachikuy. After sleeping at the foot of Huanacauri, Molina says the boys climbed the hill on the morning of the tenth. Once back in Cuzco, the initiates rested for six days according to Cobo. Molina tells us they departed for Anahuarque on the fourteenth, while Cobo simply says they left in the middle of the month. Only Molina gives a day count for the rest of the month—placing the bath at Calispuquio, delivery of arms and gifts, and the burning of the pieces of male and female firewood on the twenty-first, the ear piercing on the twenty-second, and the pilgrimage to Puquin hill on the twenty-third, where rituals were performed for several days. He adds that the feline dance lasted six days, but gives no beginning or ending date.

Despite the gaps in the combined information of Molina and Cobo, a four-week pattern is discernible:

First week    Opening ceremonies (preparation of gear) only
                 (Molina) *or*
              Opening ceremonies (llama rituals) terminating
                 with pilgrimage to Huanacauri (Cobo)
Second week   Pilgrimage to Huanacauri followed by rest (Mo-
                 lina) *or*
              Rest only (Cobo)

| Third week | Pilgrimages to three remaining hills, beginning of feline dance, bath at Calispuquio, delivery of arms and gifts, firewood ceremony (Molina) *or* |
|---|---|
| | Pilgrimages to three remaining hills, bath at Calispuquio, delivery of arms and gifts (Cobo) |
| Fourth week | Ear piercing, end of feline dance (?), counting and animal increase rituals, Puquin hill ceremonies (Molina) *or* |
| | Ear piercing, feline dance (complete cycle, Aucayo), llama and firewood ceremonies (30 of each), Puquin hill ceremonies (Cobo) |

It should be noted that Cobo's lack of dates after the middle of the month makes it difficult to directly verify a fourth week of ceremonies in his account. The activities he places after the ear-piercing rite (which occurs on the twenty-second according to Molina) seem to be end-of-the-month ceremonies—such as outsiders allowed back into Cuzco for the Aucayo rituals, sacrifice of thirty llamas, burning of thirty pieces of firewood (symbolizing the thirty days of the month?), and the Puquin hill ceremonies. The confusion with dates results from the fact that the official Inca calendar was "a day-count calendar of thirty-day months adjusted to the solar year by astronomical observation" with "the extra days . . . distributed among the months." But "the official calendar became obsolete with the fall of the Inca state, and there was a popular use of lunations which outlasted it." Molina and later chroniclers were of the opinion that the Inca calendar was lunar (Professor John Rowe, letter of November 26, 1974). For this reason he placed Inca months one month earlier in the European calendar than did Cobo and appears to be trying to fit the events of the Warachikuy into a lunar scheme. But it is difficult to understand how he concludes with Puquin hill closing ceremonies beginning on the twenty-third of the month, unless he thought they lasted for six days. He simply implies they lasted for several days (" . . . en estos dias").

As noted at the beginning of this paper, Cobo had access to both Molina's data and the earlier work of Polo. From Polo he must have derived the information on the opening ritual instructing the thirty llama herders to perform sacrifices for each day of the month, as well as the extra details on llama sacrifices on the hills, the name of the third hill (Sabauraura), the order of ceremonies performed after the return from Yavira, Aucayo rites, and the sacrifice of thirty llamas followed by the burning of thirty pieces of firewood as the penultimate ceremonies of the

month. It seems that the discrepancy between the two sources confused
Cobo, and he avoided the issue by glossing over it.

## Other Chroniclers

As for additional data provided by other chroniclers, Pachacuti (1950:
221) associates eagles, falcons, vultures, and other birds, as well as foxes,
snakes, and toads, with Huanacauri. He also says that those boys who
proved most fleet received gold and silver breechclouts, while the cowards
received black ones. Fernández (1963:bk. 3, chap. 6, pp. 83–84) claims
that the boys "fasted"—abstained from salt and chile—and were continent for the entire month of Capac Raymi, which he places in November;
that they were given one lash on each arm and leg during whippings; that
the boys had their ears pierced by old men who were specialists in the
presence of the Inca; that the sons of leaders received gold and silver
earplugs, while the other boys received plugs of wood and metal; that
after the ear piercing the boys' relatives sacrificed a llama and removed
its heart for divination by the priests (a stiff heart meaning that the boy
would be brave, while a limp heart meant that the boy would live a short
time and would not be brave or useful); that there were eight drums used
in reunions on all thirty days of the festival (additional confirmation for
a 30-day Inca month); and that after Capac Raymi there were eight days
of drinking and celebration—the first four involving only Incas of the
royal line, the last four including all social groups. Both Cobo (1956:bk.
13, chap. 26, pp. 212–213) and Molina (1947:chap. 6, pp. 118–119) inform us that the month after Capac Raymi, on the first day of the new
moon, the new knights of the two moieties of Cuzco staged a battle (called
*chocanaco* by Molina), shooting cactus fruits at each other with slings.
They even engaged in hand-to-hand encounters. The object of this contest
was to see who were the boldest and most ferocious warriors. After the
battle, in gratitude for the end of their "fast" from salt and chile begun
the first day of Capac Raymi, they dined in black tunics and tawny capes
with white feathers (of the *tocto* bird, according to Molina) in their hair.
Cobo adds that they also sacrificed a llama to the new moon.

Garcilaso (1966:1:bk. 6, chaps. 24–27, pp. 366–374) does not provide
a systematic exposition of the events of the Warachikuy (which he calls
*huaracu*), but his report contains more details regarding the ordeals
undergone by the candidates. These tests qualified them to go to war and
to set up a house. They occurred every year or every other year. Boys had
to be sixteen years of age or older. Garcilaso says that for six days they
had to observe a very strict fast, receiving only a handful of raw maize
and a jug of water apiece. At the same time their fathers, brothers, and

other close relatives underwent a less rigorous fast while praying to the Sun to bring the boys through their ordeals with honor. After the fast came the race, which Garcilaso tells us was run from Huanacauri to the fortress of Cuzco. Whoever arrived first at a banner set up as a finishing post was elected captain over the rest. Runners who placed in second to tenth place were also honored, while those who did not finish were disgraced and eliminated.

The day after the race the boys were divided into two equal groups. One had to defend the fortress against the other. After an entire day of fighting the two groups changed sides. Despite the use of blunted weapons, Garcilaso says that the boys fought with such zeal that there were severe casualties which sometimes were fatal.

When the mock battles were over the candidates were required to compete in wrestling matches, throwing contests (using stones, spears, darts, and so forth), archery and slingshot matches (for accuracy and distance), and other competitions until their use of all of the weapons used in Inca warfare had been tested. To measure their resistance to sleep they had to perform sentinel duty in watches for ten or twelve nights, during which time they would be summoned without warning. If found asleep they were severely reprimanded. Reminiscent of the whippings with slings, Garcilaso informs us that the boys were beaten on the arms and legs with osier rods; if they flinched or showed signs of pain they were eliminated with a comment to the effect that if they could not resist the blows of such light rods, they would not be able to withstand the blows of their enemies' hard weapons. Another test of nerve consisted of lining the boys up and brandishing a *macana* (club) or *chuqui* (lance) in such a fashion that it grazed their legs or swept in front of their eyes. Again, if the boys showed any sign of fear they were rejected. In addition, the boys were required to sleep on the bare ground, eat little and badly, go barefoot, and make all their weapons and footwear. Each day they were given a speech by one of the overseers of the rites in which, to quote Garcilaso (1966:370), they were reminded of:

> the deeds done in peace and war by past kings and other fam-
> ous men of the royal stock; of the courage and spirit they ought
> to show in wars to extend the empire; of patience and endur-
> ance under hardship as a proof of generosity and magnanimity;
> of clemency, pity, and mildness toward their subjects and the
> poor; of rectitude in the administration of justice; of the duty
> to prevent anyone from being wronged; and of liberality and
> openhandedness toward everyone, as befitted children of the
> Sun.

When the firstborn son of the Inca who was the legitimate heir to the throne reached the right age, he was tested with the same strictness as the rest and was not exempt from any contest except for the race for captaincy, the latter being granted to him as part of his birthright. In the hardships imposed upon the initiates, he was treated more harshly than the other candidates, the rationale being that since he was going to be king, he should outdo his peers in anything he undertook. During the entire initiation he was attired in the poorest dress possible. It is possible that Garcilaso—in his zeal for the customs of his mother's forefathers— exaggerates the latter point, for he adds that the future ruler was dressed in this fashion so that when he became king he would not scorn the poor but, rather, he would treat them with charity, remembering that he had worn their clothes and had been one of them.

After their examination, when the candidates had been declared Incas and children of the Sun qualified to wear the insignia of the nobility, their mothers and sisters shod them with footwear (*usuta*) of raw esparto, as witness that their wards had successfully completed the military exercises.

We know that this information conflicts with the versions of Cobo and Molina, who portray the candidates as wearing sandals of fine straw from the beginning of the rituals. The following information on the ear-piercing ceremony, besides providing additional facts, also conflicts with the Cobo and Molina reports. It is presented here, however, in the interest of thoroughness, especially since we do not know which version is correct.

To begin the ear-piercing ceremony, the Inca monarch—accompanied by the eldest Incas of the royal blood—addressed the novices, admonishing them (as worthy sons of the Sun) to exhibit the virtues of their ancestors and to be just and compassionate in their dealings with those below them. One by one the candidates came before their ruler, knelt, and had their ears pierced. The Inca himself pierced the ears with thick gold pins that were left in the ears, so that the lobes could heal and be enlarged. This was the principal rite, the one by which royal insignia were bestowed. Afterward the new knight kissed the monarch's hand and passed on to stand before a brother or uncle of the king, second in authority. This leader replaced the knight's esparto sandals with the fine woolen ones worn by the nobility, as a reward for his exertions and as a sign that his ordeal was over. (Garcilaso likens the latter ceremony to the bestowing of the spurs in European heraldry.) Then the second in command kissed the young man on the right shoulder, saying: "The child of the Sun, who has given proof of himself, deserves to be worshipped." (Garcilaso points out that the verb "to kiss" also means to worship, to revere, and to salute.) After this ceremony the knight entered an enclosure where other senior Incas presented him with the loincloth, which was donned for the first time as a sign of manhood. In addition to the above insignia, the youth's head was adorned with two flowers, the *cantut* (yellow, purple, and red varieties), and the yellow *chihuahua*—flowers which only those of the royal blood were allowed to wear. He also wore on his head a leaf of the green herb called *uinay huaina,* "always young," which resembled the lily leaf and retained its color for a long time. The heir to the throne wore all of the above, to which was added a yellow *borla* or woolen fringe hanging over his forehead. He was also presented with a battle axe called *champi,* as a symbol for chastisement of rebels and traitors. The flowers in his hair symbolized royal clemency, pity, mildness, and other virtues that were to be shown loyal subjects. Finally, all members of the royal line came and knelt before the heir in the presence of his father, a formality that was equivalent to swearing in the heir and successor to the empire.

Cieza (1959:bk. 2, chap. 7, pp. 33–37) gives us an account of the myths that supplied the charter for the Warachikuy. According to the variant of the story told by Cieza, when Manco Capac and a brother were living at Tampu Quiru, their dead brother Ayar Cachi came to them "flying through the air on great wings of colored feathers." The bird-brother instructed them to leave Tampu Quiru and establish Cuzco, where a sumptuous temple could be built to honor and worship the Sun. He resolved that he would remain in his bird-form on the hill of Huanacauri, where the brothers and their descendants were to worship him. If they did, Ayar Cachi promised his aid in war, adding that "the sign you will display from now on to be esteemed, honored, and feared, is that you pierce your ears in the manner you now see me."

Manco and his brother went to Huanacauri where once again Ayar Cachi appeared to them, this time to give instructions on the assumption of the fringe or crown of the empire and how to invest noble youths into knighthood. Cieza then describes the Warachikuy as given by Ayar Cachi, interspersing details of rituals reserved for the future Inca monarch. Although the overall process is similar to that described by Cobo and Molina, certain details that vary seem worthy of mention.

To begin the ceremony, the noble-to-be donned an outfit similar to that worn by Ayar Cachi on Huanacauri that first day: black, collarless shirt with red designs; a long tawny blanket; and on his head a tawny braid twisted in a certain manner. Thus attired, and observing a fast, the candidate spent an entire day gathering a sheaf of straw. Meanwhile his mother and sisters, who also fasted, were required to weave the following garments that same day: a tawny shirt and white mantle; a white shirt and mantle; and a blue shirt with fringes and cords. At this point in the narrative Cieza appears to be talking about the future monarch, for he next tells us that the youth had to fast a month; this fast was carried out in a room of the royal palace without the initiate's seeing fire or having sexual intercourse. Meanwhile, the women of the boy's family prepared chicha. The fast was over when "he who is to be ruler" emerged carrying a halberd of silver and gold, and went to the home of an elder kinsman to have his hair cut.

Directly after his account of the pilgrimage to Huanacauri, Cieza informs us that when the candidates raced down Anahuarque they carried halberds decorated with wool, as a token of their attempt when fighting to bring back enemy hair and heads. Then Cieza inexplicably has them returning to Huanacauri to gather tall-standing straw, and "the one who was to be king" carried a large golden sheaf of it, which he took to Yavira. There he donned another outfit, a golden moon pectoral, golden earplugs, and a fillet (*pillaca*) topped by a bonnet of feathers sewed like a diadem (*puruchucu*). To his halberd was tied a long golden strand that reached the ground. Thus attired, he killed a llama, the blood and flesh of which were served raw to the principal guests. This signified that if they were not brave, their enemies would eat their flesh in the same way as they had eaten the llama's flesh. Then the novices swore a solemn oath by the Sun to uphold the order of chivalry and die defending Cuzco, if that should be necessary. At the end of the ceremony their ears were pierced.

Cieza also describes the feline dance, informing us that the new knights donned the puma heads as a sign that they would be as brave and fierce as these animals. They danced in the square of Cuzco, which was encircled by a great chain of gold supported by posts of silver and gold.

Cieza closes this chapter by returning to Manco and his brother listening to Ayar Cachi's instructions regarding the above rituals of knighthood. After Ayar Cachi ended his narrative, he told Manco to found Cuzco at once. Then he and the other brother turned themselves into two figures of stone in the likeness of men. At this point we also end our narrative, hoping that the contours of the Inca Warachikuy have been rendered more solid.

To extract a summary from so many disparate sources so often at variance, one must begin with some presumption. A close scrutiny of the foregoing chroniclers' accounts, however, reveals the following distillate version of the ritual period of the Warachikuy. After preparation of costumes in October and a pilgrimage to Huanacauri in November, Inca youths underwent three weeks of initiation in December. Initiation rituals consisted of pilgrimages to the huacas of four "hills," Huanacauri,

Anahuarque, Sabaraura (or Yaurana), and Yavira, where llama sacrifices were performed. Before and after each pilgrimage—except the one to Sabaraura (although this may be the result of omission in the sources)—the initiatory party went to the principal square in Cuzco to pay homage to the Inca, the mummies of past rulers, and the assembled deities of the Inca pantheon. At each huaca and in the plaza, the guari taqui was performed, and the boys were whipped while being admonished to be brave and strong in the service of the Inca. The initiates received their halberds before the second pilgrimage to Anahuarque, where a downhill race was staged. On the last pilgrimage to Yavira the candidates received their breechclouts. After a bath in the Calispuquio springs, the youths received their shields, slings, and maces from their principal uncles. Then the young knights had their ears pierced. The last days of the month saw the performance of the feline dance and the burning of the male and female firewood. The month closed with llama sacrifices on Puquin hill. At the beginning of January the new knights staged a mock battle as a test of strength.

## Comments

From the foregoing we see that during the Warachikuy Inca youths were initiated into manhood and the society of their elders by visiting major shrines in the vicinity of the sacred city, Cuzco. That four "hills" were involved is most significant, for the neighborhood of Cuzco was divided into ceremonial quarters correlating approximately with the intercardinal points—for example, Collasuyu to the southeast, Cuntisuyu to the southwest, Antisuyu to the northeast, Chinchaysuyu to the northwest—and corresponding to the four divisions of the empire. Given these divisions, one would suspect that the youths visited one shrine from each quarter. A review of Cobo's (1956:bk. 13, chaps. 13-16, pp. 169-186) list of the huacas in the Cuzco region seems to confirm this suspicion. According to him, Huanacauri and Anahuarque were actual hills, the former in Collasuyu (1956:chap. 15, p. 181), the latter in Cuntisuyu (1956:chap. 16, p. 183). Cobo lists *Sauraura* (Sabaraura?) twice under the section relating the huacas of Antisuyu. First he tells us that it refers to a sacred round stone in the town of Yaconora (1956:chap. 14, p. 177). Later he assigns the name to three stones in the town of Larapa (1956:chap. 14, p. 178). Apuyavira is given as the name of a stone located on the Piccho hill in Chinchaysuyu. The Indians believed that it was a petrified being who had emerged from the earth and was associated with Huanacauri (1956:chap. 13, p. 174). Thus the boys visited a huaca in each one of the four quarters of the sacred valley of Cuzco. In effect, through ritual, they established domain as the future rulers of Tahuantin-suyu, "The Four Quarters of the World."

We have already noted that on the first pilgrimage to Huanacauri in November the boys were imitating the journey of their ancestors to Cuzco after the emergence from the sacred cave of Pacaritambo during the Creation. An important part of this reliving of the Inca origin myth was the performance of a festival and rituals instituted for Inca youths by the principal ancestor and culture hero, Manco Capac. There are also hints that the initiates were reenacting the Inca Creation myth. According to this myth, Viracocha (the Creator) destroyed his first creation with a flood. The visit to Anahuarque, a hill that survived the deluge, probably was performed in remembrance of this flood, with the downhill race reenacting the swirling waters. During the second creation, to call the various tribes out of the earth and make sure that they were obeying his commands, Viracocha traveled northwest along the chain of the Andes—starting at Lake Titicaca, passing through Cuzco, and eventually arriving in Manta, Ecuador. That Huanacauri, where the Warachikuy begins, is southeast of Cuzco in the direction of Lake Titicaca, and Yavira, where the four pilgrimages end, is northwest of Cuzco in the direction of Manta, suggests that the youths replicated the journey of Viracocha. This route is also the model for the biannual path of the sun—that is, from sunrise at the southern summer solstice (December 21 in the first month of the Inca year) to sunset at the winter solstice (June 21), when the sun begins its return journey as celebrated at Inti Raymi, a major Inca festival in honor of the Sun. Since the Sun was considered to be their divine ancestor and the Creator's most important servant, imitation of its movements in effect implied compliance with the Creator's divine plan as followed by the initiates' deified ancestors, with whom they interacted in the main square of Cuzco before and after each of their four pilgrimages.

In practical terms, such compliance required reverence for and loyalty to the Sun and his representative on earth, the Inca. This obeisance amounted to defending the laws of the Inca Empire as reinforced by the values of the state cult of the sun. It is most apparent from the accounts of the Warachikuy that the elders worked hard to socialize the initiates by instilling in them a sense of duty and obedience through the use of hardship, pain, and intensive instruction.

As was noted throughout the description of the Warachikuy, the taqui called guari (Huari or Wari) played a prominent role in initiation rituals. As its name implies, this dance and song was addressed to the ancient god of force, Wari. He was a most appropriate sponsor for these tests of manhood and virility, for the Incas also used the term *wari* to refer to the powerful and fecund attributes of the Sun (Molina, 1947:101-102, n. 2). It is obvious that fertility—or, more precisely, the masculine contribution to fertility—was an important theme associated with the festival—for example, performance of the ear-piercing ritual in the fields, bloodletting, llama sacrifices, animal increase rites for the llama herds, and the sacrifices on Puquin hill to guarantee that "the people would multiply and all things would be prosperous." Also, in May, the new knights were the first to harvest maize in a field dedicated to Mama Huaco, sister of Manco Capac (Cobo, 1956:bk. 13, chap. 27, p. 215; Molina, 1947:chap. 6, pp. 129-130). Molina adds that they were the first to harvest the maize in other fields set aside for the service of the Creator, the Sun, the Thunder, the Moon, the Inca, and all the royal mummies. In highland Peru, December is the month in which the rainy season begins in earnest. In Inca times the vital potato crop was sown in this month, and the first maize crop was harvested. Thus it was a time when the Incas wanted to do everything in their power to guarantee the fertility of crops and herds. Since this was also the month of the summer solstice, the full power of the divine Sun was available to guarantee the passage from one stage to another on several levels—from the old year to the new, from the dry season to the rainy season, and from the death of boyhood to rebirth as a man.

In light of the above, the following remarks by the historian of religion Mircea Eliade (1958:19) seem most appropriate. Although he is discussing Australian puberty rites, his comments appear to summarize the significance of the Inca Warachikuy as well. He points out that:

> collective initiation ceremonies reactualize the mythical times
> in which . . . Divine Beings were creating or organizing the
> earth; in other words, initiation is considered to be performed
> by these Divine Beings or in their presence. Hence the mystical
> death of the novices is not something negative. On the con-
> trary, their death to childhood, to asexuality, to ignorance—in
> short, to the profane condition—is the occasion for a total
> regeneration of the cosmos and the collectivity.

## NOTES

1. I gratefully acknowledge the help of Professor John H. Rowe in writing this paper. In addition to reading my first draft, he also provided valuable material on the Inca calendar and the historical sources for the Warachikuy. Regarding the latter, he kindly gave me copies from his microfilm of the best surviving version of Molina, a scribe's copy that, despite its spelling errors and occasional blanks, is better than any of the published editions of this chronicler.

2. I cite pages from the Morales, 1947, version of Molina so readers who do not have access to the scribe's copy may check my work against available materials. By using the scribe's copy, however, I was able to correct editorial errors in Morales, mainly native terms and place names.

3. According to Morales (1947:101, n. 2), the Inca term taqui referred to a song that accompanied a dance as well as the dance itself.

## BIBLIOGRAPHY

Cieza de León, Pedro de
1959    *The Incas of Pedro de Cieza de Leon.* Victor W. von Hagen, ed. Norman: University of Oklahoma Press.

Cobo, Bernabé
1956    *Historia del nuevo mundo.* P. Francisco Mateos, ed. Biblioteca de autores españoles, 92. Obras del P. Bernabé Cobo, 2. Madrid: Ediciones Atlas.

Eliade, Mircea
1958    *Rites and Symbols of Initiation.* New York: Harper and Row.

Fernández, Diego
1963    *Historia del Perú.* Juan Pérez de Tudela Bueso, ed. Biblioteca de autores españoles, 165. Crónicas del Perú, 2. Madrid: Ediciones Atlas.

Garcilaso de la Vega, El Inca
1966    *Royal Commentaries of the Incas and General History of Peru,* part 1. Austin: University of Texas Press.

Molina (of Cuzco), Cristóbal de
1947    *Ritos y fábulas de los Incas.* Ernesto Morales, ed. Buenos Aires: Editorial Futuro.

Pachacuti Yamqui, Juan de Santacruz
1950    "Relación de antigüedades deste reyno del Pirú." In *Tres relaciones de antigüedades peruanas.* Marcos Jiménez de la Espada, ed. Buenos Aires: Editorial Guarania. Pp. 205-381.

Rowe, John H.
1946    "Inca Culture at the Time of the Spanish Conquest." In *Handbook of South American Indians,* vol. 2. Julian Steward, ed. Smithsonian Institution, U.S. Bureau of American Ethnology Bulletin 143. Washington, D.C.: U.S. Government Printing Office. Pp. 183-330.

# 7.

# Enculturation in an Imperial Society: The Aztecs of Mexico

## FRANCES F. BERDAN

Enculturation is the process whereby each generation is equipped with the skills, knowledge, value orientations, and perceptions of a specific culture. The attainment and internalization of these cultural and social attributes allow each succeeding generation to carry on traditional patterns and activities, and to adapt these patterns and activities to new or emerging conditions.

In complex state societies, the enculturation process frequently becomes institutionalized and controlled by the polity. Structurally embedded in the political system, aspects of the enculturation process are directed and oriented to serve the needs and goals of the state.

According to Fried (1968:470), a state type of organization is made possible by the presence of social stratification, or the differential control of, and access to, strategic resources by different societal members. For present purposes, the state may be defined as "a political organization that consciously and centrally directs and controls role differentiation and complexity, as well as their consequences, in the society as a whole" (Cohen, 1970:61-62).

Fried (1968:475-476) suggests that the primary duties of the state are the maintenance of the general order and support of the system of social stratification. Such stratification would be expressed in terms of different legal rights, privileges (including access to specific occupations), and prestige, usually represented by varying modes of life-style and attire. Other functions of the state outlined by Fried include population control (in the broadest sense), the establishment of laws and judicial procedures, the protection of sovereignty (including the maintenance of military forces), and the provision of economic support for these activities.

In a state context, the enculturation process is likely to assume a highly specific form to serve these social and political ends. In particular, formal

educational institutions, or schools, emerge. At the same time, family-
and community-level mechanisms and goals of enculturation are retained,
although these will conform to some degree with those of the state.

Schools are institutions "devoted to instruction, with specialized personnel, permanent physical structures, special apparatus (of which texts
are an important part), formal and stereotyped means of instruction, a
curriculum, and rationally defined manifest objectives" (Cohen, 1970:56).
In a state society, schools are often structured to emphasize one fundamental objective: maintenance of the system of stratification. It is generally the elite who are exposed to training specifically geared to the maintenance and perpetuation of the state. These persons also, by virtue of
their status and education, gain access to the more powerful political
positions in the society. The educational process in this context must
therefore channel the individual's loyalty and commitment to the state
itself, at the same time providing necessary training for the occupation
of defined political, religious, and economic positions (see Cohen, 1970).

It may be predicted, then, that the educational systems of states would
be oriented to maintain and perhaps intensify social stratification. In
addition, these educational systems would be structured to assure a continuation of highly specialized activities, whether economic, political,
or religious in nature. Hence, one would expect not only hierarchically
arranged educational institutions, but also a wide variety of mechanisms
for the transmission of special necessary skills.

As the specific structures and goals of state organizations vary cross-
culturally, the precise form of their educational systems will likewise vary.
One important ethnographic example is that of the Aztecs of central
Mexico.

## Aztec Society

Aztec society by the time the Spanish arrived in 1519 was clearly a
state organization, exhibiting the characteristic features of states mentioned above.[1] The Aztec state was highly imperialistic, undertaking
military campaigns of conquest with the express (and seemingly singular)
goal of collecting tribute and controlling economic resources. By 1519
the Aztecs indeed controlled an extensive empire, composed of 38
ecologically distinct and ethnically diverse provinces.

The military strength to achieve the goals of conquest was mustered
by the Aztecs through the formation of a Triple Alliance. This alliance
was composed of the Mexica with their capital city of Tenochtitlan, the
Acolhuacans of Texcoco, and the Tepanecas of Tlacopan. It appears
that in the early phases of the empire Texcoco was dominant both mili-
tarily and politically. By the middle of the fifteenth century, however,

Tenochtitlan had emerged as the leading military power, and Texcoco had achieved an extraordinary reputation for progress in law, engineering, and the creative arts. Throughout the history of the empire, Tlacopan remained somewhat undistinguished in comparison with its allies.

This study is restricted to the Triple Alliance capitals, with a particular emphasis on Tenochtitlan. Within the imperial structure, the capitals manifested the greatest complexity of social, political, religious, and economic institutions. The most complex and elaborated forms of educational institutions likewise were localized in these cities. A focus on the capitals, therefore, would allow a broad perspective on the Aztec educational process. Another factor defining the scope of this investigation involves the primary source materials. Those sources that discuss the enculturation process are almost exclusively confined to Tenochtitlan.

Several themes characterized Tenochtitlan Aztec society. These are reflected in the structure and content of the educational process. The themes focus on (1) the maintenance of social differentiation, (2) militarism, and (3) an intricately developed religion permeating all aspects of Aztec life. A brief discussion of these themes will serve to place the subsequent analysis of the Aztec educational system in a sociocultural context.

## Social Differentiation

Zorita (1963a:26–36), Durán (1967:II), Sahagún (1950–1969:books 8, 9, and 10), and to a lesser extent Torquemada (1969:II, 544–545) describe a complex system of social differentiation among the Aztecs. The basic social division is that between the nobility and the commoners, with specialists, largely merchants and artisans, occupying an intermediate position.

The nobility were divided into ranks of *tlatoque,* "rulers"; *tetecuhtin,* "chiefs"; and *pipiltin,* "nobles" or "sons of nobles." These various ranks were associated with different rights and responsibilities.

The tlatoque (sing. *tlatoani*) were the supreme rulers of regions or towns. In the imperial structure, the tlatoque of conquered areas recognized and paid tribute to the still more powerful tlatoque of the Triple Alliance capitals. The responsibilities of the tlatoque (particularly of Tenochtitlan, Texcoco, and Tlacopan) encompassed the organization of military activities, the sponsoring of certain religious celebrations, and the adjudication of disputes not solved at a lower level.

Tetecuhtin (sing. *tecuhtli*) controlled a more restricted area and set of activities. A tecuhtli was the head of a "chiefly house" to which were attached commoners (*macehualtin*). These commoners were apparently resident in wards (*calpultin*) and may have included craftsmen as well as agricultural laborers. A tecuhtli, according to Zorita (1963a:28, 111), attained that title primarily through success in military activities, although it was necessary that he be a noble by birth. The status of tecuhtli brought not only honor, but also certain privileges. Among these were domestic services including the provision of firewood and water, repairs to his house, and the cultivation of his lands. All this was provided by macehualtin released from tribute to the tlatoani. The only direct obligation these commoners had to the tlatoani was service in military enterprises (Zorita, 1963a:29).

Pipiltin (all other nobles) who did not succeed to ranks of tlatoani or tecuhtli frequently attained positions in the capitals or the provinces as priests, teachers, judges, governors, and tribute collectors.

Commoners comprised the bulk of the population, engaging primarily in agricultural pursuits. All male commoners of the Triple Alliance capitals also were expected to participate in military activities and were intensively trained in the martial arts.

Artisans of luxury goods (tolteca) and professional merchants (pochteca) were apparently exempt from this military service, although the long-distance merchants frequently clashed with residents of outlying districts. These artisans and merchants, centered in the Triple Alliance capitals and surrounding cities, provided important luxury goods destined for the exclusive use of the nobility (e.g., featherwork and gold ornaments). Organized in guilds, their training focused on the acquisition of these frequently complex skills, rather than on attainment of military skills.

The distinction between commoners and nobility was theoretically established by birth. The ascriptive nature of this status system was reinforced by the religious system. Caso (1963:866) observes that not only the Tenochtitlan tlatoani, but all nobles in general were considered ultimately derived from the god Quetzalcoatl. This exclusive ancestry provided an ideological basis for distinguishing nobles from the rest of the population.

Nonetheless, ranks with special privileges and duties could be achieved by commoners, notably through success in warfare or through commitment to the priesthood. Members of the nobility class, however, tended to occupy the higher positions in the religious, military, and administrative structures (Adams, 1966:111).

Although they could attain some relatively high positions, commoners apparently could not achieve full nobility status. The closest approximation to such status was that of the quauhpilli, the generals "whose personal charge was command in war" (Sahagún, 1950–1969:book 8, 43). Although these commoners could possess economic bases similar (but inferior) to those of pipiltin, occupy high-ranking military positions, and carry the "-pilli" name suffix, their children did not inherit true nobility status, and they could not wear certain marks of rank reserved for those of noble birth.

Wolf has noted a competitive relationship between the nobility by ascription and the "nobility" by achievement:

> As this nobility of service [achievement] grew increasingly important, however, with the expansion of the Mexica domain, it also entered into conflict with the nobility of lineage over the occupancy of bureaucratic positions. During the last phase of Mexica rule an aristocratic reaction curtailed the privileges of the service nobles in favor of a renewed monopoly of power in the hands of the nobility of descent (1959:138).

This conflict may have derived, at least in part, from the increasing numbers of nobility by birth, as polygyny was permitted and common among this group. Competition over a limited number of administrative, religious, and military positions may have become a serious social problem in the early sixteenth century.

Whether noble or commoner, achievement in these arenas depended to a large extent on the individual's educational exposure, and on his abilities to attain the necessary skills and knowledge. The formal educational system of the Aztecs reserved largely for the nobility the training necessary for the performance of religious and administrative duties. Training in military skills was an important aspect of the education of both nobles and commoners.

The acquisition of special skills, especially the manufacture of luxury wares, was even more restricted, being passed from father to son in the context of specialized craft guilds (see Sahagún, 1950–1969:book 9, 69–97). Plate 1, from the sixteenth-century *Codex Mendoza,* illustrates the transmission of several of these skills (carpentry, stoneworking, painting, metalworking, and featherworking).[2]

## Militarism

From its inception in 1430, a predominant goal of the Triple Alliance had been military conquest. It is not surprising, then, to find military achievement a primary means for attaining and validating high statuses and the rewards associated with those statuses.

The capture of enemy warriors on the battlefield was the measure of military achievement. An outstanding warrior of noble status may rise to the rank of tecuhtli; such a warrior of commoner ancestry may rise into the achievement-nobility ranks mentioned above, attaining high status,

PLATE 1.  Transmission of specialized skills from father to son. From left to right and top to bottom: carpenters, stoneworkers, painters, metalworkers, and featherworkers. From the *Codex Mendoza* (Clark, 1938: part III, plate 70).

titles, and even access to goods and services otherwise reserved for the nobility.

Achievement of progressively higher ranks was accompanied by the privilege of wearing particular items of clothing not permitted to other individuals (*Codex Mendoza,* part III, 64–65). When the warrior had successfully captured four prisoners, he was given the title *tequiua.* Persons with that title attended the war councils and were qualified to serve in important military and civil capacities.

Military training, then, had two aspects. On the one hand, it assured an able military force to meet the imperial goals of conquest. On the other, it instilled the Aztec youth with personal goals of achievement. In carrying out imperial duties, he would at the same time be satisfying culturally defined personal goals.

## *Religion*

Aztec religion encompassed a multitude of deities in a specialized and hierarchical arrangement. The terrestrial accompaniment to this conception of the supernatural was likewise specialized and hierarchical in nature. There were numerous ranks within the priesthood, and the temples and deities to which priests were attached were of varying importance (Durán, 1967:II, 159–169; Sahagún, 1950–1969:book 1; Torquemada, 1969:II, 177–179, 185).

Education of the nobility and a few commoners was under the jurisdiction of specialized priests, and took place in *calmecac* ("priests' houses"). This training exposed the youths not only to the religious knowledge and ceremonial proficiencies necessary for entry into the priesthood, but also to other forms of esoteric knowledge required in the performance of high-ranking administrative duties (e.g., writing, calendrics, history and oral tradition, laws and codes).

Religious philosophy permeated all aspects of Aztec daily life. The world was viewed as a treacherous, demanding place, and a strong fatalism had developed as a cultural correlate of this conception of the world. Ethics and actions were defined in terms of these general beliefs, and transmitted to children in the form of formalized orations and admonitions.

## *Aztec Education*

Education in Aztec society focused on the themes of social differentiation (and specialization), militarism, and religion. Skill training, socialization, and moral education were structured in conformance with these themes, at the same time serving to perpetuate them. Training in all areas took into account two fundamental conceptual divisions:

(1) that between nobility and commoners,[3] and (2) that between male and female. The following discussion is structured along these lines.[4]

## Nobility: The Education of Male Children

The greatest amount of information relating to the early training of noble children is found in the voluminous Nahuatl and Spanish writings of the sixteenth-century Franciscan friar Bernardino de Sahagún. This chronicler, using Aztec informants of noble descent, is primarily describing conditions and categories pertaining directly to the nobility, or from the nobility point of view.[5]

In the *Florentine Codex* (1950–1969:book 10, 11–13) Sahagún describes Aztec age categories and the attributes associated with each category. He designates, in detail, terms pertaining to infants and very young children: *conetl* (baby), *conepil* (little child), *conetontli* (infant), and *pilpil* (child).[6] Sahagún's paraphrase of this section indicates that the pilpil is a child of five or six years of age (1956:III, 108). For these children there is no direct indication of formal attempts to train them in skills or inculcate them with morals. Rather, the "good child" is merely described as healthy, strong, and happy. Conversely, the "bad child" is sickly, maimed, and violent in temperament.

The attributes of the subsequent category, *piltontli* (boy), suggest that few overt attempts at instruction were made until a child reached this stage. The "good boy" is "teachable, tractable—one who can be directed. The good-hearted boy (is) obedient, intelligent, respectful, fearful; one who bows in reverence. He bows in reverence, obeys, respects others, is indoctrinated" (1950–1969:book 10, 13). Of equal interest are the qualities of the "bad boy"; "The bad boy (is) always inhuman, incorrigible, disloyal, corrupt, perverse. He flees constantly; (he is) a thief; he lies; he does evil, is perverse" (ibid.).

These passages emphasize qualities that are to play a large part in the continuing education of the child: obedience, respect, and honesty. Elsewhere, Sahagún (ibid., book 8, 71) provides more detail on the training of the noble child of this age. Beginning at approximately age six, the boy was allowed a certain amount of freedom beyond the confines of the house, although always accompanied by "pages." The pages were charged with assuring the boy's proper conduct while outside the house. Of particular importance were

> that his conversation should be proper; that he should respect and show reverence to others—(when) perchance he some-where might chance to meet a judge, or a leading militia officer, or a seasoned warrior, or someone of lesser rank; or a

revered old man, or a respected old woman; or someone who was poor. He should greet him and bow humbly. He said: "come hither, my beloved grandfather; let me bow before thee." . . . And when the young boy thus saluted others, they praised him highly for it (ibid.).

The importance of these same qualities for adult nobles is emphasized elsewhere in Sahagún (ibid., book 10, 19-22); they provided a focus for the young noble's instruction.

Failure on the part of the child to acquire these qualities resulted in severe scolding. One form of scolding was to compare the child to an Otomí:[7]

Now thou art an Otomí. Now thou art a miserable Otomí. O Otomí, how is it that thou understandest not? Art thou perchance an Otomí? Art thou perchance a real Otomí? Not only art thou like an Otomí, thou art a real Otomí, a miserable Otomí, a green-head, a thick-head, a big tuft of hair over the back of the head, an Otomí blockhead (ibid., p. 178).

Not only was the child shamed, but he also quickly learned to disdain the Otomí peoples.

Admonitions were an important way of instilling the noble child with cultural values. The admonitions, or *huehuetlatolli*,[8] presented the child with a moral philosophy and strict rules of conduct. Those contained in the works of Sahagún (ibid., book 6, 105-126) and Zorita (1963b:141-151) suggest a rather grim conception of the world: "Certainly it is a dangerous place, a revolting place, a boundless place, a place of no repose, a frightful place, and a painful and afflicting place" (Sahagún, 1950-1969:book 6, 105).

How does one cope in a world which offers only fear and pain? The father suggests to his son that he proceed with great caution and moderation in all things; that he constantly practice humility; that he exercise diligence, especially in the performance of religious duties; and that he make a conscious attempt to attain self-knowledge (ibid., pp. 105-126).

Also included in the admonitions are general rules of conduct relating to such things as gossip, speech, vanity, respect for elders, and honesty. More specific "rules of etiquette" also form part of the admonitions: dress and appearance, the manner of eating, gesturing, and walking (ibid.; Zorita, 1963b:141-144).

For example, a son is advised by his father as follows:

Wherever you go, walk with a peaceful air, and do not make wry faces or improper gestures. . . .

Do not seize another by the hand or by his clothing, for this
is a mark of a giddy nature. . . .

Watch well where you are going, and if you meet others, do
not walk in front of them. . . .

If you are eating with others, lower your head and do not eat
ravenously and noisily, for men will think you giddy. And do
not finish eating before the others who dine with you, lest you
give offense (ibid., pp. 142–143).

The admonitions were also one way of conveying more practical
knowledge. For example, one of the orations includes a lengthy section
describing the structure of the political hierarchy (Sahagún, 1950–1969:
book 6, 110). Elsewhere (ibid., p. 114), the role and activities of priests
are discussed.

The training of young children took place in a family context. Among
the nobility, this involved not only the polygynous nuclear family itself,
but also a wide array of nursemaids, pages, and servants (ibid., book 8,
71). Within the kinship network, the father and grandfather were particularly charged with teaching, advising, admonishing, and punishing
(ibid., book 10, 1, 4).

The education of the *telpochtli* (youth), however, became the responsibility of larger, state-level institutions. The noble youth entered a
calmecac (priests' house) for the continuation of his education (see
plate 2). The primary sources differ considerably regarding the age at
which a young noble entered the calmecac. The *Codex Mendoza* (plate
61) indicates that this took place at age fifteen; Sahagún (ibid., book 8:
71) at age ten, twelve, or thirteen; Zorita (1963*b*:135) at age five; and
Torquemada (1969:II, 222) at age five or six. Given that chastity is an
oft-mentioned virtue for persons attending the calmecac, the statements
by Sahagún and the *Codex Mendoza* would probably most closely
approximate reality. Nonetheless, it is entirely possible that the age for
admission varied with the different calmecac, or with the specific objectives of the student.

Sahagún (1950–1969:book 2, 168–176) lists seven calmecac in the city
of Tenochtitlan. Each calmecac was associated with a specific temple,
with its specialized retinue of priests:

1. Tlillan calmecac     Priests dedicated to Ciuacoatl
                        (earth mother)

2. Mexico calmecac      Priests dedicated to Tlaloc (rain
                        god)

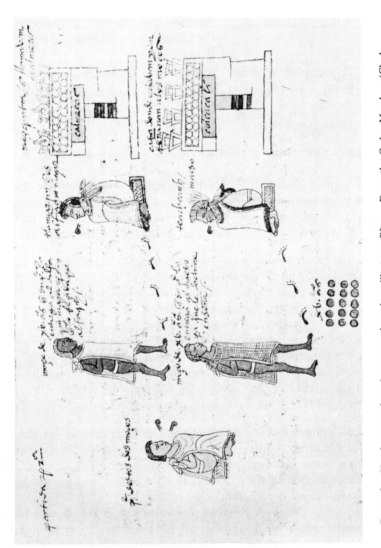

PLATE 2. Youths enter the calmecac or the cuicacalli at age fifteen. From the *Codex Mendoza* (Clark, 1938, part III, plate 61).

| | |
|---|---|
| 3. Uitznauac calmecac | Fire priests of Uitznauac temple (dedicated to Omacatl, god of revelry) |
| 4. Tetlanman calmecac | Fire priests dedicated to Quaxolotl Chantico (associated with the fire deity) |
| 5. Tlamatzinco calmecac | Fire priests of Tlamatzinco temple |
| 6. Yopico calmecac | Priests engaged in human sacrifice |
| 7. Tzonmolco calmecac | Priests of Xiuhtecuhtli (fire god) |

The education of youths in these calmecac was the responsibility of the priests.

The administration of the "calmecac system" was likewise in the hands of religious functionaries, called *teohuatzin* (literally, "keepers of the gods"). These "keepers of the gods" were hierarchically ordered. The "keeper of the gods of the Mexicans" sat at the apex of the structure:

> He was like the ruler of the lesser keepers of the gods indeed everywhere. And all the children were left in his care, that he might train them, that he might by words move them to live well. And whether men commanded, or were rich, or were leaders, or directed, all this was the charge of the Keeper of the Gods of the Mexicans. And also this one commanded in the temples everywhere; he told the lesser keepers of the gods what they might do. And if perchance any should sin, much did the Keeper of the Gods of the Mexicans take heed of it (ibid., p. 193).

Sahagún also mentions the "keeper of the god of Uitznauac," in charge of training children; and the "keeper of the gods of others." The duties of the latter centered around overseeing the priests of the calmecac and their manner of training the children. This suggests a strong centralized control over the formal education of noble youths.

Durán paints a slightly different picture of the calmecac structure. He discusses youths serving in the temple of Huitzilopochtli (patron deity of the Mexica), their activities closely approximating Sahagún's descriptions of calmecac duties. Durán (1971:85) states that attendance at this temple was restricted to youths from six wards of the city, although he does not specify the wards.

He further describes a system whereby children were dedicated to the temple of Tezcatlipoca (an omnipotent deity). Education in this temple was geared toward training children as priests, and both commoners and nobles could be dedicated to this end (ibid., p. 111). The temple of the god Camaxtli (hunting deity) also contained a formal educational adjunct where youths were trained as skilled hunters (ibid., pp. 148-149).

Given the high degree of specialization in Aztec society, it is possible that every major temple had its associated educational structure. Sahagún and Durán may have provided only partial listings, those most memorable or relevant to themselves or to their informants.

The calmecac were primarily reserved for those of noble birth. Most modern sources treating Aztec education agree on this point (e.g., Katz, 1972:204; Moreno, 1931:73-74; Davies, 1974:80-81; Wolf, 1959:142). Other authors (Carrasco, 1971:356; León-Portilla, 1963:137; Soustelle, 1961:169; Markus, 1963:288) point out that commoners could also be dedicated to the calmecac. The primary source for the latter position is Sahagún, who, in speaking of commoners, states that "When a boy was born, then they placed him in the priests' house of the young men's house. That is to say (the parents) promised (the child), gave him as a gift, and brought him as an offering to the temple of the priests' house in order that (the boy) become a priest, or a young (warrior)" (1950-1969: book 3, 49). The problem of calmecac membership is evaluated in the concluding section.

Youths trained in the calmecac were destined for a wide variety of adult activities, whether political or religious in nature. The primary sources do not clearly indicate if different "curricula" were followed by youths according to their end objectives. The training of youths as priests is most elaborately documented, and is used here as a case in point.

The specific priestly education received by an individual must have varied according to the calmecac he attended. Each deity had a different set of ceremonies and ritual paraphernalia; each placed different demands on the humans dedicated to his worship. Nonetheless, there appears to have been a general pattern of daily activity within all calmecac, which included the following:

1. Before dawn, the youths (resident in the calmecac) swept the temple courtyard.

2. The elder youths gathered maguey thorns before dawn.

3. a. While it was still dark, the elder youths traveled to the forests to gather logs for the fires that burned all night in the temples.

   b. Others in the priests' house began their work before dawn also: cultivating fields, building walls or canals.

   c. Some remained in the calmecac as guards, and to carry food to the above workers later in the day.

4. Upon completion of the day's work, the youths performed unspecified duties in the calmecac (possibly related to their education), and penances.

5. At night, the priests traveled to the countryside to "place maguey spines" as a means of penance.

6. At midnight, everyone awoke and prayed (ibid., pp. 63–65).

One wonders when there was time for the acquisition of the elaborate esoteric knowledge characteristic of Aztec culture. Yet, in this same passage, Sahagún states that great care was taken that the youths of the calmecac were taught "good discourse." Additionally, they were instructed in "the songs which they called the gods' songs. They were inscribed in the books. And well were all taught the reckoning of the days, the book of dreams, and the book of years" (ibid., p. 65). The hieroglyphic writing system of the pictorial manuscripts (codices) served only as a mnemonic device, reminding the reader of the events or information to be recounted. Specifically, "the training of the young priests in the calmecac was concerned primarily with the memorizing and word-perfect repeating of a metaphoric language peculiar to the priesthood as called to mind by the picto-ideographic ritual codices. Errors in word or act were severely punished" (Dibble, 1971:330). Histories, songs, orations, calendrics, the interpretation of dreams and omens, and other forms of esoteric knowledge were committed to memory in the calmecac. Durán (1971:293) mentions large hieroglyphic books used in the instruction of the following arts: military, religious, mechanical, astrological, law, and theology. Surely much of this information formed part of the content of the education of students not destined for service in the priesthood.

The activities of the youths in the many calmecac served to sustain the temples and the priesthood attached to those temples. The cultivation of fields provided direct subsistence support, and other daily duties of the youths served the needs of the priests in their religious duties (e.g., carrying logs for fires), as well as educating the neophyte in those same duties.

Additionally, they were taught the martial arts, particularly the use of weapons (ibid., p. 112). This instruction was especially important, in that a man of noble descent was particularly expected to be skilled, courageous, and successful on the battlefield. Sahagún (1950–1969:book 8, 72, 75) states that military training of noble youths began at age fifteen. Apparently some of this instruction took place in actual battles with enemy groups: "And then they took him to the wars. The seasoned warriors went taking great care of him, lest somewhere he might be lost. And they taught him well how to guard himself with a shield; how one fought; how a spear was fended off with a shield. And when a battle was joined . . . they taught him well and made him see how he might take a captive" (ibid.). Those who taught the noble youths the art of war were themselves accomplished warriors, for the parents of the youths requested for this instruction the *tequiuaque* (those who had distinguished themselves by capturing at least four enemy warriors).

The manner in which all duties were performed was of utmost importance. In one lengthy discourse, a noble father[9] introduces his son to the calmecac, instructing him on his behavior:

> Here is what thou art to perform, here is what thou art to do: thou art to sweep, to clean, to place things in order, to arrange things; thou art to hold vigil, to pass the night (in vigil. Do) that which thou art told to do. . . . In places not easy for running, thou art to run, thou art to proceed with agility. Be not lazy, be not slothful. Hearing it only once thou art to do (what is commanded). . . .
>
> Listen, O my son, as thou goest thou goest not to be honored, to be obeyed, to be respected. Thou art only to be sad, to be humble, to live austerely. . . .
>
> This is what thou art to accomplish, this is what thou art to do. Thou art to be diligent in the breaking off of (maguey) spines, in the cutting of pine boughs, in the insertion of (maguey) spines (in thy flesh), in the bathing in the streams. And do not gorge thyself with what thou eatest; be moderate. . . .
>
> And do not clothe thyself excessively. Let thy body chill, because verily thou goest to perform penance; for thou goest to ask (mercy) of the lord of the near, of the nigh. . . .
>
> And when the fasting setteth in . . . do not break it. . . . Do not take it as painful; be diligent in it. And take care (to understand) the writings, the books, the paintings. Enter with the prudent, the wise (ibid., book 6, 214-215).

Deviations from the ordered pattern were severely punished (Zorita, 1963b:136; Sahagún, 1950-1969: book 3, 64-65). Sahagún provides specific details:

> If at times it appeared that one perhaps drank wine, or was given to women, or committed a great (fault), then they went to apprehend him. No mercy was shown. He was burned, or strangled, or cast into the fire alive or shot with arrows. And if he sinned only lightly, they drew blood from his ears, his flanks, or his thighs with maguey spines or with a (sharpened) bone (ibid., p. 64).

Faults deserving of the latter punishment would be failure to speak well
or to greet others properly.

A primary responsibility of the priests in the calmecac was admonishing youths as to a good and proper life. As mentioned above, children
frequently received admonitions from their parents, and this responsibility
merely shifted to the priests when the youth entered the calmecac.
Undoubtedly the general content of the admonitions was little changed,
although the emphasis may have varied depending on the specific objective. That is, Sahagún (ibid., p. 68) states that the life of the priests was
most severe; those trained for the priesthood would have been instilled
with resignation to a life of hardships, of diligence, and of dedication to
a specific deity.

Students left the calmecac upon marriage, generally at the age of twenty
(Zorita, 1963b:135-136; Anonymous Conqueror, 1971:383-384; Durán,
1971:293). Those who emerged with an inclination toward the religious
life dedicated themselves to climbing the priestly hierarchy.[10] Those with
special aptitudes for the martial arts could, upon the capture of three
enemy warriors, become "masters of the youths" of the many ward schools
(*telpochcalli*) (Sahagún, 1950-1969: book 8, 76). Those destined for
bureaucratic positions, such as judges, also were required to demonstrate
a successful career on the battlefield before assuming those positions
(ibid., pp. 75-77).

## *Nobility: The Education of Female Children*

Obedience, respect, and honesty, as with noble male children, were
highly acclaimed minimal virtues for noble females. Good little girls
(*conetzintli*) were also to be energetic, virtuous, and humble. These
qualities continued to be esteemed as the girl became a maiden: ". . . the
daughter (is) untouched, pure, a virgin. The good daughter (is) obedient,
honest, intelligent, discreet, of good memory, revered, well reared, well
taught, well trained, well instructed, prudent, chaste, circumspect"
(ibid., book 10, 2-3). Moderation and tranquillity were positively valued
in the noblewoman's life, even to her dress, speech, and manner of
walking (ibid., book 6, 100). Caution in all things was also advised: "On
earth it is a time for care, it is a place for caution. . . . On earth we live,
we travel along a mountain peak. Over here there is an abyss, over there
is an abyss. If thou goest over there, thou wilt fall in. Only in the middle
doth one go, doth one live" (ibid., p. 101).

As with males of noble standing, a primary means of instilling these
virtues was through admonitions. A noble maiden was generally advised
and instructed by her mother and other, elderly, female relatives. Words

of advice, however, were also offered by her father. In addition to emphasizing prudence, chastity, and dedication to her future husband, the father also defined the skills his daughter would be expected to acquire and perform to prepare her for marriage: "What wilt thou seize upon as thy womanly labors? Is it perhaps the drink, the grinding stone? Is it perhaps the spindle whorl, the weaving stick? Look well to the drink, to the food: how it is prepared, how it is made, how it is improved" (ibid., p. 95). These same skills are mentioned elsewhere in Sahagún (ibid., book 10, 12) as attributes of the "middle-aged woman." The only information on the manner of acquisition of these skills, however, is found for commoner women in the *Codex Mendoza* (see plates 3-5). Although this does not refer directly to the instruction of noble females, the process was in all likelihood very similar (see below).

Some girls, between the ages of twelve and thirteen, devoted one year to service in the temples: "They lived in chastity and seclusion as maidens who had been assigned to the service of the god. Their only work was sweeping and sprinkling the temple and cooking the daily food for the idol and for the ministers of the temple" (Durán, 1971:83). In addition, it is documented that those girls attached to the temple of Huitzilopochtli were overseen by older women. These women directed the girls in producing cloth and other adornments for the deities, as well as other undefined religious tasks (ibid., p. 84). This suggests that some women, after serving their designated term in the temple, continued in an advisory or directive capacity.

There is infrequent mention of priestesses attached to temples. Their duties were at least in part ceremonial (see Sahagún, 1950-1969: book 2, 116). The manner in which priestesses were trained for these duties, however, is virtually undocumented.

Some noblewomen were destined for other positions of leadership and responsibility, as governors or administrators (ibid., book 10, 45-47). There is, however, no known documentation describing the nature of education provided the noblewoman to prepare her for these positions. Most noblewomen were undoubtedly intended to spend their adult lives as wives to noblemen, many of them caring for and directing large and wealthy households.

## Commoners: The Education of Male Children

As with the nobility, commoners were also instilled with the virtues of obedience, honesty, and respect. Additionally, however, the admonitions directed at commoner children emphasized diligence and hard work: "Do what pertains to your office. Labor, sow and plant your trees, and live by the sweat of your brow. Do not cast off your burden, or grow faint, or be lazy; for if you are negligent and lazy, you will not be able to support yourself or your wife and children" (Zorita, 1963*b*:145-146). The form this work took and the manner of acquiring the necessary skills are pictographically represented in the *Codex Mendoza* (plates 3-5). Although generalized for each age category, the pictorial traces the growth of male

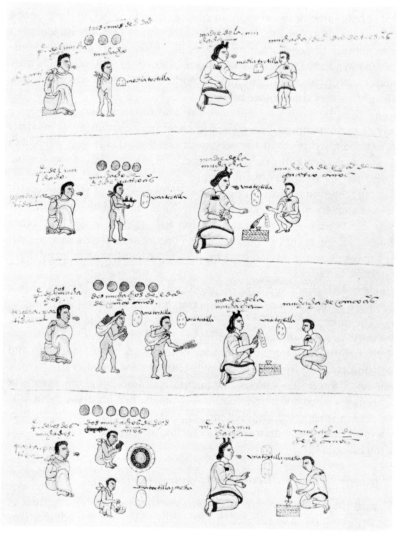

PLATE 3.   The education and duties of male and female commoner children from age three through six. From the *Codex Mendoza* (Clark, 1938, part III, plate 58).

and female commoner children from age three through age fourteen. It illustrates the ration allowed the children at each meal (one half to two tortillas) and the tasks they were expected to perform, or the punishments they were to endure for each age category. The instructor is also indicated (father for male children, mother for female children). The progression is summarized in table 1 (refer to plates 3–5).

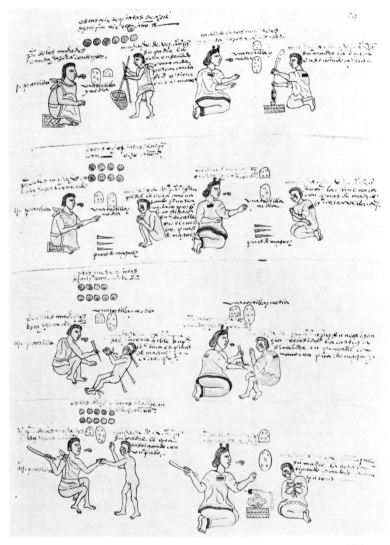

PLATE 4. Instruction and punishments of male and female commoner children, ages seven through ten. From the *Codex Mendoza* (Clark, 1938, part III, plate 59).

As the child was instructed in these techniques, he also undertook the responsibilities of performing those chores. Training in these skills took place at a household or family level. Therefore, the sequence illustrated in the *Codex Mendoza* undoubtedly varied considerably, depending on the primary means of subsistence in which each family was involved. The instance described here is clearly an example pertaining

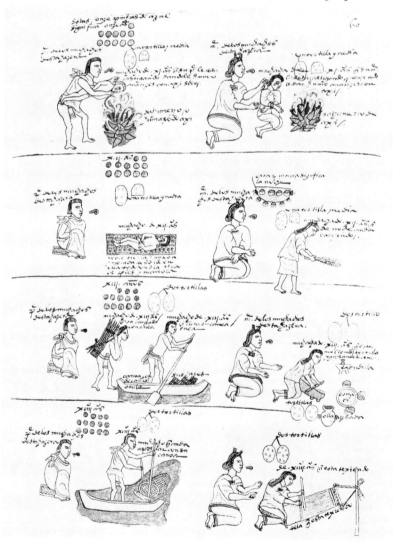

PLATE 5. Instruction and punishments of male and female commoner children, ages eleven through fourteen. From the *Codex Mendoza* (Clark, 1938, part III, plate 60).

to the mode of existence in the urbanized area surrounding Lake Texcoco. Other areas may have placed greater emphasis on agriculture or other types of production; the learning process would have conformed to that emphasis.

The education of children in these skills and in the moral underpinnings encouraging hard work and diligent efforts were the responsibility of each family. The specific details of the skills involved in these subsistence activities were undoubtedly best known and most effectively transmitted at this level. In terms of the educational process in general, the state probably took little direct interest in the transmission of these skills.

The state, however, did take an active interest in adult male commoners, as they formed the backbone of the imperial military force. Education in the martial arts was compulsory for all males. For commoners, this instruction took place in schools (telpochcalli) maintained in each ward.

A male commoner was ritually dedicated to a telpochcalli (young men's house) as a child (Sahagún, 1950–1969, book 3, 49–51). By at least age fifteen, the youth was a resident of the telpochcalli of his ward (ibid., p. 53). Monzón (1946:757) suggests that boys from ages six through twenty attended the telpochcalli, and Sahagún (1950–1969: book 3, 54) states that *pipiltotontin* (children of age five or six) slept in the telpochcalli. But at least some aspects of commoner formal education may not

TABLE 1

MALE COMMONERS

| Age | Duties | Punishments |
|-----|--------|-------------|
| 3 | — | — |
| 4 | Carry water | — |
| 5 | Carry firewood<br>Carry bundles to market | — |
| 6 | Carry goods to market<br>Collect grains in marketplace | — |
| 7 | Fish with net | — |
| 8 | — | Learn use of maguey thorns for punishment |
| 9 | — | Maguey thorns applied to body as punishment |
| 10 | — | Beaten with stick |
| 11 | — | Required to inhale "chile-smoke" |
| 12 | — | Tied hand and foot and required to lie on a wet mat |
| 13 | Carry loads of firewood<br>Paddle canoe loaded with reeds | — |
| 14 | Fish with net from a canoe | — |

have begun until age fifteen. The *Codex Mendoza* (see plate 2) indicates that a youth entered the *cuicacalli* (song house) at age fifteen. The cuicacalli was an integral part of the education of commoners and was associated with youths who slept and worked in their telpochcalli.

Attendance at the telpochcalli was compulsory for all male commoners. Each individual was expected to perform daily tasks in the telpochcalli or the community-at-large, to engage in certain ritual activities, and to acquire proficiencies in the martial arts. Duties required of the youngest youths included sweeping in the telpochcalli, laying fires, performing penances, singing, and dancing. By age fifteen, more demanding tasks were undertaken: carrying logs from the forest and traveling to war, although apparently not actively participating in actual battles.

The daily routine of the telpochcalli members is documented in somewhat less detail than that of the calmecac. According to Sahagún,

> he who was absent, who slept not in the young men's house, him they punished. And they ate in their homes. And they went about together where they had anything to do—perchance (preparing) mud (for adobes, making) walls, cultivating the soil, (digging) canals; they did these going all together, or they divided up. And they went into the forest, and gathered and carried on their backs . . . torches for the song house (ibid., p. 54).

Their daily activities centered around public works, serving especially the ward, the cuicacalli, or the telpochcalli itself.

As part of his education, a youth attended the cuicacalli. Sahagún mentions the cuicacalli infrequently, while Durán provides abundant detail. Sahagún (ibid., book 8, 43) describes the cuicacalli as the center where the "masters of the youths" supervised communal work performed by the youths. Lombardo (1973:156) indicates that the cuicacalli was a room within the confines of the royal palace where the teachers received their orders. Sahagún mentions other cuicacalli activities, notably the performance of dance and song. He further makes note of a specialized individual (*tlapiscatzin*: caretaker) in charge of the songs and the teaching of songs (Sahagún, 1950-1969: book 2, 195).[11]

Durán speaks of the cuicacalli as temple adjuncts, where there was instruction in song and dance: "In each of the cities, next to the temples, there stood some large houses which were the residences of teachers who taught dancing and singing. These houses were called Cuicacalli, which means House of Song. Nothing was taught there to youths and maidens but singing, dancing, and the playing of musical instruments" (1971:289). This same writer indicates that there were cuicacalli in all three Triple

Alliance capitals. He describes the structures as large, elaborately decorated buildings, with rooms surrounding an open courtyard, where the dances were performed. Although in general he speaks as though there were several cuicacalli, he implies that only one existed within the central ceremonial district of Tenochtitlan. He specifically locates it at one corner of the great wall that surrounded this central precinct, implying that it was a separate building, not just a room in the royal palace (ibid., p. 291).

Both attendance and activities were highly regulated at the cuicacalli. According to Durán (p. 290), males and females twelve to fourteen years old attended the cuicacalli. But the *Codez Mendoza* indicates that the age of attendance was fifteen.[12] As suggested for the calmecac, the age of admittance may have varied with different cuicacalli.

According to Durán, instruction in the cuicacalli began each day one hour prior to sunset. Boys were gathered from their wards by elders selected in their respective wards for that task. Similarly, elderly women appointed by the wards collected the girls. These different groups then proceeded to the cuicacalli. Instruction took place in the large courtyard of the cuicacalli, with the teachers observing and instructing from the center, while the students (male and female) danced about them. Apparently the dancing and singing continued well into the night, when the elders returned their charges to their respective wards.

Sahagún's description of the cuicacalli, although less detailed, is strikingly similar to that of Durán. At sunset, the youths who had worked all day in telpochcalli-administered activities bathed and prepared themselves for an evening at the cuicacalli. There they sang and danced until after midnight (Sahagún, 1950-1969: book 3, 54-55). Elsewhere, Sahagún mentions that the masters of the youths (*tiachcahuan*) and the rulers of the youths (*telpochtlatoque*) administered work activities from the cuicacalli. In the evenings, these same functionaries went to the cuicacalli for song and dance activities, accompanied by youths. When the dancing was finished, the youths returned not to their homes to sleep, but to their telpochcalli (ibid., book 8, 43).

Song and dance were essential to the proper performance of virtually all religious rituals and ceremonies. Oral transmission of vast amounts of cultural knowledge took the form of songs. Children and youths (male and female) are frequently mentioned in Sahagún (ibid., book 2, passim) as taking active part in numerous ceremonies, including the performance of songs and dances. Proper training would be a prerequisite for participation in these religious events.

Education for male commoners would have involved training in both the telpochcalli and the cuicacalli. The "masters of the youths" mentioned in connection with the cuicacalli were also associated with the telpochcalli.

A youth attending the telpochcalli, if properly raised, prudent, and of good heart, could be granted the title *tiachcauh* (master of youths). If he continued to prove himself, "then he was named ruler of youths (telpoch-tlato). He governed them all; he spoke for all the youths. If one (of them) sinned, this one judged him; he sentenced (the youths) and corrected them. He dealt justice" (ibid., book 3, 53). Persons could also achieve these positions through success in the calmecac (see above), suggesting that both nobles and commoners could occupy these teaching and administrative positions.

While some commoner youths would continue their lives in telpochcalli or cuicacalli positions, the vast majority would, upon marriage, establish households and undertake the subsistence activities in which they were trained since childhood. Additionally, as all commoner males received military instruction in the telpochcalli, they provided the state with a trained military force for the imperial expansion so important to the Aztec empire.

## Commoners: The Education of Female Children

Female commoners, like male commoners, were instructed in the virtues of obedience, respect, honesty, humility, and diligence. A mother, in admonishing her daughter, advises her to be

> cleanly and diligent, and look after the house and keep all in order as it should be, each thing in its place. Thus you will learn what you must do in your house when you marry. . . .
>
> Listen well to what you are ordered to do, and do not give a rude reply. If you cannot do what is asked of you, make your excuses civilly, but do not lie or deceive anyone. . . . If someone offers you good counsel, take it. . . .
>
> Attend to your housework, and do not frivously leave your house. Do not frequent the market place, or the public squares (Zorita 1963*b*:148-151).

The education of female commoners was aimed primarily at preparation for marriage. Girls were taught to be respectful and obedient in their future married life. They were also instructed in the skills essential for maintaining a household. Spinning, weaving, and cooking were considered of utmost importance (Sahagún, 1950-1969: book 10, 51-53). Maidens were instructed in these skills by their mothers (see plate 5 and table 2).

Inasmuch as most commoner females were confined largely to household activities, from childhood through old age, their training centered

## TABLE 2

## FEMALE COMMONERS

| Age | Duties | Punishments |
|-----|--------|-------------|
| 3 | — | — |
| 4 | Instruction in spinning cotton | — |
| 5 | Continuation of instruction in spinning cotton | — |
| 6 | Practice in learning to spin cotton | — |
| 7 | Continuation in spinning cotton; increased activity | — |
| 8 | — | Learns of use of maguey thorns for punishment |
| 9 | — | Maguey thorns applied to hands as punishment |
| 10 | — | Beaten with stick for not properly spinning cotton |
| 11 | — | Required to inhale "chile-smoke" |
| 12 | At night, instructed to sweep house and street | — |
| 13 | Instructed to grind maize, make tortillas, and prepare other foods | — |
| 14 | Instruction in weaving | — |

on the skills and moral virtues important at that household level. In terms of formal education, the state took very little interest in them, although Durán does state that females from the various wards of Tenochtitlan attended the cuicacalli (see above).

## Conclusion

By 1519, the Aztec state had developed formal school systems for the education of male nobles and commoners. The state took particular interest in preparing these persons for warfare, for positions in the religious hierarchy, or for the occupancy of political offices. In addition, the formal, standardized educational process tended to channel the loyalties of these persons to the state rather than to any subunit of the state.

One of the major functions of the state noted earlier is the maintenance of the system of social stratification. Among the Aztecs, this was facilitated by a relatively segregated school system. Nobles attended the calmecac and received training appropriate to the performance of religious and administrative duties. Commoners attending the telpochcalli were trained primarily as warriors.

The dedication of commoner youths to the calmecac may have occurred in rare instances. Yet, by the time of the Spanish Conquest, several factors militated against even those rare cases. The growing conflict between the ascribed nobility and the achievement nobility has already been mentioned. This conflict stemmed, at least in part, from the growing number of nobility by birth, without a correspondingly rapid growth in bureaucratic, religious, or economic positions. In fact, the final decades of the Aztec Empire saw a decrease in the rate of military expansion, as well as some crushing military defeats. This decrease meant a decline in the rate of growth of bureaucratic positions available to the expanding nobility. Coupled with this, an awareness of military difficulties would have encouraged the Aztecs to concentrate increasingly on military training. The most important centers for that type of instruction were the telpochcalli, attended by male commoners. Under these conditions, dedication of commoners to the calmecac would have been improbable.

A likely consequence of these forces would have been to define membership in the two schools more strictly along class lines. This would serve to intensify the stratification system. Religious and political knowledge and expertise would become the sole prerogative of the nobility, thus reserving for them the administration of the state.

## NOTES

1. See Gibson, 1971; Carrasco, 1971; Adams, 1966; Sanders and Price, 1968; Wolf, 1959; Barlow, 1949.

2. The plates are all from the *Codex Mendoza,* part III. This Aztec pictorial document was composed in post-Conquest times, although it represents pre-Conquest conditions: warfare and conquest, tribute, and daily life.

3. Information is scanty on the transmission of specialized craft skills, and discussion of such training is not emphasized here.

4. By far the greatest amount of information is available on noble males. Somewhat less data exist on commoner males, while females, whether noble or commoner, are generally neglected in the primary sources.

5. Sahagún, Durán, and Zorita are the most important primary textual sources on Aztec education; the *Codex Mendoza* is the most significant pictorial source. All were composed in the mid-sixteenth century.

6. These are placed in order from youngest to oldest.

7. The Otomí were held in very low esteem by the Aztecs.

8. *Huehuetlatolli*: old or ancient speech. This refers to a series of orations presented not only to children, but also to rulers and other important persons. See Sullivan, 1974.

9. Not only the father, but also other older male relatives were responsible for admonishing and advising the youth.

10. Details are in Durán, 1971:111-115 and the *Codex Mendoza,* part III, plate 62.

11. This suggests that the cuicacalli, like the calmecac, was administered through a centralized, hierarchical structure.

12. Sahagún (1950-1969: book 8, 71-72) states that the age for admittance to the cuicacalli was ten, twelve, or thirteen, and implies that nobles attended this school.

# BIBLIOGRAPHY

Adams, R. McC.
1966    *The Evolution of Urban Society.* Chicago: Aldine.

Anonymous Conqueror
1971    "Relación de algunas cosas de la Nueva España y de la gran ciudad de Temestitan, Mexico; escrita por un compañero de Hernán Cortés." In *Colección de documentos para la historia de México.* J. C. Icazbalceta, ed. Vol. 1. Mexico: Editorial Porrua. Pp. 368-398.

Barlow, Robert H.
1949    "The Extent of the Empire of the Culhua-Mexica." *Ibero-Americana* 28.

Carrasco, Pedro
1971    "Social Organization of Ancient Mexico." In *Handbook of Middle American Indians,* vol. 10. Austin: University of Texas Press. Pp. 349-375.

Caso, Alfonso
1963    Land Tenure among the Ancient Mexicans. *American Anthropologist* 65:863-878.

*Codex Mendoza.* Ed. James Cooper Clark. 3 parts. London.
1938

Cohen, Yehudi
1970    "Schools and Civilizational States." In *The Social Sciences and the Comparative Study of Educational Systems.* J. Fischer, ed. Scranton: International Textbook Company. Pp. 55-147.

Davies, Nigel
1974    *The Aztecs.* New York: G. P. Putnam's Sons.

Dibble, Charles
1971    "Writing in Central Mexico." In *Handbook of Middle American Indians,* vol. 10. Austin: University of Texas Press. Pp. 322-332.

Durán, Diego
1967    *Historia de las indias de Nueva España e Islas de la Tierra Firme.* 2 vols. Mexico: Editorial Porrua.
1971    *Book of the Gods and Rites and the Ancient Calendar.* Fernando Horcasitas and Doris Heyden, trans. Norman: University of Oklahoma Press.

Fried, Morton H.
1968    "On the Evolution of Social Stratification and the State." In *Readings in Anthropology.* 2d ed. M. H. Fried, ed. Vol. 2. Pp. 462-478.

Gibson, Charles
1971    "Structure of the Aztec Empire." In *Handbook of Middle American Indians.* vol. 10. Austin: University of Texas Press. Pp. 376-394.

Katz, F.
1972    *The Ancient American Civilizations.* New York: Praeger.

Lombardo de Ruiz, Sonia
1973    *Desarrollo urbano de Mexico-Tenochtitlan.* Mexico: Instituto Nacional de Antropología e Historia.

León-Portilla, Miguel
1963    *Aztec Thought and Culture.* Norman: University of Oklahoma Press.

Markus S., Mina
1963    "Estudio comparativo entre la educación nahuatl y la griega." *Estudios de Cultura Nahuatl* (Mexico) 4:281-292.

Monzón, Arturo
1946    "La educación." In *Mexico prehispánico: Antología de esta semana 1935-1946.* Mexico: Editorial Emma Hurtado. Pp. 754-764.

Moreno, M. M.
1931    *La organización política y social de los Aztecas.* Mexico: Universidad Nacional Autónoma de México.

Sahagún, Bernardino de
1950-   *Florentine Codex: General History of the Things of New Spain.* Arthur J. O.
1969    Anderson and Charles Dibble, eds. 12 books. Santa Fe: School of American Research.
1956    *Historia general de las cosas de Nueva España.* 4 vols. Mexico: Editorial Porrua.

Sanders, William, and Barbara Price
1968    *Mesoamerica.* New York: Random House.

Soustelle, Jacques
1961    *Daily Life of the Aztecs on the Eve of the Spanish Conquest.* Stanford: Stanford University Press.

Sullivan, Thelma
1974    "The Rhetorical Orations, or Huehuetlatolli, Collected by Sahagún." In *Sixteenth Century Mexico: The Work of Sahagún.* Munro S. Edmonson, ed. Albuquerque: University of New Mexico Press. Pp. 79-109.

Torquemada, Juan de
1969    *Los veinte i un libros rituales i monarchía indiana.* 3 vols. Mexico: Editorial Porrua.

Wolf, Eric
1959    *Sons of the Shaking Earth.* Chicago: University of Chicago Press.

Zorita, Alonso de
1963a   *Breve y sumaria relación de los señores de la Nueva España.* Mexico: Universidad Nacional Autónoma de México.
1963b   *Life and Labor in Ancient Mexico.* Benjamin Keen, trans. New Brunswick: Rutgers University Press.

# 8.

# Training for the Priesthood among the Kogi of Colombia

## GERARDO REICHEL-DOLMATOFF

The Kogi of the Sierra Nevada de Santa Marta in northeastern Colombia are a small tribe of some 6,000 Chibcha-speaking Indians, descendants of the ancient Tairona who, at the time of the Spanish conquest, had reached a relatively high development among the aboriginal peoples of Colombia. The Sierra Nevada, with its barren, highly dissected slopes, steep and roadless, presents a difficult terrain for Creole settlement and, owing to the harshness and poor soils of their habitat, the Kogi have been able to preserve, to a quite remarkable degree, their traditional way of life.

The present tribal territory lies at an altitude of between 1,500 and 2,000 meters, where the Indians occupy several small villages of about ten to several dozen round huts, each of about 3 to 4 meters in diameter and built of wattle and daub covered with a conical thatched roof. Each house is inhabited by one nuclear family composed of four or five people who sleep, cook, and eat in this narrow, dark space that they share with their dogs and with most of their material belongings. The huts of a village cluster around a larger, well-built house, also round in its ground plan, but provided with a wall of densely plaited canes; this is the ceremonial house, the temple, access to which is restricted to the men, and where women and children are not allowed to enter. Kogi villages are not permanently occupied; most Indians live in isolated homesteads dispersed over the mountain slopes, and the villages are hardly more than convenient gathering places where the inhabitants of a valley or of a certain restricted area can come together occasionally to exchange news, discuss community matters, discharge themselves of some minor ritual obligations, or trade with the visiting Creole peasants. When staying in the village, the men usually spend the night in the ceremonial house where they talk, sing, or simply listen to the conversation of the older men. As traditional patterns of family life demand that men and women live in not too close an association and collaborate in rigidly prescribed ways in the daily task of making a living, most Kogi families, when staying in their fields, occupy two neighboring huts, one inhabited by the man while the other hut serves as a kitchen and storeroom, and is occupied by his wife and children.

The economic basis of Kogi culture consists of small garden plots where sweet manioc, maize, plantains, cucurbits, beans, and some fruit trees are grown. A few domestic animals such as chicken, pigs, or, rarely, some cattle, are kept only to be sold or exchanged to the Creoles for bush knives, iron pots, and salt. Some Kogi make cakes of raw sugar for trading. Because of the lack of adequate soils, the food resources of one altitudinal level are often insufficient, and many families own several small gardens and temporary shelters at different altitudes, moving between the cold highlands and the temperate valleys in a dreary continuous quest for some harvestable food. Although the starchy tubers provide a fairly permanent food supply, protein sources are few, and a chronic state of malnutrition seems to be the rule. Slash-and-burn agriculture is heavy work, and the harsh, mountainous environment makes transportation a laborious task. Much agricultural work is done by women and children who collaborate with the men in clearing and burning the fields.

The objects of material culture are coarse and simple, and generally are quite devoid of ornamentation. Some heavy wooden benches, a pair of old string hammocks, smoke-blackened cooking vessels and gourd containers, and a few baskets and carrying bags are about all an average family owns. It is evident then that, to the casual observer, Kogi culture gives the impression of deject poverty, and the disheveled and sullen countenance of the Indian adds to this image of misery and neglect. Indeed, if judged by their external appearance and their austere and withdrawn manner, one would easily come to the conclusion that by all standards of cultural evolution these Indians are a sorry lot.

But nothing could be more misleading than appearances. Behind the drab façade of penury, the Kogi lead a rich spiritual life in which the ancient traditions are being kept alive and furnish the individual and his society with guiding values that not only make bearable the arduous conditions of physical survival, but make them appear almost unimportant if measured against the profound spiritual satisfactions offered by religion. After days and weeks of hunger and work, of ill health and the dreary round of daily tasks, one will suddenly be taken into the presence of a scene, maybe a dance, a song, or some private ritual action that, quite unexpectedly, offers a momentary glimpse into the depths of a very ancient, very elaborate culture. And stronger still becomes this impression in the presence of a priest or an elder who, when speaking of these spiritual dimensions, reveals before his listeners this coherent system of beliefs which is the Kogi world view.

Traditional Kogi religion is closely related to Kogi ideas about the structure and functioning of the Universe, and Kogi cosmology is, in essence, a model for survival in that it molds individual behavior into a plan of actions or avoidances that are oriented toward the maintenance of a viable equilibrium between Man's demands and Nature's resources. In this manner the individual and society at large must both carry the burden of great responsibilities which, in the Kogi view, extend not only to their own society but to the whole of mankind.

The central personification of Kogi religion is the Mother-Goddess. It was she who, in the beginning of time, created the cosmic egg, encompassed between the seven points of reference: North, South, East, West, Zenith, Nadir, and Center, and stratified into nine horizontal layers, the nine 'worlds,' the fifth and middlemost of which is ours. They embody the nine daughters of the Goddess, each one conceived as a certain type of agricultural land, ranging from pale, barren sand to the black and fertile soil that nourishes mankind. The seven points of reference within which the Cosmos is contained are associated or identified with innumerable mythical beings, animals, plants, minerals, colors, winds, and many highly abstract concepts, some of them arranged into a scale of values, while others are of a more ambivalent nature. The four cardinal directions are under the control of four mythical culture heroes who are also the ancestors of the four primary segments of Kogi society, all four of them Sons of the Mother-Goddess and, similarly, they are associated with certain pairs of animals that exemplify the basic marriage rules. The organizing concept of social structure consists of a system of patrilines and matrilines in which descent is reckoned from father to son and from mother to daughter, and a relationship of complementary opposites is modeled after the relationship between certain animal species. The North is associated with the marsupial and his spouse the armadillo; the South with the puma and his spouse the deer; the East with the jaguar and his spouse the peccary; and the West with the eagle and his spouse the snake. In other words, the ancestral couples form antagonistic pairs in which the "male" animal (marsupial, puma, jaguar, eagle) feeds on the "female" animal (armadillo, deer, peccary, snake) and marriage rules prescribe that the members of a certain patriline must marry women whose matriline is associated with an animal that is the natural prey of the man's animal. The equivalence of food and sex is very characteristic of Kogi thought and is essential for an understanding of religious symbolism in myth and ritual. Moreover, each patriline or matriline has many magical attributes and privileges that together with their respective mythical origins, genealogies, and precise ceremonial functions, form a very elaborate body of rules and relationships.

The macrocosmic structure repeats itself in innumerable aspects of Kogi culture. Each mountain peak of the Sierra Nevada is seen as a "world," a house, an abode, peopled by spirit-beings and enclosed within a fixed set of points of reference: a top, a center, a door. All ceremonial houses contain four circular, stepped, wooden shelves on the inside of their conical roofs, representing the different cosmic layers, and it is thought that this structure is repeated *in reverse* underground, the house being thus an exact reproduction of the Universe, up to the point where its center becomes the "center of the world." Moreover, the cosmic egg is conceived as a divine uterus, the womb of the Mother-Goddess, and so, in a descending scale, our earth is conceived as a uterus, the Sierra Nevada is a uterus, and so is every mountain, house, cave, carrying bag, and, indeed, every tomb. The land is conceived as a huge female body that nourishes and protects, and each topographic feature of it corresponds to an inclusive category of anatomical detail of this vast mother-image. The large roof apexes of the major ceremonial houses, constructed in the shape of an open, upturned umbrella, represent the sexual organ of the Mother-Goddess and offerings are deposited there representing a concept of fertilization.

The Kogi conceive the world in terms of a dualistic scheme that expresses itself on many different levels. On the level of the individual as a biological being, it is the human body that provides the model for one set of opposed but complementary principles, manifest in the apparent bilateral symmetry of the body and the distinction between male and female organisms. On the level of society, the existence of groups of opposed but complementary segments is postulated, based on the mythical precedency and controlled by the principles of exogamy. The villages themselves are often divided into two parts and a divisory line, invisible but known to all, separates the village into two sections. The ceremonial houses are imagined as being bisected into a "right side" and a "left side," by a line running diametrically between the two doors that are located at opposite points of the circular building, and each half of the structure has its own central post, one male and another female. On a cosmic level, the same principle divides the Universe into two sides, the division being marked by the tropical sun, which, going overhead, separates the world into a right and a left half. The dualistic elaborations of this type are innumerable: male/female, man/woman, right/left, heat/cold, light/dark, above/below, and the like, and they are further-more associated with certain categories of animals, plants, and minerals; with colors, winds, diseases, and, of course, with the principles of Good and Evil. Many of these dualistic manifestations have the character of symbolic antagonists that share a common essence; just as the tribal deities who, in one divine being, combine benefic and malevolent aspects, thus man carries within himself this vital polarity of Good and Evil.

Apart from the Mother-Goddess, the principal divine personifications are her four sons and, next to them, a large number of spirit-owners, the masters of the different aspects of Nature, the rulers over rituals, and the beings that govern certain actions. That all these supernatural beings are the appointed guardians of certain aspects of human conduct—cultural or biological—has many ethical implications that provide the basis for the concept of sin. When the divine beings established the world order, however, they made provision for individual interpretation and thus confirmed a person's autonomy of moral choice. Life is a mixture of good and evil and, as the Kogi point out very frequently, there can be no morality without immorality. According to Kogi ethics one's life should be dedicated entirely to the acquisition of knowledge, a term by which are meant the myths and traditions, the songs and spells, and all the rules that regulate ritual. This body of esoteric knowledge is called by the Kogi the "Law of the Mother." Every object, action, or intention has a spirit-owner who jealously guards what is his own, his privilege, but who is willing to share it with mankind if compensated by an adequate offering. The concept of offerings, then, is closely connected with divin-atory practices because it is necessary to determine the exact nature of the offerings that will most please a certain spirit-being. These details—some of them esoteric trivia but nonetheless functional units of a complex whole—can only be learned in the course of many years. Closely related to this body of knowledge, Kogi learning includes a wide range of infor-mation on phenomena that might be classified as belonging to tribal history, geography, and ecology, animal and plant categorization, and a fair knowledge of anatomy and physiology.

But all this knowledge has a single purpose: to find a balance between Good and Evil and to reach old age in a state of wisdom and tolerance. The process of establishing this balance is called *yulúka*, an expression that might be translated as "to be in agreement with" or "to be in harmony with." One should be careful, however, not to see in this concept a kind of romantic *Naturphilosophie*, of noble savages living in harmony with nature, but take it for what it is—a harsh sense of reality paired, at times, with a rather cynical outlook on human affairs. The concept of yulúka does not stand for blissful tranquillity, but means grudging acceptance of misfortune, be it sickness or hunger, the treachery of one's closest of kin, or the undeserved ill will of one's neighbor. A Kogi, when faced with hardships or high emotional tensions will rarely dramatize his situation, but will rather try to establish an "agreement" by a process of rationalization.

Another philosophical concept of importance is called *aluna*. There are many possible translations ranging from "spiritual" to "libidinous," and from "powerful" to "traditional" or "imaginary." Sometimes the word is used to designate the human soul. An approximate general translation would be "otherworldly," a term that would imply supernatural power with vision and strength, but otherwise the meaning of this concept has to be illustrated by examples, to convey its significance to the outsider. For example, to say that the world was created "in *aluna*" means that it was designed by a spiritual effort. The deities and the tribal ancestors exist in aluna, that is, in the Otherworld, and in an incorporeal state. Similarly, it is possible to deposit an offering in aluna at a certain spot, without really visiting that place. A man might sin in aluna, by harboring evil intentions. And to go further still: to the Kogi, concrete reality quite often is only appearance, a semblance that has only symbolic value, while the true essence of things exists only in aluna. According to the Kogi, one must therefore develop the spiritual faculty to see behind these appearances and to recognize the aluna of the Universe.

The divine personifications of the Kogi pantheon are not only continuously demanding offerings from men but, being guardians of the moral order, also watch any interaction between mortals, and punish the breaking of the rules that govern interpersonal relations. The Kogi put great emphasis on collaboration, the sharing of food, and the observance of respectful behavior toward elders and other persons of authority. Unfilial conduct, the refusal to work for one's father-in-law, or aggressive behavior of any kind are not only social sins, but are transgressions of the divine rules, and for this the offender is bound to incur the displeasure of the divine beings. Among the worst offenses are violations of certain sexual restrictions. Kogi attitudes toward sex are dominated by deep anxieties concerned with the constant fear of pollution, and prolonged sexual abstinence is demanded of all men who are engaged in any ritual activity. The great sin is incest, and the observation of the rules of exogamy is a frequent topic of conversations and admonitions in the ceremonial house.

Kogi culture contains many elements of sexual repression, and there is a marked antifeminist tendency. The men consider the acquisition of esoteric knowledge to be the only valid objective in life and claim that women are the prime obstacle on the way of achieving this goal. Although a Kogi husband is expected to be a dutiful provider and should produce sufficient food to keep his family in good health, it is also stated that a man should never work for material gain and should not make efforts to acquire more property than he needs in order to feed and house his family. All his energies should be spent on learning, on taking part in ritual, and on acquiring the necessary knowledge of procedure and moral precepts to contribute to the maintenance of the ordained world order. Now women have very few ritual functions and, except when quite old, show but little interest in metaphysical matters. To them the balance of the Universe is of small concern; they eat, they sleep, they chat and idle; in other words, to a Kogi man they personify all the elements of indulgence, of disruption, and of irresponsibility. "They are like cockroaches," the Kogi grumble, "always near the cooking place, and eating all the time!" Besides, Kogi women are not squeamish about sex and, being oblivious to the delicate details of ritual purity, appear to their men as eternal temptresses bent upon destroying the social order and, with it, the religious concepts that are so closely connected with it.

The Kogi are a deeply religious people and they are guided in their faith by a highly formalized priesthood. Although all villages have a headman who nominally represents civil authority, the true power of decision in personal and community matters is concentrated in the hands of the native priests, called *mámas*. These men, most of whom have a profound knowledge of tribal custom, are not simple curers or shamanistic practitioners, but fulfill priestly functions, taught during years of training and exercised in solemn rituals. The mámas are sun-priests who, high up in the mountains behind the villages, officiate in ceremonial centers where people gather at certain times of the year, and each ceremonial house in a village is under the charge of one or two priests who direct and supervise the nightlong meetings of the men when they gather in the settlement. The influence of this priesthood extends to every aspect of family and village life and completely overshadows the few attributes of the headmen.

To begin with, all people must periodically visit a priest for confession—in private or in public—of all their actions and intentions. An important mechanism of control is introduced here by the idea that sickness is, in the last analysis, the consequence of a state of sinfulness incurred by not living according to the "Law of the Mother." A man will therefore scrutinize his conscience in every detail and will try to be absolutely honest about his actions and intentions, to avoid falling ill or to cure an existing sickness. Confession takes place at night in the ceremonial house, the máma reclining in his hammock while the confessant sits next to him on a low bench. The other men must observe silence or, at least, converse in subdued voices, while between the priest and the confessant unfolds a slow, halting dialogue in which the máma formulates several searching questions about the confessant's family life, social relations, food intake, ritual obligations, dreams, and many other aspects of his daily life. People are supposed to confess not only the actual fault they have committed, but also their evil intentions, their sexual or aggressive fantasies, anything that might come to their minds under the questioning of the priest. The nagging fear of sickness, the hypochondriacal observation and discussion of the most insignificant symptoms, will make people completely unburden themselves. There can be no doubt that confession is a psychotherapeutic institution of the first order, within the general system of Kogi religion.

To act as a confessor to people as metaphysically preoccupied as the Kogi puts high demands upon a máma's intelligence and empathy; his role is never that of a passive listener but he must be an accomplished conversationalist, able to direct the confessant's discourse into channels that allow him to probe deeply into the troubled mind of his confidant. But confession in the ceremonial house is not the only occasion when an individual can relieve himself of his intimate doubts and conflicts. At any time, any man, woman, or child can approach a máma and ask him for advice. It is natural then that a máma obtains, in this manner, much information on individual attitudes and community affairs which allows him to exercise control over many aspects of local sociopolitical development. I know of no case, however, where a máma would have taken advantage of this knowledge for his own ends. The mámas constitute a truly moralizing force and, as such, occupy a highly respected position.

Kogi priests are the products of a long and arduous training, under the strict guidance of one or several old and experienced mámas. In former times it was the custom that, as soon as a male child was born, the máma would consult in a trance the Mother-Goddess, to ascertain whether or not the newborn babe was to be a future priest. It is also said that a máma might dream the name of a certain family and thus would know that their newborn male child would become a priest. Immediately the máma would then "give notice" to the newborn during a visit to his family, and it is pointed out that, in those times, the parents would have felt greatly honored by the knowledge that their son would eventually become a priest. From several traditions it would appear that certain families or, rather, patrilines, may have had hereditary preeminence in priesthood, and even today priests belonging to a high-ranking exogamic group are likely to be more respected than others.

Ideally, a future priest should receive a special education since birth; the child would immediately be separated from his mother and given into the care of the máma's wife, or any other woman of childbearing age whom the máma might order to join his household as a wet nurse. But occasionally the mother herself would be allowed to keep the child, with the condition that he be weaned before reaching the age of three months. From then on the child would have to be fed a mash of ripe bananas and cooking plantains, and soon afterwards would have to be turned over to the máma's family. If, for some reason, a family refused to give up the child, the civil authorities might have to interfere and take the child away by force. It was always the custom that the family should pay the máma for the education of the boy, by sending periodically some food to his house, or by working in his fields.

These ideal conditions, it might be said, probably never existed; under normal circumstances—and this refers also to the present situation—the training begins at about two or three years of age, but certainly not later than the fifth year, and then continues through childhood, adolescence, and young adulthood, until the novice, aged now perhaps twenty or twenty-two, has acquired his new status as máma by fulfilling all necessary requirements. The full training period should be eighteen years, divided into two cycles of nine years each, the novice reaching puberty by the end of the first cycle.

There exist about three or four places in the Sierra Nevada where young people are being trained for the priesthood. In each place, two, or at most, three boys of slightly different ages live in an isolated valley, far from the next village, where they are taken into the care of their master's family. The geographical setting may vary but, in most cases, the small settlement, consisting of a ceremonial house and two or three huts, is located at a spot that figures prominently in myth and tradition. It may be the place where a certain lineage had its origin, or where a culture hero accomplished a difficult task; or perhaps it is the spot where one of the many spirit-owners of Nature has his abode. In any case, the close association of a "school" with a place having certain religious-historical traditions is of importance because at such a spot there exists the likelihood of ready communication with the supernatural sphere; it is a "door," a threshold, a point of convergence, besides being a place that is sacred and lies under the protection of benevolent spirit-beings.

The institution of priestly training has a long and sacred tradition among the Kogi. Several lengthy myths tell of how the four sons of the Mother-Goddess created Mount Doanankuívi, at the headwaters of the Tucurinca River and, inside the mountain, built the first ceremonial house where novices were to be trained for the priesthood. The first legendary máma to teach such a group of disciples was Búnalyue, and once they had acquired the status of priests, they settled in the nearby valley of Mukuánauiaishi which, thereafter, became the center for the training of novices from all over the Sierra Nevada. According to several myths, it was Búnkuasé, one of the sons of the Mother-Goddess, who established the rules according to which a future máma was to be chosen and educated. Búnkuasé, "the shining one," is the personification of the highest moral principles in Kogi ethics and is thus taken to be the patron and spiritual guardian of the priesthood. It is, however, characteristic of Kogi culture that there should exist several other traditions according to which it is Kashindúkua, the morally ambivalent jaguar-priest, who is the tutelary divine personification. Kashindúkua, also a son of the Mother-Goddess, had been destined by her to be a great curer of human ills, a thaumaturge able to extract sickness from the patient's body as if it were a concrete, tangible substance. But occasionally, and much to his brother's grief, he misused his powers and then did great harm to people. Kashindúkua came to personify sexual license and, above all, incest but, as an ancient priest-king, curer, and protector of all ceremonial houses, he continues to occupy a very important place in the Kogi pantheon.

A novice, training for the priesthood, is designated by the term *kuívi* (abstinent). This concept refers not only to temperance in food and drink, but also to sex, sleep, and any form of overindulgence. This attitude of ascetic self-denial is said to have been the prime virtue of the ancient mámas of mythical times. But, as always, the Kogi introduce an element of ambivalence, of man's difficult choice of action, and also tell of outstanding sages and miracle workers who, at the same time, were great sinners.

At the level of cultural development attained by the Kogi, the teacher position is well recognized and there is full agreement that all priests must undergo a long process of organized directed training, in the course of which the novice's education is functionally specialized. The ideal image of the great teacher and master, the ancient sage, is often elaborated in myths and tales, and in their context the máma is generally represented as a just but authoritarian father figure. In the great quest for knowledge and divine illumination, the teacher never demands from his pupils more than he himself is willing to give; he suffers patiently with them and is a model of self-control and wisdom. In other tales, the opposite is shown, the vicious hypocrite who stuffs himself with food while his disciples are fasting, or the lecherous old man who seduces nubile girls while publicly preaching chastity. These images of the saint and the sinner—patterned after those of the hero and the villain, in another type of tale—are always present in Kogi thought and, in many aspects, are statements of the importance society attributes to the role of the priesthood. Some of these tales are really quite simplistic in that they tend to measure a máma's stature merely in terms of his cunning, his reconciliatory abilities, rote memory, or miracle-working capacity, but other tales contain examples of true psychological insight, high moral principles, and readiness for self-sacrifice. The image of the teacher is thus well defined—though somewhat stereotyped—in Kogi culture and is also referred to in situations that lie quite outside the sphere of priestly training and that are con-nected—to give some examples—to the acquisition of skills, the tracing of genealogical ties, or the interpretation of natural phenomena. On the one hand, then, it is plain that not all mámas are thought to be adequate teachers and to be trusted with the education of a small child. On the other hand, not all mámas will accept disciples; some live in abject poverty, others are in ill health, and others still feel disinclined to carry the responsibilities that teaching entails. Old age is not of the essence if it is not accompanied by an alert mind and a manifestly "pure" behavior, and quite often a fairly young máma has great renown because of his high moral status, while older men are held in less esteem.

The novices should spend most of their waking hours inside the cere-monial house. In former times they used to live in a small enclosure (*hubi*) within the ceremonial structure, but at present they sleep in one of the neighboring huts. This hut, which is similar to the ceremonial house but smaller, has an elaborate roof apex and the walls of plaited canes have two doors at opposite points of the circumference, while the hut of the máma's family lacks the apex and has only one door. All during their long training the novices must lead an entirely nocturnal life and are strictly forbidden to leave the house in daylight. Sleeping during the day on low cots of canes placed against the walls, the novices rise after sunset and, as soon as darkness has set in, are allowed to take their first meal in the kitchen annex or outside the máma's house. A second meal is taken around midnight and a light third meal shortly before sunrise. Even during the night, the novices are not supposed to go outside except in the company of a máma and then only for a short walk. The principal inter-dictions, repeated most emphatically over and over again, refer to the sun and to women; a novice should be educated, after weaning, only by men and among men, and should never see a girl or a woman who is sexually active; and throughout his training period, he should never see the sun nor be exposed to his rays. "The sun is a máma," the Kogi say; "And this máma might cause harm to the child." When there is a moon, a novice should cover his head with a specially woven basketry tray (*güíshi*) when leaving the house at night.

During their training period the novices are supervised and strictly controlled by one or two attendant wardens (*hánkua-kúkui*), adult men who have joined the máma's household, generally after having spent some years as novices under his guidance. These wardens are mainly in charge of discipline, but may occasionally participate to some degree in the educational process, according to the máma's orders.

Apart from the little group of people who constitute the settlement—the máma and his family, the wardens, and some aged relatives of either—the novices should avoid any contact with other people; in fact, they should never even be *seen* by an outsider. The manifest danger of pollution consists in the presence of people who are in contact with women; should such a person see a novice or should he speak to him, the latter would immediately lose the spiritual power he has accumulated in the course of his apprenticeship. It is supposed, then, that the community consists only of "pure" people, that is, of persons who abstain from any sexual activity and who also observe very strict dietary rules.

As in many primitive educational systems, the observance of dietary restrictions is a very important point in priestly training. In general, a novice should soon learn to eat sparingly and, after puberty has been reached, should be able to go occasionally without food for several days. He should eat very little meat, but rather fowl such as curassow, and should avoid all foodstuffs that are of non-Indian origin such as bananas, sugar cane, onions, or citrus fruits. He should never, under any circumstances, consume salt, nor should he use any condiments such as peppers. A novice, it may be added here, should not touch his food with his left hand because this is the "female" hand and is polluted. During the first nine years the prescribed diet consists mainly of some small river catfish and freshwater shrimp, certain yellow-green grasshoppers of nocturnal habits, land snails collected in the highlands, large black *túbi* beetles, and certain white mushrooms. Vitamin D appears to be sufficient to compensate for the lack of sunlight during these years. Three or four different classes of maize can also be eaten, as well as some sweet manioc, pumpkins, and certain beans. Some mámas insist that all food consumed by the novices should be predominantly of a white color: white beans, white potatoes, white manioc, white shrimps, white land snails, and so forth. Only after puberty are they allowed to eat, however sparingly, the meat of game animals such as peccary, agouti, and armadillo. These animals, it is said, "have great knowledge, and by eating their flesh the novices will partake in their wisdom." In preparing their daily food, only a clay pot made by the máma himself should be used and all food should be boiled, but never fried nor smoked. Shoe-shaped vessels (or, rather, breast-shaped ones) are used especially for the preparation of a ritual diet based on beans.

The boys are dressed in a white cotton cloth woven by the máma or, later on, by themselves, which is wrapped around the body, covering it from under the armpits to the ankles, and held in place by a wide woven belt. For adornment they wear bracelets, armlets, necklaces, and ear ornaments, all of ancient Tairona origin and made of gold, gilded copper, and semiprecious stones. There is emphasis on cleanliness and at night the boys go to bathe in the nearby mountain stream.

In former times, that is, perhaps until three or four generations ago, it was the custom to educate also some female children who, eventually, were to become the wives of the priests. The girls were chosen by divination and then were brought up by the wife of a máma. Aided by other old women, the girls were taught many ancient traditions primarily referring to the dangers of pollution. They were trained to prepare certain "pure" foods, to collect aromatic and medical herbs, and to assist in the preparation of minor rituals. At present, the education of girls under the guidance of a máma's wife is institutionalized in some parts, but the aim is not so much to prepare spouses for future priests than to educate certain intelligent girls "in the manner of the ancients" and send them back to their families after a few years of schooling, so they can teach the womenfolk of their respective villages the traditions and precepts they have learned in the máma's household, and be thus living examples of moral conduct.

But I must return now to the boy who has been taken into a strange family and who is now undergoing a crucial period of adaptation.

The novice is exposed to the varied influences of a setting that differs notably from that of his own family. Although the child will find in the máma's household a certain well-accustomed set of familial behavioral patterns, he is made aware that he now lives in a context of nonkin. This is of special relevance where the novice was educated for the first three or four years by his own family and has thus acquired a certain cultural perspective that, in his new environment, is likely to differ from the demands made by the máma's kin. Between teacher and pupil, however, there generally develops a fairly close emotional tie; the novice addresses the máma with the term *hátei* (father), and he, in turn, refers to his disciples as his "children," or "sons." Only after the novice has reached puberty does the apprentice-master relationship usually acquire a more formal tone.

During the first two years of life, Kogi children are prodded and continuously encouraged to accelerate their sensory-motor development: creeping, walking, speaking. But in later years they are physically and vocally rather quiet. A Kogi mother does not encourage response and activity, but rather tries to soothe her child and to keep him silent and unobtrusive. Very strict sphincter training is instituted, and by the age of ten or twelve months the boy is expected to exercise complete control during the daytime hours. Play activity is discouraged by all adults and, indeed, to be accused of "playing" is a very serious reproach. There are practically no children's games in Kogi culture and for this reason a teacher's complaints refer rather to lack of attention or to overindulgence in eating or sleeping, than to any boisterous, playful, or aggressive attitudes.

Although older children are sometimes scolded for intellectual failures, the Kogi punish or reward children rather for behavioral matters. Punishment is often physical; a máma punishes an inattentive novice by depriving him of food or sleep, and quite often beats him sharply over the head with the thin hardwood rod he uses to extract lime from his gourd-container when he is chewing coca. For more serious misbehavior, children may be ordered to kneel on a handful of cotton seeds or on some small pieces of a broken pottery vessel. A very painful punishment consists in kneeling motionless with horizontally outstretched arms while carrying a heavy stone in each hand.

In practically all ceremonial houses one can see a large vertical loom leaning against the wall, with a half-finished piece of cloth upon it. The weaving of the coarse cotton cloth the Kogi use for the garments of both sexes is a male activity and has a certain ritual connotation. But to weave can also become a punishment. An inattentive novice—or a grown-up who has disregarded the moral order—can be made to weave for hours, sitting naked in the chill night and frantically working the loom, while behind him stands the máma who prods him with his lime rod, sometimes beating him over the ears and saying: "I shall yet make you respect the cloth you are wearing!"

Life in the ceremonial house is characterized by the regularized scheduling of all activities and thus expresses quite clearly a distinct learning theory. We must, first of all, look at the general outline of the aims of education. In doing so, it is necessary to use categories of formal knowledge in the way they are defined in *our* culture, a division that would make no sense to a Kogi, but which is useful here to give an order to the entire field of priestly instruction. The main fields of a máma's learning and competence are, thus, the following:

1. Cosmogony, cosmology, mythology
2. Mythical social origins, social structure, and organization
3. Natural history: geography, geology, meteorology, botany, zoology, astronomy, biology
4. Linguistics: ceremonial language, rhetoric
5. Sensory deprivations; abstinence from food, sleep, and sex
6. Ritual; dancing and singing

7. Curing of diseases
8. Interpretation of signs and symbols, dreams, animal behavior
9. Sensitivity to auditory, visual, and other hallucinations

The methods by which these aims of priestly education are pursued are many and depend to a high degree upon the recognition of a sequence of stages in the child's mental and physical development. During the early years of training, at about five or six years of age, the child is literally hand-reared, in that he is in very frequent physical contact with or, at least, proximity to, his teacher. While sitting on a low bench, the máma places both hands upon the hips of the boy who stands before him and rhythmically pushes and bends the child's body to the tune of his songs or recitals, or while marking the pace with a gourd-rattle. During this period, the Kogi say, the child "first learns to dance and only later learns to walk."

During the first two years of training, the teaching of dances is accompanied only by the humming of songs and by the sound of the rattle; only later on are the children taught to sing. During these practices the children always wear heavy wooden masks topped with feather crowns and are adorned with all the heavy ornaments mentioned above. The peculiar smell of the ancient mask, the pressure of its weight, and the overall restriction of body movements caused by the stiff ceremonial attire and the hands of the teacher produce a lasting impact on the child, and even decades later, people who have passed through this experience refer to it with a mixture of horror and pride. For hours on end, night after night, and illuminated only by torches and low-burning fires, the children are thus taught the dance steps, the cosmological recitals, and the tales relating to the principal personifications and events of the Creation story. Many of the songs and recitations are phrased in the ancient ceremonial language which is comprehensible only to an experienced máma, but which has to be learned by the novices by sheer memorization. During these early years, myths, songs, and dances become closely linked into a rigid structure that alone—at least, at that time—guarantees the correct form of presentation.

One of the main institutionalized teaching concepts consists in iterative behavior. This is emphasized especially during the first half of the curriculum, when the novices are made to repeat the myths, songs, or spells until they have memorized not only the text and the precise intonation, but also the body movements and minor gestures that accompany the performance. Rhythmic elements are important and the learning of songs and recitals is always combined with dancing or, at least, with swaying motions of the body. This is not a mere mechanistic approach to the learning process and does not represent a neurally based stimulus-response pattern, but the child is simultaneously provided with a large number of interpretative details that make him grasp the context and meaning of the texts.

Between the end of the first nine-year cycle of education and the onset of the second cycle, the novice reaches puberty. It is well recognized by the Kogi that during this period significant personality changes occur, and for this reason allowance is made for the eventual interruption of the training process or, as a matter of fact, for its termination. Having reached puberty, a boy who fails to display a truly promising attitude toward priesthood, demonstrated, above all, by his repressive attitude toward sexuality, is allowed to return to his family. At no time is such a boy forced to stay on, even if he should wish to do so; if his master believes that the youth does not have the calling to become a máma, he will insist on his returning to his people. But these cases seem to be the exception rather than the rule; more often puberty is reached as a normal transition, and a few years later, at the age of fourteen or fifteen years, the boy is initiated by the máma and receives from him the lime container and the little rod—a female and a male symbol—together with the permission to chew from now on the coca leaves the youth forthwith toasts in a special vessel.

Ideally, a Kogi priest should divest himself of all sensuality and should practice sexual abstinence, but this prohibition is contradicted in part by the rule that all nubile girls must be deflowered by the máma who, alone, has the power to neutralize the grave perils of pollution that according to the Kogi are inherent in this act. Similar considerations demand that, at puberty, a boy should be sexually initiated by the máma's wife or, in some cases, by an old woman specially designated by the máma. During the puberty ritual of a novice, the master's wife thus initiates the youth, an experience frought with great anxiety and which is often referred to in later years as a highly traumatic event.

During the second cycle, the teachings of the master concentrate upon divinatory practices, the preparation of offerings, the acquisition of power objects, and the rituals of the life cycle. During this period, education tends to become extremely formal because now it is much more closely associated with ritual and ceremony. The youth is taught many divinatory techniques, beginning with simple yes-or-no alternatives, and going on to deep meditation accompanied by exercises of muscular relaxation, controlled breathing, and the "listening" to sudden signs or voices from within. Power objects are acquired slowly over the years and consist of all kinds of "permits" (sewá) granted by the spirit-owners of Nature. Most of these permits consist of small archaeological necklace beads of stone, of different minerals, shapes, colors, and textures, that are given to the novice as soon as he has mastered the corresponding knowledge. At that age, a novice will need, for example, a permit to chew coca, to eat certain kinds of meat, to perform certain rituals, or to sing certain songs. During this period the novices are also taught the complex details of organization of the great yearly ceremonies that take place in the ceremonial centers, higher up in the mountains.

The novices have ample opportunity to watch their master perform ritual actions, a process during which a considerable body of knowledge is transmitted to them. The seasons of the year are paced with special ritual markings: equinoxes and solstices, planting and harvesting, the stages of the individual life cycle. Now that they themselves begin to perform minor rituals, the recurrent statements contained in the texts, together with the identical behavioral sequences, become linked into a body of highly patterned experiential units. The repetition of the formulas, "This is what happened! Thus spoke our forefathers! This is what the ancient said!" insists upon the rightness, the correctness of the actions and contents that constitute ritual.

During the education of a novice there is no skill training to speak of. Kogi material culture, it has been said already, is limited to an inventory of a few largely undifferentiated, coarse utilitarian objects, and the basic skills of weaving or pottery making—both male activities—are soon mastered by any child. There is hardly any specialization in the manufacture of implements and a máma is not expected to have any manual or artistic abilities. He is not a master-craftsman; as a matter of fact, he should avoid working with his hands because of the ever-present danger of pollution.

Language training, however, is a very different matter. In the first place, since early childhood the novice learns a very large denotative vocabulary. The Kogi are fully aware that any intellectual activity depends upon linguistic competence and that only a very detailed knowledge of the language will permit the precise naming of things, ideas, and events, as a fundamental step in establishing categories and values. In part, linguistic tutoring is concerned with correctness of speech, and children are discouraged from using expressions that are too readily associated with their particular age group. As most of the linguistic input comes from a máma, the novices soon demonstrate a very characteristic verbal behavior consisting of well-pronounced, rather short, sentences, with a rich vocabulary, and delivered in an even but very emphatic voice.

While in normal child-training techniques care is taken to transmit a set of simple behavioral rules that tend to advance the child's socialization process, in training for the priesthood socialization is not a desirable goal.

An average child is taught to collaborate with certain categories of people and is expected to lend a helping hand, to share food, to be of service to others. Emphasis is placed on participation in communal labor projects such as road building, the construction of houses or bridges, or on attendance at meetings in which matters of community interest are being discussed. But priestly education does not concern itself with these social functions of the individual. On the contrary, it is evident that a máma is quite intentionally trained *not* to become a group member, but to stand apart, aloof and superior. To the Kogi, the image of the spiritual leader is that of a man whose ascetic hauteur makes him almost unapproachable. A máma should not be too readily accessible, but should keep away from the discussion of public affairs and the petty details of local power politics, because only by complete detachment and by the conscious elimination of all emotional considerations can he become a true leader of his people.

This aloofness, this standing alone, is, in part, the consequence of the narrow physical and social environment in which the novices spend their long formative years of schooling. They *are* socialized, of course, but they are socialized in a context of a very small and very select group of people associated into a unit that is not at all representative of the larger society. It is a fact that the novice learns very little about the practical aspects of the society of which he is eventually becoming a priest. Life in the ceremonial house or in the small group of the máma's family does not give the novices enough social contacts to enable them to obtain a clear picture of the wider society. It is a fact that, during the years of a priest's training period, he hardly becomes acquainted with the practical aspects of land tenure and land use, of seed selection and soil qualities, or of the ways in which gossip, prestige, envy, and the wiles of women are likely to affect society. A novice brought up quite apart from society forms an image of the wider scene, which, at best, is highly idealized, and at worst, is an exaggeration of its evils and dangers.

In Kogi culture, sickness and death are thought to be the direct consequences of sin, and sin is interpreted mainly in terms of sex. Even in those relationships that are culturally approved, that is, in marriage between partners belonging to complementary exogamic units, the Kogi always see an element of pollution, of contamination, because most men are periodically engaged in some ritual demanding purity, abstinence, fasting, attendance at nightly sessions in the ceremonial house, or prolonged travel to some sacred site. Kogi women are often, therefore, quite critical of male religious activities, being in turn accused by their husbands of exercising a "weakening" influence upon their minds, which are bent upon the delicate task of preserving the balance of the Universe. Kogi priests live in a world of myth, of heroic deeds and miraculous events of times past, in which the female characters appear cast in the role of evil temptresses. To a young priest who, after years of seclusion, finally returns to village life and community affairs, women constitute the main danger to cultural survival and are a direct threat to the moral order. Therefore, it again takes several years before the máma learns about life in society and acquires a practical understanding of the daily problems of life.

Moral education is, of course, at the core of a priest's training. Since childhood, a common method of transmitting a set of simple moral values consists in the telling and retelling of the "counsels," cautionary tales of varying length that contain a condensed social message. These tales are a mixture of myth, familial story, and recital, and often refer to specific interpersonal relations within the family setting: husband and wife, elder brother and younger brother, son-in-law and father-in-law, and so on. Other tales might refer to some famous máma of the past, to culture heroes and their exploits, or to animals that behave like humans. The stories are recited during the nightly sessions when a group of men has gathered or they are told to an individual who has come for advice. In all these stories, what is condemned is overindulgence in food, sleep, and sex; physical aggressiveness is proscribed; theft, disrespectful behavior, and cruelty to children and animals are disapproved of, and inquisitiveness by word or deed is severely censured, especially in women and children. Those qualities that receive praise are economic collaboration, the sharing of food, the willingness to lend household utensils, respectful attitudes towards one's elders, and active participation in ritual. The behavioral message is quite clear and there are no ambivalent solutions: the culprits are punished and the virtuous are rewarded. These counsels, then, do not explain the workings of the Universe and are not overburdened with esoteric trivia, but refer to matters of daily concern, to commonplace events and to average situations. They form a body of entertaining, moralizing stories that can be embroidered or condensed to fit the situation. It may be mentioned here that it is characteristic of the highly impersonal quality of social relations among the Kogi that friendship is not a desirable institution. It is too close, too emotional a relationship, and social rules quite definitely are against it.

It is evident that the counsels constitute a very simplistic level of moral teaching. These stories are useful in propagating some elementary rules among the common people; they are easy to remember and their anecdotal qualities and stereotyped characters have become household words. Everyone knows the story of Sekuishbúchi's wife or how Máma Shehá forfeited his beautiful dress. But it is also obvious that there is another, deeper level where the moral issues are far more complex.

According to the Kogi, our world exists and survives because it is animated by solar energy. This energy manifests itself by the yearly round of seasons that coincides with the position of the sun on the horizon at the time of the solstices and equinoxes. It is the máma's task to "turn back the sun" when he advances too far and threatens to "burn the world," or to "drown it with rain," and only by thus controlling the sun's movements with offerings, prayers, and dances can the principles of fertility be conserved. This control of the mámas, however, depends on the power and range of their esoteric knowledge and this knowledge, in turn, depends upon the purity of their minds. Only the pure, the morally untainted, can acquire the divine wisdom to control the course of the sun and, with it, the change of the seasons and the times for planting and harvesting. It is for this reason that the Kogi, both priests and laymen, are deeply concerned about the education of future generations of novices and about their requirements of purity. Their survival as well as that of all mankind depends on the moral stature of Kogi priests, now and in the future; and it is only natural, then, that the correct training of novices should be of profound concerns to all.

The Kogi claim to be the "elder brothers" of mankind and, as they believe they are the possessors of the only true religion, they feel responsible for the moral conduct of all men. There is great interest in foreign cultures, in the strange ways of other peoples, and the Kogi readily ask their divine beings to grant protection to the wayward "younger brothers" of other nations. The training of more novices is, therefore, a necessity not only for Kogi society, but also for the maintenance of the wider moral order.

From the preceding pages it would, perhaps, appear that, during all these years of priestly education, most knowledge is acquired by rote memory or by the endless repetition of certain actions meant to transmit a set of socioemotional messages that are not always fully understood by the novice, but have to be dealt with nevertheless. But it would be a mistake to think that training for the priesthood consists only, or mainly, of these repetitious, empty elements of a formalized ritual. The true goals of education are quite different and the iterative behavior described above is only a very small part of the working behavior of the novices.

First of all, the aim of priestly education is to discover and awaken those hidden faculties of the mind that, at a given moment, enable the novice to establish contact with the divine sphere. The mámas know that a controlled set or sequence of sensory privations eventually produces altered states of consciousness enabling the novice to perceive a wide range of visual, auditory, or haptic hallucinations. The novice sees images and hears voices that explain and extol the essence of being, the true sources of Nature, together with the manner of solving a great variety of common human conflict situations. In this way, he is able to receive instructions about offerings to be made, about collective ceremonies to be organized, or sickness to be cured. He acquires the faculty of seeing behind the exterior appearances of things and perceiving their true nature. The concept of aluna, translated here as "inner reality," tells him that the mountains are houses, that animals are people, that roots are snakes, and he learns that this manipulation of symbols and signs is not a simple matter of one-to-one translation, but that there exist different levels of interpretation and complex chains of associations. The Kogi say: "There are two ways of looking at things; you may, when seeing a snake, say: 'This is a snake,' but you may also say: 'This is a rope I am seeing, or a root, an arrow, a winding trail.'" Now, from the knowledge of these chains of associations that represent, in essence, equivalences, he acquires a sense of balance, and when he has achieved this balance he is ready to become a priest. He then will practice the concept of yulúka, of being in agreement, in harmony, with the unavoidable, with himself, and with his environment, and he will teach this knowledge to others, to those who are still torn by the doubts of polarity.

The entire teaching process is aimed at this slow, gradual building up to the sublime moment of the self-disclosure of god to man, of the moment when Sintána or Búnkuasé or one of their avatars reveals himself in a flash of light and says: "Do this! Go there!" Education, at this stage, is a technique of progressive illumination. The divine personification appears bathed in a heavenly light and, from then on teaches the novice at night. From out of the dark recesses of the house comes a voice and the novice listens to it and follows its instructions. A máma said: "These novices hear everything and know everything but they don't know who is teaching them."

To induce these visionary states the Kogi use certain hallucinogenic drugs the exact nature of which is still uncertain. Two kinds of mushrooms, one of them a bluish puffball, are consumed only by the mámas, and a strong psychotropic effect is attributed to several plants, among them to the chestnutlike fruits of a large tree (Meteniusa edulis). But hallucinatory states can, of course, be produced endogenously by sensory privations and other practices; most trancelike states during which the mámas officiate at certain rituals are produced, in all probability, by a combination of ingested drugs and strenuous body exercise. The Kogi say: "Because the mámas were educated in darkness, they have the gift of visions and of knowing all things, no matter how far away they might be. They even visit the Land of the Dead."

In the second place, an important aspect of priestly education consists of training the novice to work alone. Although a Kogi priest has many social functions, his true self can find expression only in the solitary meditation he practices in his hut when he is alone. In order to evaluate

people or events, he must be alone; he may discuss occasionally some difficult matter with others, but to arrive at a decision, he must be quite alone.
This ability to stand alone and still act on behalf of others is a highly
valued behavioral category among the Kogi, and children, although they
often learn by participation, are trained already at an early age to master
their fears and doubts and to act alone. A máma's novice might be sent
alone, at night, to accomplish a dangerous task, perhaps a visit to a spot
where an evil spirit is said to dwell, or a place that is taken to be polluted
by disease. A máma takes pride in climbing—alone—a steep rock, or in
crossing a dangerous cleft, and he readily faces any situation that, in the
eyes of others, might entail the danger of supernatural apparitions of
a malevolent type.

But what really counts is his moral and intellectual integrity, his
resolution when faced with a choice of alternative actions. The adequate
evaluation of his followers' attitudes and needs requires a sense of
tolerance and a depth of understanding of human nature, which can only
be attained by a mind that is conscious of having received divine guidance.

The final test comes when the master asks the novice to escape from the
tightly closed and watched ceremonial house. The novice, in his trance,
roams freely, visiting faraway valleys, penetrating into mountains, or
diving into lakes. And when telling then of the wanderings of his soul, the
others will say: "You have learned to see through the mountains and
through the hearts of men. Truly, you are a máma now!"

The education of a máma is, essentially, a model for the education of
all men. Of course, not everyone can or should become a máma, but all
men should follow a máma's example of frugality, moderation, and simple
goodness. There are no evil mámas, no witch doctors or practitioners of
aggressive magic; they only exist in myths and tales of imagination, as
threatening examples of what *could be.* On the contrary, Kogi priests are
men of high moral stature and acute intellectual ability, measured by any
standards, who are deeply concerned about the ills that afflict mankind
and who, in their way, do their utmost to alleviate the burdens all men
have to carry. But they are also quite realistic in their outlook. An old
máma once said to me: "You are asking me what is life; life is food, a
woman—then, a house, a field—then, god."

Reflecting back on what was said at the beginning of this essay where
I tried to trace an outline of Kogi culture, it is clear that priestly education
constitutes a very coherent system that, as a model of conduct, obeys
certain powerful adaptive needs.

Kogi culture is characterized by a marked lack of specificity in object
relations. To a Kogi, people can exist only as categories, such as women,
children, in-laws, but not as individuals among whom close emotional
bonds might be established. The early weaning of the child is only the

beginning of a series of mechanisms by which all affective attachments with others are severed. Sphincter training, accomplished at about ten months, reinforces this independence of affective rewards. A child's crying is never interpreted as an expression of loneliness and the need for affection, and a baby is always cared for by several mother-substitutes such as older siblings, aunts, or most any woman who might be willing to take charge of the child for a while. During the first two years of life, all sensory-motor development is optimized while, at the same time, all emotional bonds are inhibited. It is probable that the highly impersonal quality of all social relations among adults is owing in a large measure to these early child-training patterns.

That novices chosen for the priesthood must be exposed to a máma's teaching *before* they reach five years of age plainly refers to the observation that, at that precise stage of development, their cognitive functioning is beginning and that mental images of external events are being formed. If educated within the social context of their families, the child would develop a normative cognitive system, which has to be avoided because the cognitive system of a priest must be very specific and wholly different from that of an average member of society.

As has been said, there are no children's games, that is, there is no rehearsal for future adult behavior. Nothing is left to fantasy, can be solved in fantasy; everything is stark reality and has to be faced as such. And as the child grows up into an adolescent, these precepts are continuously restated and reinforced. The youth must eradicate all emotional attitudes, because nothing must bias his judgment—neither sex, hunger, fear, nor friendship. A man once said categorically: "One never marries the woman one loves!" Moreover, most cultural mechanisms in Kogi behavior are accommodative. The individual has to adapt himself to the reality that surrounds him and cannot pretend to change the world, not even momentarily—not even in his fantasies. The concept of yulúka, too, becomes an accommodative tool because it represents an undifferentiated state of absolute unconsciousness.

To exercise spiritual leadership over his society, the priest must be completely detached from its daily give-and-take, and it is evident that separation, isolation, and emotional detachment are among the most important guiding principles of priestly education. This "otherness" of the Kogi priest is expressed in his training in many ways: from his nocturnal habits, which make him "see the world in a different light," to his isolation from society, which makes of him a lonely observer, devoid of all affection.

The Spartan touch in Kogi culture must be understood in its wider historical perspective. During almost one hundred years, from the time of the discovery of the mainland to the early years of the seventeenth century, the Indian population of the Sierra Nevada de Santa Marta was exposed to the worst aspects of the Spanish conquest. After long battles and persecutions, the chieftains and priests were drawn and quartered, the villages were destroyed, and the maize fields were burned by the invading troops. In few other parts of the Spanish Main did the Conquest take a more violent and destructive form than in the lands surrounding Santa Marta and in the foothills of the neighboring mountains. During the colonial period, the Indians lived in relative peace and isolation and were able to recuperate and reorganize higher up in the mountains. But modern times brought with them new pressures and new forms of violence. Political propaganda, misdirected missionary zeal, the greed of the Creole peasants, the ignorance of the authorities, and the irresponsible stupidity of foreign hippies have made of the Sierra Nevada a Calvary of tragic proportions on which one of the most highly developed aboriginal cultures of South America is being destroyed. So far the Kogi have withstood the onslaught, thanks mainly to the stature of their priests, but it is with a feeling of despair that one foresees the future of their lonely stand.

## BIBLIOGRAPHY

Preuss, Konrad Theodor
  1926–  *Forschungsreise zu den Kágaba. Beobachtungen, Textaufnahmen und sprach-*
  1927   *liche Studien bei einem Indianerstamme in Kolumbien, Südamerika.* 2 vols.
        St. Gabriel-Mödling: Anthropos Verlag.

Reichel-Dolmatoff, G.
  1950   "Los Kogi: Una tribu indígena de la Sierra Nevada de Santa Marta, Colombia."
        Vol. 1. *Revista del Instituto Etnológico Nacional* (Bogota) 4:1–320.
  1951a  *Datos histórico-culturales sobre las tribus de la antigua Governación de Santa
        Marta.* Bogota: Imprenta del Banco de la República.
  1951b  *Los Kogi: Una tribu indígena de la Sierra Nevada de Santa Marta, Colombia.*
        Vol. 2. Bogota: Editorial Iqueima.
  1953   "Contactos y cambios culturales en la Sierra Nevada de Santa Marta." *Revista
        Colombiana de Antropología* (Bogota) 1:17–122.
  1974   "Funerary Customs and Religious Symbolism among the Kogi." In *Native South
        Americans—Ethnology of the Least Known Continent.* Patricia J. Lyon, ed.
        Boston/Toronto: Little, Brown.

# 9.

# The Education of the Cacique[1] in Guajiro Society and Its Functional Implications

LAWRENCE C. WATSON

The intent of this paper is to examine the institution of Guajiro chieftainship (*cacicazgo*) from the standpoint of its educational pre-requisites, particular attention being directed to the process by which a candidate is trained for the office and is inducted into the role by his predecessor. I feel that the particular form in which Guajiro political authority is transferred is intimately geared to meeting the specific and rigorous requirements of successful political functioning in this society at both the level of the individual and the social system. To demonstrate this thesis, four states of investigation are necessary: (1) a description of the institution of cacicazgo itself, as it operates within the matrilineage framework, and, also, as it articulates with the larger social system; (2) an assessment of the viability of the institution under the influences of acculturation; (3) a chronological account of the educational process involved in the transmission of authority; and (4) an evaluation of the role education plays in securing the proper performance of political functions on the part of the future office holder.

In the process, by using my own data,[2] I hope to expand on the treat-ment of Guajiro political authority by Gutierrez de Pineda (1950) and Santa Cruz (1960). In the course of the paper the latter's position that political authority, at least traditionally, can be bought through favors is subjected to serious challenge.

This article appeared in *Anthropological Quarterly* 43 (Jan. 1970), 23–38, and is reprinted with permission.

## The Cacique and Society

In Guajiro society there are approximately thirty sibs (sib as defined by Murdock 1949:47), each of which consists of several (five to eight) maximal matrilineages which in turn are divided into a number of minimal lineages. Although each minimal lineage, which may be regarded as a local descent group, has a headman who represents it and provides informal counsel and leadership, the true Guajiro cacique of far-reaching powers characteristically functions as the political representative of the larger maximal matrilineage and serves as its uncontested internal authority.

Authority at this level enjoys consensual formal recognition within the maximal lineage and in society at large, and there are well-defined rules for its transmission. Ordinarily true political functioning does not operate beyond the boundaries of the maximal lineage, which are in fact effectively defined by it. Chiefly authority is transmitted from generation to generation within one branch of the maximal lineage, the passage of power most commonly being from the incumbent to his eldest sister's son, although if this person is incompetent another sororal nephew will be chosen as successor. The chief of the maximal lineage, moreover, is the leader of his own minimal lineage, and the minimal lineage which he heads is invariably the most powerful and wealthy of all units of this order (cf. Watson 1967: 21–22).

The Guajiro cacique, as principal representative of the lineage, may be regarded as the "focus of the forces maintaining its corporate unity and identity" in the sense that Fortes (1940:252) evaluated the function of leadership in the Tallensi lineage. Indeed, because it is a tightly knit corporate group (cf. Fortes 1953), we might expect to find and do, that the Guajiro lineage places great reliance on its political authority to perform crucial activities directed toward maintenance and protection of vested interests. These include: (1) representing the collective interests of the lineage in legal disputes with other groups, whether this involves seeking recompense for injury done to a member of his group or settling a claim of damages brought against a close kinsman; (2) administering and keeping up the lineage's property in wells and grazing lands; (3) serving as a third party to adjudicate disputes arising among members of the maximal lineage; (4) acting as an executor of estates in redistributing the property of deceased kinsmen among relatives and friends (cf. Watson 1968c:10); and (5) making executive decisions, in consultation with minimal lineage heads, regarding war and peace and acting in the capacity of a temporary military leader.

The political functions of the Guajiro lineage as a corporate group, which are expressed in the institution of cacicazgo, are so essential to its identity that we can speak of it as falling logically into the category of the "political" corporation, which is characterized by the fact that members of the group are "supposed to be bound by the decisions and sanctions made by its authoritative heads" (Befu and Plotnicov 1962:315), particularly in the sense that the latter represent the interests of the group as a body of people who are jurally equivalent in the eyes of society.

An opposite, divisive tendency, however, may be detected where the institution of cacicazgo is weak. The sense of uterine affiliation beyond a certain level is not sufficient to insure cohesion where there is not a powerful leader to establish an enduring and meaningful political unity. Under these circumstances the maximal lineage fragments and isolated minimal lineages, seeking economic and political protection, attempt to affiliate with powerful maximal lineages within the sib framework on the basis of putative kinship, or with other lineages outside the sib in the capacity as retainers.

## Acculturation and Cacicazgo

Santa Cruz (1960:126) asserts that "clan" leadership in Guajiro culture is presently dying out. The author takes exception to this. Despite heavy acculturative influences, such as the shift to wage labor and agriculture, which undermines the lineage's traditional economic functions based on cattle herding, or the decline of the ancestral cult with the growing influence of Christianity, there is abundant evidence to suggest that the matrilineage retains at least its collective legal responsibility and that it is the cacique who continues to vouch for this as political representative of his group in its legal dealings with other lineages and as an arbiter of the group's internal conflicts (Watson 1967:23). A case could be made, in fact, that at present the Guajiro lineage survives almost exclusively as a politico-legal institution held together by the cacique in the absence of other integrating mechanisms.

It is important also to put Santa Cruz's discussion into proper perspective. When he speaks of the paucity of political leaders he is speaking of political figures who represent large nebulous matrilineal units ("clans") which resemble the sibs previously described. These units, strictly speaking, however, are not corporate descent groups and do not perform collective activities. But if we consider the smaller maximal matrilineage, which performs true corporate functions, we discover that one of its essential characteristics is its strong political leadership and collective legal identity (Watson 1967:27).

The allegation of Santa Cruz (1960:120) that political authority in the matrilineage can be bought from the elders with gifts and favors must also be challenged. This, in my estimation, is not a viable alternative in traditional culture; indeed, it approaches what we might expect to find if we were to accept the decline of lineage authority and the disintegration of tribal values due to acculturation. The career of José de la Rosa Fernandez, the famous cacique of the Uriana clan, is offered by Santa Cruz (1960:120) as an example of this pattern. However, I knew the old cacique well and lived with him for several months; therefore I was in a position to check the reliability of this assertion. As it turned out, José de la Rosa consistently and vociferously maintained that he had inherited the chieftainship from his maternal uncle in the customary manner after prolonged instruction. According to him, it would be unthinkable for a cacique to make no adequate provision for selecting and grooming a successor in view of the critical importance of political continuity to the lineage. He himself had already done so years before and he referred me to one of his sororal nephews, who was his designated successor. When contacted, this man declared that in the lineage he was accepted as old José's successor and even as a cacique in his own right. Significantly, conversations with other Guajiros confirmed this claim.

Gutierrez de Pineda (1950:135–137) speaks briefly about the attributes of the status of cacique: that it is inherited through the maternal line, that it is based on wealth and class position, and that the person who occupies the status demonstrates certain personality traits. She also gives a detailed account of the cacique's responsibilities. However, she does not attempt to relate or reconcile these attributes with any process by which they might be used to select, indoctrinate or socialize a candidate for political office. This paper hopes to address itself to this significant and interesting issue and to offer some tentative explanations.

## The Education of the Cacique

An attempt is made here to delineate the successive stages involved in the educational process. However, it should be kept in mind that while these stages appear functionally differentiable, there is in fact considerable overlap, and that dominant orientations of one phase may continue to be emphasized in the next one.

### Appraisal and Selection of a Candidate

Although the lineage chief chooses a successor within his immediate matri-family, he possesses the right to select any qualified individual whom he feels will best serve the interests of the whole group. In the great majority of cases this is an elder sororal nephew.

It is the responsibility of the chief, moreover, to carefully determine who this person will be; no self-respecting leader would leave such a momentous decision to chance or to the exigencies of the moment. Certain qualities of character are considered to be essential for the performance of the chiefly role and all candidates are rigorously measured against these standards. The cacique is looking for somebody who is very much like himself in matters of personality and temperament. One chief defined the characteristics he was looking for in a successor as follows:

> This person should be diligent, hard-working, and ambitious. He is a young man who carefully herds his family's cattle and increases their number through astuteness and clever management. He is a very serious person who has no time for drinking and idle pursuits. He is careful with people; he respects his elders and carries out his obligations toward them. He knows how to handle his peers and companions. He is tactful in his dealings and is the friend of all.

Essentially, the prospective cacique embodies the attributes of the Guajiro ideal self in their noblest form: responsibility, compliance, unaggressiveness, and respectfulness (Watson 1968b:118-137). And yet at the same time he is forceful and confident within the limitations imposed on him by his inherent consideration of others. His cautiousness and his sensitivity to social nuances stand him in good stead, particularly as a negotiator for his lineage in serious and delicate legal disputes. His forcefulness and even ruthlessness lie just beneath his surface amiability but are apparent in his iron-like will which serves to convince other people that he means business in spite of his desire to be fair and reasonable.

In choosing a successor from among his sororal nephews or younger brothers, the cacique begins his deliberations long before any final decision is necessary. As a rule, the cacique wishes to make at least a tentative decision by the time the projected successor is in his mid-twenties, which means that long before this he has begun to test the character of potential candidates. He does this in part by giving them gifts of livestock and observing how they manage the animals. He notices that one youth diligently herds his animals and makes them increase, while another neglects his animals or sells them to buy women or whiskey. This in itself gives an early and reasonably accurate indication of the boy's true character and his future potential for leadership.

The cacique also watches carefully to see if his sororal nephews have mastered the rules of etiquette and know how to render him, as well as other adults, the proper signs of deference and respect. One of my informants, who was already a powerful cacique in his own right, described how during his youth his uncle had indicated special pleasure with him on account of his decorous behavior:

> I remember when I was little, about twelve years old, my uncle, the chief, would come to the house of my mother. I greeted my uncle with great respect but with much affection. My mother ordered me to receive my uncle properly and then unsaddle and pasture his horse. When I came back from the fields I went to the corral to slaughter sheep so that my uncle might eat. After my uncle had eaten, he was accustomed to lie in a *chinchorro* (open-net hammock) under an *enramada* (bower). He awoke at daybreak and called me over since he had come to give me advice and tell me I was going to receive inheritance. He told me I was a good nephew and that he was satisfied with my behavior. He urged me to continue being diligent and responsible. I knew he had a special affection for me, for he did not pay so much attention to his other nieces or nephews.

After an extended period of "testing" his nephews, which may last from five to ten years, during which time he "weighs" numerous reports of their behavior, the cacique is prepared to make a tentative decision insofar as he singles out a particular person as a candidate for special advanced instruction. It must be emphasized, however, that this decision is not an irreversible one, for if the candidate subsequently shows bad qualities the cacique can drop him without feeling he has backed out of any formal commitment.

## Socialization of the Candidate in Legal Norms and Political Strategies

Characteristically, the cacique, once having made his decision, invites the candidate to come and live with him, provided the youth is not already doing so for special reasons. Under these circumstances the uncle will ask the boy's mother and father for permission to "keep" him. If, however, the uncle happens to live in the same neighborhood as the boy's mother, the candidate will continue to live at home, although he is required to consult frequently with his uncle and perform economic duties for him. Chiefly informants told me that they could not be sure they were being groomed for the chieftainship at this stage in their careers, inasmuch as the cacique would mask his intentions in order to avoid making awkward commitments he might later regret. The decision is essentially private and unvoiced.

This shift in residence actually constitutes the basis for a further and really far more demanding test of the young man's capacity for leadership, for he must now learn the mechanics and strategies of cacicazgo. If the young man fails to profit from instruction by not demonstrating proper understanding, or does not measure up to standard in matters of personal etiquette toward the uncle, he is unceremoniously sent back to his parents in a state of total disfavor and his big chance is lost.

The candidate's personal qualities, however, are more or less taken for granted at this point, so that the cacique ordinarily concentrates his efforts during this period on instilling in the young man a *theoretical* understanding of the very complicated Guajiro legal system and how a chief should interpret and manipulate it in the best interests of his lineage whose collective legal responsibility he represents to society at large.

The cacique as teacher converses at length with the candidate, usually in an informal setting while both are sitting outside the *rancheria* or resting in their hammocks. During these long discussions the older man describes in detail, and with abundant example, what acts constitute legal violations and what the cacique must do to ensure the maintenance of law and order. He explains what kinds of legal action must follow certain categories of violation and the terms under which the cacique should press for settlement in cases where a member of his lineage is the plaintiff and the defendant in the lawsuit. He also tells the candidate how to contact a legal intermediary (*palabrero*) in a serious dispute and how to employ his services effectively.

The personal qualities which a cacique should have are consistently emphasized and held up for examination by the older man. This serves to reinforce the positive character traits in the candidate that were initially identified as indicative of his suitability for political office. Tact, consideration, and respect are the cornerstones of the cacique's public personality. The man who represents his lineage in legal affairs and acts as internal judge must be an eloquent and persuasive spokesman who knows the diplomatic way of making other men accept his definition of the situation. If he is boorish and impetuous he defeats his own purpose and antagonizes other people to the point where they abandon a reasonable position and resort to violence, which it is his job to prevent.

One influential chief described how he learned the personal qualities of political leadership from his maternal uncle:

> I obeyed my uncle and showed him much respect. And I never fought with anybody because he told me this was bad—very dangerous. If my uncle saw that a kinsman wanted to fight with another, he advised him not to: "You shouldn't do

this because it leads to trouble and starts war." This I learned
from my uncle Nicolai just by watching him. I could see how
respectfully and attentively he treated his guests. I watched
how he hung their hammocks and served meals. I began to
treat people the same way.

Uncle Nicolai once told me, "Nephew, the poor should not
be mistreated for they are human beings just like us. I never
fought with anybody, even the lowest of men. I am very serious and respect others and they in turn respect me as a man
of good will. Sometimes a drunkard will act disrespectfully
toward me, but I don't pay any attention to him. However,
the next day, when he is sober, I admonish him strongly, for
clear-headed he knows he has done wrong."

## The Presentation of the Candidate to Society

After a period of apprenticeship spent in learning the theory of
cacicazgo, the young man is ready to make his debut in society as the
chosen one and companion of the cacique. Apparently this has two
purposes. First of all, it gives the candidate an opportunity to further
his learning by observing the role of the leader in action under real life
conditions. One might say that he is given the opportunity to learn the
practical application of the theory he has been taught. Secondly, it
establishes the fact that the cacique has designated a successor and
directs the proper attitudes of respect and anticipation toward the young
candidate, who now formally takes his place, albeit marginally, in
socio-political circles.

One informant remembered the day when his uncle first invited him to
attend a serious court case:

We were lying in our hammocks, just talking, when suddenly my uncle said, "Nephew, only a short while ago some
men came to see me. They asked me if I would represent them
in a legal dispute involving an abduction and I agreed to do so.
Tomorrow, I want you to come with me. It will be a good
experience for you. I want you to be ready at daybreak."
Naturally I was thrilled. In the morning we saddled our horses,
and accompanied by about twenty retainers, we set off. I felt
very important. Some of the older men of the lineage also came
and when they saw me they gave me appraising looks. They
knew I was somebody special despite my tender age.

As the above quotation suggests, one important reason for this is to
inform family heads in the lineage that a future leader has been chosen

worthy of confidence and to create conditions favorable for a rapproche-
ment by involving the candidate and the older, more influential men in
a common, unified activity.

During negotiations, the cacique, acting as intermediary, talks with
the plaintiff in order to know his wishes and then confers with the defendant to determine whether a settlement can be reached. He shuttles back
and forth between the two parties, forever urging restraint and the value
of peace and friendship: "Listen, my friend, he is only asking twenty
cows and ten horses for the abduction of his daughter. The man is within
his rights and you know the girl is really worth much more than that.
You don't want to go to war when it can be settled so easily. Just think
of your lovely wives and daughters being slaughtered in needless
bloodshed."

During the proceedings the candidate stands in the background
watching attentively. He observes exactly how the cacique conducts his
business; he remembers what gestures he uses, the proper forms of
address, the subtle phrasings of the issue, and the euphemistic circum-
locutions designed to guard against offending raw sensibilities. As one
cacique recalled from his own youth:

> When we came into the rancheria I made myself quiet and
> inconspicuous, but I listened intently to the words my uncle
> spoke and watched his behavior. I did this so I myself could
> learn to say the right words. Slowly I learned the way the old
> masters spoke when they were called upon to arrange legal
> matters.

At some point during the discussion the cacique formally introduces the
candidates to the people in the gathering, particularly to the chiefs who
are representing their respective families in the dispute. He emphasizes
the fact that this is his "favorite" nephew and implies, but does not state,
that the young man is being groomed to succeed him. He calls attention
to the candidate's fine character and enumerates his virtues, to which the
audience responds with polite signs of approval. This solemn introduction
impresses on the candidate the great responsibility of the role his uncle
has entrusted to him and he feels, if he is a typical Guajiro, a burning
desire to redeem the cacique's pledge of his excellence. This may be
regarded as a most effective technique which the cacique has at his
disposal for instilling a sense of commitment and proper motivation in
his apprentice.

The process of being introduced to society has been described by one
chiefly informant in the following terms:

When my uncle and I attended a legal case he always took pains to introduce me to men of category. He would say, "This is my nephew, José, the one I love. He is going to be a man who protects and sustains his family." After this the rich men regarded me as a person of worth. They respected me on account of my uncle. They spoke to me as though I were a brother-in-law.

Eventually, over a period of years, the candidate learns the proper role behavior of cacique through systematic and intimate observation of his mentor at work. But equally important, in the process, he establishes a reputation for himself among members of his own lineage and among politically powerful men of other lineages as a leader of the future, a man of potentially noble qualities and great promise.

## Role Experimentation

After social recognition has been accorded to him, and with maturity, the candidate begins to function as a political leader in his own right, although on a limited scale. The old cacique is more than willing by this time to delegate a certain amount of responsibility to the candidate, for he realizes that practical experience is necessary to his growth and development in the role. However, if the candidate does not handle himself well in high-powered political circles (e.g., by becoming drunk or by acting carelessly or disrespectfully) he wiil fall from the cacique's favor and will be replaced in time by a more promising successor, as there are always those who are waiting in the wings.

At first the candidate is requested to adjudicate minor disputes in the lineage or to represent strangers in a harmless legal suit involving modest demands for compensation. He feels very flattered, of course, and approaches his responsibilities with great seriousness and dedication. He begins to act like a chief: "I felt I was the defender of my family. I would tell my relatives that one day I would be chief and would serve them well. I would resolve their problems conscientiously with only their good in my heart."

A well-established cacique described to the author how he began a career as a practicing cacique:

Sometimes there were problems about marriage—civil cases —and I was requested by people to settle them myself. If it was not too serious I handled it alone, but if it were serious I had to consult with my uncle since he had more knowledge and authority than I. This was a necessary part of my education. I realized I had to start advising people sometime, because eventually I would have to govern my lineage and be its legal representative.

If he is successful in his role he soon acquires the reputation of being a promising young political leader who has "arrived." But any serious mismanagement of his office at this stage erodes the old cacique's faith in him and undermines the trust of the lineage, and as a consequence he may be forced to retire to the background temporarily or even permanently if he has made serious mistakes. One cacique reported how he had been treated by people of importance once he had successfully launched his career:

> When I went to a *velorio* (wake) where I was not immediately known people asked who I was. I would say that I was Fulano, nephew of cacique Nicolai. When they heard this they greeted me with much affection. They offered me food and rum and showed me a good time. They politely asked after my uncle. They told me, "We have heard of you. Just carry on as you are and you will be all right. Perhaps someday you will be the great man your uncle is today."

## The Social Validation of Cacicazgo

Ultimately the "apprentice" becomes a bonafide "master" and is accorded full social recognition, provided of course his career has been reasonably distinguished. He is now a political veteran and is prepared to take over from the old cacique if the latter becomes senile and loses his judgment, although in fact he ordinarily defers in deciding extremely serious matters to his old uncle. By now members of the lineage have great faith in him (optimally) and do not hesitate to seek his opinion rather than consult with the older cacique. When the latter dies he will step into the position with little shock or disruption to the lineage organization; and in all probability he has already made provisions for maintaining the continuity of authority by choosing his own successor.

## Discussion and Conclusions

It is possible to evaluate the significance of Guajiro political education for the maintenance of the political system at two distinct levels: (1) it fulfills the need for the internalization of certain personality traits that have functional value for coping with the demands of exercising political power (cf. LeVine 1960:56–57); and (2) it provides the essential conditions for maintaining the continuity of authority by securing public recognition and approval for its orderly transference; in the absence of this provision political schisms are liable to arise due to open competition for unallocated authority. Let us elaborate on these two points.

Much of the young cacique's education is designed to insure his acquisition of certain very essential personality attributes, such as respectfulness, a high sense of responsibility, caution, tact, and firmness of purpose. If at any point these qualities are not properly evidenced, the training process is terminated and the candidate falls from favor and is replaced. The data suggest that these traits, when well-developed, enable the cacique to function easily and effectively in his position. Guajiros are extremely sensitive to any indication that their feelings are not respected. Evaluation of Guajiro TAT test responses (Watson 1968a:106–107) has led me to conclude that these people wish to be taken seriously and fear being treated in a demeaning or contemptuous way since this results in loss of face. These needs are perhaps most intensely reflected in those legal proceedings in which the cacique becomes involved. It is incumbent on him, under these circumstances, to know how to read subtle social cues, how to phrase unpleasant demands in euphemistic language, and to size up personalities. Even a small blunder on his part is likely to be misinterpreted by others and hinder his chances for settling the dispute through diplomatic means.

These personality traits may be thought of as expressing a form of behavior which serves personal motivations (e.g., respect behavior as precluding contempt reactions) and yet at the same time enables the cacique to perform his political role in such a way as to maintain the fine balance of power in the lineage system (Spiro 1961:99–100; 121–122).

At another level the lengthy process of training in cacicazgo, involving the introduction of the candidate to society, the symbolic designation of his future status, and his gradual induction into the performance of the political role, may be interpreted as a mechanism for ensuring continuity of authority in a potentially divisive and unstable political situation. This would constitute a process of the type consistent with a "continuity of the existing formal order" (Leach 1954:5). Cases are known in the Guajira where competing chiefly lines rent the maximal lineage asunder when the recognized cacique had died and had not unequivocally selected and trained a successor who was acceptable to the group. The importance of maximal lineage cohesion, which is guaranteed by a powerful cacique, is apparent when we consider that a small minimal lineage alone or a maximal lineage divided is not ordinarily strong enough to protect its legal rights or vested economic interests against competitors. A small, weak group with underdeveloped political authority is considered fair prey for exploitation by powerful lineages.

A strong cacique forms the only logical focal point for lineage cohesion since he alone vouches with his wealth and control of manpower for the group's determination to support and defend its own interests. Clear recognition of this fact by other leaders serves to stabilize the balance of political forces. The introduction of the candidate to other leaders has the effect of facilitating a form of "diplomatic" recognition of far-reaching consequences.

The tendency evident in Guajiro society for political unity to be phrased in terms of a contractual relationship to authority, outside the strict limits of uterine affiliation, has been demonstrated by I. M. Lewis (1961:109) for the patrilineal Somali, also a pastoral group, one implication being that here, as with the Guajiro, scattered residential patterns and weak local contiguity makes criteria other than kinship affiliation, namely strong, pragmatic leadership, necessary to political cohesion. Levi-Strauss (1944:22-25) has similarly pointed out that among the nomadic hunting and gathering Nambicuara the strong leader provides the relatively stable nucleus around which a meaningful social aggregate centers. He demonstrates that where the institution is weak, affiliation with other leaders will be sought.

Thus, the particular form of political education in Guajiro society may be related to functional needs in society that are conditioned by the influence of certain ecological patterns which must be identified and examined in detail (nomadism, residential dispersal, competition for limited resources, etc.). In stable agricultural societies, by contrast, we may find that political authority is not predicated on elaborate training techniques due to the fact that the ecology makes for strong local contiguity and the development of sufficient kinship sentiment capable of performing the task of social integration in the absence of well-defined leadership.

## NOTES

1. The Spanish term "cacique" has been taken over by the Guajiro and is widely used to refer to traditional political authorities. It does not retain its original meaning in Spanish of "political bossism" for the Guajiro; it is most commonly used to designate the chief of a maximal matrilineage who is called "alat'laa" ("old one," "wise one") in Guajiro.

2. The author's field research was conducted in the Venezuelan part of La Guajira Peninsula, northwest of Maracaibo, from October 1964 to September 1965.

## BIBLIOGRAPHY

Befu, Harumi, and Leonard Plotnicov
1962    "Types of Corporate Unilineal Descent Groups." *American Anthropologist* 64:313-327.

Fortes, Meyer
1940    "The Political System of the Tallensi of the Northern Territories of the Gold Coast." In *African Political Systems*. M. Fortes and E. E. Evans-Pritchard, eds. London: Oxford University Press. Pp. 239-271.
1953    "The Structure of Unilineal Descent Groups." *American Anthropologist* 55: 17-41.
Gutiérrez de Pineda, Virginia
1950    "Organización social en la Guajira. *Revista del Instituto Etnológico Nacional* (Bogota) 2:1-257.
Leach, Edmund R.
1954    *Political Systems of Highland Burma*. London: G. Bell.
LeVine, Robert A.
1960    "The Internalization of Political Values in Stateless Societies." *Human Organization* 19:51-58.
Lévi-Strauss, Claude
1944    "The Social and Psychological Aspects of Chieftainship in a Primitive Tribe: The Nambikuara of Northwestern Mato Grosso." *Transactions of the New York Academy of Sciences* 7:16-32.
Lewis, I. M.
1961    "Force and Fission in Northern Somali Lineage Structure." *American Anthropologist* 63:94-112.
Murdock, George P.
1949    *Social Structure*. New York: MacMillan.
Santa Cruz, Antonio
1960    "Acquiring Status in Guajiro Society." *Anthropological Quarterly* 33:115-127.
Spiro, Melford
1961    "Social Systems, Personality, and Functional Analysis." In *Studying Personality Cross-Culturally*. Bert Kaplan, ed. New York: Harper and Row. Pp. 93-128.
Watson, Lawrence C.
1967    "Guajiro Social Structure: A Reexamination." *Antropológica* 20:3-36.
1968a   *Guajiro Personality and Urbanization*. Latin American Studies, vol. 10. Latin American Center, University of California, Los Angeles.
1968b   "Self and Ideal in a Guajiro Life History." Ms.
1968c   "The Inheritance of Livestock in Guajiro Society." *Antropológica* 23:3-17.

# 10.

# To Become a Maker of Canoes:
# An Essay in
# Warao Enculturation

JOHANNES WILBERT

## Introduction

The Warao are a South American Indian tribe that has dwelled in the Orinoco Delta since prehistoric times. An examination of how they learn to make canoes serves as an example for the study of enculturation in homogeneous societies.

The name Warao designates specifically a single person and generically the entire tribe. The word is derived from *wa*, "canoe," and *arao*, "owner." The Warao are owners of canoes. In this society, therefore, to become an expert canoe maker is tantamount to becoming a man, and the worst one can say about a man is that he is *wayana*, "without canoe." This places him on the bottom rung of the socioeconomic ladder, a pauper. It identifies him with incompetent commoners among the living and assigns him a place among the undistinguished souls of the dead.

The fame of the Warao as expert canoe builders was established in early colonial times when Sir Walter Raleigh introduced these Indians into the literature as "carpenters of canoes." According to him they "make the most and fairest houses, and sell them into Guiana for gold, and into Trinedado for *Tabacco*" (1596:52). Subsequent documentation in later

I gratefully acknowledge the comments on an earlier draft of this paper made by my colleagues Robert Edgerton, Walter R. Goldschmidt, Thomas J. La Belle, and Thomas Weisner. Clinton R. Edwards gave me advice on technical terminology of canoe making. Charlotte Treuenfels edited part of the manuscript. To all I am very indebted and thankful. The essay is written in the ethnographic present although many practices described have fallen into disuse. Most of the ethnographic data were collected among the Winikina-Warao. How far they can be generalized as representative of all Warao subtribes remains to be uncovered through future research. The field research for this paper was supported in part by the Ahmanson Foundation.

times also attests to the proficiency of Warao shipwrights. In colonial times they still were "the most famous boat-builders" who furnished "nearly the whole colony of Demarara with canoes" (Schomburgk, in Raleigh, 1970:49; Penard, 1907–1908:1,124). Eventually, Warao dugouts were in use throughout the European colonies in Guiana where English, Dutch, French, and Spanish colonists preferred to purchase canoes made by Warao craftsmen to those of any other artisans, Indian or European (Hilhouse, 1834:328; Schomburgk, 1847–1848:144). There was scarcely a traveler in the seventeenth, eighteenth, and nineteenth centuries who failed to admire Warao canoe makers as "wonderful specimens of untaught natural skill" (Bernau, 1847:34) and their products as "most excellently adapted to the wants of the Indians, though shaped and hollowed with crude implements and without any assistance from the rules of art" (Brett, 1886:166). In this century there is abundant evidence that the Warao continue to live up to their reputation for making the best dugouts, whether for domestic use on the mainland or for export to Margarita Island (Méndez-Arocha, 1963:196) and elsewhere.

In view of the antiquity of canoe making and its importance among the Warao, it is to be expected that in examining this success story we should find data pertaining not only to skill-training and technology but also to certain social and ideational dimensions of Warao enculturation which concentrate on one imperative: in each generation, to raise as many canoe makers as needed to fulfill the requirements of an environment in which canoes are essential for survival. Furthermore, the examination of the enculturation process of skill-training, socialization, and moral education as they relate to the art of canoe making should demonstrate how these processes are designed to permit the realization of the capacity of his personality in a man and "to so utilize the technology, to so implement the ideas—value, religion, philosophy—and to so act within the socio-economic organization that the traditional adjustment of the culture to the outer world is not upset" (Henry and Whithorn Boggs, 1952:261).

To sum up, there are at least four major reasons for choosing canoe making as a vehicle for probing the tribal processes of enculturation among the Warao. First, canoe making is a cultural category of demonstrable antiquity, its roots probably reaching into prehistory. Solid historical documentation covers almost four hundred years and positively establishes the dugout as an ancient artifact of Warao technology. Second, canoe making is a dominant category of Warao culture. It concerns all members of the society, especially its male members young and old, and permits a longitudinal study of enculturation from infancy through adulthood. Third, canoe making pervades all systems of Warao culture shedding light on the interrelationship of technological features with aspects of the social and the value systems. And finally, since canoe making pertains to the universal category of transportation, it lends itself to comparative studies (cf. Williams, 1972:206–207).

## The Model

A theoretical model underlies the descriptive and analytical parts of this essay (see Introduction). It shows the relationship of several factors that have an important bearing on the phenomenon of enculturation in a homogeneous tribal society. The model may also apply to the study of education in heterogeneous societies, but that is not the basic intent of its design.

According to the dimensions of the model, enculturation is studied as a process of skill-training, socialization, and moral education effected during infancy, childhood, and adulthood, in a given environment, society, and culture. The interrelationship of this process can be diagramed in the form of a cube in isometric projection (Introduction, fig. 1).

A focus on canoe making among the Warao permits us to put the whole life cycle of a male Warao into the model's frame of reference even though infancy and childhood appear to be periods of less intensity in the total learning process than do adolescence and adulthood. At least the data presently available seem to yield less information on the early life stages than on the later. I suspect, however, that these data are deceptive and that early years of child training may well turn out to be as relevant to the enculturation process as the later periods of manhood. Even the presently available data suggest that cultural conditioning of the child toward the profession of canoe making is strongly promulgated through various agents at all stages. But, to substantiate these impressions additional research through projective tests is needed. The data for the present essay were collected mainly among the Winikina subtribe of the Warao, among whom I have been engaged in fieldwork intermittently since 1954. Standard ethnographic methods were employed which included various types of interview, participant observation, and life histories.

Certain sectors of the model seem to be more closely interrelated than others. For example, the system of material culture and technology pertains particularly to skill-training which, in turn, occurs mainly during childhood and early adolescence. Socialization of the canoe maker is intensified from mid-adolescence to early adulthood, with aspects of the socioeconomic system of culture coming prominently into play in early adulthood. Finally, moral education is stressed especially during the prime of life and late adulthood, linking the ongoing enculturation processes predominantly with the value system of Warao culture. Of course, it is understood that these relationships reflect tendencies rather than sharp distinctions. In actual life, skill-training, socialization, and moral education are parallel processes occurring throughout all stages of a canoe maker's career albeit with varying emphasis. Definitions for skill-training, socialization, and moral education are given in the text at the beginning of sections 4, 5, and 6, respectively.

## Environment, Society, and Culture

### The Natural Environment

### Location, Geography, and Climate

In a process that may have taken more than a thousand years, the Warao have adapted their culture to the difficult outer world of the Orinoco Delta in eastern Venezuela, located between 8° and 10° north latitude and between 59° and 62° west longitude. This area of 17,000 square kilometers has become the heartland of tribal distribution in the Delta, but some groups have in the course of time settled in adjacent areas east and west of the Delta proper, largely along its tributaries that run into the Gulf of Paria and along the lower reaches of the Delta rivers that empty into the Atlantic Ocean.

The Orinoco Delta is a fan of alluvial deposits bounded on the south by the Orinoco River proper and on the west by the Manamo River, which branches off the main river at Barrancas, the apex of the Delta. Most of this low-lying triangle is a vast tidal swamp lacking in dry ground and stone and extending 50 to 100 kilometers inland (Liddle, 1928:20-24). The waters of the Orinoco Delta are discharged through the Rio Grande, the principal channel, and through eight so-called *caños* known as Sacupana, Araguao, Araguaito, Macareo, Tucupita, Pedernales, Cocuina, and Manamo. Connecting these major branches are innumerable smaller caños that form a labyrinthine network of navigable waterways over the entire Delta. The region is splintered by these caños into a multitude of islands of varying size that accommodate some 249 Warao settlements.[1]

The average mean temperature in the Orinoco Delta is 26°C, the humidity 60 to 80 percent. There is a rainy season which lasts roughly from May to October and a dry season from November to April, but rainy days with more or less intensive showers occur throughout the year. The annual precipitation ranges from 100 to 200 centimeters (Heinen and

Lavandero, 1973:4–11). Trade winds from a northeasterly direction sweep over the Delta almost incessantly, mitigating the hot climate of this littoral region.

## Botanical Zones

The Orinoco Delta can be subdivided into three major botanical zones: Lower, Intermediate, and Upper. The Lower Delta is the growing edge of the swamp, a coastal belt of mangroves. Typically for such environments, the soil is almost always inundated, thus providing ideal conditions for the pioneering red mangrove (*Rhizophora mangle*). A mangrove forest grows on its periphery and dies at its core. This peculiar feature is of primary importance to the Warao since the clearing that results from the dying central part of the mangrove forest is invaded by such food-producing palms as the moriche (*Mauritia flexuosa*), the manaca (*Euterpe* sp.), and the temiche (*Manicaria saccifera*), as well as by many other varieties of useful trees and plants. Thus, within the coastal mangrove belt of the Lower Delta (and within the 60-kilometer-wide tidal zone of the Intermediate Delta inland), there developed the econiche of a palmetum that has long served the Warao Indians as an abundant food basket as well as a secure home.

Twice daily the tide inundates the Intermediate Delta, nurturing the palms. The annual inundations of the Orinoco are felt here only indirectly, and the flooding of the palm groves during the rainy season is actually because of precipitation. In the dry season, when the waters of the Orinoco recede, seawater runs into the Intermediate Delta, salinating the rivers and causing a potable water problem.

Warao culture is especially adapted to life in this environment. If one were to single out the major factor facilitating the adaptation of Warao culture to the Intermediate Delta, it would have to be the moriche palm. The sago of this palm was the staple food for the preagricultural Warao during much of the year and today, when most of the Warao practice subsistence agriculture, sago continues to be an important food for many local groups.

Several varieties of trees suitable for the manufacture of canoes grow in the Intermediate and Upper Delta. The red cedar (*Colophyllum lucidum* Benth.) outranks all others in this respect, with the white cedar (*Colophyllum lucidum*) second best, and the paramo (*Symphonia globulifera*), carapa (*Carapa guianensis* Aubl.), and sassafras (*Nectandra* [?] *cymbarum*) third.

In the Upper Delta, closest to its apex, large portions of the gallery forest were cleared in colonial times for agriculture and arboriculture (coffee and cacao) by the predominantly Creole population. But the area is subject to yearly inundations of the Orinoco River which, together with pests, have rendered the plantations inoperative.

The dense pluvial forest that covers most of the islands of the Orinoco Delta has played a major role in protecting the Warao from the intrusions of cannibalistic Cariban neighbors and enterprising Afro-Europeans. Until recently the Indians considered trees sacred, and Warao culture has imposed a taboo on the felling of trees. All trees, especially the larger species, except for the sangrito (needed for firewood), are protected by specific guardian spirits who inflict epidemic disease on the families of violators. The existence of this perfect cultural goal versus the necessity of felling palms (for food) and certain trees (for the manufacture of dugouts) creates a conflict that demands a satisfactory solution. Many of the beliefs that surround canoe making serve the very purpose of maintaining the culture in a state psychologically balanced with the environment.[2]

## Zoological Characteristics

The mammalian fauna of the Orinoco Delta is rather uniform. In earlier times the Warao were reluctant to hunt the nutritionally more valuable large species such as chiguire (*Hydrochoerus hydrochoeris*), paca (*Cuniculus paca*), tapir (*Tapirus terrestris*), deer (*Odocoileur virginicus*), and peccary (*Pecari* sp.). This has changed now and all of these animals are eaten by commoners. Some priest-shamans, however, continue to abstain. Neither jaguar nor monkey is eaten, but of rodents, the small agouti (*Dasyprocta rubrata*) is much sought after as are birds such as wild turkey (*Crax alberti*) and duck (*Cairina moschata*). Of reptiles the Warao catch turtles, cayman, baba, and iguana but ignore all snakes. Fish is the most important source of protein, especially small lagoon species such as hoko (*Rivulus* sp.) or river fish such as morocoto (*Callosoma macropomus*) and several varieties of catfish. Crabs are an important seasonal supplement.

## The Human Environment

## The Society

Among the surviving tribal societies in South America, the Warao are one of the largest. They consider themselves a distinct people because of linguistic homogeneity and a shared common cultural denominator rather than for reasons of political federation. The largest social entity most meaningful and functional to a Warao is the band, traditionally consisting of several extended uxorilocal families. Bride service was required for several years after marriage. The bands average from thirty to fifty members who follow the advice and guidance of the paterfamilias.

Several bands recognize one another as belonging to the same subtribe, but beyond that unit, group allegiance is weak. Subtribes are loosely held together by three types of religious practitioner who function as intermediaries between the community and a pantheon of supernatural beings. In more recent times, missionaries and Creoles introduced the political offices of *fiscales* in charge of local groups, *capitanes* for modern riverfront communities of more than one hundred inhabitants, and *gobernadores* for larger aggregates. Besides these three political officeholders there are three different offices of religious practitioner that are the Warao elite: the priest-shaman, the white-shaman, and the black-shaman.

The kinship system of the Warao is of the Hawaiian type: all cousins are considered brothers and sisters. This reflects the customary marriage rule, inasmuch as first cousins do not generally marry each other. Instead, marriage partners are commonly chosen from nonrelated or more distantly related families of the subtribe so that endogamy prevails as long as marriageable partners are available. Descent is reckoned bilaterally.

The largest concentration of Warao Indians occurs in the Intermediate Delta, where seven to eight thousand people inhabit an area of over 10,000 square kilometers. The central sector of the zone is the home of the Winikina. In 1954 the Winikina numbered 195 individuals who lived in four settlements, along the banks of the Winikina, from which the subtribe derived its name (table 1).

Judging from the demographic sample in table 2, the Warao are a young society with 54 percent of its population below 18 years of age. The cycle of reproduction begins for the girls soon after they have participated in specific initiation rites that coincide with the onset of menstruation. Boys are usually somewhat older at marriage, and because of the existing uxorilocal rule of residence, married men move into the household of their parents-in-law. There they face a closely related group of females who condition public opinion and exert considerable social pressure. Both mates exercise free choice but final acceptability of a man by his future in-laws depends largely on his peaceful disposition and on his technical skill in the various activities essential for the procurement of a young family's livelihood. The groom considers his in-laws as his new parents, and the father-in-law especially becomes an important new agent of enculturation. Relative to the number of marriageable daughters he has, the association of a man with his sons-in-law represents a formidable work force that plays a large role in enabling the co-resident extended family to remain

TABLE 1

WINIKINA VILLAGES AND POPULATION
(1954)

| Villages | Total inhabitants | Number of dwellings | Total dwelling space[a] | Number of other structures[b] |
|---|---|---|---|---|
| Yaruara Akoho | 79 | 10 | 320 m² | 5 |
| Naonoko Hanoko[a] | 32 | 5 | 100 m² | 6 |
| Naonoko Hanoko[b] | 19 | 4 | 134 m² | 1 |
| Hanoko Buroho (La Isla) | 33 | 6 | 236 m² | 3 |
| Bure Bureina | 32 | 3 | 60 m² | 3 |
| Total | 195 | 28 | 850 m² | 18 |

[a]Occupied floor space in square meters; averaging 4.4 m² per person.

[b]Barns, kitchens, menstruation huts, temples. The house of the investigator at Yaruara Akoha is included in this category.

entirely self-sufficient. This becomes especially apparent in tasks that require team work, and canoe making is one such activity. To weld a group of young men and women into a cooperative unit the culture has to provide, of course, adequate methods of enculturation; and Warao culture is fully programmed to accomplish this goal.

## The Culture

The Warao speak a language of Chibchan affiliation. Waraoan represents the easternmost extension of this linguistic phylum of northern South America and southern Mesoamerica.

The missionaries, who established themselves some fifty years ago among the Warao, were very influential in bringing about a number of important cultural changes. For example, the intensification and diffusion of subsistence agriculture spread throughout most of the territory. Although there still exist preagricultural groups in the Intermediate Delta zone, agriculture is now practically universal among the Warao. Among the main crops planted are *ocumo*, both bitter and sweet varieties of yuca, bananas, plantains, sugar cane, maize, and rice, a cash crop.

Traditionally, however, most of the Warao were swamp foragers who relied heavily on the vegetable and animal resources mentioned earlier. Tobacco, their only psychoactive drug, was used mainly for magico-religious purposes and had to be obtained through trade with Trinidad or some of the Creole towns on the western fringe of the Delta.

Table 2

SEX AND AGE RATIOS OF LIVING WINIKINA
(1954)

| Age category[a] | Total | Percent | Males | Percent | Female | Percent | Ratio of males to females |
|---|---|---|---|---|---|---|---|
| Infants | 12 | 6 | 7 | 58 | 5 | 42 | 4:3 |
| Children | 75 | 38 | 34 | 45 | 41 | 55 | 4:5 |
| Teenagers | 19 | 7 | 12 | 79 | 7 | 21 | 4:2 |
| Adults[b] | 78 | 43 | 36 | 55 | 42 | 45 | 4:5 |
| Seniors | 11 | 6 | 4 | 36 | 7 | 64 | 4:7 |
| Totals | 195 | 100 | 93 | 48 | 102 | 52 | 9:10 |

[a]Infant, offspring below 1 year of age.
  Child, prepuberty offspring between 1 and 10 years.
  Teenager, bachelor.
  Adult, married individuals of reproductive age between 18 and 49 years.
  Senior, men and women approximately 50 years and over.

[b]Five married teenagers are listed as adults.

The Warao do not keep domestic animals for food. Hunting dogs are of considerable economic use in daily food-quest activities and as trade objects. Young birds and animals are also kept around the house to be exchanged for exotic items on periodic trade expeditions. Tame parrots, moriche birds, and monkeys are especially raised to this end.

Warao technology is little developed. Originally their only clothing was a fiber loincloth for women, and pieces of wood, bone, and shell were made into necklaces, bracelets, and other ornaments. The latter are still made but both men and women have largely adopted garments of Creole origin.

As containers for liquid the Warao used tree calabashes and for solids, baskets of various kinds. Iron pots of a casserole type are now used for cooking purposes, but traditionally the Warao lacked pottery as well as such other landmark crafts as weaving and metallurgy. Their original shelter was a dome-shaped structure in which they slept in improvised leaf-stalk hammocks. The modern rectangular stilt dwelling with thatched saddle roof is a recent introduction and was adopted for life along the riverbanks rather than in the morichales. Simultaneously, so it seems, the Warao also adopted the large net hammock of moriche fiber which now has become a characteristic piece of furniture in a Warao house and which represents one of the most sought after Warao items in trade.

For hunting and fishing purposes the Warao rely mainly on the lance, harpoon, bow and arrow, and hooks. In the early days they apparently made adzes of conch shell and axes of tortoise shell. But the equivalent tools of iron prevail in modern Warao households, together with the inevitable multipurpose machete or bush knife.

By far the most complex and most developed item of material culture is their dugout canoe. The canoe is the floating house of the traveling family, and essential to their livelihood because most life-sustaining activities in the Delta require transportation by water. The Warao trade with it, sleep, cook, eat and play in it. Eventually a man is even buried in a canoe. As a consequence, the dugout became thoroughly integrated into the technological, sociological, and ideological systems of the society, a development that turned a severely limiting factor of the habitat, namely, its dominant aquatic characteristics, into a distinct cultural advantage.

## Enculturation of a Canoe Maker
### Skill-training and Technology

Technology is a major subsystem of any given culture. It enables man to adapt to his physical environment through the production of specific goods and artifacts. Skill-training refers to the teaching of skills necessary to maintain a certain technology. Warao technology, though of little complexity, is uniquely specialized to fit the conditions of their homeland. This was particularly true in earlier times, before the advent of Afro-Europeans, when food-quest activities of the Warao centered on arbori-culture, lagoon fishing, and the catching of reptiles and shellfish. In those days the tool kit was meager: spears, bow, multipronged fowl and fish arrows, the sago hoe, the conch-shell adze, calabashes, and bell-shaped twilled baskets.

Under those circumstances the dugout canoe was then, as it is today, a major piece of equipment, especially adapted to the aquatic conditions of the Delta. While the literature frequently refers to the giant Warao canoes that could accommodate as many as a hundred passengers, it is useful to remember that it is not the very large canoes that take care of the daily needs of these Indians. The oversized craft were often made to order for European patrons who needed them to ship bulk merchandise or substantial contingents of troops. But the Warao themselves employ large dugouts, for fifty or more passengers, only on an occasional overseas trading expedition. In the Delta they make use of smaller dugouts, which often hold no more than the members of a nuclear family. The canoes are of sufficient size to tackle the windswept waters of the major caños but are still short and shallow enough to negotiate the narrow swamp channels. More important than the ability to cross wide expanses of water is the need for easy penetration of the boglands to distances of more than 10 kilometers inland, through the mangrove and hardwood belts clear into the heart of the life-sustaining palm groves.

The different sizes of Warao canoes correspond, of course, to the varying dimensions of the trees used to make them. Each type of Warao canoe is made from a single tree trunk, but canoes differ not only with respect to size. There are two classes of Warao dugouts which differ in terms of construction and use: the plain canoe and the composite five-piece canoe.

The *plain canoe* ranges in length from 2 m to 12 m. A very common medium-sized canoe averages about 6 m. The shorter craft of this class have an approximate maximum width of 50 cm; longer ones range between 70 cm and 80 cm in width. They may be anywhere from 30 cm to 40 cm deep. The thickness of the hull is an even 2.5 cm in small dugouts and 4 cm in large ones. Along the inside of the gunwale runs a rim 3 to 4 cm wide and 1 cm thick which ends at bow and stern in an inverted triangular design. Bow and stern are about 10 cm higher than the straight body, and the approximately 1.5-meter-long pointed stem at each end is relatively heavy. Both ends look identical, although the Indians know how to distinguish between the two (fig. 1:1).

The *five-piece canoe* has the same form and shape as the plain dugout, but it is invariably larger, measuring 12 m and longer, and is fitted with a plank on each side to heighten the gunwale. The planks are mounted on edge and lashed to the gunwale by means of lianas. At bow and stern these wash strakes are each connected by transverse prow boards which serve as escutcheons for painted symbols. The hull, two wash strakes, and two transverse boards are the five pieces.

Warao canoes of either class lack outriggers. The hollowed space of the vessel adds considerably to its buoyancy. Widening the hull by means of fire, hot water, and crossbeams increases the beam of the craft so that loads, even when asymmetrically arranged, do not easily cause rolling or capsizing.

Both classes of canoe are propelled by means of paddles with foliated blades and crescent handles (fig. 2), In the smaller craft the boatmen sit down in the middle and paddle from either side while sitting on thwarts. In the larger craft the boatmen sit along both gunwales and paddle only from their side. Sometimes, especially in the Upper Delta region, plain dugouts are also fitted with rectangular sails of leafstalk

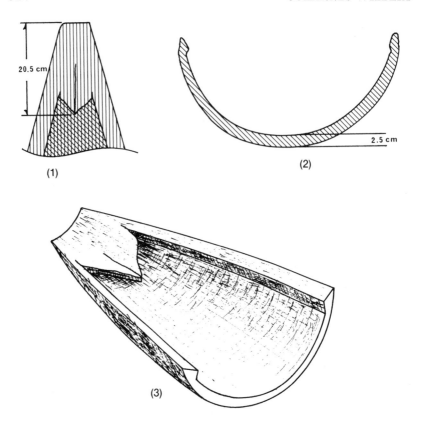

FIG. 1. Warao dugout canoe. (1) Superior prow detail; (2) cross section of hull; (3) prow section of dugout. Prototype in UCLA Museum of Cultural History (Cat. No. X70-36). Drawings courtesy Raul Lopez.

matting and triangular ones of cloth. The mast for the sail rests in a step mounted on the bottom of the boat in the forward section of the craft. The mast is further supported by two mast partners fixed above the step or by passing it through a hole in a bench board. Nowadays, larger canoes of the same class are also equipped with outboard motors.

Steering of the plain dugouts is accomplished by varying the stroke direction of the paddle. Composite five-piece canoes are provided starboard with a large paddle lashed to the stern quarter as a rudder. In the center of these seagoing vessels is a railing of beams tied together in the form of a cross. This rack is a little shorter than a man is tall and serves the shaman-captain of the vessel as support en route overseas to Trinidad: he holds onto the crossbeam mounted at elbow height. There may be as many as thirty boatmen in these large canoes.

FIG. 2.   Warao paddle. Drawing courtesy Helga Adibi.

Skill-training of the Warao boy and man has to satisfy the requirements for building canoes of all sizes and of both classes. Techniques vary in certain respects according to whether a regular-sized or an oversized canoe is envisaged and whether the trainee is a child, a young man, or a mature adult.

## Skill-Training during Infancy

Infancy lasts from the day of birth to the end of the child's first year. The Warao recognize this initial period not as an age grade but as a period in which the baby passes through five stages of motor development and a series of concomitant levels of mental achievement and status progression (table 3).

Throughout the first two months the infant rests in a baby sling, practically glued to his mother's body. Mother and child rarely leave the family corner of the communal house which is shared with two or three other matrilaterally related families. The platform of the stilt dwelling may offer a total living space of 40 m², with 10 m² reserved for each nuclear family, an average of only 4.4 m² per person (table 1). But the

Table 3

## STAGES OF MOTOR DEVELOPMENT
## IN INFANCY

| Stage[a] | Designation | Ability |
|---|---|---|
| First two months | *Horoshimo* | Suckling, sleeping |
| Three to five months | *Hiota* | Grasping |
| Six to nine months | *Hiota kabuka* | Sitting |
| Ten to eleven months | *Kabayoro* | Creeping |
| Twelve months | *Kabaka* | Standing, walking |

[a]Development stages are approximate.

family corner is of the greatest consequence to the infant as his first environment not only during the first two months but throughout the entire year and beyond.

Infancy is the period when the Warao baby is immersed in a world of women. Canoe making, in contrast, pertains mainly to the man's world in which he achieves progressively advanced status in his role as artisan. A woman's involvement in matters pertaining to canoes is more peripheral and is even hampered to some extent by negative associations attendant on her sex.

Yet, despite initial submersion in a female world, the presence of the male element soon breaks into the baby's sphere. Warao fathers frequently cradle babies in their arms and sing to them, especially when the infant has become a *hiota* and is able "to see and to laugh and to cry real tears." Sometime toward the end of this stage, the father may make a toy basketry rattle which he puts into the infant's grasping hand. The mother will also use the rattle from now on to delight the infant during his longer waking hours. He is also becoming quite frustrated with her since she leaves him behind more and more frequently while tending to her many chores. But if there is no babysitter available, the mother or parents jointly begin to take him along on short boat rides to the morichale or to the fields. By the time the infant has learned to sit up, he has taken many such rides, and the *hiota kabuka's* familiarity with canoes, as an extension of the family corner, becomes very intimate.

Another circumstance that tends to increase the infant's contact with the canoe during that third stage of motor development is the Warao belief that an infant six to nine months old must be bathed frequently so that he may learn how to stand up properly and how to walk rapidly. In fact, some mothers maintain that there ought to be several such bathing occasions during the day. Thus, one can frequently observe a mother carry her baby to the river where she seats the screaming creature in the family dugout and subjects him to extensive washing.

Toward the end of the first year of life, the crawling, and eventually walking, infant is difficult to confine to the small platform of the stilt house. Babysitting him becomes a full-time chore and parents become very inventive in discovering ways and means to keep their enterprising child in safety. The landing place with its bobbing boats exercises an irresistible attraction for the child. He wants to play with the other children. Like them, he wants to jump in and out of the moored boats. The father, seeking to keep the youngster contented in the house, carves small toy boats out of light sangrito wood. Eventually he will cut a piece of the boardlike root of the same tree and put it down on the floor of the house. This becomes the first "real" canoe for the infant, one he can actually sit in. Manipulating a miniature paddle with which his father equips him, he embarks on unchartered journeys, away from the house, through the fantasy land of infancy and childhood.

Among the many considerations of the parents is a concern for their infant's manual dexterity. Warao are right-handed as a rule, but some are left-handed or ambidextrous. This is no cause for alarm; left-handed children are not "corrected." On the contrary, naturally left-handed boatmen are appreciated on long journeys when the men paddle in rows along both gunwales of the canoe. There are also particular tasks in canoe making when it becomes an advantage to be a left-handed workman on the crew. Therefore, the parents of such a child let him be and only teach him how to hold the paddle properly. But here little goading is required. By the time a child can hold a paddle in his hands, he has observed his elders on so many occasions that paddle shaft and handle slide into the small fists almost naturally.

## Skill-Training during Childhood and Adolescence

This life period combines the ages from one to twelve years (childhood) and from thirteen to seventeen years (adolescence). The Warao themselves make these distinctions between childhood and adolescence by using different terms to refer to individuals in the different categories and by changing the personal names of postpuberty boys and girls (table 4).

Warao children seem to prefer to play outside the house as often as possible. They play "house" below the platform of the pile dwelling and various games on the dancing platform if there is one in the settlement. But by far the most attractive playground is the landing place. There they enjoy themselves for hours diving off the platform of the house nearest the riverbank and climbing back into the boats. Small children bring

TABLE 4

AGE CATEGORIES OF CHILDHOOD
AND ADOLESCENCE

| Age category | Boys | Girls |
|---|---|---|
| 1 to 12 years | *Noboto* (*nobotomo,* pl.) | *Anibaka* (*anibakamo,* pl.) |
| 13 to 17 years | | |
| a. Early teens | *Neburatu kabuka* | *Iboma hido* |
| b. Late teens | *Neburatu* | *Iboma* |

their toy paddles: bigger ones pick up real ones lying in the canoes and pretend to go on a journey. They put in so much practice time on make-believe canoe rides that by the age of three all children, boys and girls alike, know how to maneuver a canoe perfectly. Parents cannot be vigilant enough at this time. On the flimsiest pretext—for example, a canoe "accidentally" gets loose and drifts away with the current, or temiche fruit comes floating by just beyond reach—the small children push off to take care of the "problem." When the parents finally give in and let their children go in a canoe, the youngsters are euphoric. What they had been watching from infancy and had wanted so badly for themselves is finally attainable: they are able to get out onto the wide river all by themselves. It is truly breathtaking to observe a three-year-old child push off and paddle a canoe across an enormous river in full control of the craft.

Having mastered the first step toward becoming a boatman, the drive to own his personal boat soon makes the youngster eager for the time when he will be strong enough to develop his skills. In this respect, my informants consistently assured me, the process is actually a matter of imitation and copying, not of teaching. Explained one expert canoe maker: "Nobody teaches a boy how to make a paddle or a canoe." When asked why not, he replied, "Because he is a boy. Boys learn from watching. Boys just have to watch carefully."

What the informant did not tell me (but what fieldworkers, myself included, have observed) is that the canoe maker insists on having boys present when boats are being made. In other words, whereas adults may not engage in verbal instruction, they definitely require the presence of the learner when the opportunity for visual learning and instruction through demonstration presents itself. "The old Warao insists on performing this task [canoe-making] in cooperation with their children, grandchildren, and sons-in-law," writes Suárez (1968:35).

I remember one occasion when the chief of the Winikina set out to manufacture a canoe for my personal use. His wives took the girls along to gather fruit and manaca shoots but his nine-year-old son had to remain at the working place in the forest, although the prospect of eating fruit and palm cabbage tempted him greatly. Therefore, while it is true that, as one of my informants put it, "boys learn how to make canoes on their own initiative," the drive to learn must be fostered and the cue "learning through watching" must be reinforced.

The son of the Winikina chief was only nine years old, yet he had to perform several minor tasks connected with canoe building. There are also a series of precautions children have to take and taboos to observe, so that by insisting on a *noboto*'s participation the skill-training and social conditioning through which a Warao eventually becomes a master canoe maker is well under way at this early age. The paternal teacher is most understanding. He takes the relative physical immaturity of the apprentice into consideration and is forgiving if the attention span of the child is not very long, owing to the many distractions offered by a jungle environment. In fact, when the chief's nine-year-old fell asleep on a temiche leaf right next to the hull, his father smiled and walked over to him once to chase a horsefly off his bare back.

This tolerance is not shown toward an adolescent, though. At the age of fourteen a boy ceases to be a child. He can handle an axe and machete and now should participate more and more intensively in the actual production of a canoe. Otherwise he will be called lazy by his father and warned against growing up incapable of taking care of his future family. Postpuberty girls are denied the world of canoe makers for several reasons. For one, they are not considered clever enough to learn the art. They spend most of their time learning how to make hammocks and other tasks traditionally considered to be women's work. A young girl is especially dangerous to the canoe maker since she may unwittingly step into the dugout during menstruation. That would offend the patroness of canoe makers and provoke her devastating wrath.

Boys of fourteen, in contrast, make a decisive entrance into the world of canoe makers. One day the youngster will leave the settlement, axe in hand, to return with a piece of sangrito wood from which he carves his first paddle. When next the father goes into the forest to make a dugout, his son, now *neburatu kabuka,* will accompany him as assistant.

The manufacture of a plain dugout canoe takes place in three stages. First, a suitable tree has to be located, felled, and its trunk trimmed, hollowed out, and roughly shaped with an axe. The hull is then transported to the river and floated to the settlement. During the second stage the roughly hewn hull must be smoothed evenly inside and out by means of an adze. The third stage involves the hardening and spreading of the hull with fire.

A fourth stage is required for the production of a composite five-piece canoe. During this stage it is equipped with the wash strakes to increase the volume and depth of the vessel. Also two transverse prow boards have to be carved, painted, and fastened; the captain's rack is put into position midship, and the rudder lashed to the stern of the boat. Life expectancy of a well-made canoe of either class is between three and five years.

The learning process to which a young *neburatu* has to submit during the four stages is best described by detailing the technical production of a canoe.

Finding an appropriate cachicamo tree may take several days of searching in the forest. One young apprentice told me of his father who always found a tree in a very short time. "He looks around a lot," he said. And, indeed, "looking around" is a favorite pastime of the men when out on boat trips or walking through the bush. Traveling day after day by boat along the green forest edges becomes monotonous for a non-Indian. Not so for Indians. Travelers have often remarked upon the habit of the Warao of observing and studying the forest carefully as they go by. I personally have heard them comment more than once on a certain tree seen to be missing from a particular spot. To know in general where to look for a good cachicamo is half the task of finding it.

The next step is to go out and fell a tree. This has to be done during the early months of the dry season, and the boat maker who has no sons-in-law must rely on his son as helper. If he has no sons old enough, he has to engage two men from among his brothers-in-law, his brothers, or unrelated friends, for he cannot accomplish the work of felling and excavating the tree by himself. Hiring helpers, however, represents an expense inasmuch as the "owner" must provide them with food during the days of labor. Since every adult man probably wants to make a canoe for himself, it is not easy to find the necessary help. So a young father looks forward to the day when his son can take his place on the team; and at fourteen that time has come.

Very likely the youngster will be one of three men who set out one fine morning to accomplish the first stage of making a boat, the neburatu's most likely teachers being his father and his father's brother-in-law. So small a team does not usually set out to make a large canoe of 12 meters or more, let alone one large enough for overseas journeys. That requires a team of five or six men, and such teams are usually made up of a father-in-law, who functions as the expert craftsman, and his sons-in-law, the workmen. The construction of large canoes is performed with much ceremony and many ritual observances, most of which can be disregarded when constructing a small dugout.

Once the three arrive at the foot of the tree selected for the dugout, the first chore in which the neburatu participates is the cutting of trees growing around the cachicamo. The surrounding trees are felled in such a way as to form a grid on which the cachicamo comes to rest. This takes several days and serves to prevent the falling cachicamo from plunging deep into the swamp. With neighboring trees and underbrush gone the cachicamo tree can now be inspected to determine in which direction it ought to fall. This entails first identifying the flatter "back side" and the rounder "stomach side" of the tree. The father, if he is the more experienced of the two men, cuts a notch-shaped mark into the lower end of the back side of the tree, and then the men and the boy take turns cutting deep into the opposite stomach side so that the cachicamo will eventually topple on its back.

As I write this I have projected on my movie screen a tree that we filmed in 1954 during the process of making a dugout. The tree measured some 20 m in height from roots to crown. The father used as a measure the distance from the palm of his hand along the outstretched arm to the sternum, an extension I found to be 86 cm long. Applying this measure seven times consecutively along the trunk of the fallen tree, he marked with his axe the spot where his fellows severed the crown from the trunk. Thus the boat was determined to become a craft of 6 m in length. The base, which always becomes the stern of the canoe, measured 63 cm in diameter and the top 59 cm. After trimming the tree the young assistant placed two pieces of manaca on each side of the trunk to brace it firmly, and to prevent it from rocking while the work of excavating the trunk was in progress.

Excavating the trunk is work permitted the apprentice only after several seasons of experience. He is placed between the two adults and may excavate only the deeper layers, not the top ones. The first opening and the alignment of the various square excavations is a delicate procedure and must be performed by an experienced craftsman. He starts at a point one meter from the bottom of the trunk and scoops out a square piece 30 cm per side and about 20 cm deep. From the farther side of this square he measures a distance the length of his axe handle at which point he excavates a second square and lifts out the section between the two. He repeats the same operation at the other extremity of the trunk, also approximately 1 m from the end. After carefully aligning the squares at the extreme ends of the trunk, he then opens up the middle section. This first part of the actual task of hollowing out the tree is accomplished while the craftsman is standing on the ground.

The next step is performed standing astride the trunk with one foot on each edge of the shallow opening; he excavates the next layer of wood by striking diagonal blows zigzag from the middle of the trunk to the base and then from the middle to the top. This work can be executed in part by the young apprentice, as can the next step of scooping out a third layer of wood. This time the blows of the axe are directed laterally, excavating first a longitudinal groove through the middle of the trough from rear to front and then cleaving out the remaining shoulders. Two men can work simultaneously at these tasks, with the apprentice concentrating on the midsection of the boat.

The final step of excavating a tree has to be carried out by the hand of an expert. The partly hollowed out trunk is rolled on its side so that an experienced man can round out the interior of the hull. Next, he tapers the ends for about 1.25 m and rounds off bow and stern. This task has to be performed with utmost precision beginning at the stern. Facing the stern the craftsman tapers first the right side. Ideally the left side should be carved by a left-handed person. In his absence the same man must do both sides fore and aft, but the following day he must rest and overcome the pain he suffers from straining unconditioned muscles.

While his father and the adult helper rest from the strenuous five or six days of work, the young apprentice cuts manaca palms to prepare a 2-m-wide corduroy road across the swamp from the work place to the river. He is joined in this task by the women and children, who come to help by first placing the poles and then pushing the hull out of the forest into the nearest river. This concludes the first stage of the manufacturing process.

The young apprentice has had a good opportunity to practice swinging his axe with precision. He has learned how to direct a falling tree and how to use his hands to measure the thickness of the hull between them. He has also seen how the excavated parts are visually aligned and how the ends of the boat are tapered. A seventeen-year-old neburatu has usually advanced far enough in his apprenticeship that he may go out alone or with a brother or friend and try his luck with his first canoe. This often occurs immediately after he has helped his father scoop out his boat and while the older man is busy carrying out the second stage of the manufacturing process alone. By the time a neburatu thinks of marriage he has participated as an apprentice in the work crew of his father for four seasons. Under the guidance of an experienced man he carries out what he has observed for ten or more seasons. Many a neburatu prides himself on owning his own boat by the time he marries and on having mastered the rudiments of the technology involved in boat making. Of course, he would not yet pretend to be a full-fledged *moyotu*, "boat maker." For that a man needs more practice and, above all, a dream vision to receive his call to the office. Technological skill is a necessary, but not sufficient, condition for becoming a craftsman.

The second stage of production is a task carried out by the owner of the boat himself without the aid of helpers. It requires thousands of blows with the adze, an implement consisting of a transverse blade on a short handle not much longer than the width of an adult man's hand, to smooth both sides of the hull. By rolling the hull from side to side and repeatedly gauging the thickness of the walls between the flat of the hands the task is finally accomplished; the hull is smooth and even and the internal rim along the gunwale is carved.

This work is carried out within the confines of the village and the children have been watching the craftsman for weeks. The boys are called frequently to the site to observe the process, although they are not permitted to touch the tools, not only to forestall the child's damaging the hull but also to avoid provoking the spirit of the tool. Only men from neburatu up may pick up an adze. Thus, at least for the child, to learn how to handle the adze and how to finish the hull of a dugout is to learn through observation, never through practice. The adolescent will have to learn later under the guidance of his father. Again there is not much verbal instruction between father and son, but the father does correct the hand of his son and does teach him how to overcome the pain in his wrist from working with the adze. Another piece of explicit instruction occurs with respect to using the outspread hands to measure the thickness of the hull. The father remeasures the area that his son completes and, if necessary, corrects him personally.

Finally, the day comes when the carpentry work on the hull is complete. The next stage is to smooth the hull inside and out by fire. The canoe is laid on its side and the hull packed with temiche leaves. This is the moment the children and everybody in the village have been waiting for. The fire is lit and soon the hull is engulfed in a billowing bonfire. While the children jump carelessly around the fire, the boat makers themselves are busy directing the heat by adding or removing leaves at different places and by protecting strategic parts by covering them with clay. After the fire has burned down, the men scrape off the charred portion with a chip of wood. Then the other side undergoes the same treatment. This takes care of smoothing the hull and all adze scars disappear in the process. The hull is now jet black.

Next the hull has to be widened. It is propped up at both ends on two short uprights that are notched in a V at the top. Each end of the hull is firmly locked between two uprights placed on either side and tied tightly together with lianas above. This prevents the hull from slipping off its props into the fire, a mishap that could cause it to crack and thereby ruin the entire work.

The hull is filled with water, and a new heap of temiche leaves piled underneath is set on fire. From time to time the craftsman tests the temperature of the water with his hand. When the temperature is right the man climbs into the hull and begins to widen it by inserting several crossbeams of varying lengths. Starting in the middle with the longest beam, he sets one end against the rim on one side. Then he pulls up the other end of the beam slowly until there is a certain degree of resistance. He inserts a series of crossbeams of decreasing lengths toward bow and stern. When finished he jumps out of the hull and runs to each end of the boat to check the symmetry of the intended longitudinal curve of the gunwale. If it needs correction, he climbs back into the hull and applies additional heat until the sheer is perfect. If so he tips the canoe and pours out the water.

After several seasons of helping his father with the more menial tasks that accompany this third stage of the production process (maintaining and directing the fire, scraping off the charred parts, and the like), the apprentice himself is eventually permitted to step into the boat and insert the crossbeams to spread the hull. The father still determines the right temperature of the water and he indicates how far up a particular crossbeam must be pulled to reach the maximum point of tolerance, but he remains on the ground and directs the operation from either end of the hull. That is how the neburatu gets a feel for each critical task: for the evenness of the hull wall between the palms of his hands, for the right temperature of the water, and for the degree of firmness of the breaking point when the hull is spread. To see him being permitted eventually to share in his father's pride in a job well done is a moving experience.

It takes one whole night for the new canoe to cool. The next morning the branches are cut for the seats and the struts placed in position. The shiny new black boat is launched with the joyful participation of the entire village.

The technical aspects of converting a plain canoe into a seagoing five-piece vessel have already been described sufficiently for the present purpose. I return to the subject later to discuss certain nontechnical aspects.

## Skill-Training during Adulthood

Little remains for the *nebu* (young adult; see table 5) to learn about the technical aspects of canoe making other than through experience and

### TABLE 5

### STAGES OF ADULTHOOD

| Age category | Men | Women |
|---|---|---|
| Early | Nebu | Iboma |
| Late | Aidamo | Tihidamo |

seasoning. But by the time a man has made his own fourth or fifth dugout, his father-in-law and the master builder of canoes will ask him whether or not he has dreamed of Dauarani, the Mother Goddess of the Forest. By now he is a mature man of twenty-five or twenty-eight and is about to embark on a new learning experience involving the supernatural and religious dimension of canoe construction.

## Socialization and Society

Socialization as used here refers to the various processes by which a man is integrated into Warao society as a full-fledged canoe maker. "It involves . . . the adaptation of the individual to the fellow-members of his group, the achievement of a position in relation to them that gives him status and assigns to him the role he plays in the life of the community" (Herskovits, 1970:38–40). More specifically, I describe how the Warao effect socialization of the individual during childhood/adolescence and adulthood within the tribal environment, society, and culture.

## Socialization during Childhood and Adolescence

Not much can be added to what has already been said about the distinct mode of enculturation of the male Warao child. He is gradually socialized into the distinctly male domain of canoe making and encouraged to assume his place as a helper to his elder brothers and to his father. In a subsequent chapter I return to a boy's moral obligations.

The socialization process becomes much more apparent once the Warao youngster reaches his early and late teens and, of course, especially, once the adolescent enters adulthood. A young teenager (*neburatu kabuka*) frequently becomes the "alter ego" of an elder brother in his late teens (neburatu). He will function as his elder brother's confidant, his go-between with his girlfriends, and his ever reliable cover. Several such pairs from the same or from neighboring groups occasionally form one-sex gangs and roam through the territory giving expression in various ways to adolescent *Sturm und Drang*. Whether such reactions are culturally conditioned or natural, adolescent male and female Warao do not make their parents happy. The burden for disciplining a youth falls primarily upon the mother's shoulders and secondarily on the entire society. Fathers rarely take issue with the behavior of their teenage sons and daughters.

From about his sixteenth year until the birth of his first child a male adolescent adopts the identity characteristics of the tribal culture hero Haburi, the inventor of canoes. The youth adorns himself like his model with armbands made of bast and paints his face with two lines below the eyes and dots on his cheeks. His hair is cut short in the back with a crop left only on the forehead. Blowing on Haburi's flutes and playing the hero's drum, he leads the life of a restless wanderer, moving from house to house and from one settlement to another. A teenage girl finds his flute-playing irresistible and both make use of the neburatu's younger brother to exchange vows, gifts of food, and to arrange for secret rendezvous. Eventually, taking advantage of his girlfriend's isolation during her menses, the young man and his sibling companion pretend to go on yet another bird-hunting expedition, leaving the village for several weeks or months. Girls are known to have pursued their escaping paramours to beat them up and pierce the membranes of their expensive drums. All this, however, is expected behavior, typical of the vicissitudes of adolescence, and the young man moves on like Haburi whose very name means "he who roams about aimlessly." The reasons for Haburi's restlessness are explained later. Suffice it to point out here that he was tormented by remorse for having committed incest with his mother and that the dugout he invented was transformed into the mother-goddess of restored sexual order.

Fear of repeating the incestuous crime drives the adolescent youth to visit the girls of neighboring groups. Chances are that among them he may find some who are not consanguineally related to him. But under a kinship system of the Hawaiian type (which prohibits cousin marriage of any kind) and with prevailing subtribal endogamy, potential sexual and marriageable partners are scarce. But the greatest fear of the youth and of his parents is that his heart might run away with his head, that love and ignorance might trick him into an incestuous relationship, as in the case of Haburi.

What compounds these difficulties is the fact that endogamy and uxorilocal residence may eventually make it necessary for an adolescent to leave friends and relatives to find a future consort among strangers of another subtribe. Thus an adolescent's dilemma is that although he has considerable freedom in selecting sexual partners, his choice is severely limited to a very few females in the bands of his subtribe because of the constraints of social structure. For instance, of a total of twelve male teenagers in our demographic sample of the Winikina subtribe, eleven were bachelors; of the seven female teenagers only three were unmarried (table 2). Thus the eligible male bachelors were outnumbered by the marriageable females 1:4.[3] In addition, the three unmarried girls were consanguineal kin (hence forbidden) to several of the eleven bachelors. No wonder, then, that the adolescent boy empathizes with Haburi whose only potential female partners were his consanguineal and classificatory mothers. To avoid breaking the taboo he is required to roam from band to band in search of a bride.

And that is how a young man succeeds in finding a young bride instead of an older widow. To have his love returned by her is one thing; to be accepted by the bride-to-be's father is quite another. Crucial for the latter decision is the bridegroom's ability to handle the tools of a man. Does he know how to prepare a garden, hunt and fish, build a house? Above all, does he know how to make a canoe? If he is accepted by his in-laws, the young man's father-in-law may ask him to manufacture a dugout for him, and it is understood by all concerned that the canoe is compensation for a virgin bride. His firstborn child will seal this bond in accordance with the order established by Dauarani, the culture hero's serpent canoe. With the birth of the first child the adolescent's Haburi-behavior terminates. He has successfully entered the world of adults.

## Socialization during Adulthood

Thus marriage marks the boundary between adolescence and adulthood for a Warao youth. When his wife gives birth to their first child the young husband hands down the material evidence of neburatu status to his younger brother: the drum, the flutes, a necklace of jaguar bone, among other things. This gesture of passing on the paraphernalia of adolescence is associated with a good measure of trauma for the young man. It is the same trauma of separation which overshadowed his wedding day a few months earlier. All bridegrooms in Warao society are generally required to leave their parents' home and exchange the world of childhood for a strange physical and social environment. From that day a young man ceases to belong to the work team of his father where he learned the basics of canoe making. He is a *nebu*, "worker," now serving his father-in-law. He has to cooperate with his co-resident brothers-in-law sometimes even in a new settlement, there to assume junior status to those who have preceded him by marrying his new wife's sisters. Whatever remains to be learned about the art of boat making he will probably absorb from his father-in-law and brothers-in-law, the men of greatest consequence in effecting the enculturation of the newlywed.

This transitional period is a very critical time in a Warao man's life, especially if the uxorilocal residence rule should oblige him to move far away from his family of orientation, his cousins, and friends. Fortunately, this is rarely the case. With prevailing endogamy the settlements belonging to the same subtribe are usually not too distant from one another, and, under traditional circumstances, a man rarely has to move from one Delta zone to another. This is of great importance owing to the considerable differences in the physical and biological environments of the three Delta zones. A man raised in the Intermediate zone, for instance, knows best how to exploit the flora and fauna of that region. It would add considerably to the normal stress accompanying a change of residence if he had to exchange his customary outer world for a strange one as well. Compliance with his in-laws and peers is the young man's best guarantee for happiness within the new family he has joined by marriage. (I have watched such a family grow over the past two decades, and I consider them a good example for the present discussion.) To become accepted as an equal is the strongest motivation for education at this stage in life.

After establishing his family of procreation, the young family man is likely to be called upon during the first dry season to join his brother-in-law and the "owner of the house," his father-in-law, in making a new canoe. According to the prevailing custom, however, he will learn of these plans not from his father-in-law or any of the other men of the family, but rather from his wife. Of course, the initiative usually originates with *aidamo* or *moyotu,* as the father-in-law is called if he himself is a master canoe maker. But he speaks first to his wife, calling to her attention the need for a new canoe, a large one that the women could use to transport firewood. They purport to need one big enough to transport such building materials as sturdy house posts, manaca beams for construction and flooring, and temiche leaves for roofing. His wife agrees and, waiting for a good opportunity, calls her eldest married daughter and draws her attention to this need. The daughter, in turn, communicates her parents' wishes to her younger married sisters, who then explain the situation to their respective husbands. Despite the fact that there exists no avoidance taboo between father-in-law and sons-in-law, and notwithstanding that they usually communicate freely in daily life, the father-in-law would never speak directly to his daughters' husbands of labor that requires team work: for example, the clearing of a patch of forest in preparation of a new field, the construction work on houses and bridges, or the making of a canoe. He would feel "ashamed," as the Warao put it.

For her part each daughter makes sure that her husband agrees to respond to the moyotu's wish by pointing out that the work of fabricating the hull would take no longer than a week if everyone obliges.

Once the word is out that a new boat is to be made, it takes only a short time for the women to prepare a good supply of victuals (like taro and sugar cane) and to pack the boats. Then one day all the brothers-in-law with their entire families set out in three or four boats, the youngest son-in-law and his wife among them.

The small fleet voyages up one of the caños several kilometers deep into the swamp until they come to the end of the waterway. There they tie up the boats and construct small shelters that will serve as living quarters while canoe construction is under way. The moyotu and his wife or wives do not depart with the younger family members. Instead, they allow one day for the young people to set up camp and join them there the following day, arriving early in the morning.

After breakfast the men sharpen their axes and fall into file to walk to the place where they have spotted a tree of the desired dimensions. As we shall see, this is a ritually significant occasion, and the sequence in which the men walk Indian file through the forest is determined by their status and rank. First walks the master. He is followed by his sons-in-law, who take their positions according to seniority, determined in this case by the age of the wife. The man married to the eldest daughter of the master heads up the line of the nebu. This places our newlywed at the end of the line. (There were four brothers-in-law in my sample family.)

The master walks with an air of solemnity, blowing a conch shell and chanting to herald each new phase in the process of felling, trimming, and scooping out of the trunk. The workers depend on him to determine how the tree should fall; he marks the precise spot where the crown is to be severed from the trunk; he opens the first squares in the trunk and supervises the alignment of others. The actual excavation of the hull is then carried out by the workers. They line up along the edge of the trunk according to rank. The husband married to the oldest daughter puts himself in charge of the lower portion of the trunk, which is larger and tougher. Ranked on his side, according to their relative status, stand his younger peers. Thus their newlywed companion is assigned the last position at the upper end of the trunk.

Assuming the trunk to be 14 m long, it takes four men about seven days to complete the work of hollowing it out. They work for about six hours every day and, if too exhausted, sometimes skip a day. But each time they leave the camp, or return to it after work, they proceed Indian file according to status. The hardest work is allotted the eldest son-in-law, who has the first chance to distinguish himself by earning the prestige commensurate with his rank. The youngest man is usually grateful for such formalities for, as it is, he is under enough strain just to keep up with his older and generally more experienced companions. Word of his conduct will spread to the village of his parents and so he labors conscientiously to protect his father's reputation. Besides, the quality of his work on the hull is there for everyone to judge and, although nobody would dare criticize the young man publicly, there are more subtle ways to broadcast dissatisfaction.

For the work of tapering the ends of the trunk the workmen team up in pairs. The senior pair takes the hind part and completes what will be the stern of the boat. The junior pair takes charge of the bow section. Should one of them be left-handed, he is assigned to the left side of each end point, a contribution that is greatly appreciated by his teammates for the reasons mentioned. The junior son-in-law and his partner work more slowly on the hull and more deliberately than the senior workers at the stern. Therefore, as soon as the latter have completed their task, they relieve the younger men and finish the job for them.

The master builder does not participate in the hard labor of this phase of construction at all. His advice is sought from time to time. He spends some time watching the men while they work and takes responsibility for all important ritual concerns. But a very specific task for him is to provide an abundance of choice foods, especially fish and meat. The women busy themselves with tending the small children and with preparing the meals. They also assist at times with line fishing for the palatable lagoon fish that abound in the headwaters of the caño. The boys over seven or eight years of age go with their fathers to the construction site, where they watch the work in progress and perform small tasks, such as fetching drinking water or clearing away the chunks of scooped-out wood. The older boys among them, of neburatu kabuka age, may have to take an active part in hollowing out the trunk in families boasting but one or two sons-in-law.

A more important task for the older boys under the guidance of their youngest brother-in-law is the felling of a large number of skid logs for the corduroy road. Moreover, everybody has to pitch in to break camp when the work in the forest is ended and the finished hull dragged to the river.

While perfecting his technical skills as a member of his father-in-law's work team, a young man also attempts to further his own career as a master boat builder. He takes advantage of the years when his father-in-law does not need a new boat and tries his hand once again at fabricating a canoe for his own use. In the course of the years, he will have seen four or five small canoes through all three stages of construction. He establishes a name for himself among his people as a man who has at his command all the basic skills. In fact, everybody realizes that the young man is on the road to becoming a master craftsman himself.

His social status as a good carpenter is already established. Economically, he is also doing well. He owns one or two canoes and never has to borrow from his fellows. This makes him independent in the sense that he can take care of his various obligations according to his own schedule. It frees him from obligation to the owners of canoes from whom he would otherwise have to borrow boat time.

A man owns the canoe he himself constructs, although large canoes are implicitly considered by the moyotu himself to belong to his senior wife. To run down to the village landing place and push off in a friend's canoe on a short errand is perfectly permissible, but one has to obtain permission first from the owner for more extended trips. Circumstances permitting, the owner will lend the canoe with no thought of compensation. But it is one thing to borrow occasionally and another to do so consistently. This will soon severely undercut a man's prestige. People refer to him as a *wayana*, an unskilled pauper who does not even own a canoe. Whenever he needs to go on a trip he has to rely on the favor of someone who does own one. His wife is scorned because she is unable to get to the fields to bring in the vegetables. Firewood is chronically lacking in her household. As he becomes more and more dependent, his fellows will start using him as a serf, one who has no choice but to comply with the whims and wishes of others.

I observed such a man who had married exogamously but still within the same area in the Intermediate Delta where the art of canoe making is not developed by all men. His band lived in the morichales away from the large rivers and caños and canoes were of little importance to them in their moriche-oriented swamp life. The young man's in-laws, however, lived on the Winikina River, where life is unsupportable without a river craft. Not only did the unfortunate wayana have to learn how to make a living as an agriculturist, but he also had a river-oriented life. This forced him to ask constantly for help from the hands of his fellows. I have seen this wayana live the life of a beggar, humiliated, jumping to oblige every man in the village who had done him a favor. Even today, he is still considered a man without the slightest chance of ever becoming a moyotu, in this world *or* the next.

A good canoe maker, in contrast, besides enjoying the prestige that goes with technical skill, may also become well-to-do. Warao canoes continue to fetch a good price, anywhere from the equivalent of U.S. $100 to $350, depending on size. Even if a young man succeeds in selling only one canoe every second year, the sudden influx of wealth causes the standard of living of his family to soar way above the average. The wife of such a craftsman is well dressed and wears expensive bead necklaces that proclaim her husband's success as much as would a professional shingle. She owns an iron cooking pot, an axe, and kitchen knives, needles, and other metalware. He wears decent clothes, owns his machete, axe, and man's knife. These are just a few overt status symbols for gauging the level of prosperity of a competent boat maker; and there are many covert ones as well. For instance, a young boat maker does not keep for himself all that he earns by trading or selling a canoe. He gives some to his parents-in-law and his brothers-in-law. Everyone's wealth and prestige rises through mere association with the man; and that is one of the major motives for his entire effort to become an expert maker of canoes. Independent wealth and high status give him horizontal and vertical mobility.

The prestige accruing to a master craftsman and owner of a seagoing five-piece canoe is incomparably higher than for anything else he may do in his entire life and the enterprise of ultimate socioeconomic importance is an overseas trading expedition to the Island of Trinidad.[4] The best time of the year for such overseas trading expeditions is in August, when the trade winds abate and the waves are small. About fifteen men and one woman are selected for the venture. They then construct the large vessel as described.

On the last day before departure, the men stow the boat with trade goods. In the 1930s, when such expeditions were still common, goods taken aboard included mainly dogs, birds, hammocks, and baskets (table 6). Naturally, the actual value of the goods received in exchange may have deviated considerably from the expected values as represented in the table. For the Warao participants, however, these were actual values, equivalent to prices that the items listed would fetch in a Venezuelan market. The goods the Warao received in return, such as cotton cloth, men's clothing, and iron tools, were in their view equivalent to the same relative monetary value. Thus, if each of the fifteen men on board a trading boat had taken only one unit of each of the items listed, the total value, in the estimation of the sailors, would have amounted to roughly 2,000 bolivares, or U.S. $400. I say roughly because there were probably fewer than thirty dogs involved and probably more than fifteen hammocks. In any case, a sum of this magnitude represented an enormous investment, whose returns were widely distributed within the band, a fact that provided the motivation for the labor necessary to ready the boat and to muster the courage to brave the dangers of the voyage.

The prestige of the man who made it all possible rose to new heights on these occasions. Thanks to the craftsmanship of the master builder whose vessels brought the expedition to a successful conclusion each family in the band was better off than ever. Besides providing the canoe, the master would often take the rudder on such expeditions. He provided the rack and the tobacco for the shaman standing amidships to repel with abundant smoke both storm and malevolent spirits. Since the master builder was on good terms with the patroness of master builders, the steed of this goddess whose image was painted on the transverse prowboard in the stern was sent out to speed the flight of the vessel of her favorite servant. On the front escutcheon the master painted the oculus of the God of the North to guide their trip to the Island. The God of the South pulled the boat back toward the mainland again. In short, the master builder of canoes who achieved this technical and socioeconomic triumph had successfully been socialized as a master canoe maker of his society.

Contrast this exalted position with that of some Warao who fall into a certain kind of dependency relationship which parallels, in a sense, the informal serfdom resulting from general incompetence or from being a wayana. It is almost equivalent to serf peonage, quite formal, entails the loss of a considerable degree of personal freedom, and originates in the following way. The three shamanic specialists of any Warao group expect to be compensated for their curing services. When summoned by a Warao

TABLE 6

## WARAO GOODS TRADED WITH TRINIDADEAN PEASANTS

| Items | Value 1930[a] (Bolivares) |
|---|---|
| Hunting dogs (young) | 50 |
| Hunting dogs (old) | 30 |
| Amazon parrot | 25 |
| Cotorro (*Pallidae* spp.) | 10 |
| Hammock | 50–60 |
| Manioc press | 10 |
| Large basketry trays | 10 |
| Manare | 10 |

[a]Prices according to Warao men who participated in trade expeditions. Payments were made in goods of equivalent value.

in need, an agreement is entered into regarding the kind and amount of compensation. But if the patient or his family is unable to come up with the necessary remuneration, it is agreed that the patient, should his health be restored, live the rest of his life in the service of his doctor. It means that he is expected to provide the shaman with goods and to do him favors on end. The shaman, in turn, is expected to look after him and his immediate family. A man too poor to pay for the services of a religious practitioner is known by a special name that proclaims his dependency. A relationship of this kind does not degrade him intolerably, but young men find the status undesirable because it curbs their social mobility considerably. It is a dependency that cannot befall the canoe maker. He always has sufficient tobacco in the house to make the shaman come when sickness strikes and to compensate the doctor for his services. Thus, the members of his nuclear and even extended families are covered with sufficient health insurance, a benefit deeply appreciated.

To become a good family man who knows how to fulfill his obligations as husband, father, son-in-law, and brother-in-law is very much the goal of the young man who submits to the rigors of a canoe maker's life. Success in this respect makes all his effort and sacrifice worthwhile and provides the necessary motivation to excel at the specific role in which his culture has cast him.

For a considerable portion of his adult life the young canoe maker continues to produce vessels, knowing perfectly well, however, that one important feature is missing from his career. He is as yet not a moyotu, a master canoe maker. Of course, he enjoys the respect of his fellows for having acquired the technical skills of his profession. He also reaps the socioeconomic benefits commensurate with his expertise. But an established moyotu's prestige transcends all that because he has embraced the metaphysical. The true moyotu is chosen to become initiated as a workman of the Goddess Dauarani, the patroness of the master builders of canoes. This is the ultimate in the career of a master, and much effort and time are expended to achieve that goal.

There are, of course, several time-consuming prerequisites. The necessary mechanical skills have been mastered after approximately five years of marriage. Then will come the day when, while laboring on yet another boat, he has certain visions and goes forth to seek the help of an established canoe maker, the one who is to initiate him into the ranks of canoe craftsmen.

## Moral Education and Ideology

I define moral education as the teaching of the concept of correct behavior. Canoe making, particularly the construction of a large composite five-piece vessel over 12 meters long, is thoroughly imbued with the principles and considerations of those actions by which a person may be judged as being of good or bad character.

## Moral Education during Infancy and Childhood/Adolescence

During the initial period of my first fieldwork among the Warao in 1954, it was dramatically brought home to me that a large canoe is not merely an item of material culture to these Indians. I had borrowed a 9-meter-long canoe from a Winikina who had reluctantly consented to let me outfit the craft with a twelve horsepower outboard motor. (In those days motors were still a novelty.) The boat suffered from many cracks and an asymmetrical sheer, but it was the only one available and aesthetic considerations had to take second place. The life history of this dugout was known to every adult male in the tribe for it had been made by a man who had dared to cut down a large tree although he was not a master builder. The bulging gunwales proved beyond doubt that his action had not been sanctioned by the Patroness of moyotu craftsmen and that the spirit of the tree was upset.[5]

Then one day disaster struck. The chief had borrowed my canoe and gone with his family to the field. They cooked out there but the pot slipped from the burning embers, tipped over, and spilled its boiling contents all over the lower back of their nine-year-old son. The chief brought the child to me for treatment, explaining in rage and frustration that it was the canoe's fault. The restless spirit of the canoe had taken revenge on his child for having suffered construction by unqualified hands.

Warao children are held accountable for their conduct from their earliest years "as soon as they can think," that is, at the age of two or three. And it is such incidents as the one just recounted that keep them aware of the fact that canoes, especially large ones, are dangerous if not treated properly. Behavior offensive to the canoe, or rather to the spirit of the canoe, called Masisikiri, can occur as early as during a child's infancy. Since the infant cannot be held accountable as yet, it is not blamed, but some kind of disciplinary action may be taken as early as late infancy or early childhood. The child first learns to refrain from urinating or (worse still) defecating in or near the canoes. The toilet training of small children, I found, is not severe among the Warao, and nobody gets upset if the child soils the house. But both mother and father will not tolerate similar defilement of a large canoe and the child is scolded severely. Usually they are told to stay away from it altogether.

For the same reason mothers never use soap in or around the big canoes and call their children back if they notice them about to do so. To avoid all these complications the moyotu prefers to keep his canoes away from the busy landing place, where the children are bathed by their mothers, where they play, and where a young girl may inadvertently step into the vessel at the outset of her menstrual period. Women and girls are particularly dangerous for this very reason. In addition, they are also associated with other odors that are offensive to the boat's spirit, such as the smell of rancid coconut oil on their hair or the fumes of their kitchens. And so girls are taught to stay away from large dugouts, especially as long as the canoes are new, lest their actions, even their mere presence, cause damage, sickness, and death to themselves or to their kin.

Boys too must behave properly around a large canoe. Besides the restrictions pertaining to bad odors they have to learn a series of other taboos related to boat making and boat ownership. Since they accompany the men to the building sites from an early age, and since the master builder chants the spells and liturgical texts aloud, boys become aware of the fact that more transpires during canoe making than meets the eye.

One of the first things the children are told is to stay away from the felled tree and the hull under construction. The Masisikiri-spirit is still all about and will reside in the stump for all time. Children also learn that nobody may remain at the construction site at night, that even adults are afraid to face the jaguar that invariably comes in the dark to scoff at the tree that is "being devoured by the axes" of the men. Children learn to respect the jaguar as the chief haunt of their lives, for the jaguar who comes to jeer at the felled cachicamo tree is no ordinary jaguar but one endowed with supernatural powers.[6] The same is also true of other visible and invisible personages surrounding the construction site. Boys pick up fragments of this belief and value system in small increments. But by the time a young man follows a moyotu into the forest for the first time as a full-fledged workman he understands what the master has been chanting. He knows that below the technical level of canoe making there exists an ideational one, and that both together represent the true ethnographic reality of Warao canoes. Thus, when a man with full mastery of the technical skills now desirous of becoming a moyotu approaches a master, he takes the decisive step toward articulating the technical, the social, and the ideational dimensions of canoe making in his own life and mind. Throughout his childhood he has been collecting the many pieces of this metaphysical mosaic. Now he seeks a guiding hand to help him fit these fragments together.

## Moral Education during Adulthood

Teaching an apprentice to become a moyotu takes place in isolation. The initiation period may take the better part of the dry season since the learning of some of the prerequisite (nontechnical) skills takes time. The teaching environment may be a temporary shelter in the forest or simply the house of the master who usually concentrates on but one apprentice at a time. Both men abstain from food as much as possible but consume large amounts of tobacco in the form of cigars. They use only virgin fire to light these cigars. Sexual intercourse is absolutely prohibited during the period of initiation.

The apprentice is not accustomed to smoking. According to traditional practice, only shamans and the moyotu may indulge in tobacco smoking. Consumption is strictly for magicoreligious purposes. Tobacco is the food of the gods who inhabit many different sacred regions in the Warao universe, for example, the cardinal and the intercardinal points, the zenith above the earth and the nadir below, and various other places. Shamans placate these supernaturals by feeding them tobacco smoke from huge cigars. They hold the cigar in the direction in which the god is believed to reside, light it, and hold a lump of caranna resin (*Protium heptaphyllum*) to the burning end. They also mix granules of the same resin into the tobacco leaves contained in a consumable smoking tube made of the stipule of manaca. The resin smells like frankincense, a perfume most appreciated by the gods, and especially also by Dauarani, Mother of the Forest, Patroness of the master builders of canoes.

Smoking for the purpose of feeding the gods requires practice and a good measure of physical stamina. Once lit, the cigar is smoked by hyper-ventilation. The tip is ignited and the resin-treated cigar is consumed so steadily that the small flame at the top is not allowed to die. The smoke is drawn into the lungs and gulped down into the stomach. As a consequence, the shaman exhales and belches up clouds of smoke, all a sign that the spirit in whose name the tobacco is consumed is satisfied (Wilbert, 1972; 1975).

Moyotu master craftsmen learn how to smoke exacly like shamans. Their smoke offering is intended to satisfy Dauarani and the ancestor craftsmen who reside on her world mountain. The apprentice unaccustomed to tobacco starts by inhaling less deeply; only toward the end of his schooling does he feed the Goddess in the manner described.

A major part of the curriculum concerns the origin story of Dauarani, their patroness. It is a comprehensive and extensive myth cycle of Warao tradition which is presented here in brief.

### The Mother of the Forest and the First Canoe

Long before man inhabited the earth there lived in the north-western quadrant of the terrestrial disk the fishermen nation of the nutria. Two of their women, who were sisters to each other, got married to a hunter who lived in the southeastern part of the earth. The younger woman bore a son whom they called Haburi. Fleeing from an ogre who had killed their husband, the women and their infant son took refuge in the house of Wauta the tree frog (*Phrynohyas venulosa*)[7] who lived in the southwestern quadrant of the earth and who was a farmer. The mythical frog woman stretched the infant miraculously and made him grow instantly into a neburatu. Ignoring his origin, the young man unwittingly committed incest with his mothers who, in turn, did not recognize their son in the guise of the youth. Learning about his incestuous deed through his relatives, the nutria, Haburi and the betrayed women schemed their escape from the treacherous frog woman.

Haburi invented the dugout canoe, and escaped with his mothers to the northern world mountain, at the edge of the earth, which serves as the abode of the Water God, Naparima.

The canoe, however, transformed itself into a giant snake-woman and the paddle into a man. They returned as the red cachicamo (canoe) and the white cachicamo (paddle), to the

center of the earth, where the Warao had since come into
existence. The cachicamo woman became Dauarani, the
Mother of the Forest. She was the first priest-shaman (*wishi-
ratu*) on earth. Eventually she departed from earth to take up
residence on a world mountain at the end of the universe in the
southwest (where her body lives) and in the southeast (where
her soul remains). The paddle stayed in the center of the earth
with the Warao; and the moyotu are to Dauarani, their
supernatural patroness, as the paddle was to the boat. They
are her lovers and serve her by carving boats in her image out
of cachicamo trees.

This is only a summary of the origin story of the canoe related by the
master during the initiation period of the novice moyotu. As the days of
schooling under the rule of abstinence and incessant smoking pass, the
candidate is admonished by his master to live in the future strictly
according to the moral code of his trade. During the period of construction of a large canoe he must abstain from sexual intercourse, even though
the project requires two or more months to complete, eat moderately yet
smoke incessantly, offer tobacco and sago to the supernaturals promptly,
hold in reverence finished canoes especially when new, and treat properly
the tools used in carving the boat, especially the adze. All of these taboos
have to be carefully observed lest the moyotu fall in disgrace with the
goddess, thus jeopardizing the health and lives of his kin as well as his
own future happiness in this world and in the one to come.

After this preparatory period of learning, fasting, and much smoking
the spirit of the neophyte ascends one day in a trancelike dream to the
zenith. Here he meets a black psychopomp who leads him to the beginning of a celestial bridge whose span reaches from the zenith to the
world mountain of the Mother of the Forest in the southeast. The bridge
is no ordinary bridge but an enormous snake whose head rests close to
the zenith and the tip of whose tail reaches to the roots of the tree-
mountain. The reptile always keeps its jaws open and hisses when the
spirit or soul of the novice approaches. It has eight horns, four at each
end. The two pairs on the right side of the body are red and green and
those on the left side are yellow and blue. Flowers of the same color
decorate each horn and chant the ceremonial songs peculiar to the
profession of master builders of canoes. The body of the snake is
decorated all over with colorful markings and is perfumed with the most
agreeable smell of caranna resin.

Although this sky snake fills the novice boat builder with horror, he
must step on its head, shake its horns, and then pass either through its

body to exit at the anus, or walk externally over its head and body. Should the snake swallow him while he passes through its body, the novice will die. Then in a most sublime moment the novice is allowed to pass his hands along both sides of the serpent's body, and in so doing he receives the proper measure for the conformation of a perfect canoe.

On the student's return from his initiatory celestial journey the master queries him about the details of his vision. If they correspond to what is expected, the master assures the new moyotu that his initiation was successful and that he has a long life ahead of him. At the same time, however, he warns him not to break any of the taboos. Both the goddess and the sky snake watch carefully over their servant's conduct, as he makes his future canoe in the likeness of the great goddess's vagina. Also, the Masisikiri spirit of each cachicamo he transforms into a dugout will insist that he treat her in obedience to the promises of good conduct that she elicited from him prior to surrendering herself. Offenses against this code of honor bring about calamities such as accidents, ill health of children and adults, and even death of the offender's kin. The scalding of the chief's son reported above is an example of the calamity that can befall the unfortunate transgressor.

To officiate over the construction of his first large canoe as a full-fledged moyotu, the neophyte invites his fellow brothers-in-law to join him in the task of preparing the hull. But although he uses exactly the same technique as before, canoe making will never be the same after the initiation. He has now become an artist who manages the technical aspects of boat making automatically, so to speak, while at the same time his spirit roams freely and creatively, oblivious to the technology involved.

## The Ceremonial Building of a Canoe

The new master craftsman is not an ordinary man. He has been transformed during the initiation ceremony into a moyotu and is like the black psychopomp who accompanied him on his initiatory journey to the house of Dauarani. "Moyotu" is the personal name of the soul guide whose body is black like the newly fired canoe. In approaching a cachicamo the moyotu confronts not a tree but a female personage he must kill. This ritual death must only occur with the explicit consent of the victim. To obtain her permission, the moyotu engages the services of a priest-shaman who communicates with the spirit of the cachicamo in a special séance. She will tell the shaman whether she likes the master builder sufficiently to allow herself to be killed. But she surrenders only if the moyotu is a competent man, someone she knows will not abandon her once she has been converted into a canoe. She also insists on being given adequate amounts of tobacco and sago while undergoing the metamorphic ordeal. A cachicamo tree who rejects a particular master may not be felled, lest sickness, death, and disaster befall the moyotu's family and his entire village.

Even if the verdict pronounced through the shaman's mouth is positive, thus authorizing the moyotu to go ahead with his plans, he is still warned by the adult people of his group to proceed with utmost caution. They may recommend that the master restrain himself and not set his mind on too large a tree. "We don't want to suffer because of your mistakes," they say.

The men of his group draw his attention to the many precautions he should take to prevent evil consequences. They insist, for instance, that he adorn himself properly and prepare the necessary musical instruments and tools. So, while word of the pending project travels out through the mouth of the master's wife and their daughter to the workmen, the moyotu takes care of the various preparatory tasks with exquisite deliberateness.

First comes the inspection of the adze. The modern metal adze is the white man's version of an old Warao tool, the so-called *gubia,* made of the terminal spiral of a conch shell. It is considered to be as sacred as ritual paraphernalia. No child may handle it, the adolescent girl or woman may not so much as touch it. Only women past their menopause may come in contact with it and then only when explicitly asked to do so by its owner.

The master, who must inspect the adze before embarking on a new project, walks to the eastern end of his house where he keeps the tool in a special basket. Here it "rests" quietly throughout most of the year, safe from the children and away from the fumes of the kitchen. The people are very concerned as the master takes down the adze. They are afraid that he may be too hasty and fail to placate the tool when he disturbs it from its resting place.

A typical case of sickness caused by an offended adze spirit occurred among the Winikina while I was there. The young wife of a master canoe maker fell ill with high fever and pains in the back, side, and chest. Pain produced by the spirit of an adze is always "triangular," felt simultaneously in three different places. The most telling sickness caused by the adze is the stiffening of arms and legs into an L shape. At the time the officiating shaman warned the moyotu to be more careful in the future and to treat the tool with consideration. Then the shaman, after assuring the offended spirit of the master's good intentions, cured the woman with his rattle.

Such is the responsibility of the master when he prepares the adze. "Look," he will address the adze. "Don't get upset. You were made especially for excavating trees. You must recognize this and not become angry now when I make you work."

If treated with respect and awakened carefully, the adze will work of its own accord. The master only holds the tool, but the adze works by itself—"eating" the insides of the cachicamo.

Next the conch shell trumpet must be readied. They are rare instruments hard to come by and if one is not available a wooden trumpet made from the bark of a piece of mangrove aerial root may be substituted.

While the women prepare the food, the master twists moriche bast decorations around his own upper arm, wrists, ankles, waist, and forehead. The yellow ribbons identify him with the tree whose body is also marked with natural bands of a similar kind.

Finally, the day for entering the forest to face the selected cachicamo tree has arrived. Shortly before daybreak the adorned moyotu, holding the trumpet in his hand, greets the sun with a chant.

"Sun, my grandfather, we are coming to you. We will take the right road at the fork, the one that leads to your house. It is dry like sand, and clean, and without danger. The left road is boggy, covered with thorns and infested with toads and snakes and jaguars.[8] I have seen your house in my dreams," continues the chant. "I will come to talk in your house."

The master sounds the shell trumpet while the workmen line up behind him. He smokes tobacco mixed with resin incessantly, and then experiences a mystical levitation: He and his companions are lifted on the horse of the patroness of the *moyomotuma*.[9] The spirit mount's left side is white and its right side is black. The forest opens magically in front of them like a curtain as they are conveyed on the back of the flying horse along a wide pass, at the end of which they behold the cachicamo. The cachicamo appears to the master not in the form of an ordinary tree but in the shape of a maiden.

"Don't become upset," chants the master. "Be happy and smile at me. I am like your own offshoot. I am the one you accepted. I am fond of you. I came to touch your body, to caress you lovingly."

The cachicamo maiden smiles. She has been expecting the master ever since her surrender to him through the voice of the priest-shaman.

"You are a neophyte master builder," chants the cachicamo. "I can tell from your new ornaments. Do with me according to your vision: Kill me and thrust me down on the very soil that raised me."

The master is delighted, quite certain of the tree's benevolence, and confident that the children will not have to suffer because of his actions.

He says: "What I carry in my hand is called an axe. You will feel it at your waist, it will consume you."

"So this is what you call an axe. It will eat my flesh, it will make me fall down to the ground that gave birth to me."

"Poor me," continues the cachicamo maiden. "Your hands will examine my body and my roots. Looking at my body, do you like what you see? You will notice that I also have adorned body. This I did while awaiting your arrival."

Such is the dialogue developed through the master's chants while the work crew approaches the tree. The maiden enters the tree before the men arrive, and her feet become the roots, her body the trunk, her arms the branches, and her head the crown of the cachicamo.

The chanting continues all during the felling of the tree.

"Now that it is done, come take my measure. You possess the measure in your hands."

"Yes, indeed, I am the one with knowledge. I can tell you how long you are; your stretched out body measures 16 arms exactly. I make the mark so the men can cut off your head."

The master builder continues his chanting all day while crouching to one side of the work site. He also chants most of the night after the crew has returned to the camp. The exhausted men and their kind are not particularly happy about this, but they know that danger lurks all around them. Masisikiri, the maiden in the cachicamo, is upset and disturbed. Her home is now in the stump of the tree and she vacillates between it and the fallen trunk. The master must pacify her through his chanting. He has to offer her tobacco.

Then there is the jaguar. He comes during the night to the camp and to the building site to jeer at the quartered tree maiden. The master's chant keeps him at a distance.

On the evening of the fourth work day, the moyotu requests virgin fire.[10] He expects the visit of Moyotu, the sky snake with eight horns, during the following night. She appears in his dream demanding moriche sago and tobacco.

As soon as the vision disappears the master sits up in his hammock and narrates in chant form that the snake Moyotu will come to visit them in a day or two. Next morning an old woman accompanied by two or three children leave the camp to collect stipules from the manaca palm. The boys have to cut the stipules from the top because those that have fallen to the ground are impure. But cursed be the master builder who neglects to have a sufficient quantity of tobacco. The snake will arrive to inspect the body of the cachicamo and look in vain for the gift of tobacco. Her revenge is swift. One of the master's children becomes the target of her wrath. Before the day fades the child will feel the snake penetrate his body like a cool breeze.

Through the medium of the priest-shaman, summoned by the frightened master to effect a cure, everyone in the camp will learn the real cause of the child's sudden sickness. The horned serpent appears to the shaman during the séance and lets him know how disappointed she is. The entire work crew and their families begin grumbling against the master. They reprimand him for his negligence. "We have done everything according to the rules you laid down," protest the people. "But you don't see fit even to provide Moyotu with tobacco."

Should it be the master's first offense, two cigars and a large basket of sago (about 150 pounds) may rectify the error and reconcile the sky serpent. The offerings are placed beside the hull at the construction site. But it may take as long as three weeks to produce the necessary amount of moriche sago, a task that demands strenuous effort from the workers and their wives. The priest-shaman warns that nothing less will placate the offended spirit. The master builder must provide fish and meat for the families, while the men and the women work in the morichale. He also has to absorb the expense for a generous offering of tobacco, sufficient to roll at least ten giant cigars. These together with moriche sago are presented to the serpent through the shaman.

A conscientious master builder will never begin his project until he has procured the necessary amount of tobacco. The cachicamo maiden realizes this before she agrees to become his. The master's people also know it because he takes his profession seriously. Conscientiousness more than mere technical competence is what distinguishes a good master builder.

From the moment of the serpent's visit, the spirit will visit daily until the work on the hull is completed. She comes to contemplate, in company with the chanting master, the beauty of the work under construction. The men labor only during the morning hours in order to clear the site by one o'clock in anticipation of the sky snake's visit. While serpent and master admire the balanced features of the hull, they smoke tobacco and chant through the voice of the master. The snake is also gratified to observe the large basket of moriche sago the master has placed as an offering next to the hull. She looks forward to the day when the work of hollowing out the hull is complete, for then the people will present this gift of sago to her. But while construction is in progress nobody dares remain in the vicinity of the hollow log after working hours.

On the last day of work on the hull, when the younger boys, women, and children are busily cutting and placing skid logs for a corduroy road, the master shaman begins the chant of farewell. In this beautiful song the cachicamo takes leave of her branches and of the many birds who formerly lived in her crown. She says goodbye to the animals and to the stump remaining behind as abode of her soul. She also bids farewell to the bark and the excavated chips.[11] The master signals when his sentimental chant comes to an end and the arduous task of pushing the log to the river is to begin. He walks ahead of the workers chanting and forcefully blowing the conch shell trumpet down to the river.

Months later, after the expert moyotu has finally finished the carpentry work on the hull, and after the families of his people have returned from the morichale with their baskets full of fresh sago for the launching, the day arrives when the master intones the chant for firing the canoe.

This is a happy day for the moyotu. Not only did the adze in his hands work by itself, but also the hull has not buried him alive. Among craftsmen it is common knowledge that hulls of large trees sometimes rise erect before their masters and swallow them. If a craftsman has had sexual relations during the construction period he is doomed. This the Masisikiri-spirit of the cachicamo does not tolerate. The moyotu is her lover and she jealously wants to keep him, especially before he opens her with fire.

The swallowing of the master by the boat occurs in the moyotu's dream. The victim finds himself imprisoned in the dark as in a coffin.[12] He hears a voice from the outside directing him to escape through a knothole in the hull. Since all this transpires in a dream the spirit of the moyotu may eventually escape through the hole. If not, it is taken as a sure sign that the master has committed a moral offense and that he will therefore soon have to die.

To cohabit with one's wife during the period of smoothing the sides of the hull with the adze is taboo. But it can happen that the wife of a craftsman visits her husband in a dream. This is a good sign because the moyotu can gently separate the woman's legs and have coitus with her, as he will separate the legs of the cachicamo maiden when he warms her body with fire. He offers her the tobacco and the sago flour in payment for consenting to have this done to her. The master concentrates on the carved rim along the edges of the boat walls. They are two pairs of legs; the triangular sign in the bow and in the stern are the vaginas of the maiden. The feet of both pairs of legs touch midway along both sides of the canoe forming the rim. The craftsman inside the boat inserts each crossbeam, which the men refer to as penis. Only the moyotu may open the legs of the cachicamo maiden and behold her organ. But he must not contemplate intercourse with her. Being in the boat, however, means being inside her womb. From where he stands the boat has the shape of the vagina of the goddess.[13] In the presence of their wives, especially their mothers-in-law, the men call the "penis" of the boat simply "seats." The "vaginas" they call "stars."

On the morning of the day when the boat is burned, the master orders the women to begin baking sago cakes. He intends to invite the sky serpent to an agape of moriche bread and tobacco and then send her back to her celestial home. Six women are selected to build a virgin fire in a fireplace on which they bake the cakes. The offering of the gifts is performed by the priest-shaman. In fact, he and the master builder arrive at the work place early in the morning before anyone else in order to start calling the sky snake and the spirits of all the predecessors of the master who have died. It is they who have spent their lives in the service of Dauarani and now, after death, enjoy their afterlives in her divine company. All of the *moyomotuma*—that is, the serpent protector spirit and the souls of the defunct master craftsmen—respond to the invitation of their young colleague. They come to admire his boat, to eat the sago, and to smoke the ten cigars he offers them for their pleasure.

"Are you satisfied?" asks the shaman.

"Yes, this is the right way. We are very pleased."

Then the shaman urges the spirits to leave the clearing and to return to their home. There will be many women and children arriving soon, and spirit presences could be harmful.

After the moyomotuma have left, the entire population comes to admire the beautiful new boat and to praise the art of the master. From the chiefs to the smallest child, everybody receives his share of moriche bread. All the people, young and old, are beautifully adorned for this festival of the launching of the new canoe.

The actual act of launching, however, takes place only on the following day. During the night the master sings the final chant of farewell to the moyomotuma spirits, who have permitted him to complete the arduous task of successfully making a large canoe.

In the years that follow, there will be many other such occasions in the lifetime of a master boat builder. If he obeys the moral code of his profession throughout his life, he leaves earth wholly confident that his soul will again pass the snake bridge unharmed and that he will be received in the celestial village of canoe makers. Only the souls of those who have offended the patron goddess by violating her ethical standards are devoured by the sky snake and are lost.

After the craftsman has died, the people on earth ponder the outcome of this final decision for five or six days. A black soul guide has come to take his soul to the zenith, where he is allowed to rest and is furnished with his final cigar. Several days later the soul departs with lightning and thunder to its final destination in the southeast.

"Rest now," the artisan's wife or someone else close to the deceased will say. "You made many big canoes."

The soul hears this and may become sentimental, but this he must avoid. Rather he must hasten on through the sky snake without ever looking back to earth. If he passes his final test and exits at the anus of the snake, he will find there the abode of the Master Spirit of Canoe Making, a rectangular windowless house that boasts but one arched entrance facing west. Nevertheless, its interior is bathed in a blaze of light and never darkens. There is a bed and a table on which rests a bowl of water perfumed with incense. The roof of the house is beautifully decorated with six pairs of flowers at the four corners and at the center of the long sides: blue and yellow flowers at each of the eastern corners, green and red flowers on each of the western corners, and yellow and red flowers on each of the lateral sides of the roof. The stalks of the flowers are hooked on top and are the same colors as the leaves and petals. The flowers chant the same song as, and synchronize with, the song of the eight horns on the sky snake. Their perfume of tobacco smoke and incense is most agreeable to the arriving soul who is given a similar house for his own use. In it he finds a complete new wardrobe, which he puts on after taking a bath in incensed water. He has reached his heaven in proximity to the patron deity he has served so diligently throughout his adult life.

## Psychology and Symbolism of the Canoe Maker

A Warao embarked upon the career of master canoe maker engages in a learning process from which he emerges as a technician of the secular as well as the sacred aspects of his profession. He achieves the former during adolescence and early adulthood, but he commences a voluntary vision quest only as a mature individual. In making this personal decision he aims for an encounter in dream and trance with the spirit world so that he may transcend the profane physical state and attain an exalted spiritual condition. This metamorphosis is patently shamanistic and distinctly reminiscent of the initiatory complex of shamanism. He is nevertheless not actually intent on becoming a shaman, "sorcerer," or medicine man. Rather, he undergoes the initiatory ordeal and subjects himself to the hardships of a moyotu's life strictly for reasons of personal advancement.

Although not unique, the presence of an initiatory complex for non-religious practitioners among the Warao is certainly remarkable, especially since it involves an almost complete scheme of shamanic initiation with most of the characteristic features of shamanism anywhere in the world. I have described the ecological, sociological, and ideational circumstances under which a Warao man becomes a master canoe builder, and now I explore briefly by way of dream and trance symbolism some of the psychological conditions involved in the learning process. This may serve not only to satisfy our intellectual curiosity but also to furnish some pragmatic guidelines for people concerned with the future welfare of the Warao Indians themselves.

I have retraced the technical stages of boat construction to experience each through the mental eye of the sublimated moyotu. Now I turn to the symbolic features of the initiatory complex for certain covert psychological dimensions of the boat maker's world inherent in the specific milestones on his journey to his origins, his return journey to the womb.

The drive factor at work in the psychological process of learning is the boat maker's desire for personal sublimation. He chooses to engage in a vision quest that will help him transcend his human condition and interact with the supernaturals, the patron goddess, and the souls of the ancestor shamans. The perils lurking along the way are devouring monsters, the self-erecting canoe hull, and especially the sky snake. It is believed that Warao culture has placed these devourers on this path because of the original incest committed by the culture hero Haburi. The moyotu's fear of failing in his quest and of being devoured by the mother guardian motivates him to excel and to adopt the ethical code that rules the psyche on its pilgrimage from one cosmic plane to another. In short, the ophidian sky monster is the "symbolic representation of the fear of the consequences of breaking the taboo and regressing to incest" (Jung, 1967:259). Thus the Warao sky serpent functions as guardian and defender of the maternal treasure as do snakes and dragons in other cultures of the world. The serpent's main threat is the swallowing of the unworthy trespasser. But for the worthy neophyte it functions as bridge or tunnel by means of which he reaches Dauarani, the Mother.

To foster the proper climate for the test the master candidate must repress his human condition through fasting and exertion. On this minimum level of physical existence, when his body experiences a death-like state, his psyche reaches its stellar hour of ecstatic levitation. On its celestial journey to the zenith and the sky bridge, the novice's soul is sped by tobacco mixed with caranna resin. This is the moment of transcendence and judgment, of ascent to power, or conversely, of dissolution and death. During the preparatory period of learning the novice has been cued to the requirements for the realization of his upward impulse. In pushing his physical endurance to an existential minimum and by learning how to chant and to smoke "properly" he has responded positively to this cue and has accepted the challenge of the symbolic journey, the ascent to the sky.

From the zenith the path directs the neophyte's soul to the tunnel of darkness, of unconsciousness, and possible death. Usually it is not the first time the master's psyche experiences this fearful symbol. He has frequently before been "swallowed" by the unfinished hull of a canoe under construction. The hull is made from a tree that the sky snake during her visits says is shaped like her own body, in other words, serpentine. Thus we see a blend of the tree symbol with the serpent symbol on the one hand and an amalgamation of the dragon with the water and the boat on the other. In both cases, the devourer is a snake and initiation of the candidate is effected by his penetration into the snake's body.

Being enclosed in the darkness of the boat is analogous to being inside the womb of the cachicamo woman. Canoes and hollow logs are used by the Warao as coffins in which the corpse is reduced to a skeleton. The bones are reburied. Lying in the hollow envelope of his tomb the novice contemplates his own death and his own skeleton. He has reentered the womb of his primordial life in the expectation of mystical rebirth. Only if he successfully clears the Symplegadian passage through the serpent's jaws will the novice be regenerated in the germinal darkness of the monster. Within he faces annihilation. But he hopes to emerge as before through a "knothole" in the boat, this time through the rectal opening, and to proceed from one world into a new world.

The sky monster appears to the novice as a rainbow serpent, with colorful stripes on her rigid body and colors on her arching horns which mark the strata of the sky bridge. The heroic neophyte may step on the serpent's head, pass the threatening horns, and walk over the rainbow into the world beyond.

Having passed the guardian spirit the soul of the moyotu reaches his goal; a transtemporal existence in the house of the Great Mother Dauarani. He is allowed to enter this boxlike house, symbolic of the maternal body, holding in his hands the secret of boat making. Thus he is called to enjoy his reward: life in the dazzling light and splendor of his new existence. The moyotu has completed the journey back to his origin.

After his ecstatic initiatory dream the young master spends the rest of his earthly life in repeated approaches to his maternal home with each large canoe he makes. It is similar to the mystic's yearning *ex tenebris* for the light he has experienced in one sublime blinding moment of ecstasy. And it is a spark of the same creative energy of the mystics of Eastern and Western traditions which powers the psychic energy needed for the perpetuation of the art of canoe building among the Warao.

The black and white horse that Dauarani sends him to be his mount while he is still on earth symbolizes the moyotu's life between his temporal existence in the darkness of this world and his transtemporal existence in the Otherworld. It also symbolizes his position in the arena between good (white) and evil (black), a position forcing his decision at the crossroads on the path to his cachicamo maiden. Perhaps the black and white horse of Dauarani may be just another symbol of the great Mother. Its black (female) and white (male) halves are possibly indicative of the goddess's androgynous nature, which corresponds in turn to the hermaphroditism of the cachicamo tree, another symbolic double for the Mother.

Many other symbolic meanings related to the psychological process of becoming an expert canoe maker are beyond the scope of the present context—for example, the spiritual marriage to the cachicamo woman which prohibits (incestuous) fulfillment in sex and restricts the sex life between the possessed master and his wife with a jealousy characteristic of such "celestial fiancées." Nevertheless, I hope that my sketch of the psychological and symbolic areas of canoe making among the Warao supplements the technical, social, and religious data in a significant way. To me the psychic experience reveals what I believe to be the profoundly vital matrix of the canoe making complex of the Warao. Certainly, the desire to achieve technical competence, socioeconomic status, and religious bliss are prime movers of the learning process of a canoe maker. But the mystical yearning of the moyotu, as he attempts with each canoe he constructs to recapture the light that might once more dispel the "dark night" of his soul, could well be the most dynamic motivation of them all.

## Conclusions

In this essay I have focused on the processes that pertain specifically to the development of a Warao canoe maker to illustrate the question of global enculturation. By way of summary I propose now to scan the ethnography here presented for an answer to this complex question.

Skill-training of a canoe maker takes place in three distinct ways: (a) through general conditioning, (b) by the teaching of technical skills, and (c) by the transmission of esoteric skills.

The general conditioning of the Warao male toward navigation begins during infancy. The daily routine of child care introduces him to life on the water. His first toys are model boats in the family corner and communal house. A child's playground is the landing place with its moored canoes. By the time a child of either sex is three years old his familiarity with canoes, paddles, and currents is so intimate that he can be trusted to go out on the river by himself.

From the age of three on the conditioning of boys toward canoe construction becomes more intensive, quite different from that of the girls who will be required as adult women only to maneuver a canoe, which she learned to do as a child with the others. In the manufacturing process the woman plays at best an ancillary role. The father requires his prepuberty son to witness the different phases of canoe construction over and over again. But in addition to being exposed to the technical processes involved, the child also develops the realization that boat making requires esoteric skills on the part of the master craftsman. As technical skills are mastered the emphasis of the general conditioning shifts during adulthood to concentrate more on the esoteric skills. A man's aptitude for the career of craftsman which, according to the Indians, is a "natural" concomitant of being male is the result of such pervasive attitude conditioning. Casual though the general conditioning may appear to the outside observer, it is for the most part planned intentionally, a subject to which I return later on.

Technical skill-training predominates during postpuberty and early adulthood. The boy of fourteen swings his machete and axe with precision, participates progressively in the selection of an adequate tree, and is permitted to try his hand at cutting and excavating the trunk. The young adolescent also knows how to prepare the corduroy road along which the excavated hull will be dragged to the river. Approximately five years of in-service training results in skills sufficient for the eighteen-year-old to fabricate his own first canoe from start to finish. His technical proficiency improves over the next six or seven years so that skill-training per se can be said to terminate by the time a man is twenty-five years of age. Training in esoteric skills commences at this point for the properly conditioned, now technically competent, Warao. Under the guidance of a teacher he internalizes a complex curriculum of ritual and metaphysical knowledge. Among the skills he must acquire are chanting, verbalizations, and the ability to function in altered states of consciousness.

Socialization of the canoe maker occurs in four different social contexts: (a) his nuclear family and extended family of orientation, (b) the community of his childhood, (c) his family of procreation and the community of his in-laws, and (d) the subtribe of which these various groups are a part. I use the village of Yaruara Akoho as an example (table 7). A child may find as many as four "mothers" (matrilineally related women) and uncles living either in the same house as his own parents and grandparents or in close proximity. There are also one or two teenage consanguineal or classificatory brothers and sisters living in the house. All the males in the house are involved in canoe craftsmanship either as full-fledged moyomotumas or aspirants to that status. Chances are that there are four other

TABLE 7

## DISTRIBUTION OF INHABITANTS
## BY AGE CATEGORIES
Settlement Yaruara Akoho
(1954)

| Age category | Number | Percent | |
|---|---|---|---|
| Infants | 12 | 11 | |
| Children | 41 | 38 | 54 |
| Teenagers | 5 | 5 | |
| Adults | 48 | 44 | 46 |
| Seniors | 2 | 2 | |
| Total | 108 | 100 | |

small children also living in the house, and for the two or three male children among them it is wholly natural to relate to their father's team of boat makers.

Once the child is old enough to venture into the settlement and down to the landing place he finds himself in the company of more than fifty infants and children, most of whom play and travel with him in and around the canoes. With more than half the quasi permanent population of the settlement being below the age of eighteen years, the importance or the youth group as a socializing agent cannot be underestimated.

A particularly powerful socializing force is the male teenage gang made up of pairs of brothers from various settlements. For a period of three or four years the adolescent seeks acceptance among his peers and the rest of the society by identifying himself with Haburi, the culture hero, projecting on himself Haburi's fame as an irresistible lover, excellent hunter, and above all the maker of canoes par excellence. During childhood the youngster may have been called "Axe swinger" or "Machete man." Now is the time to prove it. With the arrival of the canoe making season the adolescent anxiously seeks a place on the work team of his father. The problem is that a truly meaningful position for him exists only on the team of his future father-in-law. Nevertheless, some of the uncles on his father's force are not much older than he is and serve as models for his future role.

The work team of boat makers is the strongest socializing force experienced by the Warao adolescent and young adult male. On the team of his father the adolescent son has the opportunity to establish his personal identity as his technical competence increases. But on the team of his father-in-law the young adult is assigned a rank and is expected to fulfill the role attached to that rank. He must perform well for the sake of his own nuclear family and the community to which he now belongs. His status will rise with the addition of new brothers-in-law, as he assumes increasing responsibility for each successive work role.

The ultimate socialization force in a canoe maker's life is composed of the elite of the band and the entire community of ancestor artisans so closely associated with them. The elite of his own band consists of several religious practitioners as well as several holders of political office. We have seen how the shaman elite controls the craftsmen completely. What would happen if the artisan were forbidden by the priest-shaman to cut down the desired tree? What would the result be if the priest-shaman allotted only mediocre trees to the canoe maker? He would have no opportunity to enhance his social and economic position by building large canoes and would thus be forever barred from the ranks of the elite. With his prestige as a canoe maker undermined and ultimately destroyed he would further be branded as potentially dangerous to the entire band.

By the time an adult experiences the socializing pressures exerted by the elite he has found his social identity as a canoe maker and has reached the age of thirty-five. He gradually assumes now the role of leader of his own work team. One of the imperatives of Warao culture is that canoe making is to be conducted not merely as a secular business enterprise, but rather as a religious activity. Esoteric lore as expressed to the workers of the team by the master craftsman is acquired by the artisan through association with the tribal elite, a social setting in which he submits himself to the rigors of his profession. Accordingly, he aspires to align himself with a particular deity and world direction. As a career man he seeks to become destined after death to reside on a world mountain with the ancestor canoe makers. And like the shamans, he wants to adopt from the supernaturals a special metaphoric language attesting to his elevated status. Acceptance by the band elite is an essential prerequisite for the attainment of both temporal and eternal goals.

The moral education of the canoe maker starts during childhood when he and his playmates are taught respect for the spirit of the cachicamo tree which lives on in the craft. Even during the construction of a canoe children have to show respectful behavior. They may not sit on the stump that harbors the spirit of the tree, and they must refrain from interfering with the ritual aspects involved in the making of a large canoe. From experience recounted frequently by the adults, children know that they may be smitten with disease, suffer accidents, or even meet death as a result of misbehavior. It is also known that children are the first to suffer punishment for any sin committed by the artisan and his crew.

The master canoe maker receives his instructions for proper conduct during the initiation and promises to abide by the ethical code of his profession. He must not engage in felling a cachicamo tree without having obtained prior permission from the Mother of the Forest. He must not use the adze without propitiating it properly. The supernaturals, including the ancestor canoe makers, must receive offerings of tobacco smoke and sago, and sexual intercourse during the months of construction is taboo. Any careless disregard of the prescribed set of rules governing the entire process of making a canoe, especially a large craft, is punished supernaturally—wrath visited upon the children and adults of the band, even the artisan himself "swallowed."

And so we see that skill-training, socialization, and moral education are lifelong processes of enculturation for the Warao boat maker. *Skill-training* begins with an informal conditioning during childhood, develops into postpuberty and early adulthood in-service training for practical skills, and is complemented during a man's prime and old age by esoteric skill-training. Skill conditioning takes place in the house, the neighborhood, in the forest, and on the river. At no time does instruction occur within an especially assigned area or building. The form of instruction is visual learning, demonstration, and participation in real-life situations. Verbalization during conditioning and technical skill-training is nonexistent or highly uncommon. Esoteric skills, in contrast, are transmitted and learned in the context of initiation schooling. A special room may be set aside for this purpose and a curriculum of esoteric lore underlies the training process. Instruction is predominantly verbal.

*Socialization* is effected by seeking and finding acceptance in a number of different social groups ranging from the small nuclear family, through large children's cohorts and adolescent gangs, to adult work teams and finally the tribal elite. In all these the artisan has to achieve the social status prescribed by the culture and play the role society expects.

*Moral education* is the result of lifelong conditioning imparted mainly by the parents, the father-in-law and the tribal mythology. Nonformal (noninstitutional formal) education in ethical standards and moral conduct is provided by a hired expert during a ritual initiation for canoe makers. Fear of supernatural punishment serves as primary reinforcement for proper moral conduct. There are also indications that strict alignment with ethical standards may bring mystic experience as a reward. Such an experience will make the artisan pine for repeated encounters with the Mother Goddess, a yearning that turns him into a harsh proponent of the canoe maker's code lest he jeopardize his transcendental personal (and collective) purpose of life.

There are three recognized modes of education well described in the literature. Coombs and Ahmed (1974:8) define *informal education* as "the lifelong learning process by which every person acquires and accumulates knowledge, skills, attitudes and insights from daily experiences and exposure to the environment." *Nonformal education* is defined by the same authors as "any organized, systematic, educational activity carried on outside the framework of the formal system to provide selected types of learning to particular subgroups in the population, adults as well as children." Finally, *formal education* is defined by them as referring to the "institutionalized, chronologically graded and hierarchically structured educational system, spanning lower primary school and the upper reaches of the university."

While formal education does not apply to the Warao, the definitions of the first two modes are clearly applicable but must not be understood as mutually exclusive. All preliterate societies, the Warao included, have been found to practice simultaneously informal and nonformal methods of cultural transmission. The skill-training, socialization, and moral education of a canoe maker evolve on a continuum of informal and nonformal education. As modes of enculturation they occur in parallel rather than in staggered fashion. Furthermore, informal education overlaps with nonformal education. La Belle suggests (1975:20) that the three educational modes be viewed as "modes of emphasis or predominance" rather than as discrete entities. We have seen, for example, that the conditioning and skill-training of the prepuberty Warao are directed and regulated. In turn, the novice artisan in the bush school, now a recipient of nonformal education, benefits from far more than the verbal instruction given him by his teacher. The informal education experiences acquired by the candidate through association with his fellow canoe makers and from the chants and interpretations of the master heard year after year comprise vital input to the nonformal learning process. We have a good example again in the novice canoe maker who believes that he is the recipient through a dream of the revelation of esotericc lore and especially its chants directly from the supernaturals. The teacher's role is only to correct the "spontaneously acquired" knowledge and to help the student put the various passages together. Clearly the novice has prelearned the texts through many years of association with the master artisan prior to undergoing nonformal education. The sessions with the teacher are designed to help him internalize them according to a preconceived plan. Thus we see both informal and nonformal modes of education occurring side by side, with emphasis shifting from one to the other on different occasions throughout the course of the artisan's career. The informal mode is never quite free of nonformal characteristics just as the nonformal is scarcely ever encountered without traces of the informal.

It will come as no surprise that informal and nonformal modes of education perform the function of interpreting for the Warao roles and symbolic meanings as each new identity crisis occurs. Bear in mind that canoe making represents an unconditional imperative for Warao survival and that the culture has to provide effective stimuli to prompt the male part of society to respond with the desire to undergo such identity changes. It is the genius of Warao culture that enculturation along informal and nonformal channels succeeds so well in motivating the developing craftsman by holding out new goals each time a change in personal identity becomes desirable. The culture is adequately programmed to recognize publicly the signs of accomplished growth and thereby to make the learner conscious of his new identity (Goodenough, 1961).

Despite rather traumatic experiences when the youth changes from residing with his intimate kin to live among his wife's people, the enculturation process of an artisan is continuous. It is conducted by people of the same basic culture, and adult knowledge builds organically on that of earlier life stages. Since a boy is expected to learn canoe making as a natural byproduct of being male, the learning process itself remains largely free from anxiety.

This leads me to a final comment. The informal education figuring so prominently in Warao enculturation is particularistic, affectively charged, and tradition bound (Cohen, 1971). It follows that enculturation in preliterate societies is highly culture specific. Our knowledge of cultural procedures can certainly yield important insights into the educational process per se. But the transfer of the actual technical, social, and ideational content of the curriculum from one society to another will be possible only to the extent that the societies in question are culturally similar. Furthermore, because canoe making occurs in a culture specific framework, transfer within the same society of knowledge of the canoe making process to the fabrication of some other product is quite problematic. In the Orinoco Delta I have heard of plans for such a transfer. People have assumed that the Indian's proven ability to build canoes can be redirected toward a successful program for fabricating Western furniture. Needless to say, such plans are doomed to failure. The Warao culture is completely unequipped to handle such a transfer. Nothing in the environment demands this kind of product; within the society there is no economic benefit or social status associated with the product; and there exists no traditional heaven for furniture makers. If such transfers are promulgated anyway, new markets created, and modern values established in the name of progress, the changes will be at the expense of the autochthonous culture. I am afraid that this will be the lot of the Warao and all the remaining indigenous societies of South America. Complex and teleologically functioning educational systems, the combined wisdom of untold generations, will crumble in the process of incorporating the Indians into the ambit of modern states. Any intention to "develop" these systems ought to be predicated strictly on the Indians' terms. The assumption that since these people already practice informal and nonformal education, all they really need is Western schooling is fallacious.

But even though the transfer to other processes of the curriculum content of indigenous enculturation systems is highly problematic, generalizations made on the basis of the processes involved will prove invaluable for the study of international education and for the understanding of the problems of education as a whole. To have described the intricacies of the system developed by the Warao represents the Indians' contribution to the bedeviled educators in the civilized world and our only solace.

## NOTES

1. Data are from the National Census of the Republic of Venezuela for 1960.
2. The wholesale felling of trees for timber, for swidden agriculture, for cash crop (rice), or for the palmito industry cannot be reconciled with the traditional cultural goal of forest conservation. Apparently, rather than allowing themselves to be torn apart by this dilemma, the Warao have opted for acceptance of the white man's disbelief in spiritual tree guardians; whether for better or worse, only time will tell.
3. Teenage boys usually remain unmarried several years longer than their female counterparts. Teenage girls wed soon after the onset of menstruation at about twelve. Men of high status and rank often take a young girl as a second wife.
4. These expeditions are now almost wholly a thing of the past. Trade goods are more accessible in the Delta and the Venezuelan Government has prohibited island trips to curb smuggling.
5. I am afraid that my gasoline engine did not help to improve the reputation of the boat either, although I was never openly criticized.
6. This the children learn from listening to the chanting of the moyotu and the tales men tell about it in the evening. I suspect that the canoe is related to lunar symbolism and is mocked by the jaguar, a solar animal.
7. Formerly known as *Hyla venulosa* or *Hyla tibiatrix*. The identification was made by Professor Juan A. Rivero of the University of Puerto Rico from a specimen I collected in 1971.
8. The passages in quotation marks are free translations of the recorded chants. For literal translation, see Wilbert, in press.
9. This may have been a jaguar before the horse became known to the Warao.
10. Fire produced with fire sticks through rotation, not from a kitchen fire and not one lit with matches.
11. The Warao have an ecosystemic approach to every physical and biological part of the earth. A tree does not exist in isolation. It functions, like everything else in the environment, as one part of a system of associated parts. Together they form a characteristic unit where each part is interdependent and, hence, removal of any one part disrupts and destroys the system. The farewell song of the cachicamo expresses the philosophy of partnership with nature rather than helotism.
12. The Warao traditionally bury their dead in scooped-out tree trunks.
13. Opening of the hollowed out cachicamo by fire symbolizes the defloration of her maiden spirit. As long as the boat is new, the deflowered maiden visits the craftsman in

his sleep to make love to him. She is extremely jealous and seeks to possess him to the exclusion of any other woman. A man, in order to break free from this possession, may have to imbibe a quart of rum and thus become intoxicated. The spirit lover dislikes the smell of alcohol and leaves the craftsman.

# BIBLIOGRAPHY

Bernau, J. M.
  1847   *Missionary Labours in British Guiana.* London.

Brett, W. H.
  1868   *The Indian Tribes of Guiana.* London.

Cohen, Yehudi A.
  1971   "The Shaping of Men's Minds: Adaptations to Imperatives of Culture." In *Anthropological Perspectives on Education.* Murray Wax, Stanley Diamond, and Fred Gearing, eds. New York: Basic Books.

Coombs, Philip H., and Manzoor Ahmed
  1974   *Attacking Rural Poverty: How Informal Education Can Help.* Baltimore: Johns Hopkins University Press.

Goodenough, Ward H.
  1961   "Education and Identity." In *Anthropology and Education.* Frederick C. Gruber, ed. The Martin G. Brumbaugh Lectures, fifth series. Philadelphia: University of Pennsylvania Press.

Heinen, H. Dieter, and Julio Lavadero
  1973   "Computación del tiempo en dos subtribus Warao." *Antropológica* (Caracas) 35:3-24.

Henry, Jules, and Joan Whithorn Boggs
  1952   "Child Rearing, Culture, and the Natural World." *Psychiatry* 15:261-271.

Herskovits, Melville J.
  1970   *Man and His Works.* New York: Alfred A. Knopf.

Hilhouse, William
  1834   "Memoir on the Warow Land of British Guiana." *Journal of the Royal Geographical Society of London* 4:321-333.

Jung, C. G.
  1956   *Symbols of Transformation.* Bollingen Series 20. Princeton: Princeton University Press.

La Belle, Thomas J.
  1975   "Liberation, Development, and Rural Nonformal Education." *Council on Anthropology and Education Quarterly* 6(4):20-26.

Liddle, Ralph Alexander
  1928   *The Geology of Venezuela and Trinidad.* Fort Worth, Texas: J. P. MacGowan.

Méndez-Arocha, Alberto
  1963   *La pesca en Margarita.* Estación de Investigaciones Marinas. Caracas: Fundación La Salle de Ciencias Naturales.

Penard, F. P., and A. P. Penard
  1907-  *De menschetende Aanbidders der Zonneslang.* 3 vols. Paramaribo.
  1908

Raleigh, Sir Walter
1596;  *The Discovery of the Large, Rich and Beautiful Empire of Guiana.* London:
1970    Hakluyt Society.

Schomburgk, Richard
1847-  *Reisen in Britisch-Guiana in den Jahren 1840-1844.* 3 vols. Leipzig.
1848

Suárez, María Matilde
1968   *Los Warao.* Caracas.

Wilbert, Johannes
1972   "Tobacco and Shamanistic Ecstasy among the Warao Indians." In *Flesh of the
       Gods: The Ritual Use of Hallucinogens.* Peter T. Furst, ed. New York: Praeger
       Publishers.
1975   "Eschatology in a Participatory Universe: Destinies of the Soul among the
       Warao Indians of Venezuela." In *Death and the Afterlife in Pre-Columbian
       America.* Elizabeth Benson, ed. Dumbarton Oaks Research Library Collections.
       Washington, D.C. Pp. 163-189.
In     "Navigators of the Winter Sun." In *The Cult of the Sea.* Elizabeth Benson, ed.
press  Dumbarton Oaks Research Library Collections. Washington, D.C.

Williams, Thomas Rhys
1972   *Introduction to Socialization: Human Culture Transmitted.* St. Louis: C. V.
       Mosby.

# 11.

# Becoming a *Curandero* in Peru

DOUGLAS SHARON

## Introduction

Along the north coast of Peru there is a very strong tradition of *curanderismo* (shamanic folk healing). It involves the use of a brew of the hallucinogenic San Pedro cactus (*Trichocereus pachanoi*; active ingredient: mescaline) and other "magical" plants. Curing practices include the ritual manipulation of power objects laid out on the ground in an altarlike arrangement known as a *mesa* (table). Therapy is performed in all-night curing sessions the object of which is to overcome *daño* (witchcraft). Recently, through a combination of archaeological, ethnohistorical, and ethnographic evidence, it has been possible to establish a continuum for curanderismo stretching from circa 1200 B.C. to the present (Sharon, 1974:53–63).

The major prerequisite to becoming a *curandero* (shamanic folk healer) is supernatural selection that is usually manifested as an intense psychological crisis, often including physical concomitants. Much informal instruction is also imparted to the apprentice by a veteran shaman. Reinforced by a viable cultural tradition, this training takes the form of practical assistance in curing sessions rendered to the curandero by the novice. An assistant is referred to either as an *alzador* ("raiser"), one who aids the shaman by administering San Pedro and performing other mechanics of curing rituals, or as a *rastreador* ("tracker"), one who helps the curandero clairvoyantly "see" the supernatural causes of a patient's ailment during the divinatory portion of a séance.

Continuing research on the topic of this paper is currently being sponsored by a post-doctoral fellowship from the Tinker Foundation, New York. The author wishes to express his thanks to the Foundation for its support.

The American anthropologist Gillin (1947:118) reports that the major curandero-informant for his study of northern curanderismo lived with his tutor for eighteen months while training as an alzador. The first six months were required to work out payment for a cure. During that time Gillin's informant became interested in becoming a healer so his mentor "tested" him for another year. This involved continuing to serve as an assistant while occupying a room in the master's house with bare subsistence. No details of the "final instruction" are given so we do not know whether it included more than alzador duties.

My field data indicate that service as an assistant is the only way in which apprentices learn the curing art. In other words, this appears to be a case of imitative learning. Since my material is based on the experiences and observations of only one informant-curandero, however, it is not now possible to substantiate this point.

Since World War II the north coast region of Peru has been undergoing intensive modernization, and this appears to be having a disruptive effect on local traditions such as folk healing. As a result, the social and mythical charter underlying curanderismo is perhaps not as explicit as it may have been in the past. Folk healing, however, represents an aboriginal tradition that was forced underground in the first half of the seventeenth century when the church undertook an intensive campaign to "extirpate idolatry" in Peru. Since then the art of the curandero has become a clandestine tradition shifting with the sands of time in meeting the social and psychological needs of the Peruvian people. As a result, much of the shamanic content of curanderismo has survived through syncretic accommodation with Christianity. This same eclectic adaptive capacity seems to be at work today in response to the exigencies of the twentieth century—as evidenced by the increasingly larger number of Peruvians from all walks of life who are turning to the traditional practitioner for therapy. Consequently, transmission of curing lore without the reinforcement of an explicit, overt social and mythical charter may not be an entirely new phenomenon. But the lack of detailed ethnographic information on northern curanderismo prior to the work of Gillin (1947) makes it very difficult to determine what the situation has been in the past. Given this gap in our historical knowledge regarding northern Peru, it may be instructive to note that Nadel's (1946) study of Nubian shamanism concluded that environmental or social instability caused shamanism to thrive as a coping mechanism. This seems to be the case in the contemporary Maya community of Zinacantan (cf. Vogt, 1969). Perhaps a similar situation has existed in northern Peru since the Inca and Spanish conquests of the area.

The initiatory experiences of Eduardo Calderón Palomino, a modern curandero from the Trujillo Valley of northern Peru, clearly reflect the paradoxical blend of social marginality and psychological acceptance that comprises contemporary curanderismo. Before overcoming the psychological crisis that led him to become a curandero, Eduardo experienced the mystical "call" at a very tender age—a phenomenon that is quite common in societies where shamanism is a recognized social institution. But in contrast to a simpler society where such symptoms would be recognized as the first stirrings of supernatural power that could be expressed through a legitimate social role, Eduardo's society did not provide him with an explanation or overt means of expressing his mystical vocation. Fortunately, in early postadolescence when Eduardo suffered a severe case of witchcraft, family members, who had been raised in the Andes, recognized the supernatural nature of his malady. But the role of curandero assumed by Eduardo after his miraculous recovery— although gratefully acknowledged by his many patients—is not overtly or formally recognized by his society. And yet, despite this lack of "legitimacy," Eduardo and many others like him continue to practice and transmit their art confident in the knowledge that there is a continuing need for their services. In short, theirs is a personal rather than a social charter. "Power" calls them. To explore the manner in which this ancient lore is transmitted we now turn to Eduardo's story.

## Eduardo

Eduardo ("Chino") Calderón was born in Trujillo, where his parents had settled after migrating to the coast from the Andean highlands near Cajabamba. At an early age he began working to contribute to the family economy. From the age of eight until he was fifteen he worked with his father, sold chocolates in front of local theaters, loaded cargo in the market, and butchered animals at the slaughterhouse. Having to work caused Eduardo to fall behind in his studies at school. At the age of ten he had not completed the first year of primary school. But he readily admits that he was partly to blame, for he was an adventuresome, undisciplined child who often played hooky from school to roam by the sea or through the countryside exploring the mountains, dry river beds, and sandy wastes beyond the Trujillo Valley. Often these excursions took him to the many archaeological ruins around Trujillo, where he would wander among the decayed works of man in a world forgotten by time. These adventures earned him another nickname, "Tuno" (truant, cunning rogue), which has stayed with him in his adult years.

The cause of Eduardo's restlessness during those early years, however, went deeper than mere childhood mischief. When he was very young he experienced disturbing dreams and visions. This is how he describes them:

> During my youth from about the age of seven or eight I had some rare dreams. I still remember them. I remember dreams in which I flew; my ego departed from the state in which it was, and I went . . . to strange places in the form of a spiral. Or I flew in a vertiginous manner: sssssssssssss I departed. I tried to retain myself and I could not. . . . I had these [dreams] until the age of about twelve or thirteen. . . . [Also] I have seen things as if someone opens the door and the door is closed. I have had nightmares, but not ordinary ones. I have seen myself introduced through a hole in the air and I went . . . through an immense . . . void. [I have felt] numbness in all my body as if my hands were huge and I could not grasp, I could not sustain my hand.

Eduardo did not know where to turn in coping with his unusual experiences. He was afraid that people would think he was crazy if he confided in anyone. So he learned to keep his inner world to himself handling the frightening events therein to the best of his ability, alone and unsupported.

During his adolescence Eduardo began to find respite from the tensions in his psyche as he slowly matured into adulthood. He discovered that a growing interest in his studies brought some relief. Once his native curiosity was stirred by human knowledge, he was quick to learn. He found the realm of ideas a fascinating place peopled by thinkers who had struggled—as he began to do—to understand the world around them and the people in it. As a result of this newfound motivation to learn, when Eduardo was ready for high school he decided to enroll in the Trujillo seminary instead of the public high school. He felt a deep yearning to help alleviate human suffering, and for a while seriously considered studying for the priesthood in answer to what he regarded as a "calling to serve humanity." But it was not long before he realized that the discipline and obedience required by orthodox religion stifled his personal growth. Medicine seemed to be the next best avenue of expression for Eduardo's idealism. But it was not economically feasible. In the end what had begun as a step to self-discovery became a crippling frustration.

This frustration, however, was mitigated by Eduardo's growth in another direction. His father was an artisan skilled in seven trades.

Through having to help his father in earlier years Eduardo began to acquire much skill as an artisan. In the process he became interested in sculpture and began to develop considerable talent working with clay, wood, and stone. Toward the end of his studies at the seminary it became clear to Eduardo that art provided the best medium of expression for his restless, creative spirit.

To cover the expenses of his seminary studies Eduardo worked after school in a Chinese dry goods store. By his mid-teens he was migrating to Peru's fishing capital, Chimbote, each summer to earn extra money in the newly developing fishing industry. Here his personality was tempered by rugged encounters with the world of men engaged in a perilous struggle with the elements. In addition to teaching him much about human nature, those formative years spent in the frontierlike atmosphere of Chimbote taught Eduardo a humble respect for the force and power of nature. They also hardened his stout, muscular frame forged by years of carrying cargo in the market and by weight lifting, a sport that attracted Eduardo in his adolescence.

During his last year of studies at the seminary, disappointed by the priesthood and bored by the school's curriculum, Eduardo decided to seek his fortune in Lima. After captaining his weight-lifting team in the national championships held at the capital, he enrolled in the School of Fine Arts. He attended night school, working as a bricklayer with his uncle during the day to pay for his studies.

The year spent in Lima was a most traumatic one. Eduardo soon discovered that even art, when approached as an academic discipline, bridled his impetuous, freedom-loving spirit. Before completing his first year of studies he left art school, never to return.

The trauma associated with Eduardo's experiences in Lima was personal as well as professional. While in school he married one of his classmates. But the girl's parents looked down on this poor, aspiring artist from the provinces. They succeeded in breaking up the marriage and sent their daughter to live with relatives. Eduardo, thinking that his wife had been sent to Pucallpa, went there in desperation. After a fruitless search he eventually ended up back in Trujillo where he sought to heal the wounds left by his stormy encounter with big-city life. He took up residence in a rustic seaside hamlet where he began making a living as a fisherman occasionally exhibiting his art in Trujillo. In the meantime his wife gave birth to a child that Eduardo has never seen.

Just prior to his return to Trujillo Eduardo came down with a mysterious ailment that failed to yield to modern medical treatment. This is how he describes it:

> In Lima I was studying fine arts and suddenly I began drink-
> ing and spending everything on drink. And I came down with
> a rare sickness. It happened that on one occasion I saw a cat
> on my left shoulder. It was enough that with that impression of
> a cat everything that I did went badly. I couldn't find work, I
> drank, I didn't want to do things the way they should be done.
> Then I took off wandering without a goal. Finally I decided to
> return to my home. I had just enough energy left to travel. I
> arrived home and came down with a sickness in which erup-
> tions . . . that did not emit pus broke out all over my body.
> They only emitted yellowish water and a . . . black worm stuck
> its head out and then hid. My whole body from my head to my
> feet [was affected], and I lost the power to hold things in my
> hand and to stand up. I completely lost all my strength. I could
> not sustain myself in a standing position and walked like a
> sleepwalker [when they helped me about] according to what
> they tell me.

Both of his grandfathers had been curanderos in the highlands, so
Eduardo's family, who knew about curanderismo, decided to see if a folk
healer might be able to cure an ailment the doctors had failed to alleviate.
Eduardo underwent treatment and was cured. Here is his account:

> Frankly, I didn't believe in these things. But when my con-
> dition got worse my mother and my uncle called in a friend who
> understood these matters . . . a woman who understood witch-
> craft, and especially curing. She is a great herb specialist.
> Thus one night—I could not attend [the session] because I
> could not get on my feet—they brought me a brew prepared by
> her. I spent exactly $3.00 on this. It made me throw up black
> beer as if I had recently drunk it. And I recovered from one
> day to the next. . . . They took my clothing for a session they
> had.

Although triggered by the tragedy and "culture shock" encountered
in Lima, Eduardo's experience is obviously akin to "sickness vocation"
discussed at length by Eliade (1964:33-36). It is a common phenomenon
in shamanism for the future shaman to feel himself "called" through a
serious illness that fails to respond to normal treatment and requires
supernatural intervention. "Hereditary transmission" from grandparents
is also quite frequent in shamanism (ibid.:20-23). In any case, Eduardo
recovered from a sickness of his times, thereby enabling him eventually
to cure the same malady suffered by those who share his cultural milieu.

Eduardo did not understand what had happened, but felt an urge to learn all about curanderismo. He attended a few sessions and was beginning to increase his understanding. Then a friend of his, who felt he was suffering from a love spell, decided to go north in search of a specialist capable of undoing the *enredo* or "entanglement." Eduardo offered to go along.

At the town of Mocupe they tried the "clinic" of a famous curandera. But she had become a drunkard and no longer had any power. So Eduardo and his friend went to Chiclayo in search of a healer. There they found a *brujo* (sorcerer) reputed to be a good *enguayanchero,* or maker of love spells, who used a guitar and *misha* (*Datura arborea*) with his mesa. But he also removed spells—if the price was right. Eduardo's friend was getting desperate and willing to try anything. So the two friends arranged for a séance.

The enguayanchero's therapy was successful. During the séance it became apparent that Eduardo had good "vision" (psychic insight), which aided in the cure. The enguayanchero asked Eduardo to become his assistant, but he declined. Although inexperienced in curanderismo, Eduardo instinctively knew that his nature was not inclined toward the path of darkness and intrigue.

Back in Trujillo he began to experience a disturbing restlessness and desire to return to Chiclayo. This was too much like the feeling he had after his return from Lima, except that it did not include physical sickness.

Enough was enough! Since his return from Lima Eduardo had married Maria, a fisherman's daughter. She had an uncle who was noted as a curandero working with hallucinogens and a mesa. A séance was arranged and the spell was broken.

Eduardo decided it was time to learn the art of self-defense. He began his apprenticeship under this relative. In the years that followed while earning a living as a stevedore on the docks of Trujillo's port (Salaverry), exhibiting his art in Trujillo, and fishing in Chimbote, he also gained sufficient experience as a curandero's assistant to serve as rastreador ("tracker," one who helps the curandero "see" during the curing sessions).

Eventually he developed his powers to the point where, during one momentous session, he suddenly felt that the "Christ of the mesa" had chosen him to effect a part of the curing ritual:

> One time the *mesa* called me, in the "account" [the history or power associated with single artifacts as well as the activated powers of artifacts working together] it called me. Christ called

me. He said "Come here." And he had me take the rattle and dagger in my hands and sit at the place of the *maestro* [master or curandero]. And the curandero's assistants realized that the "account" pulled me. In other words, this was the initiation in the supreme instance in which the Field of the Divine Judge [the right side of the mesa associated with the powers of "goodness" and "light"] pulled me.

After that session Eduardo decided that he had outgrown his teacher. But he did not feel ready to establish his own mesa. Instead he went north to work with famous curanderos in Chiclayo, Mocupe, and Ferreñafe. In the latter town he became acquainted with the folklore associated with two famous mountains, Chaparrí and Yanahuanga, which play a vital role in curanderismo as power spots invoked by curanderos during their night sessions. They also give concrete expression to the dualistic ideology—possibly best described as a "dialectic of good and evil"—underlying northern folk healing. Lore such as this is part of the milieu that supports curanderismo as a covert cultural institution. Here is Eduardo's description of these powerful mountains:

> Chaparrí and Yanahuanga are two of the great powers or "charms." They are mountains. According to curandero legends, they were two kingdoms: the high Yanahuanga and the wide Chaparrí. . . . They are in the Lambayeque region inland around the town of Ferreñafe. These two mountains are completely bare. The legend says that the two ancient kingdoms hated each other. One represented good, the other evil. They fought with each other. Thus it happened that Divine Providence converted them into mountains because the devil had come between them. But they vindicated themselves in order to do good to others. On one side are found the good herbs and on the other the bad herbs. The white herbs are on one side on Yanahuanga, and the black herbs are on the other side on Chaparrí.
>
> Almost all of the *curanderos* make pilgrimages to Chaparrí and Yanahuanga to look for the magical herbs. There are no mountains as bare as these two. Thus the *curanderos* have to wait for the moment when the mountains induce a dreamy state causing them to fall asleep. Suddenly the *curanderos* wake up and their steps go directly to the site where the herbs are to be found. They pick the herbs that they need, those their temperament, their idea, their "account" has "called" in their dreams, showing where the herbs can be found. And they come

down from the mountains in a tranquil state. And they return with the plants to cure others. Otherwise they can't do a thing. They have to have made a "pact" as *curanderos* in order to be able to make this pilgrimage. Otherwise it is not possible, because, if they go, the mountains begin to rumble and loosen boulders which roll down the mountainsides, causing one to run away. According to the *curanderos* who make the pilgrimage to collect the herbs, it is dangerous. One must have a special gift for bringing the herbs from there. This is developed in a "pact" that the *curanderos* make.

While in Ferreñafe Eduardo also learned of another famous pilgrimage site or "power spot" invoked by curanderos during curing séances. This is a highland region consisting of sacred lagoons known collectively as Las Huaringas. According to northern folklore, in the old days novice curanderos used to make a pilgrimage on foot to these lagoons in the company of their tutors. Once there, they were initiated by their tutors working in collaboration with veteran curanderos inhabiting the heights around the lagoons. These highland shamans were considered to be the most powerful curanderos in the north. They still enjoy this reputation today—as evidenced by the constant flow of patients they receive from all over Peru. There is reason to believe that many patients made the pilgrimage to Las Huaringas in the old days, but since World War II a new road and much attention from the media have definitely increased the traffic to the lagoons. In any case, this is what Eduardo had to say about Las Huaringas before visiting them in person with me during the summer of 1970 and again during the fall of 1971:

> I do not know Las Huaringas except through the medium of my "account," my magical herbs, my "adjustments." I "call" by means of the "charms" whose powers I "raise" on my *mesa*. I have "seen" Las Huaringas, lagoons located above the town of Huancabamba, according to the accounts of my elders. . . . There they say that one must bathe, there where all of the magical plants grow—those for good and those for evil. There one must deliver his shadow [soul]. With this one can be guided and protected from all of the malevolent powers. Las Huaringas is one of the sites of predilection for the *curanderos* and *brujos*. It is like Mecca.

The bath Eduardo refers to occurs during initiation and curing rituals performed at high noon. Regarding this rite Eduardo says that "when one works with or bathes in the lagoon, the herbs themselves 'call' one.

If he is for good, the good herbs are attracted to him and come near; and the bad also [are attracted] to him who is for evil. All this is according to the affinity of the herbs, according to their function and their application."

Eduardo's recounting of his training in Ferreñafe reveals the highly individualistic nature of the initiatory experience in northern Peru, which is a reflection of mestizo culture. As can be seen from the following, such individualism contrasts markedly with indigenous training and initiation where a relatively undisturbed cosmological and mythological system provides a clear-cut charter for the teacher to pass on to the initiate:

> But where I was really initiated was with a *maestro,* a northerner also, a man from Ferreñafe. . . . He initiated me. I had a few artifacts already and I liked the matter since I had been "pulled" by the *mesa.* . . . But I went on creating my own "accounts" because he was the one who initiated me and gave me very good advice. He said "He who wants to enter the life of a *curandero,* who likes the art, must be frank and—more than anything—create his own things. Nothing that is of another [should be his] because when a *maestro* teaches another directly it is like following the same line without creating. With his bad 'account,' they [the forces directed by the sorcerer that the teacher opposes] dominate him, and the others [his students] also go. However, you—knowing that your 'account' is your own—nobody knows you, nobody can reach you; never will they cross you on your path because you have something that is your own, not picked up from someone else."
>
> (Question: How long did you remain there with this man from Ferreñafe?) I worked with him in the highlands, I worked in Trujillo, I worked in Moche, I worked in several places. I was with him about six months. It wasn't very much time. He initiated me in the initiative sense, which is when one has artifacts and he "adjusts" them by means of his "account" within the field of the *curandero.* He "adjusted" my rattle, he "adjusted" my two staffs and my dagger and with these I began to work. . . .
>
> He made the sign of the cross over me; in other words, he initiated me in this by blessing me. He blessed me in front of his *mesa,* in front of his artifacts together with my artifacts as an initiate. Then I followed my own initiative, and from then on began to work alone creating my own and studying books, etc. And my dreams revealed certain things to me in obtaining

my artifacts, making my staffs, and in this fashion little by
little I grew in the art.

One's spirit has to bond itself with all of the artifacts that
are there, that harmonize with the esoteric, the cosmic and the
earth. The *maestro* is the one who handles the levers of that
motor, that mechanism, and I am part of the mechanism, I, as
an initiate, as part of the mechanism. In other words, I
separate myself from [that group of] the mechanism, but with
the very force of that mechanism which is the *maestro* and his
artifacts. Then I create my own world and live as an initiate
blessed by him, but with my own ideas. As he said to me
"Make your own ['account'], and with your own nobody will be
able to cross you or bewitch you. Follow this advice and you
will see."

When Eduardo returned from the north, at age twenty-eight, he was
still hesitant to practice on his own, even though he had had four years
of training. Then a cousin of his fell seriously ill. This is how Eduardo
recounted his first cure.

I came as a result of the sickness of one of my cousins . . . a
girl who was in the last stage of an ailment which was going to
drive her crazy into the streets. And my uncle was in a bad
economic situation. Then I had to intervene because he begged
me; for I didn't want to interfere. And I began to perform the
first cure of my life. . . . I don't remember all of the details of
the sickness of the girl, but it occurred in Chicama, in a town
where there are sorcerers in great quantity. The sorcerers there
abound like the sand. It is the school of sorcerers. I arrived
there to cure her. This girl couldn't look at mirrors because she
saw the devil there, she saw animals, she saw monsters, and a
series of things. It seems as if they had worked on her hair, a
thing of sortilege in witchcraft. Then in Chicama I placed two
*mesas* for my cousin and cured her. That is where I began and
was initiated with a handful of artifacts.

Thus Eduardo's career as a curandero working with his own mesa was
launched. In gratitude to God, he made a vow never to abuse his powers
and to work for good in the service of humanity. This is what he has to say
about his subsequent growth:

Then I began with force in my life in this branch of these
rites, which increased more and more as I went drinking these
brews and entering into the problem of the famous "charms,"

as they are called in *curanderismo* and witchcraft, until it
seems that they spoke to me at night, in dreams. I went along
acquiring knowledge each time that I manipulated these artifacts at night. I went along acquiring much more superior
knowledge each time: more and more and more until today as
you see me relating these things. I know so many things that
the artifacts have taught me. A mysterious thing, right? But it
exists. Now with the passage of the years . . . I have arrived at
a conclusion: knowledge is acquired by means of practice. A
logical, simple thing, right? Nobody can understand this.
However, one arrives at one single thing, so simple, which is
that practicing, practicing one reaches understanding. That is
what happened to me.

A very important facet of Eduardo's curanderismo is his role as an
artist. For as Lommel (1967:148), who sees shamanism as intimately
related to man's earliest artistic works, contends: "Without artistic
creation in some form or another, there is no shaman." That Eduardo
himself is fully aware of the relationship between artistic sensibility and
shamanism is revealed by his remarks on the subject:

The "power" of artistic sensibility in *curanderismo* is . . .
according to my evaluations, essential. In general the artist is
sensitive, extremely sensitive in this field. Because by being
sensitive he also possesses a special gamut of fantasy, which
is the supreme essence of the artist. In order to create the artist
has to have fantasy. On the contrary, in doing things he would
be nothing more than a mechanical person. . . . All that the
artist effuses toward the outside in his expressions is of a
character which is not intellectual, but spiritual. For this
reason it goes without saying that within *curanderismo* artistic
appreciations are essential, very essential because the symbols
are perceptible only to persons who really note a line, a trajec-
tory of appreciation in order to be able to dominate the distinct
phases of a curing scene. In this manner, for example, the
famous Mochicas [and] the Chimu are introducing something
from mysticism in their plastic manifestations, in their sym-
bology . . . [T]hose individuals always related art with mysticism, with the esoteric, with the mysteries.

The reference to the Moche (100 B.C.–A.D. 700) and the Chimu (A.D.
700-1475), pre-Columbian north coast cultures, is most significant.
Recent ethnoarchaeological investigation (see Sharon and Donnan, 1974)

suggests that there is a strong element of shamanism in the ceramic art of the earlier culture, that of the Moche peoples. Although there is no direct evidence at this time, it appears quite possible that the complex iconography depicted on Moche ceramics may have been produced by a class of shaman-priests. Perhaps the skills of the hypothesized Moche shaman-potters were part of a spiritual vocation somewhat similar to that of the Warao boatbuilder discussed in chapter 10 by Wilbert.

Returning to the ethnographic present, we have already noted how art helped in alleviating the first symptoms of Eduardo's shamanic "call." It seems to be no accident that, after his first cure, Eduardo's growth as a curandero paralleled his development as an artist. In the early 1960s, after several years as a practicing curandero, he had an opportunity to produce a great deal of wood sculpture for the appreciative staff of the American hospital ship *Hope*. This greatly enhanced his growing reputation as a local artist of great talent. As a result, in the mid-1960s Eduardo was hired as the artist in charge of frieze restoration when an archaeological project was undertaken to restore the adobe ruins of Chan Chan, the Chimu capital located near Trujillo. Part of the work with the project involved the production of 2,000 copies of pre-Columbian ceramics for sale to tourists. Eduardo also taught ceramics during this period. Finally, by the early 1970s, he was able to set up his own ceramic workshop. At the present time he divides his time between teaching, ceramic production, and attending to the needs of the large volume of patients who seek his services as a curandero. Through his exposure to archaeology and pre-Columbian ceramic motifs he learned much about the pre-Columbian past of the north coast. Thus, in a very real sense, Eduardo's artistry has led to a rediscovery of his cultural heritage. This has also been true of his shamanism. Together, art and shamanism have complemented his personal search for meaning.

Today, after nearly two decades as a full-fledged curandero, Eduardo is still learning and growing. His knowledge and power increase with practice and experience. He attributes this to the fact that he has never abandoned his vow. He knows that he is dealing with dangerous forces, but his faith keeps him alert and strong. In addition, his active mind is constantly probing and seeking new challenges, as evidenced by his extensive reading in theology, philosophy, psychology, art, the occult (by correspondence from the Rosicrucians in the United States), and medicine. In the latter discipline he obtained a nursing diploma by correspondence and now applies this modern knowledge in his curandero diagnosis and therapy.

But his erudition only supplements the keen insight into human nature which he has gained from wide experience in the workaday world. This experience has been obtained in a variety of jobs—fisherman, stevedore, artist, teacher, lay archaeologist.

And it has been greatly refined by Eduardo's numerous consultations and sessions with his patients. He is open, direct, and candid in his dealings with his fellows. He does not believe in keeping his knowledge a secret and freely shares his ideas with any sincere person who inquires about curanderismo. For Eduardo, his curing art is simply a matter of "vision" gained by those with a sincere desire to learn who practice regularly. But it is my own suspicion that—although curanderismo requires hard work and constant practice—curanderos are born, not made; they are the unusually gifted and perceptive members of their communities. Whatever the case, the man himself is not a common person. He sums up his own philosophy very simply: "I work under a faith more than anything, a promise that I made when I was initiated as a *curandero*—for one must make a promise, of course—a promise to serve man without thought of gain, whoever he may be, whatever his circumstances."

## Conclusion

I believe that the current situation in northern Peru verifies an assertion made by Furst and Reed (1970:280): "(A)dherents of the scientific world view fondly believe that once people become familiar with Western medicine they will quickly forget 'all that supernatural nonsense' and turn their backs on the indigenous healer. Not so." For in the north we find a Spanish-speaking, Catholic, mestizo population with a well-developed and Westernized middle class having access to the benefits of modern medicine. And yet this same middle class is strongly represented among the clientele of the contemporary curandero, who often combines the use of modern pharmaceutical products with his use of herbs and supernatural therapy. The greater majority of Eduardo's patients are middle class urban dwellers. It is apparent that the curandero is adapting to modernization. At the same time, however, he continues to command respect because his calling is firmly rooted in the cultural history and ideology of his milieu.

There are implications here for applied anthropology that I feel, sooner or later, modern planners are going to have to face. As Eduardo's story illustrates, the curandero is a health resource utilized extensively in the communities of the north. His vocation is firmly embedded in their cultural heritage. He is part of a grass-roots network established by the people. He is adapting to modern medicine. On the other hand, doctors and health facilities are in short supply and will continue to be so for some time to come given the high costs and lengthy time involved in modern medical organization and training coupled with rapid population growth. It appears that the only realistic solution to health problems in northern Peru is going to have to be a paramedical program that builds on available human resources. Something similar to the Chinese "barefoot doctor" program probably would be effective, once adapted to the culture-specific social conditions of Peru. We now have good evidence that the combination of traditional and modern medicine in China has been a success (Sidel and Sidel, 1974). But to be successful in Peru such a program will have to be built on an understanding of the fact that the transmission process must occur along a two-way street. The doctor has much to learn from the curandero and vice versa. Education offers the key to establishing such an understanding. For the members of isolated communities have to be taught the basic principles of hygiene and preventive medicine. And medical personnel must be taught the resources and beliefs of such communities to make their services relevant and acceptable to those they are meant to serve. Given recent efforts to reform the Peruvian educational system (see Drysdale and Myers, 1975) perhaps an additional innovation in medical education might be feasible.

Reciprocity between traditional and modern medicine is not a new idea in Latin America. The Instituto Nacional Indigenista of Mexico has been applying this principle for many years in its integrated program of community development. And a similar professional opinion is held by the world-renowned Peruvian social psychiatrist, Dr. Carlos Alberto Seguin. At the First National Congress of Peruvian Psychiatry held in Lima in October 1969 he had the following to say regarding Peruvian shamans:

> From the point of view of our specialization, I dare say—after many years of experience—that we have much to learn from our "colleagues" the "native curers," the "sorcerers," and "healers." We have much to learn, not just about pharmacology, for example, the use of psychotropic plants and drugs, but also in an area that psychiatry is "discovering" in our times, for example, group dynamics, group psychotherapy, family therapy as well as the manipulation of social and communal problems. These are novelties for us, but native practitioners have always manipulated them with enviable ability (Seguin, 1969:159).

In the United States the ethnopsychiatrist Torrey (1972:1) concludes from a cross-cultural survey of traditional therapists that "witchdoctors and psychiatrists perform essentially the same function in their respective cultures." He is a strong advocate of the integration of traditional and modern therapy, despite the resistance he perceives on the part of modern practitioners. As he puts it:

> Medicine can and will change. It can adapt itself to working with nonmedical therapists. Both these therapists and their techniques can be adopted and used to improve mental health services. The brew can be distilled, with the supernatant retained and the residue discarded. And this can be done despite the hoary traditions of medicine and psychiatry, feet firmly planted in the medieval guild system, voices echoing "You just can't do that!" with each footstep down the hall of innovation (ibid.:201).

Torrey (ibid.:203) asks us to "put aside our ethnocentrism and look carefully at both witchdoctors and psychiatrists." He adds: "The world has become too small to accommodate arrogance."

In considering the feasibility of learning from the past, it might be helpful to recall Eduardo's attitude before being cured by a curandera: "Frankly, I didn't believe in these things." Of course, he had a cultural heritage that, once rediscovered, was helpful in overcoming his skepticism and eventually learning curandero therapy. But, as members of the family of man, we all share the same human heritage. This is a lesson that Eduardo, and men like him, can teach us. If we are only willing to learn.

## BIBLIOGRAPHY

Drysdale, Robert S., and Robert G. Myers
  1975   "Continuity and Change: Peruvian Education." In *The Peruvian Experiment: Continuity and Change under Military Rule.* Abraham F. Lowenthal, ed. Princeton: Princeton University Press.

Eliade, Mircea
  1964   *Shamanism: Archaic Techniques of Ecstasy.* Bollingen Series 76. Princeton: Princeton University Press.

Furst, Peter T., and Karen B. Reed
  1970   *Stranger in Our Midst: Guided Culture Change in Highland Guatemala.* Latin American Center, University of California, Los Angeles.

Gillin, John
  1947   *Moche: A Peruvian Coastal Community.* Smithsonian Institution Publication 3. Washington, D.C.

Lommel, Andreas
  1967   *The World of the Early Hunters.* London: Evelyn, Adams, and Mackay.

Nadel, S. F.
1946    "A Study of Shamanism in the Nuba Mountains," *Journal of the Royal Anthropological Institute* 76(1):25-37.

Seguin, Carlos Alberto
1969    "Psiquiatría folklórica." In *Psiquiatría peruana* (Primer Congreso Nacional). Oscar Valdivia P. and Alberto Pendola, eds. Lima. Pp. 154-159.

Sharon, Douglas
1974    "The Symbol System of a North Peruvian Shaman," Ph.D. dissertation, University of California, Los Angeles.

Sharon, Douglas, and Christopher B. Donnan
1974    "Shamanism in Moche Iconography." In *Ethnoarchaeology*. Christopher B. Donnan and William Clewlow, eds. Monograph 4, Archaeological Survey. Los Angeles: Institute of Archaeology, University of California. Pp. 51-77.

Sidel, Victor W., and Ruth Sidel
1974    *Serve the People: Observations on Medicine in the People's Republic of China.* New York: Josiah Macy, Jr. Foundation.

Torrey, E. Fuller
1972    *The Mind Game: Witchdoctors and Psychiatrists.* New York: Bantam Books.

Vogt, Evon Z.
1969    *Zinacantan: A Maya Community in the Highlands of Chiapas.* Cambridge, Mass.: Belknap Press of Harvard University Press.

# 12.

# Music Education and Innovation in a Traditional Tzutuhil-Maya Community

## LINDA L. O'BRIEN

Several educational projects initiated in the last decade among the Tzutuhil-Maya of Santiago Atitlán, Guatemala, have been oriented toward innovation rather than perpetuation of traditional indigenous forms. Many of these programs have failed to reach their proximate and ultimate goals owing to the impropriety of some innovation the educator has introduced, the implications of which he does not, however, understand.

In contrast with the methods of progress-oriented innovative education, traditional Tzutuhil education is geared to the preservation and transmission of time-honored values and beliefs, expressed through customs considered primordial in origin and power. The performance and interpretation of the customs, both public and private, is in the hands of ritual specialists: *cofradía* officers, shamans, midwives, and musicians. Among their responsibilities is the accurate performance of traditional music, the syncretic character of which testifies to a good deal of musical innovation in the past. In contemporary musical practice, innovation occurs within strictly defined cultural limits. It is the aim of this paper to explore attitudes and patterns of innovation in traditional Tzutuhil musical culture.

Today the Tzutuhils number some 25,000, most of whom live in the villages on the southwestern shores of Lake Atitlán, in the department of Sololá, Guatemala. The largest of these is the former capital of the Tzutuhil kingdom, Santiago Atitlán, located on a small broken-lava terrace that forms a peninsula extending into the bay of Atitlán. It is one of thirteen towns on the Lake of which five are Tzutuhil or predominantly Tzutuhil. Santiago Atitlán's 14,000 inhabitants (who call themselves

"Atitecos" and their town, simply "Atitlán") are roughly 95 percent Indians and 5 percent Ladinos, the latter term designating the Spanish-speaking population who wear Western dress and are generally of Spanish ancestry. (This is a cultural, not a racial distinction.)

The Indian dwellings are usually stone and cane one-room houses with thatched roofs, arranged in extended-family compounds called *sitios,* in which several houses surround a central yard. Most sitios do not have electricity or water. The majority of the Indians are agriculturalists, growing corn, beans, coffee, and a few vegetables for subsistence. A small percentage are engaged in fishing or are traveling merchants, since Santiago Atitlán lies on an important trade route to the Pacific coast where tropical fruits and vegetables are grown. In 1951 the road to San Lucas Tolimán was opened, connecting Santiago Atitlán with the main highways to Guatemala City and the north.

An ethnographic study of the lake towns including Atitlán has been published by Sol Tax (1946). A valuable study of religion and world view was done by E. Michael Mendelson (1957), and illness and curing has been studied by Bill Gray Douglas (1969). Ethnohistorical material has been published by Sandra Orellana (1973; in press).

## Religion and the Cofradías

Today 78.8 percent of the Tzutuhils of Atitlán identify themselves as Catholics, but among them only a small number practice orthodox Roman Catholicism. Their belief is the traditional religion of the Tzutuhils, which has in the course of time been mixed with elements of Catholicism. The center of its practice is in the cofradías, religious confraternities or brotherhoods originally founded by the early mission-aries to aid them in carrying out the music and liturgy of Catholicism. In the chapels of these societies today, the cult and the music of traditional Tzutuhil belief are practiced.

The "cofradía community," those who associate themselves actively with the cofradías, includes roughly 32 percent of the Indians. Another 32 percent identify themselves as Catholics, but do not actively participate in cofradía or church functions, except to turn out for public festivals two or three times a year. When the missionary clergy returned to Atitlán in the 1940s, they found the beliefs of the cofradía community to be at odds with the Catholicism of the church.

To encourage orthodox belief they organized a group called Acción Católica (Catholic Action) whose creed is that of the Catholic catechism. Members of this group constitute about 16 percent of the Indian popula-tion. Converts to various Protestant sects are about 15.6 percent (Douglas 1969:40–41).

Members of the cofradía community may volunteer their services as members of the religious organization centered in the cofradías. Each of the ten cofradías of Atitlán has up to fifteen official members who volunteer for a year at a time. Cofradía *servicio,* as it is called, is a path to prestige through religious service to the community. The official members of each cofradía are led by an *alcalde* and his wife, the *xo',* in whose sitio the cofradía is housed for one year. Seven men called *cofrades* and six women called *tixels* serve under the alcalde. The leader of the whole organization is the *cabecera,* who is responsible for the orderly direction of the servicio system.

## Experiments with Innovation

In 1966 the American priests ministering to the Catholic congregation of Santiago Atitlán introduced a new musical setting for the singing of daily Mass. The music, recently composed in the style of popular Mexican mestizo traditions, had originally been written for a Spanish text of the Ordinary of the Mass. A Tzutuhil translation of it was made in Atitlán, and to this the new music was adapted. Through daily rehearsal and performance, the new Mass was taught by exclusively oral methods to the congregation. The *cantor,* who serves as organist and choirmaster, played harmonium accompaniment from a written manuscript. In the process of transmission some noticeable changes were made in the original. The Tzutuhil congregation tended to slow down the brisk meter, gradually substituting for it a sustained, unmeasured rhythm. This tendency was strongly emphasized by the cantor's harmonium accompaniment, and efforts to counteract it were altogether ineffective. Although he could demonstrate his ability to render the rhythm correctly, he was obstinate in refusing to teach it to the congregation. The mournful, wailing vocal quality in which the predominantly female congregation sang seemed to American ears inappropriate in sentiment for the liturgical celebration. It was also considered unfortunate that the new music was not drawn from Tzutuhil musical traditions. A program was therefore initiated to develop a music for the liturgy, hopefully to be based on yet-to-be-discovered indigenous Tzutuhil musical styles. For the implementation of this program I was employed to work in the parish of Santiago Atitlán.

The development of a liturgical music with an indigenous base, and the instruction of the Mass-attending congregation in its performance, were my tasks. Ideally, the sung Mass would be developed in the style of Tzutuhil accompanied song, but the existence of song in the Tzutuhil language was unknown even to longtime non-Indian residents of Atitlán, and was flatly denied by Tzutuhils. (I was not then aware of the quite common opinion of investigators that the Indians of that country have no vocal music.) Several forms of instrumental music were known, but after weeks of questioning, no information had turned up suggesting any kind of singing in the Tzutuhil language, except the recently translated Mass.

Finally one day, weeks later (after I had abandoned the original approach), my Tzutuhil language teacher said he knew a young man who sang "street songs" in Tzutuhil to the accompaniment of the guitar. I begged for an introduction, and a few days later Miguel Cuá Damián and two friends (all in their early twenties) arrived at the door of the parish office. After customary greetings, they seated themselves on a bench, and Miguel began to tune his five-string guitar. He at first played several pieces without singing. My request for a song engendered a long discussion among the three, who finally agreed to hum a song together. After a few songs done this way, Miguel gained confidence and began to sing a courting song:

> Maria Chote, Maria Candelaria,
> You must come to my house
> and be my wife
> tomorrow or the day after.
> We are made of the same water,
> We are made of the same tortilla.

This was followed by "A sad song for a widower," "A young girl says goodbye to her mother," and others. Later in the week five songs by Gaspar Petzéy Mendoza, another guitarist-singer, were also recorded, making a total of seven songs and seventeen guitar solos, recorded in three sessions. The musical style of the pieces drew largely on Hispanic sources in tonality and rhythm. While the guitar solos were rhythmically complex, both vocal and guitar parts of the accompanied songs were in straightforward ¾ meter. They consisted of one or two four-bar phrases of triadic sung melody repeated over and over, accompanied by tonic, dominant, and subdominant chords strummed on the guitar.

Without duplicating any of the melodies exactly, but imitating the style of the songs, I set melody and guitar accompaniment to the words of the Kyrie Eleison in Tzutuhil: *Kajawal Dios, tpoknak kawach.* This I performed for Tzutuhil friends who responded with amused approval. Some others were highly entertained by my experiment, even laughing aloud as I played and sang. But a demonstration of it to the *catequistas,* the lay officials of Acción Católica who regulate the teaching of doctrine and other church functions, was received with silent horror. Finally a spokesman protested: "This music is not for Church. It is bad music, and it has bad words. The young men sing it to girls with evil intentions. If we sing this in Church, passersby will say that now the Catholics are singing bad songs in Church." My protests that I had composed it, and that the words were not bad but holy, were to no avail. There could be no argument against their strong feelings. Apparently there was something profound and powerful to be learned about the Tzutuhil songs.

The failure of this experiment led me to conclude that music that would appropriately express the religious sentiments of the Tzutuhils would have to be composed by them. No one among the members of Acción Católica was a competent musician, having abandoned participation in traditional music along with traditional Tzutuhil religion in accord with the teaching of the catequistas, who knew (perhaps better than the padres) the indissolubility of the bonds between traditional belief and music. Consequently, there was little musical development among the members of Acción, who found themselves with nothing to fill the gap.

To encourage the development of competent musicians, from whose number I hoped composers might emerge, I decided to organize and train an orchestra. Unfamiliar with the combinations of instruments popular in other village ensembles, and unsure of the preferences, tastes, and talents of the proposed group, I procured a variety of familiar instruments for this orchestra: cane flutes, *chirimías*,[1] six-string guitars, a Guatemalan harp, a four-and-one-half–octave box marimba,[2] a bass drum, and a slit-drum.

To the announcement of the formation of an orchestra twenty-two enthusiastic would-be musicians—eighteen men, two boys, and two women—responded. (The two women dropped out soon afterward.) An initial attempt to instruct them in the fundamentals of Western music theory, through written notation on the five-line staff, was a complete failure, which I abandoned after two meetings.

Through demonstration and imitation in group and private lessons, the orchestra members eventually mastered their instruments. No amount of encouragement could induce them to self-directed practice at home, but their aptitude for music and the facility with which they learned were great, so that about four months later they were able to play three pieces in the town's annual fiesta parade: "Cielito lindo," "Adelita," and "Las mañanitas," old standards of Mexico.

Hoping to introduce traditional indigenous instruments into church, I proposed they learn to accompany some familiar hymns, and perhaps the Mass. The musicians were enthusiastic, but the idea was rejected by the catequistas, who considered the instruments of the orchestra inappropriate for church.

As they gained musical competence, they required less direction from me and replaced the Mexican songs with the popular music of the day, picking it up by ear. The instruments of a traditional character, chirimía, cane flute, slit-drum, and harp, were (in that order) replaced by saxophones, cymbals, clarinets, trumpets, and snare drum. A three-string double-bass viol was added first, and later on an accordion, a thermos-bottle rattle, and a bell.

From this group two members expressed interest in composing music for church, but after a few attempts became discouraged. In 1968 the liturgical music project was terminated. The Orquesta Atitlán Tzutuhil continues, however, as a popular, professional marimba band.

## The Traditional Music of the Tzutuhils

In 1972 I returned to Atitlán to study the music of the cofradía community. This group, among whom traditional Tzutuhil music, ritual, and customs are preserved, constitutes about 32 percent of Atitecos.

During the yearly cycle of celebrations, the cofradías require and sponsor the performance of traditional forms of Tzutuhil music and dance which survive almost exclusively in this context. Deeply bound up with old concepts of the nature of the world and of time, music is an integral part of the cult of the ancestral heroes, the Nawals, and of the deified Santos. Some musical genres accompany dance dramas that interpret the significance of calendric feasts through dramatization. Others accompany, or are themselves, acts of imitative magic, in which the desired effect of the rituals is demonstrated, verbalized, or symbolized. Texts of songs, and the chanted prayers of shamans and midwives, are repositories of traditional modes of thought. Together with a body of tales and the texts of dance dramas, they constitute Tzutuhil traditions of oral literature, efficacious as means of education in cultural values.

## Cofradía Musicians

Among the members of the cofradía organization are musicians of various types whose servicio is the performance of music required for the proper and complete carrying out of cofradía customs. Unlike yearly rotating posts of alcaldes, cofrades, and tixels, musicians ordinarily hold their posts for more than one year.

At the present time the cofradía community in Atitlán has at least eight servicio musicians. A single pitero (cane-flutist) who sometimes also plays the tamborón (large, two-headed drum) is responsible for the public announcements of events of religious import to the community. The pito and tamborón ensemble is most frequently observed leading a procession in which the images of the santos are carried. The tamborón alone is used to notify the town of public proclamations or notices from the cabecera.

Three *sacristanes,* semipermanent officers under the cabecera, serve as musicians for certain calendric events, during which they sing *himnos* (old Spanish hymns), accompanying themselves on violins.

The duties of the third cofrades of four of the cofradías include the care and playing of the *c'unc'un* (slit-drum)[3] housed in their cofradías. This is required daily at sunrise, zenith, and sunset, together with the burning of incense before the images on the cofradía altars. In his absence this responsibility devolves upon the alcalde of the cofradía or his wife, the xo'.

The greatest number of cofradía musicians are guitarists who play, and often sing, the "Bix Rxin Ruch'lew" (Songs of the Face of the Earth), which are considered to have been composed by the twenty-four heroic ancestors called the Nawals. The songs contain Tzutuhil myths, prayers, and moral lessons, and are believed to be imbued with the magical power of the ancestors. *Bix* singers serve the community not only in connection with public cofradía functions, but also by responding to the requests of private individuals: shamans, who require their music during private prayer rituals, usually performed in the cofradías, and other persons who require music for rituals of the life cycle, courting, dancing, mourning, or other motives.

For special occasions, non-servicio musicians are hired by the cofradías. Marimba bands from out of town often provide music for dancing in the cofradía. It is probable that this arrangement replaces a former one in which local Atiteco marimba groups, now scarce, volunteered servicio.

Chirimía and tambor players from San Pedro la Laguna are hired yearly to play for the dance drama, the *Baile de la Conquista.* A gourd-marimba from nearby Cerro de Oro comes in October to play for the Corpus Christi dance drama, the *Baile de los Negritos.*

Besides the servicio musicians, many Atiteco ritual specialists, guitarists, shamans, prayer-makers, and midwives, not currently engaged in servicio, sing chants, songs, and prayers as part of their ritual activities for private individuals or families.

## Music as a Vehicle of Education in Tzutuhil Life

The authorship of the traditional music of the Atitlán Tzutuhils practiced by the cofradía community is ascribed to twenty-four heroic men and women who lived in Atitlán in former times, or "in the beginning." These ancestors, the Old Powerful Ones (Nawals), were wonder-workers who, through the superior powers of their prayers, deeds, and music, were able to influence the forces of nature to the benefit of men. It was they who originated the religious customs, dances, songs, and prayers that the cofradía community performs, and who formed the idol of Old Mam, the powerful shaman-god who watches over Atitlán. Their lives and teachings, the substance of Tzutuhil oral literature, are the basis of moral teaching and the models of daily conduct. At the end of their lives the Nawals were taken up into the mountains to the southwest, where they were given charge of the forces of nature and certain aspects of the destiny of men. Their words and actions are regarded not only as the source of the customs but also as channels through which men can gain access to power. The exact replication of them is required for the prosperity of the people and the orderly progress of the cycles of nature.

The customs of the Nawals form two groups that correspond to the cycles of time: the years and the lifetimes of men. Each has its own subdivisions, important events, and situations that are marked by specific forms of ritual conduct, requiring prayers, the drinking of liquor, the burning of incense, and music.

Customs to ensure the orderly progress of the cycles of nature are performed on a yearly calendar by the cofradía servicio community. These rites that concern the common good are usually performed privately in the cofradías, but everyone is aware of the time and place of their performance. Customs that correspond to the events in the life of a particular individual, the "rites of passage," are determined by his personal *suerte* (destiny). These are the concern of individuals and their families. Those who hold servicio posts perform the calendric customs in the cofradías and make available in the cofradía houses a place for life-cycle rites. Ritual specialists, shamans, midwives, and musicians engaged both in servicio and private practice, cross between the two groups and serve them both.

The customs they perform are spoken of as "the heart and center of the world," the "ancient source of power and contentment," and "the roots of life." As the focus of common activity, they are a strong unifying force. They are also the means by which a child learns traditional teachings about the significance of life and the world and discovers the meaning and means of fulfillment of his own personal suerte.

The clear recognition of one's destiny to be a musician usually comes to a man during the early years of adulthood. No special training precedes this, but from the first moment of his life he absorbs the cofradía musical tradition through the customs of the Nawals.

The universe into which a Tzutuhil baby is born is shaped by the path of the sun, Dios Titixel (Grandfather God). The dome of heaven through which he travels is supported at the four solstice points, the "four corners of the earth," by spirits who live on and inside the sacred mountains.

Stretched out between the mountains is the earth, with Lake Atitlán in the center. Directly below the zenith of the sky, at the very center of the cosmos, is the town of Santiago Atitlán.

All of the visible world of nature—the sky and the surface of the earth—is formed by the body of a cosmic deity called Face of the Earth. On his back men live and walk, and corn, trees, and herbs grow. His nose forms the mountains, his arms embrace the world, carrying it carefully "like water in a basin." He is Lord over a company of subordinate nature spirits, including the Nawals, who perform tasks at his command. Diverse aspects of his power are signified by his names: Green-Mountain World, Face of the Earth, Mountain-Plain, San Martín, Diego Martín, Juan Martín. The sun, his highest manifestation, is called K'ij (Sun or Day), Dios Titixel, Dios Padre del Cielo (God the Father in Heaven).

At the moment of his birth into the center of the cosmos, the Tzutuhil baby is given an unchangeable suerte by the sun. Some particulars of his suerte can be read in the events of nature and the conditions of his delivery by the midwife, but the greater part of it will be revealed to him as his life unfolds, in signs and dreams. So pervasive and dominating will be its influence on his life that his parents take great care before his birth to secure a favorable suerte by the proper performance of the customary prayers and songs of the Nawals.

Before his birth the midwife chosen by the parents begins her rituals of petition to the spirits of childbirth enshrined on the cofradía altars. The parents and their children attend in the cofradía as she offers candles, incense, and liquor to San Martín and the images of the other Santos on the altar before beginning her prayer. On one such occasion which I witnessed in the cofradía San Nicolás, the midwife took the sacred bundle of San Martín from its box near the altar and, cradling it in her arms, danced and rocked it while she prayed. At the end of the prayer she sang a song to the spirits of childbirth. The meaning of her actions, prayer, and song was clear to those who knelt behind her. The powerful customs the ancestors had taught were once again being performed. The familiar melody came directly from them and was filled with their power. The sacred words carefully named each spirit of pregnancy, childbirth, and midwifery, forgetting no one who might show displeasure at the time of birth:

O Martín, Martín, Martín,
O Nicolás, Nicolás Martín,
O ancient miss, O ancient virgin,
O ancient mamma, O Martín, Martín, Martín.

Here is your son, here is your daughter.
Lullaby before your spirit,
Lullaby before your soul, Martín.
O lords of women, lords of the daughters.
O Martín, Martín, Martín.

From the beginning of his life the process of socialization by which the infant learns to become a member of his culture, and the future musician an educator in its values, is intimately linked to traditional music.

When the moment of birth arrives, the midwife's softly changed prayers are among the first sounds to reach his ears. Within a few hours the rhythmic beating of the c'unc'un rises up from a nearby cofradía in daily salutation of the sun. Adults stop and kneel to kiss a bit of earth and direct a prayer to the source of light, warmth, and suerte.

During infancy, at the time of a crisis of health, the baby will probably be taken by the mother to the cofradía San Juan, where the images of spirits of maternity and women's affairs, the "Marías," occupy the right side of the altar. In this sacred place, the "navel of the world," a shaman engaged by the parents will chant prayers before the wooden box containing objects for ritual use left by the ancestors, which relate to the affairs of women: different aspects of maternity and the arts of weaving. Among them is a velvet cloth to which are attached three small painted wooden heads resembling cherubs, representing the spirits of childbirth. Beneath each head a small skin bag representing the uterus is sewn. Covering the baby with the velvet cloth, the shaman lays the ailing infant in the sacred box, called "the cradle" (cosol) and rocks it gently while he improvises a song to the accompaniment of the c'unc'un played by a cofrade:

O María, María Isabela,
O María Candelaria,
O María Dios,
O you are holy, you are the creator, the
    genetrix, O Dios Jesucrist.
Lalala lala lilalala.
O my dear, O my mother,
O crib, O cradle, dear,
O light, O life,
O wisdom.

In some cases the shaman instructs his clients to engage a guitarist-singer to attend. If a singer is present at the ritual, he waits for the officiating shaman to instruct him to play. He is expected to choose a melody from a standard repertory, appropriate in its title to the situation that occasioned the prayer ritual. At the blessing or curing of an infant, his melody would be one of the songs entitled "Of San Martín" which appeal to the spirits of nature. If inspired or requested he will also sing, drawing his textual material partly from a standard repertory of phrases and partly from his own imagination. He constructs a text related closely in theme to the intent of the ritual.

As it goes through the first years of life, carried here and there on its mother's back, it learns to associate musical sounds with specific places, events, and times, a fundamental concept of Tzutuhil music, reinforced through the yearly cycle of customs. In its childhood, as its awareness grows, it sees and hears the reenactment of the annual ancestral celebrations, dramatizing the relationships among cosmic forces and human agents. Songs and stories, chants and ritual speeches teach it the origins and significance of places and things in the world.

As its language skills develop, it learns to distinguish the language of vernacular speech from the specialized, elevated, and obscure language of ritual speech, song, and prayer, and the obscure language "of Jesucristo," a form of Latin sung by the sacristanes during Holy Week. It sees that strong emotions of sorrow, weeping, and wailing, unacceptable in other contexts, are allowed expression when singing and dancing in the cofradías.

Later in childhood the traditional skills are learned: the primordially established tasks of men and women, performed in faithful imitation of the Nawals, to gain their ultimate blessing on the enterprise. From songs and prayers done in preparation for this task, it understands that the milpa must be laid out in the pattern in which the sun divides the sky; and that its profits must be similarly divided; that the ears of corn have guardian spirits, and that one must show reverence for the growing things in nature. Calendric customs including guitar music, the c'unc'un, and dancing assure the coming of the rains and the heat of the summer sun for the growth of the crops. Apprentice fishermen invoke the protection of San Gregorio, their special patron, through shamans, prayers, and songs. Songs "of the drowned" and "of the dead" tell of the afterlife.

In imitation of the ancestral women, Maria Warp-beams and Maria Heddles, the young girl sets up her loom for the first time, knowing it to be a replica of the loom in the sacred box of the cofradía San Juan.

Later in their teens, it is customary for young men to go in small groups to the street near the house of the girl one of them is courting. One of their company will play the guitar and sing courting songs, the texts of which are standardized dialogues between the young man and the girl, expressing the customary attitudes and conduct appropriate to the various stages of courting. Through the songs the magic power of the Nawals is brought to bear on the listening girl and her parents, influencing them in the young man's favor.

Many young men acquire enough musical proficiency to learn the courting songs, and later add more guitar pieces to their repertory for private entertainment. Until he responds to a supernatural call to servicio, however, a guitarist does not achieve the status of ritual specialist.

Marriage is the mark of social maturity, when a man may elect to begin servicio to the community as an *alguacil*. In this capacity, he serves the cabecera for a year. His most significant duty comes during the rituals of Holy Week. At that time, fasting and continent, he walks with twenty-three alguacils to the Pacific coastlands to gather tropical fruits to be used in the rituals of Old Mam. With them goes a guitarist who sings and plays on the way, instructing them in the significance of the ritual. While the rhythmic strumming encourages their footsteps, his songs tell them that they are the representatives of the Holy Earth. Acting the role of women, they bear the fruits of fertility to the center of the earth, where the festival is celebrated. The greatest of the calendric celebrations, these equinoctial rites are performed to the accompaniment of much traditional music. Sounds of the marimba accompany the dancing of the alguaciles, flute and drum accompany the procession back to town. To onlookers, the rites signify the sacred meaning of male and female, flute and drum, the seeds in the Holy Earth.

## The Origins and Significance of Music

The antiquity of the customs is a fundamental value in Tzutuhil thought, intimately related to the nature of time expressed in their mythology, according to which the order of the cosmos was originally established by the Nawals at the beginning of time. The ancestors, now in charge of cosmic forces, expect and require the continual reenactment of the customs and periodically return in human form to renovate and reaffirm them. If the customs and the magic power with which they are imbued should be lost, the Tzutuhil people would lose the power to influence nature in favor of men, the economy of exchange would be destroyed, and with them, the order of the cosmos and the Tzutuhil people.

Tzutuhil mythology guarantees the antiquity of the music. In the stories of the ancestors, they are cited as its composers. In the words of one storyteller: "The first men formed the *sones*:[4] Francisco Sojuel formed the "*son* of Maximón," Diego Pablo formed the "*son* of the cofradía Santa Cruz," Diego Pablo formed the "*son* of María Castellano," Esteban Ajcot formed the "*son* of Santiago Tzutuhil." The women formed the "*son,* sad song of the elders."

In Tzutuhil belief, old music is not left to the vagaries of oral transmission, but is renewed by the ancestors when they return to earth. Francisco Sojuel, the leader of the twenty-four, is believed to have lived most recently about seventy years ago. The music is renewed not only by their return, but by the direct contact with the ancestral spirits which occurs in the dreams of musicians. These beliefs guarantee the antiquity and authenticity of the music and provide a basis for the authority of musicians.

## Becoming a Musician

A man decides to become a cofradía musician in response to a call revealed to him in signs frequently given in dreams. In such dreams a spirit, one of the Nawals or Santos, instructs him to volunteer his service to the cofradías as a musician in fulfillment of his preordained suerte. Musicians frequently said they protested inability to play an instrument or to sing. Some musicians had repeated dreams of this sort in which the spirit taught them to play and sing. Sometimes a cofradía official, in response to a musician's own dreams, will approach him with the request that he fill a vacant post as musician. Eventually the number of signs is sufficient to convince him of the irreversibility of his suerte. With this conviction the musician offers himself for cofradía servicio.

There is no formal music instruction given to him. His art is a gift from the spirits. Musicians were unanimous in denying having learned to perform their music from any human source.

The music he plays influences the spirits in favor of men. Its effectiveness derives from a form of imitative magic by which the musician activates and directs the power of the Nawals through his music, which casts spells and breaks them, cures disease, calls the spirits of the dead and defends against them, and brings rain or sun.

The antiquity of the music is one of its primary values. Musicians repeatedly assured me of this quality of their music: "This is old, old, old; it is from the Nawals, from the past."

The accurate transmission of the music is facilitated by the uniformity and simplicity of the style, and the limited instrumentarium. Further, the repertory is considered closed, that is, complete and not open to the addition of new compositions.

These conservative attitudes toward music are inimical to innovation, and they are no doubt responsible for the survival of musical instruments and styles that originated as long ago as the colonial period and for the archaic quality of the language of the texts.

## Innovation in Tzutuhil Music

In spite of the conservatism of their tradition, the contemporary music of the Tzutuhils is an amalgam of alien and indigenous elements. The acceptance and innovative reorganization of nonindigenous musical forms in the past is testified to by the syncretic, acculturated character of traditional music. The various genres of this music contain easily recognizable elements of Spanish, African, and other Western musical styles and instruments. Some stem from probable colonial Spanish ecclesiastical and secular sources. Others, such as the popular marimba *sones,* have roots in the *ladino* styles of the eighteenth and nineteenth centuries. Nonindigenous and indigenous elements are welded in this music into an integral whole in which harmonic, tonal, and rhythmic characteristics of the originals have been modified by the Tzutuhil musician, operating under his own aesthetic, into a unique style.[5]

The impression that a variety of alien cultural influences converged upon the Tzutuhils in the past, leaving them with a heterogeneous collection of styles and instruments, is a superficial one. The integrity of Tzutuhil musical culture is founded on a system of prototypes that signify or symbolize cosmological concepts. The deliberate adaptation of nonindigenous musical practice to traditional use is founded on the recognition of common prototypes and contexts.

A clear example of this is contained in the adaptation of musical instruments. Tzutuhil musical vocabulary contains two terms for musical instruments. The drum, described as female, is called *k'jom:* "instrument played with the hands." The cane flute, a male instrument, is called *xul:* "instrument played with the breath." These terms have been extended to include the nonindigenous instruments, classifying those whose shapes resemble female anatomy, which are also played with the hands, as k'jom: marimba, guitar, and violin. The word "k'jom" is related in meaning to the verb *ok'ej:* to cry, to lament or weep, which describes the singing of women. Similarly, the term "xul" is extended to other instruments played with the breath, of phallic shape and male significance: the chirimía, clarinet, saxophone, and trumpet.

The material forms and playing techniques of the nonindigenous instruments are evidently perceived as analogous to the indigenous prototypes, the cane flute and drum, and the differences are overlooked or ignored. On the basis of this analogy they are identified with traditional instruments in name, significance, power, and ancestral origin. The Tzutuhils believe that the k'jom and xul were created by the ancestors at the beginning of time. As the cycles of time repeat and the ancestors return, the k'jom and xul are transformed in material shape, but their significance is unchanging. Thus the accommodation of nonindigenous instruments is accomplished without violence to the system of Tzutuhil symbolism. In spite of the emphasis placed on the exact reproduction of the ancient customs, a certain kind of change is expected to occur through the repeated cycles of time. These changes occur on the level of superficial details, without affecting the basic symbolism or significance. This attitude underlies a variety of acculturative changes accepted and integrated by the Tzutuhils into their cultures.

Equivalence of contexts also serves as a basis for adaptation, identification, and assimilation of nonindigenous music. It seems likely that acceptance of the church music of the past, so evident in contemporary styles, is based on an equivalence of contexts. The church is today considered somewhat like a special cofradía chapel for Jesucristo, who has entered the Tzutuhil pantheon as one of the Santos. The probability is that church music in Atitlán has in the past largely consisted of Gregorian chant sung by the whole congregation, and homophonic hymns sung by the sacristanes. This has led to the identification of these two musical styles with the cult of Jesucristo. No other musical genres are considered by the cofradía community to be appropriate to this cult, nor are these styles used in any other context. The experience of the recently returned priests with the newly composed Mexican Mass supports this theory, since the effect of the congregations' singing was to change it to resemble the rhythm of Gregorian chant. Even the members of Acción Católica, including the cantor, were influenced by this concept, despite their intent to reject forms of traditional music.

In a similar way, the Spanish association of San Martín with the sending of rain has resulted in the identification of that saint with the Tzutuhil rain god, the greatest and most eminent of the nature deities. Today songs to San Martín to plead for rain resemble litanies in textual structure, and Gregorian chant in musical style. They are sung in a language that contains unintelligible bits of Latin and garbled names of Catholic saints.

In this connection it is interesting that in Tzutuhil experience the music of the church originates with the priests: ritual specialists, whose role may be understood as equivalent to the music-making ritual specialists in their own servicio community. This would account for the ready acceptance of their music as originating with the Nawals, based on the authority ascribed to the dream experiences of musicians.

Composition of music is an activity believed to be accomplished by the ancestors. The repertory of pieces ascribed to them consists of fewer than twenty quite similar skeletal melodies with semifixed harmonic implications. From these formulas discreet songs are constructed by the individual musician, using rhythmic and melodic variation. Improvised melodic ornamentation, and with vocal music, textual improvisations, are also added by the musician according to his skill and choice.

The amount of improvised variation and ornamentation depends upon the limitations of his skill and his instrument, but their style, and much of their content, are determined by the common practice of musicians. The spontaneous composition of texts allows for great amplitude of improvisation in vocal music. It is not uncommon for musicians to acquire new improvisations in dreams.

Since the musicians have no formal instruction, no written manuscripts, and no teachers, there is no device for the correction of discrepancies in their reproduction of the style. The musician may freely choose to incorporate nonformulaic elements of the music he hears, exclude or forget others, and add his own. Gradually the tradition is modified through the choices of succeeding generations of musicians. The musical evidence suggests that these choices are influenced and enriched by borrowing from popular styles.

It is clear that for traditional Tzutuhil musicians the concept of equivalence extends to deep structures associated by analogy with patterns of traditional cosmology. The recognition of analogous patterns in alien and indigenous musical instruments, contexts, styles, and structures allows for their identification and substitution. Differences that fall outside the analogy are considered insignificant.

The acculturation process of Tzutuhil music is one of incremental syncretism, in which the adaptation of alien forms in terms of an indigenous counterpart results in identification of the alien form with the ancestral tradition, into which it is assimilated. Once part of the tradition, it is tenaciously preserved in its accepted form and not subject to deliberate modification. This process, together with the improvisational practice of Tzutuhil musicians, and the changes inevitably following on oral transmission, accounts for the high degree of innovative reorganization of music evident in Tzutuhil musical culture.

## NOTES

1. A *chirimía* is a type of shawm (or oboe) introduced by Spanish colonists.
2. The box marimba (*marimba de cajas*) has a chromatic keyboard and gourd-shaped boxes for resonators, in place of the traditional gourds.
3. Commonly known in other parts of Guatemala as *tun* (a Quiché word), the *c'unc'un* is a so-called slit-drum made of a hollow log with closed ends, into the side of which an H-shaped slit is carved, forming two tongues that, struck with a stick, produce two pitches

approximately a fourth apart. In central Mexico it is known as *teponaztli,* in Yucatan as *tunkul.* There are six in Atitlán, where it is associated with the sun and with maternity.

4. The Son guatemalteco is the national dance of Guatemala.

5. In the following paragraphs, I have freely drawn on the discussion of innovation in Barnett (1953).

# BIBLIOGRAPHY

Barnett, Homer Garner
   1953   *Innovation: The Basis of Cultural Change.* New York: McGraw-Hill.

Douglas, Bill Gray
   1969   "Illness and Curing in Santiago Atitlán, a Tzutuhil-Maya Community in the Southwestern Highlands of Guatemala." Ph.D. dissertation, Stanford University.

Mendelson, E. Michael
   1957   *Religion and World-View in Santiago Atitlán.* Microfilm Collection of Manuscripts on American Indian Cultural Anthropology, no. 52. Chicago: University of Chicago Library.

O'Brien, Linda Lee
   1975   "Songs of the Face of the Earth: Ancestor Songs of the Tzutuhil-Maya of Santiago Atitlán, Guatemala." Ph.D. dissertation, University of California, Los Angeles.

Orellana, Sandra L.
   1973   "Ethnohistorical and Archaeological Boundaries of the Tzutujil-Maya." *Ethnohistory* 20 (2): 125–142.
   In   "The Introduction of the Cofradía System in the Lake Atitlán Region of Highland Guatemala." *América Indígena.*
   press

Tax, Sol
   1946   *The Towns of Lake Atitlán.* Microfilm Collection of Manuscripts on Middle American Cultural Anthropology, no. 13. Chicago: University of Chicago Library.

# 13.

# Urbanization, Cognition, and Socialization of Educational Values: The Case of the Guajiro Indians of Venezuela

LAWRENCE C. WATSON

## Introduction

In a recent attempt to use a Darwinian paradigm to study personality, Robert LeVine (1973) has asserted that in any social system certain kinds of behavior come to be selected out as valued through normative definition because they have maintenance or survival functions for the system as a whole or for some important part of it. In this scheme the role of parental socializers is one of transmitting to their children an adequate cognitive organization for appropriate, normatively defined behavior, thus propagating adaptive behavior intergenerationally and insuring the maintenance of society within certain parameters in a state of equilibrium with its environment. Transmission may also involve the socialization of relevant new behavior brought about by changes in the larger system which are perceived to impose new requirements for behavior. This basic process has been likened to a mechanism in a Darwinian model for the preservation, duplication, and propagation of the positively selected variants (cf. LeVine, 1969:504).

LeVine (1973:128) argues, however, that despite theoretical congruence, "slippage" may occur between the normative environment and the content of socialization, particularly in a complex sociocultural system characterized by cultural plurality and/or in periods of rapid social change (see also Inkeles, 1961, 1969, 1972; and Inkeles and Levinson, 1969). Under such circumstances, parental socializers may experience uncertainty and confusion interpreting the requirements of the larger changing environment and hence may be unable to transmit appropriate adaptive behavior in the course of socialization.

LeVine (1973:127 ff.) suggests several possible causes of faulty transmission of environmental information: (1) the socializer may simply be ignorant of the broader context of life and the relationship between environmental events and the child's behavior; (2) the sharp discontinuity between past and present environments and the frustration of adapting to change may lead the socializer, despite his desire to change, to fall back on old but maladaptive solutions in socializing the child to cope with his new reality; and (3) under the stress of change and the uncertainty it brings, the socializer may be dominated by unconscious wishes and fears to the extent that these motivate his socialization strategy and prevent him from perceiving and/or utilizing important environmental cues in an objective, instrumental way.

I propose that the foregoing model may help to delineate some of the reasons why Guajiro Indians who have recently migrated to Maracaibo experience difficulties adjusting their educational practices to fit the prevailing demands of the urban sociocultural environment. I also argue, however, that the discrepancy between normatively defined requirements for behavior and educational transmission, while it may characterize Guajiro migrants in the early phases of urbanization, represents merely a temporary stage in the transition from one stable system associated with tribal society, where an adaptive "fit" exists between the normative environment and the aims and content of socialization, to another form of stable adaptation between education and social reality, which has been achieved in the acculturated Guajiro urban community. As we shall see, the swing toward accommodation to the urban system on the part of acculturated Guajiros is accompanied by the development of a cognitive organization that enables them to properly assess and interpret the demands of the new normative order. This is suggested to have profound implications for the socialization of positively selected behavioral variants in the following generation (cf. Watson, 1972b).

Thus, to understand the lack of adaptive change in the urban migrant's socialization strategy in the early transitional phase of adjustment, we must consider it in relationship to (1) the socializer's tribal background, and (2) the adaptive reorganization of perception and socialization which accompanies the acculturative process in the more advanced phases of urbanization.

The following observations forming the remainder of the paper have been drawn from an analysis of subject responses[1] to a standardized interview and to selected tests[2] that were designed to tap aspects of cognitive organization related to how the subject perceived normatively defined environmental success and his plan for achieving it. Among urban subjects it was especially important to determine their ability to distinguish prestigious jobs in the urban occupational structure and to identify properly those behavioral strategies linked to their attainment, especially the crucial role played by formal education in this respect.

## The Tribal Society: Adaptive Fit in a Stable System

The sociocultural environment that Guajiro migrants leave behind can be characterized as a unified system from our standpoint, one in which the objectives of socialization serve to meet normatively defined behavioral requirements that have explicit as well as unstated maintenance value for the functioning of critical economic, social, and political institutions. The typical socialized adult in this culture exhibits certain overt behavioral traits as part of his phenotypic personality[3] which permit him to conform to the specifications of social roles within culturally accepted limits of deviation.

Let us briefly examine Guajiro society as a relatively stable sociocultural system in equilibrium with its environment and consider this factor in relationship to other variables in our model, namely, normatively defined behavior, cognition, socialization, and personality.

The Guajiro are a tribe of seminomadic cattle herders who inhabit the arid Guajira Peninsula in the area of northwest Venezuela and northern Colombia. In addition to keeping cattle, these people also raise sheep and goats, and in certain favorable regions practice limited agriculture. During the annual cycle the Guajiro migrate from more or less permanent base camps that they occupy during the rainy season to a series of temporary campsites during the long dry season where limited water and pastures are available. The men and boys do the herding. Because of the scarcity of environmental resources and the danger of theft and loss of livestock through negligence, utmost responsibility and careful adherence to routine represent expected qualities of behavior, recognized by the Guajiro themselves, which are essential to meeting the obligations of economic role behavior (Watson, 1968). The presence of these correlated attributes supports the theoretical formulations linking economic and socialization variables hypothesized and tested cross-culturally by Barry, Bacon, and Child(1959).

The women and girls, whose sphere of work is in the home, do the cooking, keep up the rancho, and care for the small children. But above and beyond this, they are also in charge of milking the animals and processing dairy products for family consumption.

The society is crosscut by approximately thirty matrilineal sibs, which in turn are segmented into lineages. Each matrilineage is represented in legal and political matters by a chief who heads up the highest-ranking family line. The Guajiro lineage is a tightly-knit corporate group (cf. Fortes, 1953) of a basically political character (Befu and Plotnicov, 1962), which, in addition to its political functions, also possesses vested ownership over various wells and pasturelands. Of particular politicolegal importance is that the lineage customarily assumes collective legal responsibility in the eyes of the society for the acts of its individual members.

Given the prevailing collectivistic orientation described above, it is not surprising that a compliant, cooperative mode of socially adaptive behavior generally characterizes the interpersonal relations of close matrilineal kinsmen, nor is it unexpected that all in the lineage unite in showing respect to the chief and that they obey his authority (Watson, 1970a:24).

Guajiro matrilineages stand in potentially inimical relationship to one another. Any violation of the legal rights of a member of one lineage by the member of another is countered by a legal suit that the chief of the plaintiff's lineage initiates in the group's behalf; if the suit is not resolved by compensation of damages, feuding between the lineages is likely to follow, for ultimately each lineage is a law unto itself in the absence of any centralized political authority. In serious legal disputes the services of impartial intermediaries (*palabreros*) are obtained to negotiate a peaceful settlement (cf. Gutiérrez de Pineda, 1950). The acephalous political situation, with the ever-present threat of feuding as the ultimate means of legal arbitration, has serious implications for interpersonal behavior in the sense that it makes it necessary for Guajiros to maintain an attitude of guarded care in their dealings with members of other lineages. Such behavior, it may be argued, serves to inhibit ill-considered displays of aggressiveness that could lead to misunderstanding and conflict, with its potentiality for activating political and military involvement.

Guajiro society is rigidly stratified in terms of differential access to wealth in resources, social prestige, and political power. This is true even in the lineage itself where particular family lines control most of the important resources (including armed manpower in retainers) and supply successors to the lineage chieftainship. Basically there are four distinct social classes; these include (1) chiefly families who possess vast wealth in livestock, as well as political and military power; (2) commoner families related to the nobles, who have their own independent economic holdings, but who nevertheless rely on the nobles' political and military authority for protection from outsiders; (3) servants and retainers, who are poor people bereft of resources who have indentured themselves to chiefly families in return for economic and political support; and (4) slaves, who have been captured in war, sold to their owners, or born to their position.

Because of the demands of the class system, the need to acquire and maintain wealth has become a significant motivating factor in many spheres of behavior. And to some extent, social mobility through the accumulation of valued property is possible for the enterprising individual, thus providing sufficient reinforcement for the behavior in question.

Young boys, particularly those from chiefly families, are socialized to be responsible and ambitious herders so that they will maintain and even increase their family's holdings in cattle, for in doing so they help to insure the continuance of the family's favored social and political position in society, which in large measure is based on wealth. Failure on the boy's part to demonstrate these virtues may result in his being disinherited by the maternal uncle (or other ranking members of the matrilineage), with such an eventuality forcing him to start his adult life without any security in cattle or other livestock. This is a dismal situation in Guajiro society and is fraught with the possibility of severe loss of status, for to be poor and dependent is regarded as a humiliating and contemptible situation. It is understandable, therefore, that Guajiros expend much energy striving to secure and/or enhance their social position.

Polygyny is the preferred pattern of marriage, although only wealthy men are ordinarily able to afford more than one wife. In polygynous marriages co-wives usually live apart, each with her own mother and sisters in a matrilocal arrangement. Among chiefly families, however, one regularly finds the avunculocal household because of the customary practice of the nephew receiving his education from his maternal uncle and succeeding him to political authority, which necessitates a pattern of common residence.

In Guajiro society marriage represents a contractual arrangement of economic and sometimes political character between two families, in which a bride payment in cattle, horses, mules, and jewelry is made by the groom and his kinsmen to the parents and matrilineal relatives of the prospective bride. This transfer of property puts the stamp of legality on the marriage. Informal liaisons resulting from abduction or elopement, in contrast, are defined as illegal and are strongly condemned by the Guajiro; indeed, if a young couple cohabits without a bride payment exchanging hands, the woman's matrilineal kinsmen will bring a suit of damages against the male offender, inasmuch as he has violated the exclusive sexual and domestic rights they hold in her and which they alone transfer to a man under conditions of formal marriage.

The bride must enter marriage as a virgin. Her sexual purity, in fact, may be regarded as the sine qua non for a successful marriage. If a woman is discovered by her groom to be impure on her wedding night, the latter will demand a refund of part of the bride payment as compensation not only for her essential loss of value, but also for the deception perpetrated against him, which is an offense to his dignity (after all, he bought her in "good faith," believing her to be virginal). As a precaution against this happening, young unmarried women (but especially those from chiefly families) are carefully chaperoned before they marry and are prohibited from having any intimate social contact with men, under threat of severe punishment (Watson, 1972a).

In the process of socialization, Guajiro children may be treated with great harshness to insure that they learn correct behavior. The emphasis in socialization is placed on the child's acquisition of compliant, respectful attitudes toward parental and lineage authority, and rigid control over impulsive behavior, particularly sex and aggression. Misconduct is punished by ridicule, beatings, whippings, and deprivation of food; in extreme cases punishment may assume the form of burning the child with a hot branding iron or suspending him upside down from the rafters of the house. Disinheritance is the ultimate sanction.

The mother is the principal agent of discipline. The maternal uncle may also perform the functions of a disciplinarian in extreme cases and he assumes considerable authority over his adult nieces and nephews (cf. Watson, 1967; Wilbert, 1970). The father, by contrast, has only a very limited role in this sphere.

Apparently most Guajiro children in the traditional culture become effectively socialized into the expected modes of behavior by the time they reach adolescence. By that time, they exhibit such desired traits as obedience, self-control, and a willingness to work hard and carry out their assigned responsibilities. Nevertheless, Guajiros appear to experience an underlying resentment of the need for compliance and restraint in everyday life because of the powerful constraints it imposes on their capacity to exercise personal freedom. Well-developed psychological defenses, which are culturally patterned, transmitted, and learned, however, enable the individual to cope with his forbidden needs and feelings (Watson, 1974).

As we can see from this brief ethnographic summary, a basically stable fit exists in traditional Guajiro society between normatively defined behavior (having adaptive value for critical role performance) and the actual strategy and execution of childhood socialization considered in its broadest sense. It can be argued that the effect of this deliberate socialization is to create phenotypic personality traits that enable the socialized individual to adapt to the behavioral requirements of normatively defined roles. The personality traits that are modally and adaptively significant among the Guajiro are, as we have seen, the tendency to repress aggressive and sexual feelings, a high sense of responsibility in performing routinized tasks, and a marked attitude of compliance-conformity. The crucial roles that to some degree involve the expression of one of several of these key dispositions include various kinship dyads in the lineage (e.g., bro-bro, mobro-siso); herdsman and provider; political follower; the husband and wife relationship; and lineageperson to members of other lineages.

## Urban Society and the Recent Migrant: A System in Disequilibrium

It is almost a truism to say that drastic changes occur in the lives of Guajiros who leave their tribal culture and migrate to Maracaibo. Traditional institutions fall into disuse, the old rules no longer apply, and new roles must be mastered for which the Guajiros have little or no previous training. The recent migrant, in other words, must quickly learn to adapt his behavior to a complex system of normative prescriptions, utterly dissimilar from the operating characteristics of his tribal culture. And yet, successful adaptation is essential if he is to alleviate psychological stress, maintain adequate self-esteem, and acquire security and stability in his new life.

Previous studies have delineated some processes of sociocultural change that take place in the early phases of urbanization (cf. Watson, 1968, 1970b, 1972; Watson-Franke, 1970, 1972). Nevertheless, several general points must be stressed. It is sufficient to mention here that wage labor supersedes the traditional pastoral economy based on livestock; in the process wage labor undermines many of the institutions linked to cattle herding, such as the extended family organization, the matrilineage and the institution of chieftainship, the social class system, and the custom of bride payment. Under urban conditions, the pattern of forced male absenteeism created by the fluctuating and temporary job market for manual labor gives rise to unstable family arrangements characterized most typically by a strong matrifocal emphasis. It is paradoxical, however, that while her responsibilities for holding the family together are critical, the urban Guajiro mother cedes much of her traditional economic control to the husband and her older children owing to the disadvantage of having few marketable skills, being a woman and uneducated. Even young children, for that matter, often are better equipped than she to provide some income to the family.

Our intention is to show how the tenuous and uncertain relationship that the Guajiro migrant assumes toward urban society prevents him from accurately interpreting the normative requirements of his new environment. Lacking proper environmental information or the ability to use what information he has deprives the Guajiro of an adequate basis for properly assessing his child's behavior in formulating a viable socialization strategy. It is proposed that the three potential causes of imperfect transmission of normative information in unstable systems, which were identified in the introduction, may provide an explanation of considerable utility for understanding underlying processes affecting the breakdown of educational transmission in the emerging Guajiro urban community.

## Ignorance of the Broader Environmental Context

With their limited experience of city ways, urbanizing Guajiro migrants have had neither enough time nor a sufficiently large number of relevant encounters to learn the meaning of significant environmental events that affect their lives. One may talk, in this connection, of a failure on their part to develop an appropriate cognition for identifying and understanding institutionalized strategies to meet prevailing urban needs and goals, especially a cognition for properly defining the critical role of formal education in occupational success.

The migrant's very inability to speak Spanish seriously reduces his capacity to communicate with the Venezuelan culture of Maracaibo, thus depriving him of corrective feedback for reappraising his own working assumptions about urban life and the solutions he has adopted for coping with environmental pressures. But even if he does know some Spanish, the migrant is apt not to be literate or to know the language well enough to be able to utilize effectively such vital sources of information as newspapers, radio, or television. We must bear in mind, too, that the migrant's prior experience has in no way conditioned him to look for information from the kinds of sources where it is customarily found in the city.

In addition to the above-mentioned limitations, the migrant's range of experience is also restricted because he is often unemployed or holds an unskilled occupation that provides little opportunity for cognitive development adapted to the wider urban scene. Moreover, since his manifold anxieties and insecurities doubtlessly make the thought of expanding experiential boundaries threatening, the migrant probably tends to find it comforting to encapsulate himself in the Guajiro barrio that he knows and where the adaptive change expected of him is not so great as it would be outside the barrio.

These problems, generally, are even more acute for Guajiro women than for men because there is less immediate pressure (e.g., economic) for them to confront the larger urban world "outside" and adapt their behavior to existing normatively defined expectations governing performance. This has enormous implications in the sphere of education, since the Guajiro woman is the one who usually bears the brunt of socializing the children in the home. Significantly, recent migrant women and those who for various reasons had remained relatively unacculturated made it clear in interviews that their conception of the basic requirements of urban culture was extremely limited, especially in the sense that they did not recognize the role of formal education in conveying the skills and knowledge that in the long run enhanced their children's chances of achieving occupational advancement. At the most, they saw education as conferring only immediate and practical adaptive skills such as literacy and Spanish language fluency that would make it easier for their children to find and hold unskilled employment. Many of the Guajiro mothers who were studied, furthermore, could not identify even in the simplest terms what kind of attitudes and disciplines were necessary for the student to learn if he were to perform successfully in school.

On the basis of interview and test results, the typical migrant mother was judged to lack awareness of the strategic means-ends relationships between environmental events and thus could not effectively socialize adaptive behavior, the situation being especially acute in her limited understanding of formal education.

It should be mentioned, however, that the ignorance of the broader environment was not necessarily dependent on recency of contact with urban culture. It was noted that several long-time Guajiro residents of Maracaibo had failed completely to adjust to urban life for various reasons.

## The Sharp Discontinuity between Past and Present Environments

Because of the oftentimes rapid, traumatic change that occurs in their lives when they leave the traditional society and migrate to the city, Guajiros do not quickly or effectively develop a cognition for interpreting their environment which is likely to be positively reinforced in their new experience. The sharp discontinuity of experiential change, which creates cognitive dissonance when formerly valued behavior is negatively reinforced, causes many Guajiros, despite their desire to adapt, to fall back on old modes of thinking and problem solving, although these, of course, may help serve the psychological function of resolving some of the cognitive dissonance that has been engendered; these solutions, in any event, represent poor bases on which to predicate socialization and therefore they have little value in aiding the socializer to reappraise either the correctness of his own educational methods or his children's intellectual and social development.

Confronted with the awareness of the denigration of his customary behavior in the city and at the same time conscious of the extreme difficulty if not impossibility of acquiring a more adaptive identity, the Guajiro migrant frequently alleviates his identity dissonance by not only over-estimating traditional patterns of behavior, as we have suggested, but also by rejecting urban behavior as negative and demeaning. This can be seen as the psychological basis behind the decision of many Guajiro mothers to subject their daughters to the puberty confinement ceremony in the traditional manner at the expense of the latters' formal education. When asked to explain the reason for this practice, for example, many mothers responded that they felt formal education had a corrupting effect on the girl's moral character, whereas the *encierro* (confinement) effectively served to instill the traditional moral virtues.

The old values, when they are held to, not only determine the choice of general educational strategy (e.g., choosing the *encierro* over school or choosing plantation work over higher education) but they also affect the content of what is actually socialized. Some of the following behavioral modes can be cited as examples of psychological dispositions that are defensively favored in the socialization choices of Guajiro migrant parents, and which, while they are adapted to the exigencies of tribal culture, do not sufficiently prepare children to meet many normative expectations in urban life.

*Dependency-compliance.* —We note that many Guajiro socializers train their children to be dependent and compliant in the erroneous belief that this enables the child to master his new situation. These traits, as we have seen, have positive adaptive value in the traditional sociocultural setting, particularly in the lineage and authority spheres; these same traits, however, are manifestly nonadaptive in a competitive, individualistic urban society where a person must aggressively and self-reliantly pursue his individual happiness, often at the expense of others' well-being. There is no collective entity in the city which can provide the individual with security in return for, and commensurate with, his submission to its decisions.

*Nonsociability.* —In the traditional Guajiro view, foreward, sociable behavior is potentially disruptive for it leads people to take liberties with each other, giving rise, so the thinking goes, to breaches of etiquette eventuating in legal disputes and even feuding. Since sociability is explicitly dangerous, one mission of socialization is to suppress feelings of sociability in the child so he will not initiate relationships and compact involvements that could get him and his family into difficulties. In Maracaibo, however, this kind of socialization produces intended behavior that hinders the child from making a proper interpersonal adjustment in the school and neighborhood and forces him into the position of being a social isolate. The sociability he needs to make acquaintances and elicit interpersonal support, which is so crucial to morale in an area like the school, is denied to him by the very training he receives at home.

*Unaggressiveness.* —Earlier we indicated that this behavioral modality, typical of the tribal personality, is normatively defined and thus positively rewarded in the context of intralineage interpersonal relations as well as in interlineage political settings. Its reward value consists, principally, in precluding the display of aggressiveness that is believed to result in unmanageable conflict and social disruption. In the city, though, this no longer really obtains with the breakdown of tribal institutions and the cessation of their actual functioning as social realities. If anything, the individual must learn to defend and protect himself aggressively from attack by other people and to find pressure points in social relations for working his own advantage by imposing his ideas and selling their merits. In all, it is advantageous for a person to conduct his affairs aggressively and assertively in the city to avoid losing out to the superior resourcefulness of his competitors.

The foregoing points paint a rather bleak picture, to be sure. But this drastic change in environments resulting from migration, while it tends to have disruptive consequences for socialization, is not entirely negative in its effects on child training. It must be pointed out that certain aspects of favored traditional behavior actually seem to have considerable adaptive value in the city. The traditional emphasis in Guajiro socialization on developing impulse control and attitudes of deferred gratification, particularly in managing scarce, valuable economic resources such as livestock, is a case in point and might be interpreted to confer the appropriate response tendencies, involving staying power, to persevere in the struggle to attain the difficult, long-range goals that are so characteristically urban values. When this factor is considered in relationship to the value of achieving wealth and social status, which plays such an important role in traditional socialization, we have a series of convergent assumptions about life whose direct carryover has a potential and obvious adaptive importance to affect the course of educative acculturation. The conflict of these traits with other, less adaptive ones, however, presents serious problems and tends to detract from the positive influence these patterns of thought and behavior might otherwise exert on socialization and character development.

## The Influence of Unconscious Needs

The difficult life circumstances of many migrant Guajiro women in the city—and we are talking especially about the woman in this context—create insecurities and anxieties that make the satisfaction of certain psychological needs an ever-present concern. Confronted with unemployment, abandoned or neglected by the husband, and thrown on the mercy of her children whose earning capacity exceeds hers, many a Guajiro woman faces a set of circumstances which renders her vulnerable to the need to seek emotional and material support from her children as compensation for her own incapacities and deficiencies.

But since these dependency needs run counter to her self-image of being a capable, resourceful maternal figure in the traditional sense (thus creating identity dissonance), these needs are repressed into the subconscious even though in that state they continue to motivate behavior.[4] This is reflected in the tendency for unacculturated mothers who have been abandoned and who are economically vulnerable to adopt, without consciously realizing it, the strategy of socializing dependent and nurturant responses and encouraging their children to feel emotionally helpless without them.

The successful inculcation of dependent attitudes in the children, of course, administers to the mother's need for nurturance and provides psychic relief for her powerful but suppressed "helpless" identity. This complex process may even subvert the mother's conscious recognition of the need for her child to be assertive, self-reliant and independent in many urban institutional and interpersonal settings. Thus, in this fashion unconscious psychological states may cause the socializer to misperceive or ignore highly essential environmental information that she might otherwise acknowledge and act upon systematically in her choice of socialization methods. I have spelled out the complex implications of this basic dilemma in several other works (Watson, 1970b, 1972b, n.d.), detailing how several vulnerable subjects, fearful of losing their children and being thrown upon their own meager resources, encouraged their children to act helpless and dependent and to be fearful of the outside world. Consciously these women realized, at least to some extent, that their children needed to be self-reliant and assertive in school and in contacts outside the home if they were to have success, and they asserted that they had trained their children to behave in this way. The failure of the children to "turn out as expected" was, according to their rationale, owing to their children's inherent characterological defects, not to any mismanagement of the education they had given them. As it was, they could not admit even to themselves that the socialization choices they made might have been predicated on selfish needs and were ultimately maladaptive for their children's future well-being outside the closed system of the family.

The children of these unacculturated migrant parents show certain predictable deficiencies understanding their environment which can be attributed to corresponding deficiencies in their socialization. First of all, many of them inaccurately or inappropriately define the nature of urban occupational success, and some continue to overvalue traditional economic roles. The inability to distinguish prestigious from nonprestigious occupations is often marked, as is an ignorance of the attributes and qualifications associated with urban occupational statuses. Second, they lack an understanding of basic coping strategies appropriate to meeting normative requirements in the city; at the same time, they often subscribe to maladaptive tribal methods and values. Third, these children are generally found to have only a limited notion of the role of formal education in crucial urban means-ends relationships; indeed, at the most they may be said to recognize that formal education confers limited skills of immediate practical value for dealing with basic survival problems. Fourth, their cognition of forms of adaptive behavior related to education possesses only the most simple and limited kind of awareness of proper study habits and preferred classroom demeanor. Last, it is not surprising that many of the children of unacculturated mothers place domestic and familial responsibilities (which may be taken as a reaction to the mother's dependency needs) before educational goals and individual achievement.

In summary, we have argued that the transmission of knowledge on the part of Guajiro socializers in the early phases of urbanization is not properly articulated with the normative demands of the urban system owing to the inability of the socializer to interpret his new environment correctly and to rid himself of traditional ideas and values, to say nothing of subconscious conflicts, that hinder his perception and understanding of significant environmental information. Thus, we can, we believe, speak of the "culture" of the migrant Guajiro community as representing essentially an unstable fit with the larger urban sociocultural system and for that reason those who are products of socialization in this milieu encounter difficulties adapting their socialized phenotypic behavior to the requirements of the larger urban order. The faulty cognitive model of urban behavior possessed by these Guajiros and transmitted to their children tends to be too simple and insufficiently organized to permit the individual to master effectively the more demanding aspects of his objective environment.

## Urban Society and the Acculturated Guajiro: Reintegration and Adaptive Fit

As Guajiros become increasingly acculturated to urban life along such critical dimensions as Spanish language facility, literacy, and experience in urban occupations, they acquire a familiarity with and, in time, an understanding of the essential operating characteristics of their chosen environment, embodied in valued goals and the normatively defined strategies leading to the attainment of these goals.

Our research indicates that there is a steady progression toward increasingly sophisticated cognition as Guajiro subjects become more acculturated in the sense of taking on the behavioral manifestations associated with urban life. There is, it seems, an association between observed behavioral indexes of acculturation and the presence of a cognitive structure sufficient to activate it, although the relationship between these two sets of variables is too complex to be defined precisely.

In addition to acquiring a proper "intellectual" cognition of the urban system, acculturated urban Guajiros also experience changes in their immediate economic and social environment which make them more secure and thus less inclined to socialize behavior in their children which serves needs associated with vulnerability, helplessness, and deprivation, and so on. We might mention, in this connection, (1) the tendency for the family to shift from an unstable matrifocal type to a more stable conjugal variety, in which some of the former matrifocal emphasis is lost, and (2) the financial security and earning power that the husband or consort brings to the family, this being a function of his close association with and concern for the family, and the likelihood that he commands an occupational skill having stable market value commensurate with his urban experience.

The change to a more orderly family system, associated with urbanization and acculturative variables, may in itself be the consequence of several processes; in part, it may arise out of the assimilation of a cognitive model defining what a successful middle-class urban "Venezuelan" family should look like. We suggest that family life in the urban Guajiro community may change, then, not only because of obvious "etic" factors such as greater economic stability, for instance, which diminishes the need for enforced paternal absenteeism; it may change because of "emic" factors, too, exemplified by a learned cognition of the normatively defined bases of urban family life, most particularly the need to be respectable in this area, poverty notwithstanding.

Looking at highly acculturated urban Guajiros who have made a successful adjustment to city life, we find that since their lives are no longer ruled by massive psychological insecurities tied to a deprived or dependent sociocultural status, they can begin to orient their own behavior and that of their children toward meeting objectively defined standards of performance and accomplishment that have currency in behavioral contexts outside the family where a person's social worth is ultimately judged. One of the most characteristic features of socialization in highly acculturated families is the united concern shown by both parents for inculcating in their children socially adaptive, purposive behavior that they recognize to be defined by prevailing urban norms; another feature of socialization is the manner in which they subject the child to a disciplined regime of training to insure his proper acquisition and demonstration of such behavior.

A most significant change resulting from urban acculturation is the socializer's full recognition that formal education is a central element in any course of action whose purpose is individual advancement. Whereas unacculturated subjects often misperceive the role of education or ignore its critical significance in making socialization choices, highly acculturated subjects possess an accurate and developed cognition of the meaningful application and advantages of education in urban occupational and social contexts. The orderliness and complexity of this aspect of cognition suggest that acculturated Guajiros have been able, as Wallace would say, to maximize the organization of their urban mazeways (cf. Wallace, 1961, 1970), developing a perception of reality that takes account of adaptive, normatively defined means-ends relationships and their activation.

It is now possible to summarize some of the specific aspects of cognitive organization having to do with education and its perceived relationship to occupational success in the city. Since this cognition, according to our analysis of the interview data, constitutes the basic criterion by which socialization choices are evaluated and reappraised, it becomes the mediating psychological variable that accounts for the adaptive fit between socialization and the normatively defined environment that exerts demands on individual behavior.

We might start off by pointing out that those Guajiro socializers who had become acculturated to urban ways were capable of properly identifying urban occupations and making accurate discriminations between different occupational categories (e.g., professional v. skilled trades) on the basis of such relevant criteria as income, prestige, education, and culture. Their recognition of the value of the benefits to be derived from professional employment, moreover, was informed by an understanding of the manifold privileges and powers (e.g., access to high society and political offices) conferred upon those who were able to attain professional status. On the other hand, they rejected lower, unskilled occupations because these positions were associated in their thinking with low income, powerlessness, and insecurity. Their complex conceptualization of occupational success was accompanied by a full awareness of the proper educational tracks, often involving special university and technical training, that led to different but valued professional and/or skilled positions. Indeed, acquiring the proper education was generally seen as the single most essential ingredient in the attainment of occupational status, with its material and social advantages.

Scholastic success, in turn, depended, they felt, on the ability to activate certain types of strategic behavior. Some of these behavioral modes were of a basic character adapted to successful urban striving in general, such as self-reliance, impulse control, confidence and assertiveness, ambition, and discipline; but others were related specifically to the demands of the classroom and showed that the socializer was aware of what behavioral operations were involved in studying, learning, and mastering academic or technical subject matter. Thus, they recognized the importance of such factors as (1) regular classroom attendance; (2) attentiveness in class; (3) the need for a disciplined routine of study in the home; (4) the systematic review of material for examination and other performance purposes; (5) an interest in reading outside the strict confines of the subject matter itself; (6) the utilization of library resources for study purposes; (7) the advantage of studying with more knowledgeable students; (8) the conceptual understanding of the subject matter, for a greater contextual awareness, as opposed to mere rote memorization; (9) the need for the socializer to give encouragement to the student and to desist from burdening him with work or involving him with activities that take him away from his classwork; and (10) the responsibility of the parent to seek corrective feedback from the teacher so that he may properly reevaluate his child's study habits. The highly acculturated, urbanized Guajiros felt that if the child and parent could only cooperate in developing a coordinated plan of action in which these operations were realized, it would greatly enhance the child's chances of passing his examinations and graduating in a position where he was prepared to enter the next step of his education.

At the same time, the cognition of these socializers included the perception of the strong relationship that existed between social adequacy and educational success. Thus, many of the subjects recognized the need for the student, if he were successfully to pursue his education and attain his occupational objectives, to develop those social skills (e.g., friendliness, tact, timing) which would enable him to make friends, engage in successful impression management, manipulate others, and build up useful contacts that he could exploit for future gain. They assumed, and probably correctly so, that intellectual and performance skills in themselves did not guarantee success if the individual were not able to sell himself to others and utilize their influence and assistance to his own advantage.

In addition to using a standardized interview, which yielded the data on which the aforementioned discussion was based, a modified Thematic Apperception Test was administered to these subjects to elicit supplementary information, which, it was hoped, would provide a partial check on the interview material. As it turned out, the results of the test tended to reaffirm the importance that the acculturated subjects in the interview attributed to valued occupational goals and the crucial role played by education in their realization. Self-reliant study habits and assiduous preparation were mentioned frequently as forming the basis for scholastic success. Much of the real emphasis in the TAT stories, however, seemed to center on the persistent conviction, already briefly alluded to, that parent and child were capable of working together in harmony to achieve success in the civilized urban world: the parent by conveying a proper definition of society's requirements (including the need for an advanced education) and rendering material and spiritual support; the child, for his part, by complying with well-meant parental advice so that he developed the proper behavioral characteristics and skills that would insure him a bright future.

It remains to be mentioned that the adaptive cognition of Guajiro parental subjects, which was hypothesized to constitute the basis on which much of their socialization strategy would be predicated, is generally replicated in the cognition of their children. If anything, the latter's mazeway organization may be even more elaborate and complex than that of their parents. Moreover, the cognitive organization of these child subjects tends to be more highly developed and better adapted to urban normative requirements than that of children of less acculturated Guajiro parents. These points strongly suggest that (1) cognition does, in fact, constitute the basis for socialization choices, and that (2) parental socialization may be a very important variable for determining whether children learn or fail to learn the proper operating characteristics of their environment.

## Conclusions

It would appear that if we are to talk about the adaptive fit between socialization and a normatively constituted environment responsible for sociocultural maintenance, one of our principal tasks is to define the conditions under which the successful learning of an appropriate cognitive set occurs. A model for studying the complex relationships posed by that problem has been tentatively suggested. This model emphasizes five variables and their dynamic interrelationship:

1. The normative environment must be properly identified in its operational aspects, especially in the form of roles that are performed in crucial institutional settings.

2. The adult socializer's perception of his normative environment must be studied. To what extent does his cognition take account of the relationship of his own behavior to significant environmental demands expressed as norms? In periods of rapid change it may be difficult if not impossible for the individual successfully to acquire a cognition relevant to the new situation.

3. We must determine the extent to which the individual socializer uses his cognition as a basis of formulating and reappraising socialization choices. It is possible that because of psychological conflicts or situational

constraints, a person may not actually use his cognition in formulating his socialization strategy.

4. The effects of socialization must be measured by assessing the cognitive organization of those who have been socialized. Theoretically, we should expect a strong correlation between the socialization of adaptive cognition and its acquisition by the socialized individual; we may actually find, however, that for some reason the child fails to accept or to internalize what he has been taught (he may, for example, rebel against the parent or he may be counter-influenced by his peer group, etc.).

5. Finally, we must determine if the socialized adaptive cognition mentioned above really enables the individual to perform required behavioral operations in his environment. The empirical demonstration of this eventuality, nevertheless, may not be possible in a rapidly changing society where socialization which was adaptive only a few years ago is no longer effective in meeting the challenges of the present.

If we consider the situation of the Guajiro migrants in Maracaibo, comparing them to tribal as well as to thoroughly urbanized Guajiro, the above model may offer some likely bases for defining the operation of cognitive processes in socialization and adaptive learning which accompany the wholesale acculturation that we associate with urbanization.

## NOTES

1. Urban subjects included sixteen Guajiro women, who fell into different acculturative groupings, and nineteen of their children. All of the mothers were represented in the sample by at least one of their children. Data on the tribal culture were based in part on previous in-depth research with fifteen subjects, including adults and children; this material, however, has been supplemented with interview material garnered from at least ten subjects in the course of the present research project.

2. A modified TAT test was utilized, in addition to an Occupational Inventory Evaluation (OIE) which I devised to elicit information regarding the subject's ability (1) to identify urban occupational categories, (2) to discriminate between jobs of different prestige, and (3) to discuss the skills and knowledge required to hold these various jobs.

3. LeVine (1973:121–122) refers to the personality phenotype as the "observable regularities of behavior characterizing an adult functioning in a variety of settings comprising his environment. The personality phenotype of an individual includes his pattern of performance in social roles, in formal and informal settings, in interaction and alone, in coercive and free-choice situations, under stressful and relaxed conditions, in verbalization and actual behavior. It includes his conscious attitudes and values, his skills, competence, and knowledge, his preferences and tastes in recreational and hedonistic activities. If the individual is functioning normally, his phenotypic personality is a stable organization of characteristics that affords him satisfaction of his perceived needs, enables him to meet social demands and take advantage of sociocultural opportunities, and protects him from excessive anxiety."

4. But it is clear that the woman will give her actual behavior as such an acceptable rationale, which may be wholly at variance with the motivation behind it.

# BIBLIOGRAPHY

Barry, Herbert, M. K. Bacon, and Irvin Child
  1959    "Relation of Child Rearing to Subsistence Economy." *American Anthropologist*
          61:51–63.

Befu, Harumi, and Leonard Plotnicov
  1962    "Types of Corporate Unilineal Descent Groups." *American Anthropologist* 64:
          313–327.

Fortes, Meyer
  1953    "The Structure of Unilineal Descent Groups." *American Anthropologist* 55:
          17–41.

Gutiérrez de Pineda, Virginia
  1950    "Organización Social en La Guajira." *Revista del Instituto Etnológico Nacional*
          (Bogota) 2:1–257.

Inkeles, Alex
  1961    "Modal Personality and Adjustment to the Soviet Socio-Political System." In
          *Studying Personality Cross-Culturally.* Bert Kaplan, ed. New York: Harper
          and Row.
  1969    "Social Structure and Socialization." In *Handbook of Socialization Theory and
          Research.* David A. Goslin, ed. Chicago: Rand McNally.
  1972    "National Character and Modern Political Systems." In *Psychological Anthro-
          pology.* Francis L. K. Hsu, ed. New edition. Cambridge, Mass.: Schenkman.

Inkeles, Alex, and Daniel J. Levinson
  1969    "National Character: The Study of Modal Personality and Sociocultural
          Systems." In *Handbook of Social Psychology,* 2d ed., Vol. 4. Gardner Lindzey
          and Elliot Aronson, eds. Cambridge, Mass.: Addison-Wesley.

LeVine, Robert A.
  1969    "Culture, Personality, and Socialization: An Evolutionary View." In *Handbook
          of Socialization Theory and Research.* David A. Goslin, ed. Chicago: Rand
          McNally.
  1973    *Culture, Behavior, and Personality.* Chicago: Aldine.

Wallace, Anthony F. C.
  1961    "The Psychic Unity of Human Groups." In *Studying Personality Cross-
          Culturally.* Bert Kaplan, ed. New York: Harper and Row.
  1970    *Culture and Personality,* 2d ed. New York: Random House.

Watson, Lawrence C.
  1967    "Guajiro Social Structure: A Reexamination." *Antropológica* 20:3–36.
  1968    *Guajiro Personality and Urbanization.* Latin American Studies, Vol. 10,
          Latin American Center, University of California, Los Angeles.
  1970a   "The Education of the Cacique in Guajiro Society and Its Functional Impli-
          cations." *Anthropological Quarterly* 43:23–38.
  1970b   "Urbanization and the Guajiro Matrifocal Family: Consequences for Sociali-
          zation and Personality Development." *Antropológica* 27:3–23.
  1972a   "Sexual Socialization in Guajiro Society." *Ethnology* 11:150–156.
  1972b   "Urbanization and Identity Dissonance: A Guajiro Case." *American Anthro-
          pologist* 74(5):1189–1207.
  1974    "Defense Mechanisms in Guajiro Personality and Culture." *Journal of Anthro-
          pological Research* 30(1):17–34.
  n.d.    "Conflict and Identity in a Guajiro Urban Family." MS.

Watson-Franke, Maria-Barbara
  1970    "Zur Desintegration eines matrilinearen Verwandtschaftssystems: Die Position
          des Mutterbruders bei den Guajiro." *Antropológica* 25:3–20.
  1972    *Tradition und Urbanisation: Guajiro Frauen in der Stadt.* Acta Ethnologica
          et Linguistica, No. 26, Series Americana, No. 6. Vienna.
Wilbert, Johannes
  1970    "Guajiro Kinship and the Eiruku Cycle." In *The Social Anthropology of Latin
          America: Essays in Honor of Ralph Beals.* Walter Goldschmidt and Harry
          Hoijer, eds. Latin American Studies, Vol. 14, Latin American Center, University
          of California, Los Angeles.

# The Contributors

Marina Anguiano, Instituto Nacional de Antropologia e Historia, Mexico

Frances F. Berdan, Department of Anthropology, California State College, San Bernardino

Peter T. Furst, Department of Anthropology, State University of New York at Albany

Nancy Brennan Hatley, M.A., Latin American Studies, University of California, Los Angeles

Sandra McCosker, Department of Anthropology, California Academy of Sciences

Kalman Muller, National Anthropological Film Center, Smithsonian Institution

Linda L. O'Brien, Ph.D., Ethnomusicology, University of California, Los Angeles

Gerardo Reichel-Dolmatoff, Latin American Center, University of California, Los Angeles

Douglas Sharon, Latin American Center, University of California, Los Angeles

E. Richard Sorenson, National Anthropological Film Center, Smithsonian Institution

Nicolas Vaczek, National Anthropological Film Center, Smithsonian Institution

Lawrence C. Watson, Department of Anthropology, San Diego State University

Maria-Barbara Watson-Franke, Latin American Center, University of California, Los Angeles

Johannes Wilbert, Department of Anthropology and Latin American Center, University of California, Los Angeles

# Index

Acapulco, 104
Acolhuacan Indians, 238
Agency for International Development (A.I.D.), 67, 75
Ailigandi language, 30
Amazon River, 6
*American Journal of Sociology,* 191
American Museum of Natural History, 173
Anahuarque shrine, 14
Animals: Agouti (paca), 276, 308; armadillo, 267, 276; cattle, 209, 399; deer, 97, 109, 112, 123, 124, 126, 131, 134, 136, 138, 142, 143, 172, 178, 267, 308; dogs, 114, 128, 265, 311; horses, 349, 399; jaguar, 106, 174, 267, 308, 335, 341; llama, 14, 214, 215, 216, 217, 218, 220, 222, 223, 224, 226, 228, 233; marsupial, 267; monkeys, 308; mules, 399; opossum, 114, 120, 176, 177; peccary, 267, 276, 308; pigs, 208, 209; puma, 267; tapir, 308
*Anthropological Quarterly,* 289
Araucanian Indians, 1
Atiteco Indians, 18, 377-393
Atratro River Valley, 29
Aztecs, 2, 20, 103, 106, 116, 175; art, 173; caste system, 239-241; cosmology, 175; drum, 178; education, 14, 178, 237-264; education, commoners, 253-261; education, 14, 178, 237-264; education, commoners, 253-261; education, nobility, 244-255; Mexican enculturation of, 237-264; militarism, 241-243; religion, 243, 246-253; rituals, 258-260; Triple Alliance, 238

Behavior systems: achievement, 89-90; imprinting, 11; nurturance, 86-87; responsibility, 90-91; self-reliance, 88-89; sociability, 87-88

Birds, 308; eagles, 124, 173, 179, 267; turkey, 117
Birth of Tayaupá (Sun Father), 116-122
Bushmen, 4
Byron, George Gordon, 6

Cajabamba, 361
Calderón, Eduardo Palomino, 17, 18, 361-375; adolescence, 362; artist, 370-371; background and childhood, 361-362; cures, 369; education, 363, 365-369; health, 364; herb medicine, 366; initiation, 367-368; marriage, 364-365; philosophy, 372
California Academy of Sciences, 30
Callispuquiu, 220, 233
Canoes, 16-17, 303-358; ceremonial building of, 339-346; origin, 337-338; prices, 331-332; psychology and symbolism, 346-349; sizes, 313; trees used to construct, 307-308
CARE, 80
Career training, 15-19
Catholic. *See* Christianity
Ceremonies, animal, 228; athletic competition, 229; Aztec rituals, 258-260; canoe building, 339-346; Cobo version contrasted with Molina version, 214-228; costumes for, 214-215, 216, 218, 219, 221, 223, 224, 226, 230, 231, 232; ear piercing, 230; *guarachico,* 214; Inca Warachikuy initiations, 213-236; Inna Mutiki, 83; Inna Suiti, 83; Kogi religious ceremonies, 265-288; llama blood, 223; music, 217-218, 223, 234; Piba Uwe, 83; Tatei Neiya, 124-128, 134-173; Warao initiation rites, 336
Chan Chan, 371
Chaparri, 366